SCHREBER:
FATHER AND SON

SCHREBER:

FATHER AND SON

by
Han Israëls

INTERNATIONAL UNIVERSITIES PRESS, INC.
Madison   Connecticut

This book is a translation by H.S. Lake of *Schreber, vader en zoon*, Han Israëls'
Ph.D. thesis, University of Amsterdam, 1980.

Copyright © 1989, Han Israëls

All rights reserved. No part of this book may be reproduced by any means, nor
translated into a machine language, without the written permission of the publisher.

Library of Congress Cataloging-in-Publication Data

Israëls, Han.
  Schreber : father and son / by Han Israëls.
     p. cm.
  Bibliography: p.
  Includes index.
  ISBN 0-8236-6011-7
  1. Schreber, Daniel Paul 1842–1911—Mental health. 2. Paranoia—
Patients—Germany—Biography. 3. Paranoia—Case studies.
4. Schreber, Moritz 1808–1861. 5. Fathers and sons. 6. Mentally
ill—Family relationships. I. Title.
RC520.S33I87 1989
616.89′7′00922—dc 19   88-35654
                                                                      CIP

Manufactured in the United States of America

CONTENTS

INTRODUCTION

The subjects of this study are Moritz Schreber (1808–61), physician and educator of Leipzig, and his son Paul Schreber (1842–1911), "the most frequently quoted patient in psychiatry."[1]* Moritz Schreber was an orthopedist and wrote many booklets for laymen on health, gymnastics, and child-rearing. Paul Schreber was a lawyer, became insane in middle age, and wrote a book about his delusions which has become popular among psychiatrists.

In this introduction I shall give an outline of the role played by Moritz and Paul Schreber in the literature, and of what I shall have to add to it.

1. PAUL SCHREBER

Paul Schreber was born in Leipzig in 1842. He grew up with his brother and three sisters close to the orthopedic clinic owned and run by his father. He studied law, also in Leipzig, and then embarked on a successful career in the judiciary of the kingdom of Saxony. He married at a relatively late age and had no children. When he was forty-two he was a candidate for the Reichstag. He lost the election, spent several months in a psychiatric clinic suffering from hypochondriacal complaints, apparently recovered completely, and resumed his legal career. At the age of fifty-one, shortly after accepting a senior post in the judiciary, he again had to be admitted to a psychiatric clinic. He was completely taken over by delusions and felt that he was being persecuted by supersensible powers. After a few years he man-

*Notes appear at the end of each chapter or section.

aged to adapt reasonably well to ordinary life and believed that he would again be able to live outside the clinic. In this his opinion differed from that of the doctors at the clinic, and so, being an experienced lawyer, he embarked on a series of actions at law in order to gain his release, being ultimately successful after several years. He then spent four years living with his wife and adopted daughter in Dresden, then again became severely psychotic, was again admitted to hospital, and died four years later, in 1911, in a clinic in Leipzig.

During the period in which he was engaged in legal proceedings to secure his release from the clinic, his intellect functioned perfectly, though he had not been able to abandon his ideas of being persecuted by supersensible powers. From the initial chaos of voices which he heard and frightening and painful experiences seemingly affecting his body, he developed in later years a complex view of the world, which, however, he would not discuss with his psychiatrist. He believed that he was being persecuted by God and by dead souls. He was to turn into a woman in order then to be impregnated by God. At the same time, he said, God was trying to make him go mad.

In order to allow the rest of mankind to share in his supposedly superior theological insights, he wrote a long and detailed account of those experiences which he had had in the clinic that could only be explained in supersensory terms. This was published in 1903, at his own expense, as a book entitled *Denkwürdigkeiten eines Nervenkranken* (translated as *Memoirs of My Nervous Illness*).

The book did not—as its author expected—bring about a revolution in the religious thinking of his fellow human beings. No one reading the countless fantastic details in the *Memoirs*—such as how Paul Schreber once swallowed the soul of his psychiatrist, how little men tried to pump out his spinal cord, or how he was surrounded by "fleeing-improvised-men" who dissolved into nothingness as soon as they had passed beyond his range of vision—no one reading all this can escape the thought that Paul Schreber was mad. Yet equally inescapable is the impression that what one is reading is the work of a mentally deranged man who describes the delusions he has experienced with great precision, intelligence, and integrity. For this reason, it was not long before the *Memoirs* attracted the attention of psychiatrists. In this way, one of Paul Schreber's other expectations was all too accurately fulfilled: in the *Memoirs* he wondered what consolation the future would bring for his years of suffering in psychiatric clinics, and supposed "that great fame will be attached to my name surpassing that of thousands of other people much better mentally endowed" (D. P. Schreber, 1903, p. 293; 1955, p. 214.) In the next section I shall outline how this prediction came true.

2. LITERATURE ABOUT PAUL SCHREBER

It is said that on publication of the *Memoirs* Paul Schreber's dismayed relatives bought up as many copies as possible. They were not in time, however, to prevent it from being reviewed quickly in various psychiatric journals. The reviews generally were favorable: "Anyone who takes an interest in the psychology of paranoiacs is recommended to read this book, which provides us with an account of the origin and development of a highly complex delusional system such as we are rarely given by our patients" [(Schultze, 1905].) Paul Schreber's case was raised to the status of a classic by the detailed analysis which Sigmund Freud wrote about it in 1911. "The Schreber case" then appeared so frequently in psychoanalytic literature, particularly after the Second World War, that when the English translation of the *Memoirs* appeared in 1955, its translators were able to refer to Paul Schreber as "the most frequently quoted patient in psychiatry" (Macalpine and Hunter, 1955, p. 8).

However, it was not until later that Paul Schreber achieved his true fame. Canetti (1972, p. 21) called the *Memoirs* "the most important document in psychiatry bar none." Various schools of psychiatric thought have used the book as a source of examples: "There has scarcely been a single new view of psychosis that has not been presented with reference to the Schreber case, which has been a sort of public forum for the discussion of paranoia" (Racamier and Chasseguet-Smirgel, 1966, p. 3). And all these psychiatrists found in Paul Schreber the confirmation of their own views that they were looking for. Freud, for example, believed that Paul Schreber "ought to have been made a professor of psychiatry and director of a clinic" (Freud and Jung, 1974, p. 343). For in the *Memoirs* Freud detected latent psychoanalytic insights. The psychiatrist Morton Schatzman, too, found (1973a, p. 1) that the true significance of Paul Schreber's book had escaped his contemporaries, for "nobody grasped the meaning of his message." However, Schatzman used the *Memoirs* for an attack on Freud.

It is not only psychiatrists who have honored Paul Schreber as the messiah of their own beliefs: there are plenty of others in that twilight area between genius and lunacy who have done the same. In "Critique of Phallocentrism: Daniel Paul Schreber on Women's Liberation," A. Wilden, an author with feminist-socialist sympathies, opined that Paul Schreber deserves a place "among the great mystics and the great utopian socialist philosophers" (1972, p. 302). Bernard This, writing on the race theories of the national socialists, saw in Paul Schreber "an informant who is particularly aware of this furious madness" (1973a, p. 3). More recently, Paul Schreber was even taken seriously by a theologian: "Schreber's theology is not a 'caricature'; it is a radical attempt at a new religious insight. Blessedness comes not through authority, but in erotic, ecological harmony" (Bregman, 1977, p. 133).

The following list may give some idea of the variety of authors who have studied the *Memoirs*: psychoanalysts, C. G. Jung, an Adlerian, Jacques Lacan and various of his structuralist-Freudian followers, Marxist structuralists, a graphologist, dramatists, and an opera director. In 1973 two new German editions of the *Memoirs* appeared (it is a book of over five hundred pages), followed in 1974 by an Italian translation and in 1975 by a translation into French.

The *Memoirs* have two qualities that make them such an attractive subject for interpretation. To begin with, their manifest message—the theological doctrine—need not be taken seriously, so that any interpreter can try to find the text's "deeper" significance. In the second place, the *Memoirs* are so full of mad details that the possibilities for interpretation are legion; and the sincerity and preciseness with which Paul Schreber wrote down his psychotic experiences are beyond all doubt.

One might wonder whether the modern view, according to which madness is invested with a sort of superior rationality—a rationality which only has to be divulged by the interpreter in order to reveal itself as the brilliant precursor of, as it happens, the interpreter's own revolutionary theory—one might wonder whether this view of madness is all that much more reasonable than the now vanquished naive picture of madness as nothing more than incomprehensible chaos. The great diversity of the latent insights of genius that have been ascribed to Paul Schreber must at any rate give some cause for doubt.

But be that as it may, the diversity of interpretations of the *Memoirs* is so great that I shall confine myself to only one current in this vast body of literature, the current that seems to me to be the most interesting and rewarding, namely that in which the central theme is the relationship of Paul Schreber to his father. The father is also of interest in his own right.

3. THE FATHER, MORITZ SCHREBER

Moritz Schreber (1808–61) from 1844 onward ran an orthopedic clinic in Leipzig, where his patients were chiefly children with malformations of the spine. Closely linked with his profession were his efforts to improve the general level of health in the population. He was actively involved in the foundation of the Leipzig *Turnverein* (gymnastics club) and wrote a bestseller on indoor gymnastics. His other books for laymen on health, and particularly about child-rearing, were not so successful. Not that he lacked the necessary enthusiasm: he drew up a grandiose plan whereby one of his educational booklets was to be distributed free in all the German states, but even this did not come to very much. Consequently, his name does not appear in books of reference about the history of education. However, this was not to prove his final disappearance from the public eye.

Moritz Schreber's name is still more or less a household word in the German-speaking countries in that an allotment garden—a small plot of land on the outskirts of a city that is owned and tilled by a city resident—is commonly called a *Schrebergarten*. Some years after his death, an educational association was founded in Leipzig to organize lectures and eventually to provide a children's recreation ground. More or less coincidentally the name chosen for this association was "Schreber Association," (Mittenzwey, 1896, p. 67, 68) in memory of the "excellent medical educator." Later the association did acquire a recreation ground, which was then christened the *Schreberplatz*. Some years after this, children's gardens were laid out on its periphery. These, however, only really became a success when their cultivation was taken over by the children's parents. In popular parlance these gardens were known as "Schreber gardens." Subsequently, when other Schreber Associations were founded in Leipzig and elsewhere, they were devoted more often than not to allotment gardening rather than to educational aims.

Thus Moritz Schreber himself never had anything to do with allotments, even though newspaper items about allotments report that he left money to the city of Leipzig to establish gardens, or that he propagated "his idea of the small garden on the edge of the city" in enthusiastic speeches made even far away in foreign countries (Bankhofer, 1977). Thanks to Schreber Association commemorative pamphlets and occasional articles on the Schreber gardens, Moritz Schreber's name as an educator has also survived. In this connection he is always honored in general terms as one who warned against too intellectual an upbringing, and who was far ahead of his times in asserting ideas of this kind.

In recent years Moritz Schreber has quite suddenly re-emerged as an educator even far outside Germany, principally as the result of the work of two American authors. Recent characterizations of him as a "torturing pedagogue" (Calasso, 1974a, p. 524) or as "a 19th century Dr. Spock" (*Psychotherapy Review*, 1974) can be expanded as far as one desires. This recent fame as an educator is due to the literature on his son.

4. LITERATURE ABOUT FATHER AND SON SCHREBER

In the literature about Moritz Schreber connected with the allotment gardens, little attention is paid to his two sons: the elder, Gustav, who committed suicide, and the younger, Paul, who ended his life in a psychiatric clinic. It is exceptional enough for a journalist to write that some of Moritz Schreber's descendants were hit "by heavy blows of fate" (W., 1908). Conversely, the father at first had little place in the psychiatric literature about Paul Schreber. Freud (1911a, p. 68 = 1911b, p. 78) only made more or less passing reference to the "excellent father" who had probably had a favorable influence on his son's illness.

It was not until 1959 that a psychoanalyst first paid any real attention to Paul Schreber's father. This was curiously late: after all, psychoanalysts are always interested in their patients' younger years, and Freud had already reported that Moritz Schreber had published work on child-rearing. There, then, lay the possibility of discovering something about Moritz Schreber in the role of Paul's father. This was first done by the psychoanalyst W. G. Niederland, with fascinating results.

Niederland's way of looking at Moritz Schreber was quite different from that of the authors of the allotment tradition: he characterized Schreber senior's educational ideas as "studiously applied terror" (1959b, p. 386 = 1974, p. 70). He wrote at length about the instructions Moritz Schreber gave parents for the upbringing of their children. One example will suffice. In order to prevent children leaning forward while writing, Schreber invented what he called a *Gerade-halter* (straightener: literally, a "straight-keeper"; Fig. 1), "which after repeated tests on my own children and on the pupils in my orthopaedic clinic . . . has shown itself to be most satisfactory" (D. G. M. Schreber, 1858a, p. 203). Such devices are interesting enough in themselves, but Niederland made his material truly fascinating by the parallels he drew between Moritz Schreber's educational practices and the delusions subsequently experienced by his son. In his *Memoirs* Paul Schreber described at length what terrifying physical experiences he underwent, experiences that were called "divine miracles" by the supersensory voices he was able to hear.

> One of the most horrifying miracles was the so-called *compression-of-the-chest-miracle,* which I endured at least several dozen times; it consisted in the whole chest wall being compressed, so that the state of oppression caused by the lack of breath was transmitted to my whole body [D. P. Schreber, 1903, p. 151 = 1955, p. 133].

This sounds as if it might be an exaggerated account of the experience Paul Schreber may have had as a child when being made to use the "straightener." Niederland made the parallel very convincing by adding numerous similar examples which I shall later discuss in detail (pp. 293 ff.). Niederland's work on father and son Schreber has since come in for much praise in the psychoanalytic literature.

It was more than ten years before an obvious conclusion was drawn from the parallels that Niederland had discovered between Paul Schreber's upbringing and his delusions. To explain Paul Schreber's persecution mania, Freud had had to invoke complicated psychological mechanisms: according to Freud, Paul Schreber had secret homosexual feelings for his father, and the persecution mania was the result of surpressing these, first by way of denial (I do *not* love my father) and then by projection (I do not love my father, I hate him, because *he* hates *me*); and finally, according to Freud's scenario, Paul Schreber raised his father into an avenging God. In the early 1970s Morton Schatzman, an American psychiatrist strongly influenced by R. D. Laing, used Niederland's parallels to produce a much simpler explanation: the God by whom Paul Schreber was persecuted was in reality his father, by whom he had been persecuted as a child. Schatzman's book about the Schreber case, *Soul Murder* (1973a), has been translated into many languages, including Japanese, and has elicited a consid-

Fig. 1. The "straightener." (From D. G. M. Schreber [1858a, pp. 203,205].)

erable reaction which includes stage plays and articles on Moritz Schreber with headlines like "The Dr Spock of the 1840s" (Cohen, 1973).

There are thus two completely separate genres of literature on
Moritz Schreber: the earlier genre of laudatory writing connected more
or less directly with the Schreber allotment gardens, and the modern
psychiatric literature in which Moritz Schreber's ideas of child-rearing
are seen as the height of repression.

5. MY OWN WORK

From the work of Niederland and Schatzman it is clear that an
interest is now being taken in the circumstances in which Paul Schreber
lived before the onset of his mental disorder. Niederland says:

> If there existed a biographical outline of Schreber's life before he
> fell ill at the height of an impressive professional career, it would
> be relatively easy to give an anamnestic account of the events which
> ultimately led to his hospitalization (and eventual death) in an insane
> asylum. So far, no such account is possible [1959b, pp.384-385].

It is that biography that I present in this book. During visits to the
region where the Schrebers lived, the former kingdom of Saxony, now
part of the German Democratic Republic, I found that it was not
particularly difficult to discover much more about the lives of the
Schrebers than had hitherto been known. It also emerged that descendants of the Schrebers still live there and still keep many family papers,
without knowing anything of the fame, or notoriety, which father and
son Schreber currently enjoy in Western psychiatry.

The first half of this study is devoted to the biography. This covers
the whole of the family in which Paul Schreber grew up, and the period
from 1808, when his father was born, to his own death in 1911. The
biographical part is concluded with a summary designed as a narrative
table of contents of what has been set out in detail in the preceding
chapters. The second half of the book concentrates on Moritz Schreber
and the extent and nature of his public reputation: the reputation he
acquired through his own work and through the allotments named after
him, and finally his role in recent psychoanalytic literature and in the
work of the psychiatrist Morton Schatzman.

My work is essentially different from most other writing on the
case of Paul Schreber. Other authors try to contribute to the explanation

of Paul Schreber's mental disorder; that is, their aim is to make a positive contribution. My work is entirely negative in regard to the theory: I produce much new information, but I do not offer any new explanation. And on the existing literature I have almost nothing positive to say: it is my view that the biographical literature is full of errors, I have misgivings about Schatzman's interpretation of the Schreber case, and I shall have even more disparaging things to say about the psychoanalytic literature.

In most of psychiatry, theory is formulated so that it will always be possible to find evidence to fit it, but also so that it is difficult to imagine how the theory might be refuted. Hence the lack of any decent polemic between the various schools of thought in psychiatry: Insofar as other theories are irrefutable, all one can do is keep silent about them or confine oneself to the occasional snide remark. In the case of the Schrebers this situation has been summarized as follows by Schalmey: "From the theoretical angle the development of the controversy about Schreber appears unsatisfactory. The number of different general hypotheses . . . is increasing without it being possible to decide in favor of any one hypothesis" (1977, p. 165). In this situation it can do no harm to make the theoretical field easier to survey by pruning, by means of a strictly negative approach.

I do not object to *all* theory. The very case of father and son Schreber contains an element that goes beyond the naked facts. I refer to the parallels between father Schreber's system of child-rearing and son Schreber's delusions. However, precisely because this is so convincing, the research that has to be done to determine what may be concluded from it must be all the more painstaking.

Not only do I not offer any new insights: my work is not even on an original subject. Many publications in the social sciences begin with a statement to the effect that the—always fascinating—subject to be discussed has so far unjustly failed to receive the attention it is due, and that in the publication in question an—always modest—attempt will be made to begin to set this state of affairs right. This seems to me a weak argument for the choice of a subject for scholarly study. If the social sciences aspire to more than mere historiography, it seems to me unlikely that (theoretical) progress is to be achieved through covering ever more subjects. In this thesis I do the opposite: I write about a subject about which much has already been written. If I were to come up with new biographical information about an unknown

nineteenth-century educator and his equally unknown mentally deranged son, that new information would be unimportant.

A publication from the genre to which I have just referred generally ends with a statement to the effect that it is only a first step
toward a proper study of its subject; the author then expresses the hope
that subsequent authors will continue the good work. (Subsequent
authors then embark upon their own studies of new and so far unjustly
neglected subjects.) It is my hope that with this book I have achieved
quite the opposite: I hope that with the information I present here I
have been able to nip a particular type of publication in the bud,
namely, the sort of literature in which Moritz Schreber is presented
as the Dr. Spock of the nineteenth century.

6. MY RESEARCH

This section of my introduction does not really belong in this
book at all, strictly speaking. This book is about the Schreber family;
this section is about my search for information on the Schrebers.
Nevertheless, I include the following paragraphs because I believe they
are interesting and possibly even instructive.[2]

Research in an extremely hierarchically organized state like the
German Democratic Republic presents certain specific problems which
I can illustrate here with a lament about my attempts to gain access
to the archives of the psychiatric clinic in which Paul Schreber spent
the last four years of his life. I began in 1977 with a letter to the clinic.
I received no reply. In the summer of 1979 I went to the clinic myself.
There I was informed that I needed the official consent of the *Kreisarzt*
(district medical officer) in Leipzig. At the office of the *Kreisarzt* I
was told that such matters had to be dealt with in writing. I therefore
quickly wrote a letter to him. This elicited no response. Four months
later I wrote again. Once again there was no reaction, and several
months later I wrote a third letter, again with no result. In the summer
of 1980 I again went to the office of the *Kreisarzt*. Since many sub-
ordinates proved unavailable, I found myself being directed straight
to the deputy *Kreisarzt*. He informed me that my letters had all arrived,
but that the *Kreisarzt* himself had no authority to take a decision
regarding my request, as he was subordinate to the *Bezirk* (region) of
Leipzig. My request had therefore been passed on to the *Bezirk*. At
the offices of the *Bezirk* authorities I was then received by a friendly
lady who informed me that my request had, several months previously,

been forwarded to the health ministry in Berlin, and that that ministry would now be contacting the health ministry in The Hague to discuss the matter. This lady further informed me that I had gone along the wrong channels: I ought in the first place to have addressed myself to the Dutch Ministry of Health; they would then have contacted their colleagues in the G.D.R., and when I had thus received consent from the East German ministry, everything would have gone forward "with no trouble at all."

The surprises of an impenetrable bureaucracy can sometimes also be unexpectedly pleasant. When I first wanted to go to Leipzig, I rang the embassy of the G.D.R. in The Hague to ask whether perhaps I needed any special permission to visit libraries in Leipzig. The ambassador informed me then that foreigners were not allowed to visit libraries in the G.D.R. at all—at least, not unless they were officially invited by a university in the G.D.R. Upon hearing this, I explained my need to M. Razc, a man not noted for his prejudice against East European regimes. He later phoned me and told me how I might be able to get an invitation from the Karl Marx University in Leipzig. I had to send in a proposal to the Ministry of Foreign Affairs in The Hague; this proposal would then be forwarded to the Netherlands embassy in East Berlin, and there the matter would be put to the G.D.R. authorities. After consent had been given by the government in East Berlin, Karl Marx University would then be free to issue an invitation. Without much hope of success I sent a proposal to the Ministry in The Hague. I heard nothing from them, and in a few weeks I had forgotten all about it. Instead, I decided simply to try and find out whether the information given me by the East German ambassador about libraries in Leipzig was correct. It proved not to be so: on the contrary, as a foreigner I should have no difficulty whatsoever. Many weeks later I was telephoned by the Ministry of Foreign Affairs in The Hague. They had just received a telegram from the Dutch embassy in Berlin: I was expected in Leipzig in a few days' time. They were unable to tell me anything more than the name of the hotel where I would be met. Arriving a few days later at the hotel in Leipzig, I still knew nothing, not even who was going to pay my hotel bill. It soon emerged that not only was Karl Marx University going to pay for my hotel, I was also going to receive an amount per day that I was scarcely going to be able to spend (there is not much to be had in the shops in East Germany, and the basic needs for survival are extremely cheap). But the most important thing was that I received first-class assistance in the university library. In a few days there I learned more about reference works than in many years in Amsterdam.

In Leipzig I found the descendants of Schreber senior.[3] The search for them may give an idea of how important a role coincidence plays in this sort of affair. On my first visit to Leipzig I found an article by an orthopedist in the city about Moritz Schreber—an article in the tradition of the Schreber gardens. I found the orthopedist's name in the telephone directory. I wrote to him from Amsterdam; he then sent me another article on Moritz Schreber that he had published in collaboration with the Leipzig art historian G. W. Kilian in 1958. On my next visit to Leipzig this orthopedist introduced me to Herr Kilian. One of the interesting things in what Kilian had written was a footnote in which he had thanked a descendant of Schreber senior for allowing him to see family papers. I asked Herr Kilian if the lady was still living, and, if so, whether he had her address. He was unable to supply me with an answer to either question: nearly twenty years had gone by, but the lady had been old even then. However, he was able to tell me that she had been a teacher at the Leipzig conservatory. At the conservatory I was told that the lady in question had been dead for ten years, but they did still have her last address, where I was directed to the flat in which she had lived. The people who were living in the flat gave me the name of someone who had had something to do with the old lady's estate when she died. This brought me to a lady aged about forty, who proved to be a great-great-granddaughter of Moritz Schreber, and who was able to direct me to the more important, i.e., older, members of the family. This story can also serve as an illustration of how important it is to get in touch with authors who have written on one's subject. The following story illustrates the same things: the role of coincidence and the importance of contact with writers.

Although the descendants were my richest source—they had kept much that was related to the family history, including letters, photographs, paintings, poetry, family trees—I did not find among them anyone who had personally known Paul Schreber. How I did eventually find someone who had known him, I shall now relate. In 1973 the well-known German magazine *Der Spiegel* carried a long article about father and son Schreber, prompted by recent publications on the subject. This article was read by Herr R. Troitzsch, who was then eighty-five. Having read it, he wrote a long letter to the publishers of one of the books referred to in the article. It was a letter of singular interest: as a boy of fourteen he had known Paul Schreber and his mother—they were distant relations. I, as it happened, wrote to the same publishers. Not that that is how I found Herr Troitzsch: that would have been too easy. Neither he nor I received an answer from the publishers. However, a third person addressed himself to the same publishers, namely Dr. F. Schweighofer, a graphologist. He was looking for manuscripts by the Schrebers. The publishers were unable to help him in that regard, but they did send him the letter they had received from Herr Troitzsch, who was by now eighty-six. In his search for manuscripts Dr. Schweighofer also approached Dr. Baumeyer, one of the most important writers on Paul Schreber. Dr. Baumeyer, with whom I too was engaged in correspondence, advised Schweighofer to get in touch with me. Schweighofer was then so kind as to give me the address of Herr Troitzsch, by now eighty-nine.

7. ACKNOWLEDGMENTS

I could not have accomplished my research without the help of a great number of people. The descendants of Moritz Schreber in Eastern Germany were extremely helpful and gave me access to all the information I wanted. I want to mention here especially Mrs. I. R. and Miss R. J. and the whole R. family in K.; Mrs. R. J., then living in L.; and D. J. and C. J. in Z. Mrs. Inez Roesler not only gave me access to interesting information but also turned out to be an extremely skillful researcher herself. I remember gratefully the excellent memory of Mr. Rudolf Troitzsch in Bendestorf. Mrs. E. B. in B. gave me an invaluable collection. I cannot say how much I thank all these people; I hope that I have used the material they gave me in a decent way.

The help of a great number of archives and libraries has also been indispensable. There are some librarians whose assistance has been so exceptional that they must be mentioned by name; Peter Daniels of the psychiatric clinic in Amsterdam, Mr. R. B. Knottnerus of the University Library in Amsterdam; Mrs. Heidrun Smers of the Psychiatric Hospital in Leipzig-Dösen; Ms. Carola Bots of the Psychoanalytic Institute in Amsterdam; and Dr. H. Bräuer of the Municipal Archives in Karl-Marx-Stadt.

I thank the following people for severely but rightly criticizing the style of this text: my parents, Aagje Aaij, Carolien Bouw, Dr. med. G. Friedrich, H.S. Lake, Mrs. J. van der Pot, and Mrs. B. Wienstein.

Especially do I thank my thesis adviser J. Goudsblom, who gave me the self-confidence to accomplish this project.

In 1981 a preliminary English translation of my Dutch thesis was made by H. S. Lake. One of those to whom I distributed copies was Dr. Morton Schatzman in London. He told several people about my work. One of them was a friend of his, the eminent Freud historian Peter Swales in New York. Swales distributed several copies of this preliminary translation. He gave one copy to a journalist on the staff of the *New Yorker*, Janet Malcolm, who was then carrying out research for her book *In the Freud Archives*. Janet Malcolm gave a copy to Dr. Kurt Eissler. It was Dr. Eissler who advised me to contact International Universities Press. I thank these people more than I can say, especially Drs. Schatzman and Eissler. Dr. Schatzman is criticized in the last chapter of this book. Dr. Eissler is so prominent in the field of psychoanalysis that he needs no introduction here; in this book no group of scientists is so severely criticized as a number of psychoanalysts. We scientists often say that criticism is a good thing. Very few of us are able to *act* in accordance with that belief. Schatzman and Eissler have shown that they belong to those few.

NOTES TO INTRODUCTION

[1] His full name was Daniel Paul Schreber. It is under this name that I have included his citations in the bibliography. In the literature he is almost always referred to as Daniel Paul Schreber, and sometimes as Daniel Schreber. However, during his lifetime he was always known as Paul Schreber. (Friedrich, 1932; see also note 7 to Chapter 3 below). His father Moritz was officially Daniel Gottlob Moritz Schreber; he too appears in the bibliography under his full name.

[2] What follows in part repeats what I published in the Dutch literary magazine *Maatstaf* (May/June 1978).

[3] I am not the first author from the Western European psychiatric tradition to be in touch with descendants of Moritz Schreber. During the 1950's the West Berlin psychiatrist Dr. Baumeyer corresponded with a grandson of Moritz Schreber who lived in Leipzig; this correspondence did not bring much new information to light. Baumeyer never met this man and was unable to telephone him as the cold war was then at its height. This grandson appears not to have known that members of the family still had much material on the Schreber family history: either that, or he was disinclined to mention it to Baumeyer. Several authors have also been in touch with Paul Schreber's adopted daughter. She has important material but is not inclined to release it for publication. My own contact with her has been exclusively by letter.

PART 1

THE SCHREBER FAMILY

In this biographical part of my study I give an account of the life of Moritz Schreber, his wife, and his five children. The emphasis will be on Moritz Schreber and his son Paul Schreber. By and large, I shall disregard the two most interesting features, that is, Moritz Schreber's ideas on education and Paul Schreber's religious mania. There is already a considerable literature on these subjects, and I need all the space available to me to present my new material on the Schreber family in anything like complete form.

1

THE SCHREBERS

A biography commonly begins with a brief account of the subject's antecedents. In the case of the Schrebers this is all the more necessary because Paul Schreber was well informed about his family tree (D. P. Schreber, 1903, p. 73 = 1955, p. 86) and because in due course it will become clear that that knowledge left its mark on his insanity. One reason why the Schrebers were so knowledgeable about their genealogy was a scholarship established in Oschatz in the year 1600 by a certain Wolfgang Schreber (C. S. Hoffman, 1815, p. 636). This scholarship was later administered by the municipal authorities in Oschatz and awarded to the student who could demonstrate that he was the most closely related to Wolfgang Schreber. In the family, not surprisingly, it was referred to as the Schreber family scholarship; it operated for over two hundred and fifty years. There is still in existence a family tree drawn up by Moritz Schreber's father to support his son's claim to the scholarship.

The best Schreber family tree was drawn up in 1932 by G. Friedrich, a great-grandson of Moritz Schreber. It is based on two earlier pedigrees: the one drawn up in 1812 by Moritz Schreber's father, and one compiled by Moritz Schreber himself in 1852. The latter of these—particularly interesting because Paul Schreber undoubtedly was familiar with it—has regrettably been lost.

The Schreber family history unfolded almost exclusively in the kingdom of Saxony. In the seventeenth and eighteenth centuries the Schrebers were part of the intellectual bourgeois upper classes, as witnessed by their occupations: councillor, burgomaster, advocate, rector. Moritz Schreber's father characterized his ancestors as "scholars" (J. G. D. Schreber, 1812).[1]

3

Fig. 2. Daniel Gottfried Schreber (1708–1777).

1. MORITZ SCHREBER'S GRANDFATHER

Moritz Schreber's grandfather, Daniel Gottfried Schreber (1708–77; Fig. 2), was a professor of economics, mainly at Leipzig.[2] From his first marriage a son was born, Johann Christian Daniel Schreber (1739–1810), who took a doctorate under Linnaeus, later became a professor at Erlangen, acquired a very considerable reputation in the field of biology, and is still remembered in the history of that science. There is a monument to him in the park at Erlangen.[3]

Shortly after the birth of Johann Christian Daniel his mother died. Daniel Gottfried Schreber remarried. His second wife was Henriette Philippine Rosenkranz. This marriage resulted in the birth in 1754 of Gotthilf, the father of Moritz Schreber. He, therefore, was fifteen years younger than his later so academically successful half-brother. Five years later a little brother for Gotthilf, Benedikt, arrived, and two years after that their mother died. In the family tree of 1932 her cause of death is given in quotation marks as "fever and hysteria."

2. MORITZ SCHREBER'S FATHER

Moritz Schreber's father, Gotthilf Schreber,[4] is the author of a text I found entitled "Kurze Geschichte meines Lebens" (A short history of my life). This brief autobiography was written when he was well over seventy, and the sixteen large pages are full of all kinds of self-pity and a list of his own ailments: a recurrent eye disorder, pleurisy, a "bad foot" which once kept him indoors for three months, typhoid fever, and much else besides.

Between the ages of twelve and eighteen Gotthilf Schreber lived with his uncle, who was deputy rector of a school at Rossleben at which Gotthilf was also a pupil. He then returned to his father in Leipzig, the city where he was to spend the rest of his life. He attended lectures at the university in history, mathematics, ethics, law, and other subjects. Four years after his return to Leipzig his father died. His half-brother in Erlangen laid claim to all the desirable things in the inheritance (according to Gotthilf Schreber's own account of his life). He and his brother were left with only five or six hundred thalers apiece, and that was used up in a couple of years. (At this time a carpenter's mate in Leipzig earned about a hundred thalers a year [Saalfeld, 1974, p. 421].) Gotthilf's efforts to find a job were in vain,

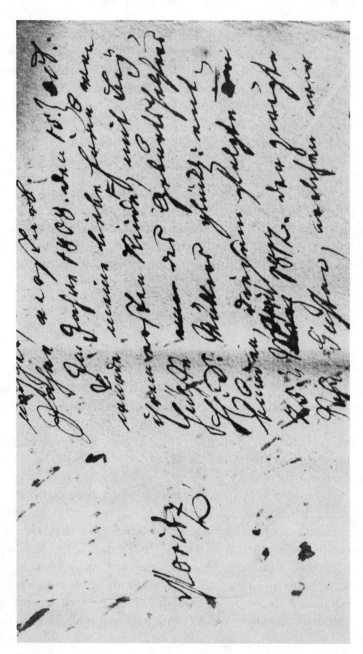

Fig. 3. From J. G. D. Schreber (1830, p. 11).

and he "discovered all too well how worthless and fickle were human nature and kind promises" (J. G. D. Schreber, 1830, p. 7).

Later he was apprenticed to an advocate, eventually setting up his own practice. He did not make a fortune: as a student his son Moritz would later be dependent on scholarships. In 1802, at the age of forty-seven, Gotthilf Schreber married the twenty-two- or twenty-three-year-old Friederike Grosse,[5] of whom he wrote that she was "appropriate to my inclinations and nature." "In the year 1808, on the 15th Oct.,[6] my dear wife was happily delivered of her first child, with the assistance of the obstetrician Dr. Müller" (J. G. D. Schreber, 1830, p. 11). The child's name, "Moritz," is entered in the wide margin of the autobiography which Gotthilf seems to have used for recording things he had earlier forgotten (Fig. 3).

There is no further reference to his son, even though in the meantime over twenty years had elapsed since his birth. Is this the indifference toward children that was general in those days, or is the preoccupation with himself, and particularly with his own misfortunes, typical only of Gotthilf Schreber?

I have been unable to find an autobiography of any length by Moritz Schreber. In fact, he probably never wrote one, since he died relatively young and it is a custom which has regrettably declined steadily over the years, probably as a result of a growing feeling that it is an arrogant form of writing. If Moritz Schreber had written an autobiography, its tone would undoubtedly have been quite different from that of his father's: not so full of self-pity and more on the lines of "tired but satisfied." Moritz would also certainly have had a lot more to say about his children: in the nineteenth century children came increasingly to be the object of constant parental concern, and Moritz Schreber was the archetype of such parents.

Four years after Moritz Schreber, a second son, Gustav, was born; he died of a "hot fever with great spasms"[7] four years later. Gotthilf Schreber died in 1837 at the age of eighty-two. His wife followed him in 1846.

NOTES TO CHAPTER 1

[1]More information on the Schreber family prior to the nineteenth century may be found in Lübbing (1952), Siemens, (1966), and Tabouret-Keller (1973). This (1973b, 1973/4) obtained his information from Tabouret-Keller.

[2]Schilling (1964, p. 5) gave quite a different grandfather for Moritz Schreber, namely Daniel Gustav Schreber, Doctor of Law, town clerk, 1720–78, married to

Clara née Rauth, 1727–91. It all sounds highly respectable; moreover, Schilling worked with church records. The only thing is: these are not Moritz Schreber's grandparents.

[3]Daniel Devreese (a psychologist in Ghent) is working on a thesis in which he hopes to establish a link between the language used by the supernatural voices heard by Paul Schreber during his illnesses, the *"Grundsprache"* (basic language), and the language of the publications of Daniel Gottfried Schreber and Johann Christian Daniel (von) Schreber. More on these two is to be found in Tabouret-Keller (1973, pp. 291–295).

[4]Gotthilf Schreber's full name was Johann Gotthilf Daniel Schreber; this is the name, for example, with which he signed the "Short history of my life."

In the literature he is often referred to as "Gottfried" instead of "Gotthilf." This error springs from Ritter (1936a, p. 9), and subsequently appears in the work of Brauchle (1937, p. 243), Kleine (1958, p. 161), Tabouret-Keller (1973, p. 288), and elsewhere. This (1973b, p. 9) carried it over from Tabouret-Keller. Niederland (1974) gave the correct name "Gotthilf" on page 4 and the erroneous name "Gottfried" on page 63.

The name "Gottfried" also appears in a report dating from 1842 (see note 11 to Chapter 3). This report—drawn up on the instructions of no less a person than Moritz Schreber, and now in the municipal archives of Leipzig—was doubtless not known to Ritter. It was, however, known to G.W. in the *Leipziger Tageblatt* in 1908, who thus gave Moritz Schreber's father a name which was not his.

Kleine (1958, p. 161) and Bankhofer (1977, p. 15) erroneously credited Gotthilf with a doctorate.

[5]Friederike Grosse's full name was Friederike Karoline Grosse (D. G. M. Schreber, 1833b, p. 11). Not Frederike Grosse (Tabouret-Keller, 1973, p. 288).

Schilling (1964, p. 3) gave her surname as "Gross" instead of "Grosse." This is probably not merely a slip of the pen: I have also seen this version of her name in the highly official national socialist pass issued to one of her descendants.

She was born on 1 April 1779 (G. Friedrich, 1932), not in 1766 (Tabouret-Keller, 1973, pp. 288, 295, and hence also in This, 1973/4, p. 9). Tabouret-Keller did not give her source and in a letter to me wrote that she thinks she deduced her dates from other dates which she does not specify.

[6]Mangner (1877, p. 4) had Moritz Schreber born a day early (14 October). Ackermann (1943, p. 287) and Dr. A. (1943, p. 218) had him born a year late (15 October 1809). So we also know who Dr. A. is.

[7]According to all the literature Gustav was born, not after but *before,* Moritz Schreber, and he was already dead when Moritz Schreber was born (e.g., Brauchle, 1937, p. 243, Niederland, 1960, p. 494). This mistake goes back to Ritter (1936a, p. 9).

Tabouret-Keller (1973, p. 288) called Gustav "Daniel Gustave" and gave his dates as "probably 1796–1799" instead of 1812–16; she did not name a source. This (1973/4, p. 9) carried over the date 1796 from her, at the same time leaving out the word "probably."

2

MORITZ SCHREBER UNTIL HIS MARRIAGE
(1808–38)

1. YOUTH (1808–26)

> I was born at Leipzig in 1808, the son of the best and most beloved
> of parents, my father Johann Gotthilf Daniel, advocate, and my
> mother Frederique Caroline, née Grosse; I pray to Almighty God
> that they may live as long and happily as possible.

So wrote Moritz Schreber[1] in the curriculum vitae which accompanied
his thesis (D. G. M. Schreber, 1833b, p. 11). His earliest memory
probably dates from 1813: as a five-year-old he looked for "bullets
and other war souvenirs with his father on the battlefield of the Battle
of the Peoples" (the battle of Leipzig), as Ritter (1936a, p. 9) was
told by Moritz Schreber's daughter Anna toward the end of her long
life. In his "Short History of My Life" Moritz's father gives a less
light-hearted description of the events of the battle, at which Napoleon
was defeated. A typhoid epidemic was raging in Leipzig: Gotthilf
Schreber related how, in his own house, someone succumbed to the
disease "on the very day on which the city was bombarded and stormed
by the Russians, Prussians and Swedes. To what distress, fear, worry
and horror we were subjected in all this simply cannot be described"
(J. G. D. Schreber, 1830, pp. 14–15.).

At the end of April 1816, when Moritz was seven years old, his
little brother Gustav died, as mentioned above, and Moritz was left
an only child. Referring to his relationship with his parents, his daughters
were later to say:

Some letters still in our possession show that there was a profoundly
affectionate relationship between our father and his parents, and from
his own stories we know that his childhood and youth were very
happy [Siegel, 1909b, p. 205].

The letters referred to here may be, or may include, two letters which
Moritz Schreber wrote to his parents when he was a young adult,[2] to
which I shall return.

In Leipzig Moritz Schreber received both his elementary and his
gymnasium education (D. G. M. Schreber, quoted in Kloss, 1862, p.
11). His elementary schooling took place in the "schola civica ur-
bana," where he became acquainted with the "primis religionis ac
literarum elementis' (D. G. M. Schreber, 1833b, p. 11). His gymnasium education took place at the famous Thomasschule, which he
attended from the age of ten until he was seventeen. The names of the
masters are recorded in his curriculum vitae (*ibid.*, p. 11).

2. STUDENT YEARS (1826–33)

On September 23, 1826 Moritz Schreber was enrolled as a student
of medicine at the University of Leipzig. To begin with, he attended
lectures in philosophy and anthropology, besides chemistry, experi-
mental physics, botany, and natural history lectures, and lectures on
a whole range of medical subjects. Among his tutors [3] were numbered
Professor W. A. Haase, his future father-in-law; Professor A. K. B.
Bock, the father of the future Professor C. E. Bock, who was about
the same age as Moritz Schreber, in whose life he was later to play
a recurrent role; and Professor C. F. S. Schwägrichen, who gave him
free tutorials in botany and natural history for a year, for which Moritz
expressed his deeply felt gratitude in his curriculum vitae (*ibid.* p. 11).
There are signs that Moritz Schreber did not have an easy time
of it financially during his student days. On 3 November 1826 he wrote
a short letter in Latin to the Rector Magnificus, saying that he would
very much like to study medicine and was already attending lectures
but lacked sufficient parental assistance, and asking whether he might
not therefore be allowed to take the examinations before receiving a
scholarship (D. G. M. Schreber, 1826). His request was evidently
granted: on 3 September 1828 Moritz Schreber took his baccalaureate
in medicine. And in 1828 Professor Schwägrichen, from whom Moritz
was receiving free tuition, wrote a note declaring that Moritz Schreber

was attending his lectures: this note was necessary because Moritz's father wanted to apply for the "Schreber Family Scholarship," and the administrators of the scholarship, the municipal authorities in Oschatz, wanted him to furnish evidence that Moritz was a genuine student. They also wanted a birth certificate; see Figure 4.

Moritz Schreber was awarded the scholarship, which was for three years. Beginning on St. Michael's Day (September 29) 1829, it amounted to 17 thalers and 12 groschen annually (J. G. D. Schreber, 1829). For comparison: the carpenter's mate was now earning about 130 thalers a year (Saalfeld, 1974, p. 421). Moritz was also indebted for funds to the "Ordini Medicorum Gratioso," who provided him as a poor student with "stipendiis" (D. G. M. Schreber, 1833b, p. 12).

On October 15, 1831 he was given the "prima censura ab ordine medico," the first judgment by the order of medicine.[4] From 1831 until 1833 he was "occupied practically and literarily" (D. G. M. Schreber, quoted by Kloss, 1862, p. 11). He was an assistant at several hospitals (Schilling, 1964, p. 4).[5] On July 12, 1833 he defended his medical thesis, written in Latin, on a medicine for inflammation of the respiratory organs.[6] It was to accompany this thesis that he wrote the curriculum vitae already referred to, which is included in a text by Professor E. H. Weber (1833, pp. 11,12), who appears to have been his adviser.

About Moritz Schreber's student days there is—besides a certain amount of unreliable information[7]—one story that is probably true, since it comes from C. H. Schildbach, who although not an "old friend" (Tabouret-Keller, 1973, p. 296) was somebody with whom he worked quite closely during his latter years.

> Daniel Gottlob Moritz Schreber . . . was in the first few years of his time at the university a small, meagre figure. It was only then that he took up gymnastics, which he thereafter practised with the same energy and tenacity to which he owed so many of his successes in other fields. In this case he was to reap the first rewards himself, for soon his body developed in height and breadth in such measure that when he left the university he had far outstripped the average dimensions of the male physique[8] [Schildbach, 1862a, p. 5].

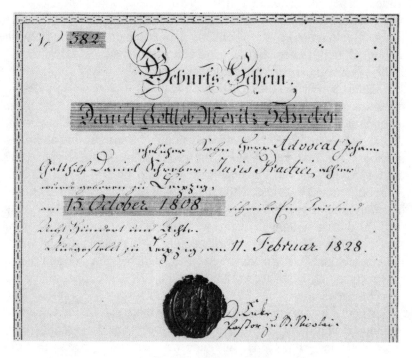

Fig. 4. Birth certificate.

3. PERSONAL PHYSICIAN TO A RUSSIAN NOBLEMAN; STUDY VISITS TO BERLIN, PRAGUE, AND VIENNA (1835–36)

Quite soon after finishing his thesis Moritz Schreber became personal physician to a Russian nobleman. Schreber described this episode as follows:

For further training, namely at the larger places of medical education, such as Berlin, Prague, Vienna etc., he accepted a post as a travelling physician which took him to the chief cities of Germany and to various parts of Russia [D. G. M. Schreber, quoted in Kloss, 1862, p. 11].

Such a sequel to a course of study in medicine was not uncommon.[9] The Russian nobleman's name was Stakovich[10]; his property was near Chernigov in the Ukraine, not far from Kiev.[11] With Stakovich Schreber visited "several of the mineral baths of Germany" and "central and southern Russia" (Heindl, 1859, Band II, p. 396); he also spent several long periods in Dresden.

It was from Dresden that he wrote long letters to his parents in September 1835. These letters have already been referred to on page 10; it was probably from them that his daughters concluded that "there was a profoundly affectionate relationship between our father and his parents" (Siegel, 1909b, p. 205). They confirm my impression of Moritz's father as a man who complained about his many ills. His son writes:

> Regarding your cramps, dear Father, why don't you rub in some corn brandy every evening? May you soon be well again! [D. G. M. Schreber, 1835b, p. 2].

> I beg you again, dear Father, to be sure to tell me in every letter how your foot is, and your health in general. [D. G. M. Schreber, 1835a, p. 3].

Elsewhere in these letters Moritz, now about twenty-five years of age, is at some pains to reassure his parents as to his own well-being, apologizing at length for his forthcoming absence from a wedding:

> Nevertheless I am confident in hoping that despite [my absence] you will both celebrate the festival with just as much pleasure; my spirit will float happily around you (my body will drink one or two small glasses to the health of the happy couple); but I do insist that you

only think of me with joy—you especially, dear Mother, must take
this to heart! [D. G. M. Schreber, 1835b, p. 2].

The relationship with the Russian nobleman Stakovich was evidently not particularly close. In Dresden they stayed at separate addresses. It was Stakovich's desire to see his doctor once or twice a
day, and Moritz spent the rest of his time—if we are to believe his
letters—visiting tourist attractions and paying his respects to people
whose names I have usually been unable to decipher. It all makes a
relaxed impression. On one occasion he asked his parents "perhaps,
if the opportunity arises, to send my white boots with the cabman, *not*
carriage paid" (D. G. M. Schreber, 1835a, p. 3).

These letters are the only surviving autobiographical documents
concerning Moritz Schreber's private life. All the other material presents quite a different picture of his personality, one more of "a man
of enthusiastic will, of the most tireless endurance" (Politzer, 1862,
p. 2). This last impression is confirmed by a story related by Schildbach, Moritz Schreber's later associate, when he records that Schreber
took "a post as a travelling doctor with a Russian":

> During this travelling about his gymnastics had been neglected, and
> when he and his patient eventually arrived at the latter's estates in
> southern Russia his limbs had grown so round that folds of fat were
> already in evidence on his arms. Even after almost twenty-five years
> he painted for me, with the most vivid colours, the horror with which
> he was seized at this discovery. At once he had parallel and horizontal
> bars erected in the garden and did exercises daily, to the speechless
> amazement of the onlookers from the local populace [Schildbach,
> 1862a, p. 5]

Schreber also took the opportunity offered by his post as a personal
physician "to make a scientific journey to Vienna, Prague and Berlin
on his way home, spending some time at each of those places to further
his training" (Heindl, 1859, Band II p. 396). He returned to Leipzig
in the autumn of 1836.[12]

4. PRIVATDOZENT AND GENERAL PRACTITIONER (from 1836 onward)

"Having returned to Leipzig in 1836, he lived for his doctor's
practice, his literary activities and his teaching work as a tutor at the

university" (D. G. M. Schreber, quoted in Kloss, 1862 p. 11). As a *Privatdozent* in the faculty of medicine,[13] Moritz Schreber was connected with the University of Leipzig from 1836 until 1854.[14] The income of a *Privatdozent* consisted solely of fees paid by his students, and as it was customarily considered slightly improper to give many or large lectures, it was a profession generally reserved for those with private means or some other substantial source of income. Moritz Schreber, then, was not only a *Privatdozent* but also a general practitioner, a profession which in those days did not commonly provide more than a very basic income for a man at the beginning of his career (Engelsing, 1978, p. 41). We may assume that Schreber either reduced the size of his practice or gave it up altogether when he took over an orthopedic clinic in 1844.

Apart from his work as a *Privatdozent* and family doctor, Schreber referred to a third occupation after 1836: "literary activities." The first trace of this that I have been able to find is his first book, *Das Buch der Gesundheit* (The book of health), completed in September 1838. By this time he was a married man. I shall therefore turn now to his wife, Pauline Haase.

NOTES TO CHAPTER 2

[1]Moritz Schreber's full name was Daniel Gottlob Moritz Schreber. However, in most of the literature his second forename appears as "Gottlieb" instead of "Gottlob."

The question of whether it was "Gottlob" or "Gottlieb" has exercised the minds of other writers too: Niederland (1959a, p. 152), O. Mannoni (1974, pp. 629, 631). Before Gerhard Richter published his umpteenth book about the Schreber Associations in 1939, he decided to pay a visit to Moritz Schreber's only surviving child, the ninety-eight-year-old Anna, to resolve the question once and for all. The following quotation is from an account of this meeting:

> [I was] . . . then greeted by Frau Anna Jung in person. The purpose of my visit was to establish whether Schreber was called Gottlieb or Gottlob. Frau Jung assured me: Gottlieb, Gottlieb. When I thereupon told her that it was otherwise on his books, Frau Kunio rummaged about in the bookcase and Frau Jung gave her various documents. However, documentary evidence was not to be found. I was told he had always been called Moritz. We agreed to leave it at Gottlieb in the Festschrift [G. Richter, 1939a].

Despite this, "documentary evidence" does exist. Kilian (Kilian and Uibe, 1958, p. 335) looked it up in the register of baptisms for the church of St. Nicholas in Leipzig, where the name appears as "Gottlob." The same name appears in Moritz Schreber's autobiographical writings (1833b, p. 11; Kloss, 1862, p. 11). Thus there is much more to argue in favor of "Gottlob."

The literature provides us with virtually all the possible permutations of the correct name "Daniel Gottlob Moritz Schreber," or "Moritz Schreber" for short. Here is a selection:

—Daniel Schreber (Daniels, 1975, p. 1331)
—Gottlob Schreber (O. Mannoni, 1974, p. 632)
—Gottlieb Schreber (*Deutsche Schreberjugend,* 1979, p. 1)
—Daniel Gottlieb Schreber (Bauer, 1937, p. 235; Buchheim, 1966, p. 180; Tabouret-Keller, 1973, pp. 295, 296)
—Daniel Gottlob Schreber (O. Mannoni, 1974, p. 631; Melman, 1980, p. 4)
—Daniel Moritz Schreber (J. G. D. Schreber, undated family tree; Daniels, 1975, p. 1339)
—Gottlieb Moritz Schreber (Kleine, 1958, p. 160; Kleine gave the impression that he was quoting from *Personalakten* (personal files); more on the reliability of Kleine in note 9 to Chapter 4), (Elliott-Smith [1973, p. 4] wrote "Gottlieb Morritz Schreber")
—Gottlieb Daniel Moritz Schreber ("Polizeiamt der Stadt Leipzig 105").

[2]In this note I shall show that the letters from Moritz Schreber which daughters of his had in their possession in 1909 may be the ones he wrote to his parents in 1835 which I found in the archives of the oldest Schreber Association in 1977.

As I have said, in 1909 two of Moritz Schreber's daughters, Klara and Sidonie, were in possession of some correspondence between their father and his parents. Klara died in 1917 and Sidonie in 1924. Neither had any children; the letters probably passed to their sister Anna. In 1929 Walter Bernhardt wrote a paper on Moritz Schreber as the final part of his work for his degree. It seems that he borrowed from Anna some letters by her father and omitted to return them. This at least is a possible inference from the following account of a visit to Moritz Schreber's by then extremely elderly daughter Anna in 1936 by Gerhard Richter, a prominent member of the first Schreber Association. Anna

> thanked me for our successful efforts to retrieve the letters written by her father (accounts of journeys) which she had lent *Studienassessor* [title of a fully qualified secondary school teacher] Bernhardt years previously, and which she calls *family heirlooms*. At my request she gave me these letters in trust and for our information; I promised her that I should bring them back to her undamaged in a few weeks. The family will then decide whether we may already have some of these letters for our archives now, while the rest we are in all likelihood to receive later [G. Richter, 1936a].

Richter met with at least a measure of success in this respect, for in his book of 1939 (1939b, p. 86) he was already able to write that his Schreber Association's archives possess "two letters from Dr. Schreber to his parents." It was in the same archives that I found the letters to which I referred earlier, written to his parents from Dresden in 1835 and fully justifying the description of "accounts of journeys."

Ritter (1936a, p. 9) wrote of Moritz Schreber: "his childhood was bathed in the sunshine of the deep love of his parents for one another and the deepest, truly devoted paternal and maternal love. Oral communication by Frau A. Jung, née Schreber, Leipzig; cf. Richard Siegel: Freund der Schrebervereine, 5. Jahrg. 1909, Heft 10."

It is thus unclear whether this text by Ritter is based on the passage by Siegel quoted in the text, or on statements made by Anna Jung. Even if we are to assume the latter, we must be wary of attaching too much value to such statements: is it possible for a descendant to make a good assessment of a parent-child relationship more than a century after the event?

It would not be necessary to spend so much time on this were it not for the fact that Tabouret-Keller (1973, p. 296) wrote:

> The information [about the life of Moritz Schreber] that has seemed to me the most valuable is that gathered in 1934–5 from *Anna Jung, geborene Schreber,* eldest daughter of Daniel Gottlieb Moritz and, we are told, still in full command of her faculties. It is she who describes to us the earliest childhood of Daniel Gottlieb, to whom "all his

mother's love was consecrated'', bereaved of a child as she had been since the premature death of her first son. His childhood was bathed in the sunshine *(übersonnt)* of the deepest and most truly devoted *(treubesorgt)* paternal and maternal love.

Later Tabouret-Keller wrote of Ritter that he was the person ''who, as I have said, was able to hear the testimony of Anna, the eldest of the daughters. I have deliberately kept to the actual terms of these texts, confining myself in most cases to translating passages from them'' (1973, p. 297). Now that is certainly not a good idea: quite apart from the fact that Ritter was careless in his quotations (see note 8 below, note 17 to chapter 4, and note 1 to chapter 5), it is only in respect of the first four sentences of his book that he claims that they are based, or partially based, on statements made by Anna.

³Details of his tutors and subjects are to be found in his curriculum vitae (1833b). Ritter (1936a, p. 24) stated:

> It would have been interesting for Schreber's biographer to follow the details of his intellectual development. However, here all the sources fail us, his study-books have disappeared, there have never been lists of his own or borrowed books, and even the efforts kindly undertaken by the University of Leipzig, for which I should like to express my gratitude here, have remained unable to provide evidence about Schreber's teachers.

Curiously enough, it is precisely to the University of Leipzig that I owe my own knowledge of Schreber's tutors. In the excellent catalogue of the United States Army Library one of the university librarians was able to find for me the reference to the work in which Schreber's curriculum vitae is to be found.

Elsewhere Ritter wrote of Schreber's undergraduate years:

> there are no details about his years at the university, and all we can do is assume, by inference from the universality of his intellect which later becomes clear in his many writings, that apart from his medical studies he also devoted himself to philosophical, psychological and educational studies [1936a, p. 10].

Ritter's speculation is accurate as regards philosophy. There is no evidence, however, that Schreber studied psychology or education. Since Ritter, some authors have simply stated that apart from medicine Schreber also read philosophy, psychology, and education (Brauchle, 1937, p. 243; Milczewsky, p. 25; Bankhofer, 1977, p. 15). According to Kuppe (1976, p. 88) those were the only subjects he studied.

Niederland (1959a, p. 152) wrote that Moritz Schreber ''specialised in orthopedics''; Croufer (1970, p. 216) carried this over. Here Niederland is anticipating later events in Schreber's life. In 1844 he took over an orthopedic clinic, but there is nothing to point to any particular interest in orthopedics before then, as Uibe (1959, p. 216) had observed.

⁴The quotation is from E. H. Weber (1833, p. 12), who gave the date as ''October 1831.'' I found the exact dates of the examinations in the archives of what is now the Karl-Marx-Universität in Leipzig. These archives, however, do not tell us exactly which examination Moritz Schreber took on 15 October 1831: a curious omission, in the opinion of the director of the archives, Prof. Schwendler.

⁵I do not know where Schilling obtained his information. However, where I have been able to follow up his data I have found his article to be generally very good; so that I am inclined to give this particular piece of information some credence.

⁶The date of the degree ceremony is given in the archives of the University of Leipzig as 12 July 1831. However, someone has crossed out the year ''1831'' and written next to it ''muss wohl 32 heissen'' (must mean 32). In fact, however, it should

be 1833; see, for example, the title-page of the thesis (D. G. M. Schreber, 1833a). Schilling (1964, p. 23) also gave 1831 as the date of Schreber's doctorate. In a document drawn up in 1842 to Schreber's instructions (see note 11 to chapter 3) it is stated that he took his doctorate in February 1833; this is also mistaken.

I have not read the entire thesis. The text contains no autobiographical references.

[7]One of the less reliable stories, for example, is that when a student Moritz Schreber was one of those who "with fanatical enthusiasm worked intrepidly at strenthening the national feeling and fought and suffered for modern liberal reforms in all spheres" (Siegel, 1908c, p. 205). Gerhard Richter repeated this bombastic wording in his own books (1914a, p. 5; 1925, p. 5; 1939b, p. 14).

Other references to Moritz Schreber's student days which have no evidential foundation include the statement that "he attended to his studies with the greatest zeal" (Fritzsche, 1903, pp. 1–2; 1911, p. 179).

[8]In the following passage Ritter claimed to be *quoting* Schildbach: "Whereas in the first years of his time at the university Schreber was still a man of small and meagre figure, when he left the university he had far outstripped the average dimensions of the male physique" (1936a, p. 10). However, this is not a quotation but a (considerable) condensation. Niederland wrote of Moritz Schreber: "Even in his college years he is described as having been '*von dürftiger Gestalt*' (of very poor physique) and possibly having suffered from pulmonary tuberculosis in adolescence" (1974, p. 5). I do not know where Niederland got this idea of tuberculosis.

There is something to know about life at the Thomasschule. One of Moritz Schreber's classmates describes setting up a secret gymnastics group with a few classmates. Later, when they went up to the university in 1826, these boys joined a *Burschenschaft*, where they continued to engage in their gymnastics activities.

Unfortunately it is far from certain that Moritz Schreber was one of their number. The author in question signed himself merely "E. Bdt."; the list of names of those who joined the Leipzig *Burschenschaft Germania* in 1826 includes that of Carl Eduard Burkhardt (Leonhardt, 1928, p. 185), who was thus almost certainly "E. Bdt."; however, the same list does not contain the name of Moritz Schreber. In addition, it will be recalled, Schildbach (1862a, p. 5) stated quite definitely that Moritz Schreber first started gymnastics when he was a student.

Nevertheless I shall quote a passage from this piece by Schreber's classmate, first because gymnastics was later to become very important to Schreber, and second because the article gives a good idea of how treasonable (because it was nationalist in spirit) gymnastics was considered to be in the Saxony of 1825:

> We practised [it] in as great secrecy as possible—for we feared interdiction and punishment—and only trustworthy boys from the top two classes were admitted into the gymnastics club; it flourished quite splendidly; on Wednesday and Saturday afternoons we would walk out to Stünz, do vigorous exercises on the horizontal and parallel bars, later we would have a very frugal supper with a small glass of milk or brown beer, and then we would make our way back to town with much song and dance. It was not long before we had equipped ourselves with student-song books [*Commersbücher*], from which we learned the gymnasts' and patriotic songs by heart and practised them with amazing aptitude [Bdt., 1859, p. 70].

[9]For example Schildbach, Schreber's later assistant and successor, spent several years as a *Reisearzt* (travelling physician) after qualifying (Brehme, 1889, p. 9). J. C. A. Heinroth, who will receive passing attention below (see page 23), also became personal physician to an itinerant Russian nobleman upon completing his studies, on his way home spending some time in Vienna to study further—thus exactly paralleling

Moritz Schreber's career up to that point (*Allgemeine Deutsche Biographie,* 1880, Band 11, p. 648). Niederland (1974, p. 87) cited another such case.

[10]On seeing the name "Stakovich," anyone who has read the *Memoirs* will at once be alerted: the head of the sick Paul Schreber was once filled with the souls of 240 Benedictine monks led by a father "whose name sounded like Starkiewicz" (D. P. Schreber, 1903, p. 49 = 1955, p. 71); "a Viennese nerve specialist" bore the same name.

[11]My source for Chernigov is Schilling (1964, p. 4). At least: Schilling referred to "Tschornigow/Russland." Where he got this information I do not know. Nevertheless I do not doubt its authenticity. Chernigov is not far from Kiev, and from Moritz Schreber's letters of the period (1935b, p. 2) it is clear that the Russian nobleman's estates were in that region. Schilling, however, probably never saw these letters.

According to the *Illustrierte Zeitung* (1862, p. 80) and Schreiber (1894, p. 2), Moritz Schreber did not become a personal physician until 1835.

The following observations by Schütze may properly be placed under the heading of curiosities. He wrote of Moritz Schreber's experiences

> as travelling physician in the service of a Russian aristocrat. Above all, in Russia the young doctor had . . . come to the realization that the simplest, strongest and healthiest people were to be found precisely where they were still in communion with nature and the soil [Schütze, 1936a, p. 11 = 1936c, p. 528]

[12]I have taken this dating from Schilling (1964, p. 4): "In the autumn of 1836 he returned from *Tschornigow/Russland* to Leipzig." How Schilling arrived at this dating I do not know. It was between Chernigov and Leipzig, incidentally, that the study visits to Berlin, Vienna, and Prague undoubtedly took place: the source for this (Heindl, 1859, p. 396) was drawn up according to information provided by Moritz Schreber himself (1858c). According to the *Leipziger Tageblatt* (J., 1861, p. 5813) Schreber first visited Berlin, Vienna, and Prague, and only then became a personal physician; this is unquestionably false.

[13]Moritz Schreber "qualified as a *Privatdozent* in 1837," according to the *Leipziger Tageblatt* article of G.W. of 1908, generally so well informed: in this case, however, it was mistaken, since Schreber became a *Privatdozent* in 1836.

According to Hirsch, (1887, p. 279), Schreber was *"Privatdozent* in internal medicine and medication science [Heilmittellehre]." I do not know where Hirsch got this information, though it is true that in 1840 Schreber published a booklet entitled *Die Normalgaben der Arzneimittel* (Standard medicament dosages).

It was undoubtedly in his function as a *Privatdozent* that Schreber wrote a letter which is undated and difficult to decipher, in which he informs the recipient, who is addressed merely as "Dear Friend," that there is scarcely any literature on the subject in question (which is clearly of a medical nature). At the same time he sent his correspondent two books from his library (one of which was entitled, in English, *Memoirs*) in which he might perhaps find something on the subject.

[14]More precisely: in 1855 his name no longer appeared in the university yearbook as a *Privatdozent.* The Leipzig directories were somewhat later in noting the change: in 1856 his name no longer appeared in the list of *Privatdozenten*; in 1858 the fact that he was a *Privatdozent* was no longer recorded in the entry for his name. Tabouret-Keller wrote: "It was during this same period (between 1840 and 1843; I have been unable to establish the exact year) that Schreber gave up his work as a *Privatdozent*, on account of a chain of events that is difficult to elucidate" (1973, p. 301). As we have already seen, he in fact gave up his work as a *Privatdozent* sometime in the

eighteen-fifties. I was curious to know what complex "chain of events" (concours de circonstances) Madame Tabouret-Keller had discovered. She wrote to me (16 January 1979) that this "chain of events that is difficult to elucidate" meant that she did not know why he gave up his work as a *Privatdozent*. (Her "source" was undoubtedly Ritter [1936a, p. 23].)

3

PAULINE HAASE: BACKGROUND, MARRIAGE TO MORITZ SCHREBER, EARLY YEARS OF MARRIAGE

1. PAULINE HAASE (b. 1815)

Pauline Haase[1] was the daughter of a professor of medicine at Leipzig, Wilhelm Andreas Haase, mentioned above as one of those who taught Moritz Schreber. For many years he was also the university's rector magnificus. Pauline, therefore, came from a family of considerably higher standing than her future husband. Not that the Haases could boast any particularly illustrious ancestry: though grandfather Haase had also been professor of medicine, his father had been a brandy distiller. Much more distinguished, and richer, was the family of Pauline's mother, whose maiden name was Wenck. It was from this side of the family that Pauline's parents inherited two manorial estates—estates to which as an old woman Pauline was to allude as follows:

> Of course in the old days being the lord of the manor was something grand, but now you're just rabble. In the old days they would have been entitled to have themselves buried in Leipzig with a coach-and-four and veiled horses, and all the people including the local dignitaries would walk alongside [Oral statement recorded by the wife of one of her grandsons (K. Jung, 1907)].

The Wencks and the Haases must have known each other well.

As professors at Leipzig, Pauline's grandfathers were colleagues, and when referring to her parents she related the story that Professor Wenck was supposed to have said: "If one of the Haases comes along wanting Julie for a wife, give her to him." She continued: "And then a Wilhelm Haase really did marry Juliane Wenck."[2] More detailed information about the two families is to be found in the *"Ahnentafel der Familie Wenck und Haase"* (Table of ancestors of the Wenck and Haase family) (G. Friedrich, 1932–33).

Regarding her birth Pauline told a story which was likewise recorded by her grandson's wife:

> Grandmama was born on 28 June 1815, ten days after the battle of Waterloo; prematurely, as she herself said, because of the rejoicing at the victorious battle. According to her it was only nine days later that they heard the news and celebrated it with punch. In the process, she said, her mother "over-exerted herself with the lemon-squeezers" [K. Jung, 1907].

The house in which Pauline was born was called *"Die Feuerkugel"* (the fireball).[3] She was later often to repeat the story

> of how her parents lived at The Fireball for some years, and how the windows of Goethe's room were frequently pointed out to them. She was very proud of the fact that in the whole of Leipzig she was the only one to know this, so one day she had to be driven there to show the committee of the Leipzig Goethe Society exactly which windows they were, so that they could put the memorial plaque between them [*ibid.*, 1907].

The same story appeared in obituaries of Pauline Schreber (*Leipziger Tageblatt*, 1907a; Siegel, 1907c, p. 126) and a poem written by Paul Schreber to celebrate her ninetieth birthday (D. P. Schreber, 1905, p. 1). The poem also recorded the names of the houses in which the Haases lived later: *Hohmanns Hof* (Hohmann's Court), *Schwarzes Brett* (Black Board), and finally *Das Fürstenhaus* (Prince's House).

> No coincidence that, to take that house:
> Usually only the professors were tenants.
> Prince's House! How the proud name reverberates
> Full of memories in your soul!
>
> [D. P. Schreber, 1905, p. 2]

Pauline had two brothers and two sisters.[4] Both brothers died when about fifty without having married; curiously, this is all we are told about them by the family tree.[5] "Grandmama's [Pauline's] parents had had a very grand life. The daughters had a governess and the sons a private tutor. In the evenings the manservant always walked in front with the lantern" (K. Jung, 1907). The children received their education at home. Paul gave a brief account of it in his poem for his ninety-year-old mother:

> School was disdained: it was held to be grand
> To keep in its stead a magister.
> He praised, reproved if the occasion arose,
> He taught you and with you your siblings,
> Everything that is part of an education:
> World history, natural history, foreign languages—
> Your head was burdened almost more than was just:
> It is still noticeable now, in your old age.
> Despite this you have always loved books:
> But who your valiant teachers were,
> Apart from Hauthal, Reichardt and Krüger,
> That I could probably only learn from you yourself,
> For there can hardly be any other witnesses still alive.
> They have all passed on long since:
> It will soon be eighty years and more.
> Since a start was made with your education.
>
> [D. P. Schreber, 1905, p. 1]

Visitors, too, were received at the home of Pauline's parents:

> Learned men went in and out;
> Conversing cheerfully and congenially
> Was your parents' joy; and Father did not
> Scorn a good feast with his glass of wine.
>
> [Ibid., p. 2]

The "learned men" included Professor J. C. A. Heinroth, still well known on account of his psychiatric publications, and the criminal law specialist Professor C. J. G. S. Wächter (Siegel, 1907c, p. 126); both are accorded entries in the *Allgemeine deutsche Biographie* (General German biographical dictionary).

But it was not only the intellectual that interested the Haases: cultural matters in general seem to have played an important part in

Haase family life. I have referred to the way Goethe's old rooms were frequently drawn to the children's attention. The Haases also made music at home, and "concerts at the Gewandhaus were hardly ever missed" (D. P. Schreber, 1905, p. 2). From 1835 the famous Gewandhaus orchestra was conducted by the young but already world-renowned Felix Mendelsohn-Bartholdy, at that time still unmarried. Mendelssohn was to be important to Pauline until her old age. Probably he also visited the Haases at home.[6]

> Dear Grandmama [i.e. Pauline] used to look down on the present *Gewandhaus,* concerts with great scorn. In her day, Mendelsohn had conducted in person. Schumann too. They had sung from the manuscript scores. . . . Once in the forties the bishop and cardinal had been at the *Gewandhaus.* Probably in honour of Mendelsohn's engagement to be married [K. Jung, 1907].

This last supposition is false: Mendelssohn had become engaged in 1836, and married in the following year. A year after that, and also a year after her father's death, Pauline married the poor and undistinguished *Privatdozent* and family doctor Moritz Schreber, who had also lost his father the previous year.

2. MARRIAGE (1838) AND FIRST YEARS OF MARRIAGE OF MORITZ AND PAULINE SCHREBER

Pauline's son Paul wrote the following verses about her earlier suitors:

> Every now and then a suitor would appear,
> Ready to unite himself with you for life;
> One exalted man swore solemnly
> That he could find happiness only with you.
> Rejection was painful for the poor man,
> And for you too it is not one of your pleasant memories;
> But it would not have done to take on
> The unloved one's yoke of marriage purely out of compassion.
> So it went on, until the right man came along;
> When he, a young doctor, spoke of love,
> When he summoned up the courage for a proposal,
> Then to be sure there was no need for long reflection.
> Near Machern, under a viaduct*
> —the "Lightning" was just passing at full steam—
> Your heart throbbed mightily once more:

"Yes"—it was out, and you were promised for life.
And when the steamy mist had drawn away
It was soon clear as daylight to others too
That Amor once again had drawn his bow,
That Miss Haase was now a bride.

*Note for other readers: in those days (early 1838) the railway line from Leipzig to
Dresden had only been completed as far as Machern. Every now and then excursion
trains were laid on to give the people of Leipzig an opportunity to try out the great
innovation of the railway [D. P. Schreber, 1905, p. 2].

Needless to say, the young doctor who asked for Pauline's hand
at the beginning of 1838 was Moritz Schreber. The wedding took place
on 22 October 1838 in St. Nikolas' Church in Leipzig (*Zentralstelle
für Genealogie*; D. P. Schreber, 1905, p. 2).

Before his marriage Moritz Schreber had lived at *Hainstrasse
354, Fleischergasse 242*, and *Thomaskirchhof 105*. These high numbers in such a relatively small town as Leipzig was then—the population in 1830 was something over forty thousand (*Leipzig* 1914, p.
20)—are explained by the fact that they are not street numbers.

At the end of 1838 or the beginning of 1839 the young couple
moved into an apartment in a house variously described as *Brühl 317*
(Leipzig university yearbook, 1839) and *Theaterplatz 4* (Leipzig directory, 1840 and 1841) or *Theaterplatz 5* (Leipzig university yearbook, 1841). Evidently numbering the houses by streets was introduced
in that year. It was here that their first child, Gustav, was born on 27
July 1839. Their second, Anna, was born on 30 December 1840, "in
a house . . . which stood near the old theatre, where a department
store is now going up on the corner of Brühl and the Richard-Wagner-
Strasse," as she herself later recorded (B. 1940). The next addition
to the Schreber household was not their third child. I quote from the
poem for Pauline Schreber's ninetieth birthday:

The first pain entered your young married life.
Your mother died. The flat became too small;
It was a matter of taking in your youngest sister;
You were obliged—otherwise it would not have been possible—
To resign yourselves to a new apartment.
Your choice fell on the Thomaskirchhof.
[D. P. Schreber, 1905, p. 3]

Pauline's mother died in 1841. The family moved to a flat at

Thomaskirchhof 22 and Pauline's youngest sister Fanny went to live with them. She was then thirteen or fourteen, and married ten years later. I have not discovered whether she lived with the Schrebers all that time, and indeed it is only from Paul Schreber's poem that I know she lived there at all. We may assume that the death of Pauline's mother meant a large legacy for the Schrebers. There is no other way I can explain the fact that from 1844 onward Moritz Schreber is listed in the Leipzig directories as the owner of business premises in the Leipzig shopping street *Brühl* (No. 54–55). But now back to Paul's poem; he wrote of this flat on the *Thomaskirchhof*:

> Two little children you had already brought with you.
> A boy and a little girl were there
> When, before it was really expected,
> The stork ventured to come again;
> That is when I appeared.

> [*ibid.*, p. 3]

Paul Schreber was born on 25 July 1842.[7]

3. THE "FORMER LUNATIC" IN MORITZ SCHREBER'S FIRST BOOK (1839)

I shall have only relatively infrequent occasion to quote or summarize passages in Moritz Schreber's books. The books themselves can be found without any great difficulty, and summaries are usually less interesting than the original. In this biographical part of my study I shall use Moritz Schreber's work only to the extent that it contains references to the Schrebers themselves.

A borderline case is to be found in *Das Buch der Gesundheit*, Moritz Schreber's first book published in 1839, which offers general advice for a physically and mentally healthy life. Here (pp. 198–202) Schreber presents, as an instructive tale, a "Confession of a former lunatic." This is a life-history which Schreber claims to have heard from a "scholar" he once met in the south of Germany, a scholar who, however, "when giving his narrative at the same time expressed the wish that he might see it published on some suitable occasion." The psychoanalyst W. G. Niederland (1974, p. 64) suggested that this story might be autobiographical. Before I discuss the arguments in favor of this suggestion I shall summarize the "confession."

"Born of extremely upright parents I enjoyed a very sound education in which at most only somewhat more discipline might have been desirable in some respects." The subject had a congenital tendency towards melancholy and at the age of twelve began to suffer from an *idée fixe* which is not specified. At the age of sixteen or seventeen attacks of melancholy began in which "all sorts of black thoughts tormented me, particularly an urge to commit criminal acts which was in all the more glaring opposition to my otherwise very genial nature."

He neglected his work, was uncharitable towards those around him, and then suffered agonies of remorse. True melancholy

> broke out again in increased measure when I had already reached the age of manhood, after I had attained circumstances which more than ordinarily turned the circle of my thoughts away from the outside world and towards itself. . . . Madness roared through my brain day and night. The quite peculiar and exceedingly troublesome headache which this brought on multiplied my suffering with oft-recurring attacks. . . . The urge to evil became ever more terrible and was rekindled and inflamed by every opportunity which presented me with the possibility of committing a misdeed. . . . Those about me noticed some signs of neglect in my otherwise hard-as-iron body, and now and then somewhat more absences of mind and a more sombre aspect than usual, it is true, but they attributed this to physical ill-being. . . . This ghastly condition lasted more than two years. . . . Then finally I collected together the last remains of my spiritual strength and determined forcibly to suppress every malicious thought as soon as it appeared.

After a long struggle he regained his love of God and his peace of mind. End of story. Schreber added a brief comment: this story may be unusual, but it can teach us that every bad tendency must be suppressed from the very beginning, and that the human will is capable of great things if it perseveres. The former lunatic, he tells us, now lives "fully reconciled with God, the world and himself, and has been for many years satisfied and happy in the bosom of his family, enjoying on account of his steadfast and upright character the respect and love of all who know him."

Niederland said of this story that "In its veiled language the account reads like an autobiographical record the content of which corresponds essentially to the previously mentioned entry in the Sonnenstein report" (1974, p. 64). This "entry in the Sonnenstein report"

is a note on Moritz Schreber found in the reports on his son Paul which
were drawn up by the Sonnenstein psychiatric clinic; it reads as follows:
"His father (originator of the 'Schreber garden allotments' in Leipzig)
suffered from obsessional ideas with homicidal tendencies"[8] (quoted
by Baumeyer, 1956, p. 62). The note was made by a psychiatrist more
than thirty years after Moritz Schreber's death.[9] It almost certainly
refers to the last ten years of Moritz Schreber's life, when he was
suffering from a peculiar "head complaint" which I shall discuss
below (pp. 59–60). Some time before the onset of this complaint, an
iron ladder had fallen on him, striking him on the head. However,
Moritz Schreber does not appear to have known whether the complaint
was a result of the ladder accident or of "a severe nervous breakdown"
(Fritzsche, 1926, pp. 13–14). A curious doubt in view of the fact that
he was quite convinced that he led the healthiest possible sort of life.
But the fear of a severe nervous breakdown would be understandable
if one accepts the premise that he recognized the head complaint from
his earlier years, from the story of the former lunatic.

The literary device of describing his own experiences as though
they were the experiences of another is not uncommon in the work of
Moritz Schreber (see p. 88).

4. FAILED AMBITIONS: CHILDREN'S HOSPITAL AND
EXTRAORDINARY PROFESSORSHIP (1839–43)

Moritz Schreber was now in his early thirties, a family doctor,
Privatdozent, author, husband and father. He was also evidently full
of surplus energy, as some ambitious plans from this period show. The
first of these was the foundation of a children's hospital in Leipzig.
The best source here is an obituary which refers to

> the failure of his favorite project of this time . . . which was the
> establishing of a children's hospital. Both numerous written appli-
> cations addressed to the relevant authorities in 1839 and 1840, and
> his personal efforts in the right quarters, met only with polite refusals
> [*Illustrierte Zeitung,* 1862, p. 80]

I have been unable to find any other record of this project.[10] There
then followed his unsuccessful application for an extraordinary professorship:

> For some time he had hopes of an extraordinary professorship. At

least, in September 1842 he declined to become an official citizen, pointing out that he had applied to the Ministry of Culture for a professorship to be conferred on him and that he hoped for a decision by Christmas. However, as these hopes did not materialize, despite the fact that he had a full professor as a father-in-law, in May 1843 he voluntarily put himself forward to become a citizen, and received civic rights on 20 May 1843. [W., 1908].[11]

Not all Moritz Schreber's ventures into public life were failures. In the early 1840's, for example, he was secretary to the *"Société Française de Leipsic."* To be precise, there is a copy of the *Dictionnaire de gallicismes* by Zitz-Halein of 1841, revised by C. F. Fliessbach, president of the same *Société Française*; the book's red leather cover is stamped with the following text: "Dedicated to my true friend Herr Dr. med. Moritz Schreber, Secrétaire de la Société Française de Leipsic, as a mark of the most sincere affection and gratitude, from the editor."

From 1839 on Schreber also belonged to the *"medizinische Gesellschaft"* (medical society) of Leipzig (Leipzig directory, 1839, pp. 95–96). Perhaps he was introduced by his father-in-law Professor Haase, who had been a member for some time. Another member of this society was to prove of vital importance in connection with a turn in Moritz Schreber's life: Ernst August Carus.

NOTES TO CHAPTER 3

[1]Her full name was Louise Henriette Pauline Haase; see, e.g., *"Acta der Frau,"* etc. Her gravestone gives the name as "Luise" instead of "Louise."

[2]These were stories told by Pauline and put into writing shortly after her death by a granddaughter-in-law (K. Jung, 1907). Here, as elsewhere in this biographical part of my thesis, I make use of writings by members of the family which were in many cases also intended principally only to be read by other members of the family. There are, of course, certain objections to the use of this kind of source. Romein (1946, pp. 204–205) opined that autobiographies are full of pitfalls for biographers on account of the sophisticated distortions introduced by their authors, and in a sense one might say that the same is true, or truer, of the kind of family writings used here, since here one also has to contend with distortions introduced because the writer has to take account of all the sensibilities of his readers, i.e., the other members of the family.

However, I believe there to be advantages to this kind of material which compensate for the disadvantages. In the first place: interest in the life of the Schrebers springs chiefly from curiosity as to the things that might have played a part in shaping the life of Paul Schreber. In this respect stories which can be established to have been current in Schreber family circles are far more interesting than possibly objectively accurate stories which may not have been known to Paul Schreber. For example: the details of the Schreber family tree would hardly be of much significance if we knew that the Schrebers themselves were not acquainted with their ancestry. A second advantage in this kind of material lies precisely in the distortion or coloring to which the "facts" are submitted, which tells us something about author, informant, or readership. Thus, in all Pauline's stories about the rich and well-connected life led by her parents, we may perhaps detect a silent reproach aimed at her husband, who was not even to reach the grade of professor.

³More detailed information about this house, and about the Haases' later houses in Leipzig, Hohmanns Hof, and Schwarzes Brett, is to be found in Grosse (1897, pp. 288–289; 1898, pp. 361, 736).

⁴According to the *Zentralstelle für Genealogie* in Leipzig, there were ten Haase children. Presumably the five extra children all died in infancy.

⁵It is curious that there is nothing in the family tree about Pauline's brothers, since the person who drew it up (G. Friedrich, 1932–33) undoubtedly used information provided by the two men's niece, Anna Jung. For example, if her uncles had had ordinary jobs, surely Anna would have known about it?

⁶Siegel (1907c, p. 126) simply said that Mendelssohn *"verkehrte"* in (was a regular visitor to) Pauline's parents' house. The notes made by the granddaughter-in-law on this point are singularly unhelpful. Part of the passage to which I refer has already been quoted. In full it reads as follows:

> Dear Grandmama used to look down on the present Gewandhaus concerts with great scorn. In her day, Mendelsohn conducted in person. Schumann too. They had sung from the manuscript scores and (Mendelsohn in the Fürstenhaus) and she had known personally such great artists as Clara Schumann, Jenny Lind, and Madam Schröder-Devrient [K. Jung, 1907].

The *Fürstenhaus* was the name of Pauline's parents' house: it looks as if the writer made a note in brackets, "Mendelsohn im Fürstenhaus," to remind herself that the story concerned was to be inserted at that point.

⁷According to the *"Polizeimeldebuch"* (the police register of births, deaths, residence, and so on) of Chemnitz, Paul Schreber was born in 1872.

His full name was Daniel Paul Schreber, which is how it appears in almost all the literature concerning him. I prefer to call him "Paul Schreber"; just as I prefer to call his father "Moritz Schreber" instead of "Daniel Gottlob Moritz Schreber." In the *Memoirs* the author's name is given as Daniel Paul Schreber; the same name is found in certain official documents. However, there is no doubt that the most commonly used version of his name was Paul Schreber, or P. Schreber, even on official occasions such as the signing of a letter regulating a bequest (A. Jung *et al.*, 1907). During his candidacy for the Reichstag in 1884, he was referred to exclusively as Paul Schreber. Those who knew him personally, too, always referred to him as Paul Schreber.

In the literature concerning him it is not uncommon to find him—erroneously—as Daniel Schreber or just Daniel (Shulman, 1959, p. 180; Elliott-Smith, 1973, p.4; O. Mannoni, 1974, p. 632; Meijer and Rijnders, 1976, p. 9; Fortuin, 1976; Schweighofer, 1976, p. 81; Eigler, 1978).

⁸This misunderstanding crops up constantly in the literature: Moritz Schreber was not the "originator" of the Schreber allotments in Leipzig.

⁹Meijer and Rijnders (1977, p. 23) made of this that Moritz Schreber suffered as an adolescent, by his own testimony, from attacks of melancholy and bloodlust.

¹⁰It is undoubtedly true that Moritz Schreber tried in vain to establish a children's hospital: his daughters tell the same story (Siegel, 1909b, p. 208; Fritzsche, 1926,

p. 13). However, I am not quite so sure about the dates given (1839 and 1840). In an article based on statements made by his daughter Anna we read: "This must have been in the early forties" (Fritzsche, 1926, p. 13). Schilling (1964, p. 8) placed this affair in 1843 (see also Note 9 to Chapter 4). I do not know what foundation he has for this; however, he must have been able to see material unknown to me—see note 11 to Chapter 2.

According to Tabouret-Keller (1973, p. 301) Moritz Schreber's efforts to found the children's hospital occurred "two years after his return, in 1840." But as Tabouret-Keller herself accurately recorded (*ibid.*, p. 297), Schreber had already returned from his travels abroad in 1836.

¹¹This article from the *Leipziger Tageblatt* of 1908 has never been used in subsequent literature. This is a pity, since the author (G.W.) is the only one who evidently did research in the Leipzig city archives. These contain the following document:

No. 5191
Leipzig
30 September
1842
Herr Dr. med. Daniel Gottlob Moritz Schreber appeared here in answer to a summons. It was explained to him how according to the general municipal statutes he is obliged to obtain citizen's rights here. Upon this Herr Dr. Schreber stated
> that he has applied to the ministry of culture for appointment to an extraordinary professorship in medicine and that he hopes to receive the relevant resolution by Christmas this year, on account of which he requests that until then he be excused the formalities for acquiring citizen's rights.
As regards his personal circumstance Herr Dr. Schreber stated
> that he was born in wedlock in Leipzig on 15 October 1808, the son of the advocate Johann Gottfried Daniel Schreber. He went to St. Thomas's School in this city, studied here from 1826 until 1831, took his doctorate in the medical faculty here in Feb. 1833, and has been married since 1838 to Louise Pauline Henriette Haase of this city, and they have three children.

Read out and approved by
D. Jerusalem, city councillor and sworn recorder

Leipzig
15 May 1843
Herr Dr. Schreber appeared here of his own free will and stated:
> I hereby wish to withdraw the recourse previously entered by me in the matter of acquisition of citizen's rights and request that citizen's rights be granted me.
Read out and approved, also jointly signed as follows:
Dr. med. Moritz Schreber.

The errors in this document should be noted: the name of Moritz Schreber's father, the date of his doctorate, and the order of his wife's forenames.

To the modern way of thinking it may seem odd that Schreber should himself ask for a professorship; but at the time it was by no means unusual. Where Karl Biedermann, a contemporary and compatriot of Schreber's, noted that he has been given an extraordinary professorship (1886, pp. 61, 62), he stated expressly that it was granted him without his having asked for it.

4

MORITZ SCHREBER'S SUCCESSFUL YEARS
(1844–51)

1. THE START OF THE ORTHOPEDIC CLINIC (1844–47)

In 1844 Schreber took over the orthopedic clinic of E. A. Carus. Some ten years older than Schreber, Ernst August Carus had studied medicine at Leipzig and then become a country doctor. Because of weak health, however, he was forced to exchange that profession for an extraordinary professorship in Leipzig. Besides this chair he also had a "Poliklinik für chirurchische Kranke" (Outpatient clinic for the surgically ill). "He also established in his house an orthopaedic clinic, in which the indigent from near and far sought and found the liberation from their infirmities which they desired. However, this clinic remained a private affair" (Adelmann, 1854, p. 10). This clinic can never have been particularly large, considering that running it was a job which Carus did alongside the surgical clinic and his professorial duties. In 1844 he was appointed to a chair at Dorpat (Tartu, in Estonia); it was then that Moritz Schreber took over his orthopedic clinic.[1]

One of his daughters was later to remember, with reference to the beginning of his work for the clinic:

How conscientious Dr. Schreber was then re-equipping Dr. Carus's orthopaedic clinic is illustrated by the fact that he beforehand (in 1844) undertook, in the company of the mechanic Reichel, a journey to Paris lasting several weeks, in order there to become familiar with the latest equipment for orthopaedics. Schreber needed Reichel as a practical man for orthopaedic equipment [Fritzsche, 1926, p. 13].

33

Moritz Schreber himself said: "From 1844 he was head of the orthopaedic and remedial gymnastics clinic in Leipzig. Later he undertook
two journeys for study purposes to Belgium, England, France, part of
Italy, and Switzerland"[2] (quoted by Kloss, 1862, pp. 11–12). Moritz
Schreber's passport for one of these journeys still exists. It is a large
sheet of paper, issued in Leipzig on 25 May 1846 and valid for two
months, made out in the name of "Dr. med. Moritz Schreber von
hier," the reason for its issuance being given as "travelling for pleasure
through Bavaria to France and back." The passport also contains a
"Description of the Person":

Age: 37
Height: tall[3]
Hair: fair
Brow: open
Eyebrows: fair
Eyes: brown
Nose: medium to long
Mouth: average
Beard: brown
Face: long
Complexion: healthy
Chin: round.

The back bears a number of stamps: Würzburg 29 May, Stuttgart 31
May, Paris 9 June and 11 June. Next to the Paris stamp of 11 June
there is a note to say that Schreber is returning to Saxony by way of
Valenciennes (on the border with Belgium).

Carus's orthopedic clinic in Leipzig was at Burgstrasse 15[4]; Schreber moved it to his own house at Königstrasse 4,[5] where he held his
surgery from 9 until 10 in the morning and from 3 until 4 in the
afternoon. His later associate Schildbach described the clinic rooms
as "rented town premises" (1861, p. 12).

For his old mother Paul Schreber composed the following lines
about this house:

the Königstrasse
Was only to touch the growth of the family,
Which, even if not in immodest measure,
Had nevertheless already led to there being four.

The fourth child was Sidonie (pronounced as four syllables, the stress falling on the second); she was born on 4 September 1846.

> When in addition the worry of strange children;
> The clinic had brought them in to you;
> There was no less vexation and trouble with them,
> But they were cared for as your own.
> Thus the household had grown large and larger,
> And with it the number of servants;
> It became necessary to look for somewhere else
> Where in future one might live on one's own.
>
> [D. P. Schreber, 1905, p. 3]

The new home was to be an enormous building. It is the subject of the following section.

2. THE HOUSE IN THE ZEITZER STRASSE (from 1847 on)

In 1847 the Schrebers moved to a house "outside the *Zeitzer* Gate." This building plays an essential role in the history of the Schreber family: Moritz Schreber lived there until his death, and it was there that he did most of his writing; the Schreber children grew up there—Paul was four years old when the family moved—and even after Schreber's death in 1861 it remained more or less the center of the family: Schreber's widow Pauline lived there until her death in 1907, albeit from 1874 onward in a house built in the garden at the back. All five Schreber children also spent some part of their adult life there: Sidonie, indeed, spent her entire life there until the house was demolished in 1915.

This was the same spot where, on his mother's birthday more than fifty years later, Paul Schreber was to read aloud his version of the building of the house:

> A home on its own plot of land was decided upon;
> . . .
> Almost countrified was its position in those days,
> The houses were only scattered, there where today
> The thronging of the big city is now almost a plague.
> Under construction! *Those* were happy times!
> Imagining a spot and a space for everyone.
>
> [D. P. Schreber, 1905, p. 3].

Das Heim Dr. Schrebers und seine gymnaftisch-orthopädische Heilanstalt
zu Leipzig um das Jahr 1850.

Fig. 5. Dr. Schreber's home and gymastic-orthopedic clinic in Leipzig around 1850. From Siegel (1909b, p. 206). See note 7.

In 1846 building work commenced (Schildbach, 1861, p. 12) on the house which Moritz Schreber "laid out and equipped superbly, especially for the purposes of the clinic, and to which he moved, with the clinic, in June 1847'' (Schildbach, 1877, p. vii). Initially the house was outside the town proper: the address was *Vor dem Zeitzer Thore 2* (outside the Zeitzer Gate, No. 2); later it became part of the *Zeitzer Strasse* (at first No. 43, subsequently No. 10).[6] Figure 5 shows the house. Figure 6 is a drawing of the ''corner of the Zeitzer and Hohe Strasse, February 1865, drawn from Zeitzerstrasse 10 *exactly* from life by Klara Schreber,'' according to a handwritten note on the back of the frame. Klara was the fifth and last of the Schreber children; she was born on 25 January 1848.

In 1861, i.e., at the end of Moritz Schreber's life, Schildbach described the layout of the house as follows:

> In the raised ground floor there is the very roomy, heated gymnasium with changing-room, in the basement the likewise heated bathroom with shower, rain-bath and inclined upward-facing shower. The first floor has, facing east ['gegen Morgen'] the rooms for me and my family, to the south ['gegen Mittag'] the living-room and the dormitory for the patients, and on the west side two small rooms, one with side-chamber, for those in-patients wishing or needing private rooms. The second floor is occupied by Herr Dr. Schreber. Immediately adjacent to the house is a large, shaded garden [Schildbach, 1861, p. 12].

There is not much other information to be found about the second and highest floor, occupied by the Schreber family. I quote from a newspaper article on the occasion of the hundredth birthday of the eldest daughter Anna (whose married name was Jung), where it refers to 1848:

> By that time the physician and orthopaedist Dr. Schreber was already living in the house which he had built for himself just outside the town in unspoilt countryside, at the edge of a garden which stretched as far as the Flossplatz, where today the great office block on the Adolf-Hitler-Strasse, where it joins the Hohe Strasse, is going up. ''We could see the church towers of 14 villages from here'', says Frau Jung [*Neue Leipziger Zeitung*, 1939].

The following is also based on Anna's recollection: her father's ''study

Fig. 6. *Zeitzer Strasse*, 1863; drawing by Klara Schreber.

in the Zeitzer Strasse was three flights up in the left-hand corner; the gymnasium was downstairs'' (G. Richter, 1935).

Between 1859 and 1877 patients came to the clinic literally from all over the world, even from as far away as Java, Russia, Egypt, and South America (Schildbach, 1877, p. xv). Add to this the colossal dimensions of the building which housed it (see Fig. 5), and one might easily suppose that the whole thing was an enormous operation. Wrong. The clinic and the living quarters for the Schrebers (and from 1859 for Schildbach and his family as well) took up far less than the entire building.[7] The clinic itself consisted of a large gymnasium, a shower-room, and accommodation for inpatients, whose numbers did not exceed more than four to seven children.[8] There were also outpatients, whose numbers I have not been able to determine reliably. In 1859 Moritz Schreber seems to have had remedial gymnastics sessions for outpatients only once a week—though this period was a nadir in the size of the clinic (Schildbach, 1864, p. 4).

> The clinic . . . never attained any significant dimensions, because Schreber was unwilling to go beyond the extent of a family circle with the number of his patients, apart from which he avoided with the greatest anxiety anything that might in any way have smacked of quackery [*Illustrierte Zeitung*, 1862, p. 81].

One wonders why Schreber built such an enormous structure for such a small clinic. In the passage just quoted the clinic's small size is attributed to his modesty and his deliberate policy. I should prefer not to exclude the possibility that it was the result of a gigantic miscalculation, and that he had in fact dreamed of a very large clinic.

3. MORITZ SCHREBER AND THE LEIPZIGER TURNVEREIN (1845–51)

Before 1845

Reference has already been made to Moritz Schreber's gymnastic activities: how as a student he developed his meager physique, and how some years later in Russia he exercised to get rid of his fat. In note 8 to Chapter 2 I quoted one of his former classmates who described how during the mid-1820's boys from the senior forms would meet secretly to do gymnastics. From that account it is apparent that gymnastics was a sort of philosophy: a philosophy of the revolutionary-nationalistic-song-singing variety. After the Napoleonic era gymnastics had been prohibited on account of this political complexion. By the middle of the 1830's, however, it was already being introduced in some schools in Saxony (Kötzschke and Kretzschmar, 1965, p. 327; H. E. Richter, 1863, p. 487; D. G. M. Schreber, 1843, p. 35). In this climate in the 1840's, it was quite possible for a group of about twelve respectable citizens of Leipzig, including Moritz Schreber, Professor Carl Ernst Bock, and Professor Karl Biedermann, the three future founders of the *Leipziger Turnverein,* to do exercises together (H. E. Richter, 1863, p. 487). Moritz Schreber's daughters were later to recall of their father: "For a while during the forties he did gymnastics with professors Biedermann and Bock and others, at six o'clock in the morning in a garden in the *Inselstrasse* belonging to Professor Bock's father-in-law" (Siegel, 1909b, p. 205).

Of the three founders of the *Leipzig Turnverein* just named, Schreber, Bock, and Biedermann, the first two had known each other for some time: as medical students in Leipzig they had been contemporaries, and after that they are both listed among the ten or so *Privatdozenten* in medicine at the university of Leipzig; moreover, as professor of medicine, Bock's father had been one of Schreber's teachers. Referring to collaboration between Schreber and Bock, Schildbach sang the former's praises as the true inventor of *"Heilturnen,"* gymnastics for orthopedic purposes: "Schreber created it through constant studies, which with Prof. Bock he tried out on his own body" (Schildbach, 1862a, pp. 5–6).

Schreber, Bock, and Biedermann not only exercised together: there were also points of contact on the political plane. Biedermann, who was slightly younger than Bock and Schreber and was professor of philosophy at Leipzig, had gradually started moving into politics. In 1845 he became a *Stadtverordneter,* or member of the city council: he was the most prominent of a number of moderate liberals. At this time Bock and Schreber were also city councillors. I shall return to this in the next section, which is devoted to political events of the period.

Moritz Schreber had not only been doing gymnastics with friends even before the founding of the *Turnverein* in 1845, he had also defended the sport in a little book published in 1843 entitled *Das Turnen vom ärztlichen Standpunkte aus, zugleich als eine Staatsangelegenheit dargestellt* (Gymnastics presented from a medical viewpoint and as a matter for the State). It is dedicated to the "Supreme Assembly of the Estates of the Kingdom of Saxony." In it, Schreber described the advantages of gymnastics from the health point of view and suggested a number of measures which the government might take, particularly regarding gymnastics as an obligatory subject in the school curriculum. The result was polite but noncommittal: "apart from a statement from what was then the ministry of culture, that they would henceforth be keeping an eye of the matter, there was, however, not even the slightest further result to be discerned" (Schildbach, 1862a, p.6), wrote Schreber's later associate.[9]

1845–51

The summary of Moritz Schreber's activities in and on behalf of the *Turnverein* in Leipzig is based chiefly on a chronological survey in the club's *Festschrift* of 1895 (pp. 2ff.).

On 23 July 1845 Professor Bock called a first preparatory meeting. Some twenty people attended, of whom five, including Moritz Schreber, took upon themselves the task of drawing up statutes for the new club. A week later they met again, the *Turnverein* was officially established, and Schreber was elected to the *Turnrat* (committee or council). An appeal to the citizens of Leipzig then appeared in the *Leipziger Tageblatt*, and a great public demonstration was planned for 17 August, with speeches in the *Schützenhaus* followed by gymnastics on the gymnastics ground. This gathering was postponed, however, because Leipzig had become the site of revolutionary chaos (see next section). Three days later the *Leipziger Tageblatt* published a long extract from the booklet by Schreber referred to above. Finally, a week later than originally planned, the demonstration took place: the *Leipziger Tageblatt* for 26 August recorded that two days previously Biedermann, Bock, and Schreber had given talks to an audience of several hundred people. Schreber had spoken on gymnastics as a means of curing infirmities. Subsequently the assembled gathering had repaired to the gymnastics ground, where there was a demonstration of gymnastics.

During the months which followed, a polemic centered on the *Turnverein* unfolded in the pages of the *Leipziger Tageblatt*; one anonymous writer tried to make the whole business politically suspect, whereas another declared that that was quite wrong: in the *Turnverein*, he wrote, "it is also not true, as some appear to believe, that under the mask of physical exercises, in a quite secret and surreptitious manner, demagogues will be trained and highly subversive plans hatched. Nay, nothing like that" (*Leipziger Tageblatt,* 27 November 1845, p. 3446). In Leipzig at any rate, gymnastics was a matter for a highly respectable class of people:

> At the end of the first year of its existence, 1845, the club already numbered 187 members, viz. 15 lawyers, 7 doctors, 2 civil servants, 6 writers, 15 booksellers, 87 businessmen, 8 artists, 5 teachers, 5 professors, 3 technicians, 17 handicraftsmen and 17 students [Euler, 1895, p. 37].

On 27 March 1846 Moritz Schreber took over the presidency of the club from Biedermann. On 14 July 1846 it is recorded that "The president, Dr. Schreber, pointed out in answer to a written query from the government to the committee that the *Verein* did not pursue any subsidiary objectives whatever" (*Festschrift,* 1895, p. 6). "Subsidiary objectives" (Nebenzwecke) here unquestionably mean "political aims."

At the First Saxon Gymnastics Festival held from 30 October to 1 November 1846, two members of the Leipzig club took part; one of them was Moritz Schreber. The club already possessed a square where it could practise its exercises; in 1847 a gymnasium was built. In the *Leipziger Tageblatt* for 8 April 1847 (p. 925) we read that the club had issued shares for this purpose, that it was on a sound financial footing (with an annual grant from the city of two hundred thalers and a further thousand thalers coming in as subscriptions)[10] and that matters concerning the building were in the hands of five gentlemen, one of whom was Moritz Schreber. The new gymnasium was opened on 12 August 1847, on which occasion Schreber made a speech.

The year 1848 will be discussed at greater length in the next section. Moritz Schreber was able to stop a demonstration by the *Turnverein* planned for 18 March 1848 (Ritter, 1936a, p. 18).[11] This undoubtedly spared the club political difficulties in the years that followed. The *Festschrift* recorded, for 2 August 1848, a

> [n]otice from president Schreber to the Ministry. According to which within the *Verein,* which numbers 770 members, there is a choral society with 30, a gymnastic arms drill team ['Turnwehrmannschaft'] with 80 and a firefighting and rescue squad with 180 members [1895, p. 7].

A *Turnverein* of 770 members was very large for those days.

In 1849 the gymnasium was enlarged (Schildbach, 1862a, p. 6). Moritz Schreber again made a speech, the manuscript of which has been preserved[12]: he said that he is pleased at the club's rapid growth, especially in such difficult times for the sport generally; he expressed the opinion that governments should make gymnastics compulsory in schools; and he closed by saying that gymnastics clubs are essentially apolitical.

At the end of 1851 Schreber resigned both from his official functions in the *Turnverein* and from the club itself. The official explanation is that he did so for health reasons, and indeed it was in 1851 that he began to suffer from the peculiar head complaint to which brief reference has already been made and which I shall discuss at greater length below. Nevertheless, the fact that he left the club altogether seems to indicate something in the nature of a difference of opinion. It was at about this time within the *Verein* that a school of thought gained the ascendancy to the effect that gymnastics must not be a means to an end (the improvement of physical well-being) but an end in itself (Euler, 1895, p. 37).

After 1851

The break with the *Turnverein* was not a permanent one:

> Unfortunately in 1851 Schreber was obliged by considerations of health to withdraw not only from all public affairs but also from the running of the turnverein, but his heart remained true to the cause, and he not only constantly returned to the subject of gymnastics in his medical and educational writings, but also, at Christmas 1859, sought through an address written with great spirit and verve to win over to gymnastics the generality of students; and when at least two student societies in Leipzig have started demanding that their members take part in the exercises of the turnverein, this is, in part at least, Schreber's work[13] [Schildbach, 1862a, p. 6].

On 11 January 1856, moreover, he was made an honorary member (*Festschrift*, 1895, p. 46). In 1860 he made another speech to the *Turnverein*, the text of which, hardly legible, has survived. Also in 1860, on 5 December, he addressed the thirteen *Turnvereins* of the Leipzig region on the subject of the fundamental rules of gymnastics;

the text of this address also appeared in print (D. G. M. Schreber, 1860c).

4. SOME RELIGIOUS AND POLITICAL EVENTS OF THE 1840'S

This section deals with a number of religious matters which caused feelings to run high in the Leipzig of the 1840's, and with some related major riots.

Interest in the lives of the Schrebers springs chiefly from the hope that information about what Paul Schreber lived through in his normal life may shed light on the deranged ideas which occur in his *Memoirs of My Nervous Illness*. In this section I shall be pointing out several "religious" matters in the Leipzig of the very young Paul Schreber which may perhaps have a bearing on some of the religious figures in the *Memoirs*. The most important of these, the God-figure, has a great deal to do with reality, namely with Paul's father—a circumstance which, since the work of Freud, Niederland, and others, can scarcely be called into doubt. I want here to point out real events which may perhaps have something to do with the Wandering Jew and the unpleasant Catholics who turn up in the *Memoirs*.

The Wandering Jew brings me to a novel and a play, unpleasant Catholics to the Saxon hatred of Catholics. The Saxon hatred of Catholics brings me to the riots in Leipzig to which it contributed. In those riots Paul's father, as a member of the civil guard and city councillor, also played a modest role. This, briefly, is the subject of this section.

The Wandering Jew

The concept of the Wandering Jew plays a part in Paul Schreber's *Memoirs*. Sometimes God destroys the world, only one man being spared, a man known as the Wandering Jew (ewige Jude).[14] He is then supposed to turn into a woman and bear children to repopulate the world. Paul Schreber thought that he was predestined to be the Wandering Jew (D. P. Schreber, 1903, pp. 53–54 = 1955, pp. 73–74).

The Wandering Jew, as Paul Schreber knew, is an old mythical theme. There was Jesus, groaning under the weight of the Cross, wanting in his exhaustion to lean against a house; this was forbidden him by the owner, a Jew, whom Jesus then cursed, condemning him to wander the world until the Day of Judgment. Subsequently the Jew turned up in a wide variety of places: in 1542 he was seen in Hamburg, in 1575 in Madrid, and so on. The theme has frequently been used in literature, as in a novel by Eugène Sue entitled *Le juif errant*.

I mention this work because Prado de Oliveira (1979b, pp. 261–269) drew attention to all kinds of parallels between it and the *Memoirs*. At the same time he passed rather lightly over the question of whether Paul Schreber knew it. All he had to say is that:

> *Le juif errant,* was published between 1845 and 1847 in the pages of *Constitutionnel*, in Paris. It immediately brought fame for Sue and subsequently went through numerous editions, being as popular in the second half of the last century as the novels of Balzac or Victor Hugo [*ibid.*, 1979b, p. 263].

Paul Schreber was, as his *Memoirs* demonstrate, an educated man. However, almost all his references are to the products of German culture, and it is therefore not especially illuminating in this context to point out that Sue's novel was as widely read as those of Balzac and Hugo.

Despite this, the assumption that *Le juif errant* was not unknown in Germany is quite correct. The *Leipziger Tageblatt* provides a nice illustration of this at the end of 1845. In the issue of 26 December (p. 3797) there is an announcement of the première of the drama *Der ewige Jude*, based on the novel by Sue.[15] Two days later the paper's reviewer wrote that "The whole world has heard talk of Sue's wandering Jew, the whole world wants in a couple of hours to get at least an idea of it" (H.L., 1845).

Prado de Oliveira also looked to Sue's novel for an explanation of the Jesuits who play an unpleasant part in the *Memoirs*. However, the unattractive roles played by both Jesuits and other Catholics in the *Memoirs* also have their parallels in the real world in which Paul Schreber lived.

Anti-Catholic feeling[16] *and riots*

According to the Augsburg Confession of 1530 Saxony was a Protestant land. In the days of Moritz and Paul Schreber the predominantly Evangelical Lutheran population was headed by a Catholic royal house. When in 1830 the government failed to give its full support to the celebration of three hundred years of the Augsburg Confession—certain parades and processions were prohibited—this led to a certain amount of unrest. Then a curfew was imposed, after which a party spreading into the street was enough to trigger off enormous riots during two days in which the authorities were conspicuous by their absence. The homes of a number of senior police officials and a member of the city council who had placed an order with an handicraftsman from outside Leipzig were broken into and property destroyed. Herr Brockhaus's new cylinder press almost suffered the same fate, and there was also havoc in a number of brothels. After two days of rioting a citizens' militia was formed (the beginning of the later civil guard, the *Communalgarde*), which saw to it that normal law and order was restored. There was renewed serious rioting in 1831.

The most spectacular year for riots in Leipzig was 1845. Besides political affairs there were again religious problems. "However, in the Germany of those days, and especially in Saxony, people were almost even more excitable and suspicious in matters of religion than in matters of politics" (Biedermann, 1886, p. 234). Jesuits were officially prohibited in Saxony. There was great uproar when a Jesuit mark appeared on a Catholic church and the authorities did nothing about it. At about the same time more latitudinarian Protestant groups were beginning to spring up. The Saxony government proclaimed a ban on religious meetings. A brother of the King, suspected of harboring Catholic sympathies, stayed in a Leipzig hotel. After that the situation erupted: singing and catcalling outside the hotel, no *Communalgarde* to break up the assembly, a stone through a window, then without warning a salvo from the military garrison which cost several passers-by their lives; great commotion, the authorities nowhere to be seen for a week, "running" of the town only by daily popular gatherings led by the radical Robert Blum (later to find his way into the history books on account of the way in which he was executed in Vienna in 1848). That, in telegrammatic terms, was the pattern of the rioting in Leipzig in 1845 (Biedermann, 1886, pp. 234–238). The popular meetings took place in the *Schützenhaus*, causing the postponement of the recruitment meeting which Moritz Schreber and his gymnast friends were to have held there.

It was these events of 1845 which became the earliest memories of Paul Schreber's sister Anna, eighteen months older than he. That is what emerges from a newspaper article about Anna when she reached her hundredth birthday in 1940, though either Anna or the journalist appears not quite to have understood the situation. The old lady well remembers times long ago. The serenade, for example, which enthusiastic Leipzigers gave Prince Johann, who was living in the Hotel de Prusse. The fact that the civil guard did not prevent it was afterwards deprecated by Dresden. That is probably her youngest childhood memory, followed by those of the turbulent year 1848 [A.L., 1940].

I shall therefore go straight on to the events of 1848 and continue the quotation about Anna:

At that time her father, the spiritual author of the Schreber movement, the physician and orthopaedist Dr. Daniel Gottlieb Schreber, was himself in the civil guard—'which was the done thing', says his daughter today—and the children admired him in his uniform [*ibid.*, 1940].

Two years previously Anna had already told the same journalist this kind of thing about 1848.

At that time my father was in the civil guard. On Holy Saturday he didn't come home, which was enough to make us fearful of trouble, especially as barricades had been put up at the Café Français—now Kaffeehaus Felsche. And of course that is where Commandant Gontard was shot and killed, a very honourable and respected man. Another memory I still have of that time—I would have been eight years old [actually seven]—was when one night we were woken up and had to put on our clothes because the volunteers were supposed to be coming. But they didn't come, and we children thought the assembly in the front hall in the middle of the night was grand fun. When our father wore his uniform we were quite especially proud of him [A.L., 1938, also quoted in G. Richter, 1939b, p. 24].

These riots were one side of the events of 1848 as they took place in Leipzig; the other side was the municipal authorities, which themselves protested, albeit very cautiously, to the Saxon government. It was a protest by the entire city council, both *Stadtverordneten* and *Stadtrath*; at the initiative of the moderate liberal councillor Karl Biedermann a petition was submitted to the king in Dresden asking, among other things, for a lifting of the censorship—something that in those days had become a real possibility. The king reacted with irritation, troops were later concentrated around the "rebelling" city, but in the end nothing happened. One of the city councillors who supported the petition was Moritz Schreber.[17]

Another councillor was Professor Carl Ernst Bock, who, as we have seen, was one of the founders of the *Turnverein*. The frequency with which the same names keep cropping up in different contexts is conspicuous. There are other examples: a brother of Moritz Schreber's father-in-law was also a councillor, as was Robert Blum, who also happened to be the secretary of the theater where *The Wandering Jew* was put on. Professor Bock also had a senior post in the civil guard. The reason for this frequent recurrence of the same names is not only that Leipzig was at that time quite a small town by modern standards—in 1840 the population stood at fifty thousand (*Leipzig im Jahre 1904*, p. 35)—but also that the section of the community that got into the news was in those days proportionately smaller than in our own times.

Moritz Schreber as "Communalgardist" and "Stadtverordneter"

It has already become clear from Anna Schreber's recollections of 1848 that her father was a member of the civil guard. Such militias were established throughout Saxony in 1830. Officially, the idea was that all able-bodied men would join, but this still meant that the guard in Leipzig only numbered a few thousand members. Moritz Schreber's function was probably not of any great importance; otherwise Anna would not so immediately have linked the uniform with 1848, when undoubtedly as many members of the corps as possible would have been mobilized.

We have also seen that Moritz Schreber was on the city council. He was a city councillor from 1846 until 1851: first, in 1846, as a substitute member, from 1847 until 1850 as an ordinary member, and in 1851 as vice-president, according to the Leipzig directories.

At this time city councillors were elected every three years on the basis of indirect partial franchise (see *Sächsische Vaterlands-Blätter*, 1845, p. 833). There was not yet a true party system. There was, however, among the town councillors of Leipzig, a radical faction led by Robert Blum. It would also be correct to speak of a moderate liberal faction whose most prominent member was the Karl Biedermann who has already been mentioned. His political opinions are precisely known from his own autobiography. Moritz Schreber's political views are not known, but I assume he belonged to Biedermann's faction. They did a lot together on the gymnastics side, they came from comparable professional backgrounds, and were later both pro-Prussian.

The *Leipziger Tageblatt* carried reports of city council meetings. For example, on 7 February 1850 Moritz Schreber expressed the opinion that Leipzig houseowners had to have a disporportionate number of soldiers billeted in them, and on 27 March 1850 he spoke on the question of whether appointing a supply teacher at school X might not encourage absenteeism by the other teachers.[18]

5. THE SCHREBER FAMILY PORTRAIT (1851)

Still in the possession of their descendants is a painting of the Schreber family signed "Aug. Richter 1851"; see Figure 7. The only information that can be found concerning this portrait is that obtained by examination of the painting itself and from the signature. First something about the painter, August Richter, whose life history is curious, to say the least.

August Richter (1801–77) lived for most of his life in Dresden. From 1830 on he was a lecturer at the academy of art there, being styled extraordinary professor. At first he painted grand biblical scenes, but from 1835 onward he did drawings which are now sought after on account of their supposed signs of a beginning impressionism. From 1839 signs of mental illness became stronger, and in 1845 he was relieved of his post and admitted to the Sonnenstein psychiatric clinic at Pirna, not far from Dresden, the clinic where over fifty years later Paul Schreber was to write his *Memoirs*. Later Richter even had his own studio in the clinic.[19]

The question of why Moritz Schreber should have his family painted by someone suffering from mental illness is not easily answered. A positive appreciation of mental illness—as in the typically nineteenth and early twentieth-century idea of an association between genius and madness—is lacking in Moritz Schreber's writings. It is possible that he knew Richter's work: when Richter was lecturing at the art academy in Dresden, Schreber more than once visited the city as Stakovich's personal physician. He wrote, "I also once visited the brilliant picture gallery, though without meeting Mlle. [illegible]; perhaps I shall see her when I go up there again" (D. G. M. Schreber, 1835b, p. 1).

This August Richter

Fig. 7. The Schreber family portrait, signed "Aug. Richter 1851," in the possession of descendants of Moritz Schreber.

must be distinguished from another living artist of this name, whose circumstances we do not know since after two requests by letter we have been favoured with nothing less [presumably the writer means: nothing more] than a polite acknowledgement [Nagler's *Künstler Lexikon*, 1835–52, vol. xiv (between 1841 and 1846), p. 430].

Perhaps, then, the solution is that the portrait is by this other, unknown August Richter.

Resemblances between the Schreber children as depicted in the painting, and children portrayed in illustrations in books by Moritz Schreber will be discussed in the chapter on day-to-day life in the house in the *Zeitzer Strasse* (p. 87).

NOTES TO CHAPTER 4

[1]Kilian wrote of Carus and Schreber: "Although there is no evidence, it may be assumed that they knew one another and that they had professional and social connections with one another. People knew about each other in rising Leipzig" (1977, p. 1). This caution, then, is unnecessary: both were members of the Leipzig medical society. This paper by Kilian of 1977, "Die Anfänge der Orthopädie in Leipzig," is the only reasonably detailed text on the earliest stages of the orthopedic clinic. According to Kilian (*ibid.*), Carus had taken it over from Jörg; however, there is no evidence for this.

Schreber took the clinic over in 1844; the chief source for this date is Schreber himself (1852a, p.iii; quoted by Kloss, 1862, p. 11). Schildbach, Schreber's later associate and successor in the clinic, and thus someone who ought to be in a position to know, gave various dates: 1843 (1864, p. 3), 1844 (1862a, p. 5), and 1845 (1861, p. 4).

The clinic was a private establishment. This means that Moritz Schreber was not appointed its director (Meijer and Rijnders, 1977, p. 23); nor did he found it (Macalpine and Hunter, 1955, p. 1). Gasch (1896, p. 50) referred to Schreber's " 'Orthopaedic Clinic' founded on 20 February 1848"—wrong on two counts. Nor was it a university institute (Lacan, 1971, p. 99), neither did Schreber buy it "together with his friend Dr. Schildbach" (Schilling, 1964, p. 9); in due course Schildbach bought it from Schreber.

[2]According to the quotations of Moritz Schreber and his daughter cited in the text, he thus undertook three study trips for the clinic; one before the takeover and two afterward. Of course, it is also possible that his daughter is mistaken, and that the journey she thinks of as having taken place before the takeover actually consisted of the two journeys which took place after it. In the later literature only the daughter's testimony is accepted: there is no talk of two or three, but only of one journey, before the takeover (e.g., Ritter, 1936a, p.15; G. Richter, 1939b, pp. 16–17).

[3]Niederland referred, without a shred of evidence, to Moritz Schreber's "small size—he was probably not more than three-quarters of an inch over five feet tall" (1974, p. 6). Meijer and Rijnders wrote: "but he remained a small man: 1.56 m" (1977, p. 23). Evidently they zealously and almost accurately converted Niederland's "three quarters of an inch over five feet tall," and for convenience's sake left out the "probably" and the "not more than." On the other hand, the fact that Schreber is

described in his passport as "tall" must be seen in the perspective of the times: Friedrich Engels, whose height was 5 ft 9 in, was "large" in his official police description (Kliem, 1977, p. 11).

⁴At the time when Moritz Schreber took over the clinic it was not in the *Schlossgasse*, as Schildbach (1877, p. vii) wrote. It had been there only until 1842 (see *Leipziger Adressbücher*).

⁵The house at Königstrasse 4 is listed in the *Leipziger Adressbücher* as "Reimer's Garden . . . Dr. Drechsel's house." Schildbach (1877, p. vii) gave the house number as "22" instead of "4." Perhaps the numbering in the *Königstrasse* was changed between 1844 and 1877.

⁶The later names of this street reflect the political history of the country: the *Zeitzer Strasse* was later rechristened the *Adolf-Hitler-Strasse*, became the *Süd-Strasse* (South Street) for a few years after the war, and has since been called the *Karl-Liebknecht-Strasse*. The exact situation of the clinic building is shown in the outline plan (Fig. 8). (The *Hohe Strasse* was later extended westward.) Schilling (1964, p. 10) placed the house diagonally opposite its actual position.

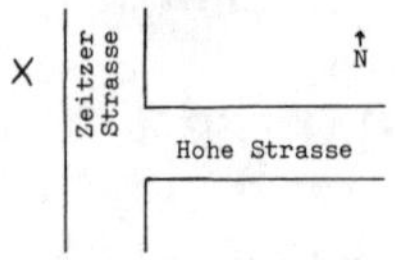

Fig. 8

⁷I have only indirect evidence to show that the clinic and living quarters for the Schrebers (and the Schildbachs) did not take up the entire building. In Moritz Schreber's day it was not yet possible simply to look in the Leipzig directories to find out who lived at any given address. This capability was introduced in 1863. I have chosen the year 1868, as by that time the clinic had more than recovered from the temporary decline in the numbers of patients resulting from Schreber's death in 1861 (see Schildbach [1864, pp. 4–5; 1877, p. ix]). In 1868, apart from the clinic and the names of Schildbach and Frau Schreber, there are eleven other names listed at *Zeiter Strasse* 10. It is not possible to tell the sizes of the households which these names represent.

This means that the caption to Figure 5 is somewhat misleading, since it gives the impression that the building consists solely of the clinic and Moritz Schreber's personal accommodations. In all the other literature, too, where there are constant references to the "world renown" which the clinic is supposed to have enjoyed, there is no mention of the fact that it was quite modest in size (see Ritter [1936a, p. 16], Schütze [1936b, p. 1889], Brauchle [1937, p. 246], Tabouret-Keller [1973, p. 302], and Mangner [1884, p. 10]; for an exception, see the *Illustrierte Zeitung* [1862, p. 81]).

⁸The figure of four to seven inpatients is based on the following data: On 30 March 1852 there were seven *"Pfleglinge"* (foster-children) in the clinic, aged between ten and eighteen years—five girls and two boys (D. G. M. Schreber, 1852b). When Schildbach went to the clinic in 1859 (1864, p. 4), he found *"only 7 orthopedic beds."* From 1859 to 1861 there were always four inpatients (Schildbach, 1877, p. xiii).

"With the boarders from the orthopedic clinic we were about ten or twelve children," according to two of Schreber's daughters (Siegel, 1909b, p. 207); ten or twelve minus the five Schreber children leaves us with five or seven patients. In view of all this information I find the figure given in an obituary of Schreber's widow somewhat exaggerated: "The conscientious care of . . . twelve to fifteen children from the clinic who as non-residents [of Leipzig] had board and lodging in the clinic, claimed all her time and energy" (Siegel, 1907c, p. 126).

⁹Every biographer has probably at some time or another felt the need to depict

his subject as something of a martyr. Add to this the arrogance of biographers who think they also have an insight into the "social context"—people who have read that after the Napoleonic era gymnastics was prohibited in Germany—and with his little book on gymnastics for the Supreme Assembly of the Estates of the Kingdom of Saxony Moritz Schreber becomes a hero swimming against the tide of stupidity of his times. Let us look at two examples of this.

According to Schilling, promoting gymnastics was

> in the years between 1815 and 1848 a downright act of foolhardiness. . . . Under these conditions of milieu it took a great deal of intrepidity to write a memorandum to the Saxon government in the way Schreber did in 1843. . . . The extent to which Schreber thus made himself unpopular in government circles becomes apparent from the fact that in the same year the city of Leipzig council refused approval for him to establish a children's hospital, an incredible decision by which the common good was ruthlessly suppressed behind petty personal animosity [1964, p. 8].

Rubbish. To utter a plea for more gymnastics was by no means "foolhardiness" in the Saxony of 1843. Let us compare this with the following passage from the *Sächsische Vaterlands-Blätter* of 1843:

> It is scarcely credible, but even so the sad truth is unhappily making itself all too evident: *The University of Leipzig still has no gymnastics ground!* In Saxony, where now there is such great and praiseworthy enthusiasm everywhere in evidence for the sport of gymnastics, in Saxony, where every grammar-school and many intermediate schools and other educational establishments, indeed, where even many of the villages of the Erzgebirge and Voigtland have their own gymnastics centres, the university should really not have to do without a gymnastics ground [p. 559].

A second author who makes Moritz Schreber and his booklet of 1843 an unsung hero was Professor Kleine (1942, pp. 175–81; 1958, pp. 159–163). First he described a grumpy police official poring over Schreber's booklet under orders from the Saxon Assembly: He takes the view that private citizens have no business interfering in matters which are the sole concern of the state authorities; he mutters that that fellow Schreber has clearly got time to waste, and that the police would be well advised to keep a quiet eye on him. Kleine then gave a detailed description of Schreber's reaction when he heard that his booklet had met with a negative response: "In downcast mood he made his way to the little summerhouse he had put together in his garden." Moritz Schreber never had a home-made summerhouse (*Laube*) in his garden. However, the idea that he had one is not total nonsense: there is a definite connection between homemade structures of this kind and Moritz Schreber: They are both associations immediately called to mind by the word *Schrebergarten*, i.e., allotment. But the Schreber gardens did not come into existence until long after Moritz Schreber's death. What Kleine did here is to take something connected with "Schreber" and, without further ado by way of researching the period in which that something came into being, weave it into the events of 1843.

But now back to Kleine's text. Here we have Schreber pondering in his "summerhouse":

> The government obviously feared that gymnastics would do too much to strengthen the self-confidence of the workers and the bourgeoisie.
>
> But if the government in its prejudice was going to forbid its adult subjects to do gymnastics and physical exercises on public gymnastics grounds, then he would teach his compatriots how to keep their bodies healthy and how to make them stronger through gymnastics at home, within their own four walls.

Well . . . there was no question of gymnastics on public gymnastics grounds being forbidden. And when Kleine had Moritz Schreber philosophizing about indoor exercises in 1843, he is presumably thinking of Schreber's bestseller of 1855, *Indoor Gymnastics*. Yet ten years before that, Schreber and others had already opened a public gymnastics ground. Back again to Kleine's insight into the workings of Moritz Schreber's mind in 1843:

> If in its short-sightedness the government refused to approve money for places of recreation out in the open, so that the people of the city could spend their free time there, then he himself would exhort the inhabitants of Leipzig to lay out small, attractive gardens for themselves outside the city.

Schreber had not made any request to the government for money for recreation grounds. And as regards the small gardens, which just like the "summerhouse" were something that was only later to be linked with the Schreber name, this is another case of projection back into the mind of Schreber himself. Let us have a last look at Kleine's Moritz Schreber:

> He himself, who year in year out looked after the many crippled town children in the orthopedic clinic of which he was the director, knew better than anyone how essential fresh air and sunlight were, precisely for the healthy development of young people.

But Schreber *had* no orthopedic clinic—that was not to come until 1844.

What status did Kleine accord his story? He said that he is practicing the writing of history "in poetic form, without however damaging the intrinsic historical truth [die innere geschichtliche Wahrheit]" (1958, p. 7). Now "intrinsic truth" is a rather difficult concept. What it clearly does *not* mean here is "intrinsic in the facts." What it means here is: intrinsic in certain associations called up by the word "Schreber" and intrinsic in Kleine's compulsion to paint his hero as a martyr.

Incidentally, Kleine is not an East German writer, as I long thought. Yet my mistake is understandable: he opens with a quotation from Schreber: "Only a people possessed of perfect physical health possesses the strength for political action." Which is in the same sort of genre as the slogan that confronted me whenever I mounted the steps to the municipal archives in Leipzig: *"Gesundheit und Lebensfreude—unser humanistisches Ziel!"* (Health and the joy of living—our humanistic objective!). Moreover, I first came across this book (the 1958 edition) in an East German library, and was struck by the apparently socialist sentiment in the "self-confidence of the workers" quoted above. Yet the book was published in West Germany. In the 1958 edition, however, there is nothing to show that it had already appeared at an earlier date, with a slightly different title: not *Ärzte in den Sturmen der Zeit* (Doctors in the storms of time) but *Ärzte kämpfen für Deutschland* (Doctors fight for Germany). Year of publication: 1942. Then too, the workers were self-confident. In his 1958 edition Kleine wisely omitted such minor sentences as "These men's heads and facial shape often clearly show the Nordic stamp" (1942, pp. 10–11).

Let us return for a moment to the quotation from Moritz Schreber that Kleine used as his motto: "Only a people possessed of perfect physical health possesses the strength for political action." Kleine gave no indication of the source: That is not necessary in the case of a motto. Although I cannot, of course, reel off by heart every sentence ever written by Moritz Schreber, I am disinclined to believe that this is really from his pen. "Politics" is a word which is virtually absent from his works. An advantage of this mistake is that it is possible to see exactly how Kleine hit on Moritz Schreber. His information is clearly taken from Ritter's thesis: his grumpy police official, reading from Schreber's gymnastics booklet, quoted precisely the same words as Ritter. But then how does a medical man like Kleine come to read a philosophical thesis such as Ritter's? The answer is fairly plain: a commemorative article on Moritz Schreber appeared in the medical journal the *Deutsches Ärzteblatt* in 1936; in it the author referred to Ritter's thesis. In the same article, moreover, we find the words: "The times of political disunion had shown Schreber that 'only a people possessed of perfect physical health possesses the strength for political action' " (Schütze, 1936a, p. 1167). And Kleine, understandably, thought that this was a quotation from Moritz Schreber. In fact it was a quotation from Ritter: "Always and everywhere [Moritz Schreber] found that only a people possessed of perfect 'physical' health possesses the strength for political action" (1936a, p. 17).

[10]In other words, not only was the club receiving a subsidy, the city had already helped in the acquisition of a gymnastics ground. Milczewsky's observation on the founding of the *Turnverein* may thus be relegated to the status of martyrdom fantasy: "a slap in the face for the bureaucrats. But curiously no 'active resistance' followed" (n.d., p. 30). More realistic, it seems to me, is the observation made by Schreber's daughter Anna. On the subject of the negative attitude toward gymnastics in the 1840's, she is reported as saying "that at that time gymnastics and the physical training so dear to her father's heart were still often regarded as tomfoolery. Girls on skates were an exceptional sight" (*Neue Leipziger Zeitung*, 1939).

[11]I do not know how Ritter knows this. Schreber's daughter Anna later recalled that "As a peaceable citizen Schreber prevented the young Turnverein from joining in the demonstrating in the revolution of 1848, and thus saved it from dissolution" (Fritzsche, 1926, p. 13). However, I know nothing of a demonstration in Leipzig in 1848—only that there were *rumors* of one.

[12]The text was given in full in Bernhardt (1929, pp. 29 ff.)—for the first time, as Bernhardt proudly observed. It also appeared in Juhnke (1975, pp. 13–17). Juhnke, one of the few authors to know the work of Bernhardt, likewise announced proudly that he was publishing this speech for the first time.

[13]The cautious "in part at least" (zum Theil wenigstens) had already disappeared by the time this passage was repeated by Ritter (1936a, p. 18). Nor did it reappear in Schatzman (1973a, p. 12), who obtained his data from Ritter.

[14]"Wandering Jew," and not "Eternal Jew," as the English translation of D. P. Schreber's book has it (D. P. Schreber, 1955, pp. 73, 74).

[15]This date is difficult to reconcile with the dates given by Prado de Oliveira for the publication of Sue's novel, which, indeed, was published not between 1845 and 1847 but in 1844–45.

[16]Niederland too (1974, p. 86) pointed to politico-religious problems as the reality behind the Catholics in the *Memoirs*, though what he referred to are problems of the seventies and eighties.

[17]It is not indisputably certain that Schreber supported Biedermann's petition; but I consider it improbable that he was one of the two right-wing councillors who left the hall before the vote—after which the vote to support the petition was carried unanimously.

This detail comes from the autobiography of Karl Biedermann (1886, p. 252). This is also my chief source for my description of the unrest in Leipzig in 1845 and 1848. One thing should be noted here, however: according to Biedermann (*ibid.*, pp. 257–258) there were no riots in 1848 at all. This mistake is not so very surprising: it was in his interests that "his" petition should reach the king from a city that behaved with dignity.

Riots in 1845, no riots in 1848: that is Biedermann's picture of Leipzig. In the majority of Schreber literature we find the reverse: nothing about the unrest of 1845, but plenty of gratuitous observations about 1848: "It was 1848. . . . . It was the first time Schreber [Paul] had been mixed up in political agitation" (Croufer, 1970, p. 219). Another example:

> 1848 was the year of revolution. In Leipzig as elsewhere the seas ran high; Schreber [Moritz] was a convinced democrat and in his heart of hearts he welcomed the (just) revolt of the people. But he had too much experience of the world not to see the senselessness of these petty, splintered riots [Ritter, 1936a, p. 18].

This sort of wording always looks safe. Phrases of the vagueness of "in Leipzig as elsewhere the seas ran high" are always somewhere near the mark. And who will ever be able to prove that Moritz Schreber did not think just as Ritter wrote: approval in his inner self, but a realization of the pointlessness of the popular revolt? And yet it is all wrong. As I have said, the events that took place in Leipzig in 1848 have to be seen from two quite distinct angles: on the one hand there were the riots, which were not secretly welcomed by Schreber—on the contrary, as a member of the civil guard he was actively involved in their suppression—and on the other hand there was a petition from the city authorities which, far from being pointless, deserved his vote as a city councillor.

Niederland wrote of these turbulent times as follows: "There is evidence that the Schreber family was in political difficulties during the 1840s, especially during the revolutionary years 1847 and 1848" (1974, p. 99). I asked Niederland what evidence he had for this assertion, apart from the vague information given by Ritter. He answered that as someone who fought for social and educational reforms, Moritz Schreber was politically suspect in the eyes of the authorities. But who are "the" authorities? To some extent Moritz Schreber himself, in his capacity as a city councillor—probably a relatively moderate one—was one of their number. And was he really a fighter for "social" reforms?

In the chronology at the end of the French translation of the *Memoirs* we find for the period 1845–48 the following: "W. Niederland has pointed to certain difficulties which the Schreber family experienced with the Saxon authorities at this time." This passage would have given a truer picture if the words "certain difficulties" had been placed in quotation marks.

[18]There is undoubtedly much more new material of this kind waiting to be found in the reports of council meetings in the *Leipziger Tageblatt*.

[19]The fact that August Richter continued to paint after his admission to Sonnenstein in 1845 refutes everything written about him in the literature of the history of art. "It may be assumed that his creative work ceased after 1843" (Koetschau, 1924, p. 157). A letter from the museum of the history of Leipzig to the owner of the painting amounted to more or less the same thing:

> An August Richter appears in the dictionary of artists (1801–73, lived chiefly in Dresden, significant as a portrait and historical painter), though on account of illness he is supposed not to have done any more creative work at least after 1845. Clearly, therefore, he cannot be the painter of your picture.

My knowledge that Richter continued to paint after his admission for psychiatric treatment has its foundation in an article on him entitled "Ein Atelier im Irrenhaus" (A studio in the lunatic asylum), which in turn is based on statements made by his sister, in *Die Gartenlaube* of 1867. I came across the article quite by accident while leafing through the magazine. Evidently it is not known in the literature of the history of art (see the bibliographical references in *Allgemeines Lexikon*, 1934, pp. 282–283).

The article in *Die Gartenlaube* is signed merely with the initials "E.P." The author wrote that he has also written a book about August Richter. If we can discover what name these initials stand for, perhaps we shall be able to find out something new about August Richter.

5

MORITZ SCHREBER'S LADDER ACCIDENT
(1851) AND HEAD COMPLAINT

In the first half of 1851 Moritz Schreber was in the gymnasium of the orthopedic clinic when a heavy iron ladder fell on him, striking him on the head. This accident was held at least partly responsible for his curious head complaint from which he began to suffer several months later (certainly before the end of 1851).[1] His daughter Klara later wrote about "the incident in the gymnasium when an iron ladder fell on father's head, which might have caused his peculiar head complaint which started a few months later" (Krause, 1900, quoted in Baumeyer, 1956, p. 68.)

Schreber himself was evidently unsure whether the ladder accident was the actual cause of his head complaint. Fritzsche drew on Anna Schreber's account for the following passage:

> Even today there seems to be no clear explanation for Schreber's head complaint. We do not know precisely whether it was the consequence of an iron ladder falling on his head while he was doing gymnastics or whether it was a severe nervous breakdown. We do know, however, that Schreber suffered from it for many years. If on the one hand this suffering crippled his creative powers and hence his pleasure in his work, on the other hand his work distracted him, and Schreber possessed unflagging energy; he gave evidence of that throughout his life. Happily this severe head complaint grew appreciably less troublesome in the last years of his life [1926, p. 14].

Schildbach went into somewhat greater detail on the consequences of Schreber's head complaint, after praising the "vigorous and thorough training of his body" by much gymnastic exercise. "True, in the somewhat strained region of the eyes his face bore the traces of endured severe bodily complaints and lacked fullness and healthy colour" (1862b, pp. 16–17), but then gymnastics cannot be a cure for everything, said Schildbach. Even so:

> he exercised out of himself much ill humour and irritability, many a feeling of physical unease and ill-being, for to him his gymnasium was the best pharmacy, for himself as well as others. But the congestions of the brain which soured the last ten years of his life were probably the consequence of an external injury which he sustained six months before the onset of the suffering when a heavy object struck him on the head.

The onset of this head complaint meant a break in Moritz Schreber's life: he found himself forced to lay down all his public functions. "Unfortunately in 1851 Schreber was obliged by considerations of health to withdraw not only from all public affairs but also from the running of the turnverein" (Schildbach, 1862a, p. 6). There were also consequences for the orthopedic clinic: "In 1851 while practising his profession Schreber sustained an injury and was never again in perfect health. He was thereby obliged to cut back both his work for the clinic and the clinic itself as far as possible" (Schildbach, 1864, p. 4).

The head complaint also had repercussions for family life: often Schreber would retire for hours at a time, refusing to see his children. I shall return in greater detail to the consequences of the head complaint for the clinic and the Schrebers' family life in the following chapters, which deal with day-to-day life in the *Zeitzer Strasse* and the everyday practice of the orthopedic clinic. The fact that Schreber's literary productivity did not suffer as a result of the head complaint—on the contrary, it was during these last ten years of his life that he wrote the major part of his total output—seems to indicate that it was no ordinary headache, but that there were tensions of some kind which only made social relationships difficult for him: the note on Moritz Schreber, made by a psychiatrist over thirty years after his death, viz., that he suffered from "obsessional ideas with homicidal tendencies" (quoted in Baumeyer [1956, p. 62]—see page 178), would seem to confirm this.

NOTE TO CHAPTER 5

[1] 1851 was the year of the accident and the onset of the head complaint. Ritter (1936a, p. 14) placed the accident much later:

Towards the end of the 1850s* Schreber had a serious and fateful accident; in the gymnasium a heavy iron ladder fell on his head. subsequently he was often confined to the house for half a day at a time by a chronic head complaint which recurred for many years and whose exact medical diagnosis we do not know.

*Establishing an exact date appears impossible despite every attempt to find it.

This dating of the accident and the head complaint has been adopted in all the literature since Ritter; e.g., White (1963, p. 214), Schilling (1964, p. 4), Croufer (1970, p. 219), Tabouret-Keller (1973, p. 299), This (1973–74, p. 14), Niederland (1974, p. 58), Colas (1975, p. 86), the appendix in D. P. Schreber (1975, p. 386), Meijer and Rijnders (1977, p. 24), and S. M. Weber (1973, p. 8). Weber would even have it that the head complaint was the cause of Schreber's death.

Perhaps Ritter's dating appears so convincing because of the impressive footnote: "Establishing an exact date appears impossible despite every attempt to find it." Tabouret-Keller made even more of this note than it says: "The exact year escaped both documentation and Anna's memory" (1973, p. 299). The really remarkable thing about Ritter's dating is that it appears nowhere in the earlier literature. What does appear there is the dating 1851—even in literature used by Ritter himself (1936a, pp. 12, 19), viz., where Fritzsche wrote that Moritz Schreber (who, it will be recalled, had died in 1861) "for the last ten years of his life suffered from an exceptionally severe head complaint" (1926, p. 13). Considering the unanimity with which the accident and the onset of the headaches are nowadays considered to have taken place at the end of the eighteen-fifties, it may be interesting to look at some further quotations from which 1851 emerges. Siegel, for example, wrote that Moritz Schreber "was for the last ten years of his life tormented by a severe head complaint—caused by an iron ladder having fallen on his head" (1907c, p. 126). Then there is Schildbach, according to whom Schreber was "frequently interrupted in his ordinary activities by suffering during the last ten years of his life" (1877, p. ix). Then again:

The majority and the best of his writings appeared in the last ten years of his life, though it was precisely during that period that he suffered severely from the consequences of a concussion caused by an iron ladder falling on his head [Der Freund der Schreber-Vereine, 1908, p. 211].

The date of the accident is important for the following reason. In the (false) dating at the end of the fifties Niederland saw some interesting parallels with Paul Schreber's Memoirs. In that book the name "Casati" appears (D. P. Schreber, 1903, p. 49 = 1955, p. 71). According to Niederland (1974, p. 88), the explorer Gaetano Casati was important to Paul Schreber for various reasons, one of which is that at about the same point in his life as Paul's father, that is, three years before his death, he had a serious accident. Moreover, and more importantly, Niederland saw (1959a, pp. 162–163) an interesting parallel between Paul's father's age when he had his accident (he would then, according to the false dating, have been fifty or fifty-one) and Paul's age at the start of his second and most important period of illness: fifty-one.

Since Niederland's report, the age at which Moritz Schreber suffered his accident has thus been narrowed down to simply "fifty-one" (White, 1961, pp. 59, 60, 62; Shengold, 1961, p. 436; Croufer, 1970, p. 219; This, 1973–74, p. 14).

The usual general objections to the drawing of parallels between sets of figures—objections arising chiefly out of the circumstances that there is almost always some sort of remarkable correspondence to be found between sets of figures—are confirmed by this accident with the ladder: here again, where an essential datum is incorrect, there are striking parallels.

Yet the fundamental thought underlying Niederland's parallel is not all that crazy: that Paul Schreber's father played an essential role in his life, and that fateful moments in the father's life may have instilled anxiety in the son at the moment at which he realized that he was precisely the same age. Alongside this theoretical consideration there is an empirical one: twenty-five years ago J. R. Hilgard wondered, in a letter to F. Baumeyer, whether Paul Schreber's father might not have an accident at the age of forty-two—because Paul's first period of psychosis began when he was aged forty-two. Curious, since at the time when Moritz Schreber had his ladder accident he was indeed forty-two years of age.

6

FAMILY LIFE IN THE SCHREBER

HOUSEHOLD

1. INTRODUCTION

So far I have simply related bare facts of the Schrebers' life, just as though I were unaware that nowadays in the social sciences it is more or less generally accepted that "value-free" description is an impossibility, that the author's own values play a part in every description, and that therefore the best thing an author can do is to come out into the open with his value judgments.

I shall illustrate my doubts about this critical view by reference to the considereable volume of literature on the family life of the Schrebers. At first sight this appears to support the critical view: a reader faced with the diverse genres of literature about the family would not easily, without the name "Schreber" being mentioned, realize that it was all about the same family. The best known genre is that of modern psychiatric literature, in which the Schreber family is depicted as groaning under the yoke of the domestic tyrant Moritz Schreber. This "domestic tyrant literature" reached its peak in the work of the psychiatrist Morton Schatzman. A second large genre has its origins in the Schreber Associations, the allotment gardening clubs. Here Moritz Schreber appears as the perfect paterfamilias. Schreber the despot and Schreber the exemplary head of the family—it would seem to be proof enough of how inevitable it is that the author's attitude determines the nature of the description. However, it seems to me that this is not a matter of inevitable coloring, but rather that in both genres the authors have too easily adapted the facts to their own taste.

In both genres, for example, systematically determined information is lacking. In the allotment tradition we look in vain for the curious educational contrivances invented by Moritz Schreber (for an exception, see K. Pfeiffer [1937, p. 16]). On the other hand in the work of Schatzman et al. there is a total absence of all passages in which Schreber argues in favor of letting children follow their own instincts to a greater extent than was then the norm (see Israëls [1980, pp. 344, 345]).

Not only are certain facts absent from both genres, but others are systematically exaggerated, either favorably or unfavorably, depending on the circumstances. The following passage from the allotment tradition will serve as an example. Ritter wrote of Moritz Schreber's family life that "Everything was governed by strict rules: one rose very early, did some gymnastics, bathed and swam before starting work. In winter this sometimes even meant breaking up the ice" (1936a, p. 12). This ice also turns up in similar later writing, as in Brauchle: "The Schreber family were so hardened that sometimes in winter it was even necessary for the ice to be broken up because Schrebers wished to bathe" (1937, p. 244). Exactly the same story can also be found in Schatzman's work (1973a, p. 36) and similar literature (e.g., Tabouret-Keller, 1973, p. 298). In the allotment literature it is used to illustrate the family's physical toughness; in the writings of Schatzman et al. it is an example of the unrelenting harshness with which Moritz Schreber treated his children. Here it looks as if the author's standpoint automatically determines the place to be assigned to such a detail. In reality, however, this story goes back to a considerably less spectacular piece of information: in the first years of his marriage Schreber "even occasionally had the ice broken up and bathed for a minute in the ice-cold water" (Siegel, 1909b, pp. 205–206).

The apparently so complete contradistinction between Schreber the despot and Schreber the perfect father also has a common element: In both genres he is accorded the chief role in the family. To some extent this is a distortion, both in the allotment literature and in the work of Schatzman et al. In the idealizing literature the focus of interest is the man whose name lives on in the Schreber allotments; it is not surprising, therefore, that in stories about his family all the emphasis is placed on *his* role in it. Similarly Schatzman et al., when reconstructing the circumstances in which Paul Schreber grew up, concentrate almost exclusively on Moritz Schreber and his approach to education. This is because Moritz Schreber's educational publications are taken as the sources for his family life. Even so, this great emphasis on Moritz Schreber is certainly not all distortion: the state of affairs is one which is susceptible of description less tainted by value judgments: the Schrebers were a strongly patriarchal family, like most others at that time.

There is so much literature about the Schrebers, and it is so full of value judgments, that I shall devote this chapter to an examination of the various genres.

I shall have little criticism of the allotment literature, since the genre is now virtually forgotten. There is one exception to this, however: unfortunately, Alfons Ritter's thesis of 1936 has been used in much modern literature.[1] It is therefore worth the effort to identify and examine the best writing in this genre. This is based on conversations with Moritz Schreber's daughters; it is scarcely possible to offer a critique of such works because there is of course no way of ascertaining whether what the daughters said has been reproduced faithfully.

I shall be far more critical of the psychiatric literature. This is not simply because I deprecate the negative attitude which such psychiatrists adopt toward Moritz Schreber. Indeed, something of a malevolent eye is probably desirable when looking for the social causes of mental illness. But in the psychiatric literature written sources have been used exclusively, and it is therefore possible to examine critically the way in which those sources have been employed.

The various genres will be discussed in chronological order, beginning with the allotment literature. This will be followed by a number of psychiatric genres; I shall end with additional factual data.

2. SCHREBER FAMILY LIFE ACCORDING TO THE ALLOTMENT LITERATURE

The best writing in this genre consists of two articles based on statements by Paul Schreber's sisters. "Memories of Dr. Moritz Schreber," with the subtitle "Compiled by R. Siegel from recollections by his daughters," appeared in 1909 (1909b). These memories were written in the "we-daughters" form: a deceptive style since the subtitle indicates that the article was written by Siegel.[2]

The second major article is "Episodes from the life of Dr. Moritz Schreber" and dates from 1926; the author, H. Fritzsche, indicated that it is based on statements made by Moritz Schreber's eldest daughter

Anna. Fortunately he did not write in the "I-Anna-remember" form. Not that he is overflowing with critical acuity: the tales told him by Anna serve as illustrations of the fact that

> our Schreber [Moritz] was not merely a hard-working doctor and scholar, not merely a clear, far-sighted brain, but at the same time also a modest, simple, true man, a loving husband and father, and a thoroughly upright character without guile, and all of this brings him so near to our hearts that it is not only with pride but rather with love that we call him the spiritual father of the Schreber Associations [1926, p. 13].

I have also made use in this section of various other texts: interviews with Anna on her ninety-eighth and hundredth birthdays, accounts of the visits Gerhard Richter paid her, a story which H. Fritzsche (Fritzsche and Brückner, 1903) heard from Pauline Schreber, an obituary of her, and a text by Klara. In places where they fit into the picture painted by this idealizing genre of the allotment literature, I have also used certain sources which are not actually part of that literature: an occasional remark by Moritz Schreber's colleague and successor in the orthopedic clinic C. H. Schildbach, the poem which Paul wrote for and about his mother, a letter from Klara to her brother's psychiatrist, and publications by Moritz Schreber.

I begin with a series of quotations which all testify to how healthy living and bourgeois virtues prevailed in the Schreber family: lots of physical exercise, healthy asceticism, domesticity, a Christian spirit, and benevolence toward those less fortunately placed.

Lots of physical exercise

"Our father liked a *brisk, austere* and *robust* life as the heart of good health and vitality. Exercise in the fresh, open air, bathing, swimming, gymnastics etc. were to him a necessity of life" (Siegel, 1909b, p. 205). According to Schildbach, Moritz Schreber's "skill and endurance in walking, dancing, riding, swimming, skating and games of dexterity were equally excellent, as in gymnastics, jumping, vaulting, sprinting and long-distance running" (1862a, p. 5). "Whenever Schreber went upstairs he would take two or three steps at a time, and in the garden the children would often see him turning cartwheels"

(Fritzsche, 1926, p. 13). "He also regularly went walking, bathing and swimming, and indeed in the first years of his marriage he even occasionally had the ice broken up and bathed for a minute in the ice-cold water" (Siegel, 1909b pp. 205, 206). Part of the last quotation has already been quoted in connection with its subsequent exaggeration to show that the whole family was forced to go swimming in freezing water. However, Moritz Schreber certainly did see to it that his children took good healthy exercise, as his daughter Anna is reported as saying that "He was also greatly interested in ensuring that his children took exercise in the fresh air, and he was especially fond of skating, which at that time was not yet very popular" (H.B., 1940).

The other daughters had similar stories to tell of their father:

He did gymnastics with us and in the evening he would do indoor exercises with us [Siegel, 1909b, p. 207].

On holiday we sometimes had to step out strongly. Of course he was also in favour of swimming and bathing, only regretting that in those days the baths were not yet open to the feminine sex. He was very keen that we should skate; very often the whole family went skating [Siegel, 1909b, pp. 207–208].

"The whole family"—evidently Frau Schreber went too. Not that she joined in all her husband's sporting activities: Paul Schreber recalls for his mother that

To Rudelsburg and Kösen,
You went there too,
You in the trap, your bridegroom on foot.
[D. P. Schreber, 1905, p. 4]

Actually, it is not really surprising that Frau Schreber rode in the trap: Rudelsburg and the health resort of Kösen are some thirty miles from Leipzig.

Healthy ascetism

The emphasis on physical exercise is part of a more general attitude to the body, in which Moritz Schreber stressed not only physical fitness but also the superiority of mind over body, not giving in to "comfort-seeking" desires. This somewhat ascetic attitude is nicely illustrated by the following domestic scene:

> He hated comfort and called it coddling the body. For example, one day he answered mother, in reference to a winter fur, with "Not under fifty". But when, when he was in his fiftieth [actually fifty-first] year, at Christmas 1858, mother gave him one, although he did his best not to hurt her feelings he was unable to hide the fact that he would really much rather return it. And that is what happened [Siegel, 1909b, p. 207].

Other characteristics of Moritz Schreber also fit into this picture: "Schreber lived very moderately and as a rule went to bed at 10 o'clock" (G. Richter, 1935); "He was an early riser, but was also in the habit of going to bed betimes. Coffee was drunk at six in the morning"[3] (Fritzsche, 1926, p. 13); "In matters of food and clothing he liked things *simple*. For health reasons no meat was served one afternoon a week, and likewise hardly ever in the evenings, except for Sundays and holidays"[4] (Siegel, 1909b, p. 208). Food was not the only matter in relation to which Schreber observed moderation: "He drank very little spirituous liquor. Only on Sundays would he drink a small glass of wine with his sons" (Fritzsche, 1926, p. 13).

Domesticity

The little alcohol which Schreber drank was consumed principally at home in the family circle: he was not one for going out in the evenings.

> He devoted all the free time he allowed himself to his family. Every now and then he would play billiards for an hour at the Harmony before supper, but the rest of the evening would be spent in the family circle. We would go into the garden, play and do gymnastics, and talk and read about the day's events and about topical matters [Siegel, 1909b, p. 208].

> Schreber did not cultivate much company. He was absorbed in his family, though now and then he was to be seen in "the Harmony" [Fritzsche, 1926, p. 13].

It seems that his infrequent visits to the café even made Schreber rather ignorant of the ordinary affairs of the world:

He did not drink beer. One day when despite this he went to a hostelry with Fleischer [his publisher], he asked with astonishment: "Goodness, do women go into hostelries nowadays?" Fleischer answered: "My dear doctor, do you live in Leipzig or in some village or other?" [G. Richter, 1935].

Neither was Schreber a keen card-player: "Schreber was not much interested in cards: he played only to kill time. He did like music, however, and himself played the piano" (Fritzsche, 1926, p. 13).

A Christian spirit

One of the bourgeois virtues of Schreber's day was a Christian attitude to life, and doubtless such an attitude prevailed in the Schreber household. The Schrebers were Lutheran (*"Polizei-Amt der Stadt Leipzig 105"*), as were most of their compatriots. However, I do not think religion played a very dominant role in the Schrebers' life: Moritz Schreber wrote little on religion and expressly warned both against too early religious instruction and against church-going by young children (D. G. M. Schreber, 1858a, p. 154).[5]

At Easter 1856, to mark her Confirmation, the then fifteen-year-old Anna was given at text entitled "Paternal words to my dear Anna," signed "Your father Schreber, also on behalf of your mother" (D. G. M. Schreber, 1909). "On their Confirmation day my father had presented my brothers and my eldest sister with his "paternal words," with the recipient's full name." (Klara Krause, quoted in Siegel, 1909a, p. 75). In his "paternal words" Schreber explained that God's commandment is that we should wish for what is good, and gives rules for practising good by way of self-conquest.

Benevolence toward those less fortunately placed

Besides all the virtues already mentioned—physical exercise, healthy asceticism, domesticity, and a Christian spirit—there was also an atmosphere of benevolence toward the less well-off. This is illustrated by a story told by the two younger daughters.

From father and mother we learned to give *alms* with a good grace. Father emphasized that this was only of value if it meant self-denial. So for a while we would do without butter at breakfast, for example;

and the farthings saved went to make a poor child happy at Christmas [Siegel, 1909b, p. 208].

The children were also taught to behave properly toward the servants, according to the younger daughters:

> We were made to join in the domestic chores for educational reasons; for our father emphasized that the girls, in particular, ought to have done every job about the house at least once, so that they would learn how to judge properly both the jobs themselves and how well the servants did them. For the same reasons also our brothers once had to clean and polish their own shoes for a time [*ibid.*, p. 208].

Despite all this, there was no question of any radical dismantling of class barriers. Hence my description "benevolence toward those less fortunately placed": it indicates the nature of the virtue, but at the same time the great moderation with which that virtue was exercised. The same applies to the other virtues: Moritz Schreber was in favor of plenty of physical exercise, but believed that aching muscles are a sign of overexertion (D. G. M. Schreber, 1857c, p. 33); the Schrebers usually ate no meat in the evenings, but it was only later writers who turned this into what almost amounts to a vegetarian régimen (see note 4). In the same way Schreber was later accounted by East German writers a "man full of ideas for social reform" (Loeffler, 1955, p. 8). But in fact a world in which staff did all the work in the house was to Moritz Schreber something which he took for granted: servants were simply part of the social décor.

It was not only with respect to the less fortunate outside the family that positions in the hierarchy were perfectly clear: Within the family itself there was also a definite order of rank, with the father undisputedly at the head. How far this was more pronounced in the Schreber family than in others at this time is virtually impossible to say. Certainly Moritz Schreber was someone who emphatically stood out from the crowd, chiefly on account of his many publications, but to what extent did that affect the children? Much later the eldest daughter Anna was to recall that her father's exceptional consequence only dawned on her quite late, when she was already twenty years old: "I only realized my father's intellectual stature in the last year of his life, 1861" (quoted by A.L., 1940); "It was not until the last year of his life that I really understood my father and realized his stature, for before that I had

been really quite childish and, physically too, sensitive and tender''
(quoted by A.L., 1938). Childish normality is the keynote of Anna's
statement that: ''When our father wore his uniform we were quite
especially proud of him'' (quoted by A.L., 1938).

In the family hierarchy the father was followed immediately by
the mother. The place of the children and servants would also have
been clear, though the relationship between these two groups cannot
be ranked in quite the same straightforward manner: as the representatives of parental authority the staff were unambiguously senior to the
children, and anything the children ''desire of the servants, they may
only ask for,'' as Moritz Schreber wrote (1861a, p. 69). On the other
hand, both children and staff must have been aware from which group
those who later would assume the positions of master and mistress of
the house would come.

What is not so clear is how the four to seven resident patients
fitted into the family. In 1856 Schreber handed over the boarding side
of the business to someone else; up till then the boarders had probably
had much the same sort of place in the family as the Schreber children
themselves. According to Sidonie and Klara their father ''in every way
encouraged our playing and rushing about in our large courtyard and
garden; with the boarders from the orthopaedic clinic we were about
ten or twelve children'' (Siegel, 1909b, p. 207). Probably the boarders
also ate with the family. Their bedrooms, however, were on a different
floor from the Schrebers' in 1861; this may also have been the case
earlier. It is difficult to say how far their complaints (chiefly spinal
abnormalities) and their long orthopedic treatment meant that the life
these children led was different from that of the Schreber children.

The influence of Moritz Schreber's head complaint

So far we have seen the Schreber family portrayed in the idealizing
literature as a veritable haven of virtue. However, the same works also
have much to say about a less idyllic aspect of Schreber family life,
namely the effect which Moritz Schreber's head complaint had on it.
The fact that it was possible for such matters to penetrate this writing
indicates, indeed, that it was not merely a question of ideological
glorification; it is also an indication of the great impression which
Schreber's illness left on those around him: all the children who expressed themselves on the subject of their family life remarked on it.
As Sidonie and Klara recalled,

. . . when an iron ladder struck our dear father on the head and an
enduring chronic head complaint often took him away from his job
and the family for hours at a time and banished him to painful silence
and loneliness, in these difficult hours too his wife was his faithful
helpmeet [Siegel, 1909b, p. 205].

Anna remembered of her father "that in the last ten years of his life
he suffered from an exceptionally severe head complaint, so that at
times his family feared for his sanity" (Fritzsche, 1926, p. 13).

His wife was "the only one allowed to be with him when the
nerves in his head tormented him too much. Then not even the children
he loved so much were allowed to see him" (Fritzsche, 1926, p. 13).
"His head complaint had got better in recent months. But when it was
bad, the children were often not allowed to go to him for a whole day"
(G. Richter, 1935). In an obituary of Schreber's wife we read that

As her husband had been plagued by a severe head complaint in the
last ten years of his life, caused by an iron ladder falling on his head,
she retired from all social intercourse in order to live only for him,
her children and her husband's work [Siegel, 1907c, p. 126].

Paul referred to this in more poetically veiled language for his mother:

But then the skies suddenly clouded,
Protracted illness gnawed away at your husband;
From then on, a touchstone of your love,
It cast deep shadows on your life's path.
What you suffered and were deprived of in those days
—The world was shunned, even in the house there were
    barriers—
That, truly, none other needs to say,
Often you yourself still linger in thought about it.
                    [D. P. Schreber, 1905, p. 3].

This affair seems also to have played a part in Paul Schreber's mental
illness. That at least is the implication in what his sister Klara wrote
to his psychiatrist in 1900:

It is incomprehensible to me how he (Schreber) mixes up facts with
misstatements and obscurities, for example in what he said about the
illness of our good father. . . , just because they fit in with his
present delusions; and that he does not mention in these notes things
which he knew earlier when he was well. For instance, he does not

mention the incident in the gymnasium when an iron ladder fell on father's head, which might have caused his peculiar head complaints which started a few months later [Krause, 1900, quoted by Baumeyer, 1956, pp. 67–68].

Moritz Schreber the writer

As already mentioned, Moritz Schreber's head complaint did not prevent him from writing. On the contrary, it was after its occurence that most of his work appeared. The idealizing literature contains two nice stories about the way family life and Schreber's writing activities were connected. In both, his wife Pauline played an important role as a faithful assistant. The first of these stories was recounted in note 5, where Sidonie and Klara are reported as having said of their father: "He discussed everything with our mother; she shared in all his ideas, plans and designs, she also read the proofs with him when his writings were published" (Siegel, 1909b, p. 205).

The second runs as follows:

One day she [Frau Schreber] was watching some boys playing about in a clay-pit opposite the house—where St. Peter's church now stands—and was enjoying the spectacle. Suddenly the "holy Hermandad" [the police] appeared and that was the end of the fun, the end of the youthful, joyous play which the policeman saw as a trespass. The boys took to their heels, but Frau Schreber hurried to her husband's study and told him what had happened, and he thereupon wrote his famous last essay "Children's games and their significance for health and education" [Fritzsche and Brückner, 1903, p. 51].

This story turns up incredibly often,[6] and is, moreover, probably true: Fritzsche and Brückner wrote that the eighty-eight-year-old Frau Schreber herself was the one who told the story.

I shall return to Moritz Schreber's writing activities at the end of this chapter.

Travel

Filtering out as much useful information as possible from the material supplied by the idealizing allotment literature, I shall end this survey of the Schreber's family life with accounts of journeys undertaken by Moritz Schreber and his family. Some of these have already been mentioned in passing. After a conversation with his daughter, Anna, Fritzsche wrote:

> He seems to have liked travelling. He went on cures to Gastein and Carlsbad. In 1859 or 1860 he travelled to Lake Garda with his publisher, Fleischer (Leipzig), he also visited Heligoland, and we find him with his family in Saxon Switzerland and in Thuringia. On his journeys, as at home, Schreber led a moderate, almost ascetic life [1926, p. 13].

Kösen and Rudelsburg—where Schreber walked and his wife rode in the trap—lie exactly on the border between Saxony and Thuringia. Saxon Switzerland is to the east of Dresden.

To some extent it is possible to reconstruct a picture of the Schreber family outings. Sidonie and Klara recalled that "On our frequent family walks he would draw our attention to the nature surrounding us, and when the opportunity arose he would make us do tests of courage. On holiday we sometimes had to step out strongly" (Siegel, 1909b, p. 207). Anna, too, made passing references to family outings when talking about her father being tormented by his head complaint: then

> not even the children he loved so much were allowed to see him, [the children] whose childish questions he answered patiently, whose attention he drew, with his educator's perception, to the beauties of nature, whom he taught to understand nature, whom, for example, he made find out why the trees leaned towards the east [Fritzsche, 1926, p. 13].

In his poem for his mother, Paul wrote the following lines about a family trip:

> To the Lausche and to the monastery mount Oybin,
> There the two of you once went, with three children;
> To sit astride the border stone
> Was then my greatest delight.
> When I went there for the second time,
> I took pictures of it,
> After fifty years
>
> [D. P. Schreber, 1905, p. 4].

The health resort Oybin lies about a hundred and thirty miles east of Leipzig, on the border between Saxony and Austria (Bohemia). The hill called "Lausche" is in the same district. I do not know whether the "fifty years" in these verses must be taken literally, i.e., whether the trip took place in 1855 or shortly before. It may be that Oybin was one of the resorts which Moritz Schreber visited at the end of his life, in about 1860. I am happy to leave the drawing of conclusions from Paul's proclivity for sitting astride frontier stones to the psychoanalysts. The reader who finds this a rather feeble remark should now read the following pages on the inferences made by the psychoanalyst Maurits Katan.

3. PSYCHIATRISTS ON SCHREBER FAMILY LIFE

I shall begin my survey of the psychiatric literature about the family life of the Schrebers by examining the work of the psychoanalyst Maurits Katan.

Maurits Katan on Paul, Gustav, Anna, and their mother

In 1959 Katan described in detail how he discovered traumatizing events which took place in the Schreber family. In 1975 he summarized his 1959 findings as follows. It should be noted that Katan refers to Paul as "Schreber."

Schreber's father had "granted" his oldest son [Gustav] the privilege of acting as guardian, which means that he had assigned him the task of watching his younger brother [Paul] in order to keep him from masturbating. Schreber's brother misused the privileges which his father had granted him by performing a homosexual attack on his younger brother. From the delusional material (Katan, 1959, p. 370) I was able to enlarge my construction. The sister who was next in age to the older brother [Anna] discovered what had gone on between the two boys and told their mother. In the discussions that followed, the older brother showed himself very resistant and refused to give up his privileges unless his mother and his sister would assure him that they would not divulge anything to the father. The mother was so afraid of the father's wrath if he heard about what had happened that she readily convinced the older daughter that she must not tell the father. Once these conditions had been accepted, the brother promised not to repeat his homosexual attack on Daniel Paul. The

younger Schreber [Daniel Paul = Paul] felt indignant about what
he regarded as a plot against him. Especially because of the mother's
attitude, the older brother now escaped a well-deserved punishment.
On the occasion of Daniel Paul's complaints, his mother explained
to him that she could not continually be with him to protect him
against his brother, that the other children also needed her attention
[Katan, 1975 p. 364,365].

Inversely proportional to these spectacular findings is Katan's
source material, which consists of nothing more than the beginning
of the *Memoirs,* the book already analyzed so often in which Paul
Schreber explained how, as a mentally sick adult, he had the kingdom
of God revealed to him. Katan's sensational discoveries are merely the
result of a spectacular method of reasoning, better described perhaps
as a rather uncritical method.

Let us look first at some relatively lucid examples of Katan's
reasoning. In the kingdom of God an important role is played by a
certain Professor Flechsig, the psychiatrist who treated Paul Schreber
at the beginning of his illness and who is later, in supersensible form,
supposed to have had an uncommonly detrimental influence over him.
Paul Schreber recorded how by supersensible means he heard names
of Flechsig's ancestors: "Abraham Fürchtegott Flechsig . . . and a
Daniel Fürchtegott Flechsig; the latter lived towards the end of the
eighteenth century" (D. P. Schreber, 1903, p. 24 = 1955, p. 56).
Katan opined that

> There is an unmistakable connection with the first names of
> Schreber's father. [Daniel Gottlob Moritz] . . . it is as if in this
> respect Schreber treats Flechsig as though the two have the same
> father, i.e., *as though they were brothers* [1959, p. 367].

From this he concluded that Flechsig was in reality Paul Schreber's
brother Gustav. Katan did not know the names of Paul's distant for-
bears, but they include several that are not unlike "Abraham
Fürchtegott" and "Daniel Fürchtegott." Names not unlike "Fürchtegott"
include not only the "Gottlob" of Paul's father but also the "Gotthilf"
of his grandfather and the "Gottfried" of his great-grandfather. The
name "Daniel" occurs not only in Paul's father's name but also in
Paul's and in his grandfather's and great-grandfather's names. As regards the name "Abraham," Katan wrote (*ibid.,* p. 354) that it suggests

the Biblical father-figure. Now the Bible is not short of names of people who were also fathers, and the typically Biblical name "Abraham" may also perfectly well be linked with names such as "Solomon" (a Schreber of three generations before Paul) or "David" (four, five, and six generations before Paul). These names fit in better with Paul's statement that one of these Flechsig ancestors lived in a more remote past. Looked at this way, Flechsig—descended from Paul's distant forebears—is more of a father-figure than a brother.

Another example of Katan's logic: He has already established that Paul's supersensible psychiatrist Flechsig is actually his brother Gustav. As a mentally sick adult Paul Schreber heard other things about his psychiatrist's ancestors. For example, he heard of quarrels in a distant past between members of the Schreber family and members of the Flechsig family; both families were supposed to belong to "the highest heavenly nobility," and the Schrebers were fond of embellishing themselves with the pompous title of "margraves of Tuscany and Tasmania." From this Katan concluded as follows:

> Does not this adornment with titles sound like child's play, in which two boys boast between themselves and each one tries to outdo the other by assuming still higher titles?
> On the other hand, was this play so innocent? [*ibid.*, p. 366].

In short, Katan took the use of pompous titles heard by the mentally sick Paul Schreber to suggest child's play in reality. What happens in the second sentence of this quotation is typical: having suggested child's play as a hypothesis, Katan at once goes on to inquire into the details of the game, so that the cautiously worded hypothesis has already tacitly been promoted to the status of a premise for everything that follows. viz., a new train of reasoning designed to discover the precise nature of this child's play. In this regard—camouflaging the weakness of a hypothesis by at once taking it as the point of departure for the next train of reasoning—it would almost be fair to speak of a "Katan method." In the following quotation we see it happen within a single sentence: "Presumably his brother [Gustav] tried to masturbate him, but we do not know how far this act went" (*ibid.*, p. 373).

Katan even managed to find support for his reconstruction in the quite different publications of Niederland, in which Moritz Schreber is represented as a domestic tyrant. Let us see what Katan wrote in 1975 about his constructions of 1959:

I believe that *my* constructions do not contradict the facts which, thanks to Niederland, have become known about Schreber's father. Therefore I conceive of this information regarding the father as corroborating the correctness of my constructions [1975, p. 365].

However, one can scarcely conceive of what information Niederland could have found in the writings of Moritz Schreber to contradict Katan's constructions. A plea for sexual relations between brothers? Or a statement by Moritz Schreber that the problems Katan discussed did *not* arise in his own family? No, even that would not be sufficient, since according to Katan the father was unaware of what had occurred between his sons.

The repercussions which Niederland's publications have for Katan's findings are even sadder. According to Katan, father Schreber was told nothing of the problems in his family; in 1959 Katan observed in this connection: "In addition, the father was frequently absent" (1959, p. 371). However, this last assertion does not rhyme with the picture of Moritz Schreber given by Niederland, who represented him as an authority always present and always managing affairs. It is not surprising therefore that in his later summary in 1975 Katan quietly dropped the 1959 reference to the father's frequent absence. The tragic part of this is that on this particular point it so happens that Katan was largely right: after 1851, it will be recalled, or in other words from the time when Paul was aged nine onward, the father frequently retired because of his head complaint.

To the more theoretical objections to Katan's way of reasoning we may add a few empirical ones. Katan started from the plausible assumption that the figures in Paul Schreber's later theological delusional world must have had their origins in persons who played an important part in Schreber's real life; as a psychoanalyst he believed that these persons are to be found in the family in which the patient has grown up. He therefore made the hierarchy in the insane kingdom of God correspond to the hierarchy within the Schreber family. In doing this, he assumed a family constellation of a kind which may well be correct for twentieth-century Americans like Katan (i.e., father, mother, and children), as he did in a passage in the *Memoirs* where there is a reference to "the next higher in rank" in God's kingdom. Katan inferred that "Since this person was only the next higher in rank to [Paul] Schreber, it must have been his two-year-older sister, Anna" (1959, p. 373). For, Katan claimed, "the structure of the family was such that, after the parents and his brother [Gustav], the authority rested in the next child, who was a sister [Anna]'' (*ibid.*, p. 374). However, this family hierarchy which Katan so glibly assumed did not in fact obtain in the family of the Schrebers, which was considerably more intricate in its make-up. Besides parents and children, it will be recalled, there were also the young inpatients at the clinic, domestic staff, and possibly Paul's fifteen-year-older aunt Fanny Haase.

In other words the family hierarchy was much more complicated than Katan assumed; moreover, the opportunity for forbidden sexual games was naturally greatly enhanced by the presence of those members of the household forgotten by Katan. I shall say nothing of the attraction of an aunt fifteen years older than Paul, particularly as I do not know whether Fanny Haase lived with the Schrebers for the whole of the period preceding her marriage in 1851. The young inpatients were certainly not all as well brought-up as the Schreber children. And finally there were the domestic staff: Moritz Schreber gave the following advice for the prevention of masturbation in children: ''Above all, work preventively by eliminating all laxity and effeminacy, by attention to your children's association with other children, with the servants etc'' (D. G. M. Schreber, 1861a, p. 65).

To conclude all this criticism of Katan, a consideration of a more general nature: It may be that the reader has formed the opinion that so much criticism of such a bad article is a little overdone. But in the more than twenty years since it first appeared, that article has never been criticized, nor has there been any lack of praise for Katan on account of it: in 1974 it was partially reprinted in Niederland's book *The Schreber Case*; in 1978 that book appeared in a German translation as part of a series under the general editorship of the famous psychoanalyst Mitscherlich; in 1975 Katan was able to publish a laudatory account of his own article; and in 1979 a translation of the entire article appeared in French in *Le cas Schreber,* on which occasion it was referred to by the introducer as a *''très importante étude''* (Prado de Oliveira, 1979a, p. 10).

It is perhaps a pity that opinions in the social sciences are not formed according to Popper's principle of ''conjectures and refutations''—bold hypotheses such as Katan's being tested for their tenability and, in this case, rapidly being consigned to the dustbin of science. In fact, opinion-forming in the social sciences is more like what it ought to be in the world of literature: the bad studies are simply ignored, and only the good ones attract much attention. We thus have the paradoxical situation in which a recognized classic such as that by Ariès on childhood is far more often ''refuted'' than any other book of its genre. However, we can hardly wish for the Popper principle to apply absolutely to the social sciences: there is simply too much rubbish being bandied about for that. Nevertheless, it does seem to me that some sort of shift toward the methods of the ''real'' sciences would be a good thing; that is why I have paid so much attention to Katan. All we must hope for now is that the usual mechanism of the social sciences does not start operating in Katan's case: it must not be thought that a text which has been considered at such length must also be worth closer study.

Moritz Schreber as a domestic tyrant

The situation is quite different in the next psychiatric genre to be discussed, namely, that in which Moritz Schreber is represented as a domestic tyrant: whatever I have to say about it, that literature is certainly worthy of study. The following quotation is typical of the genre when in a more well-considered vein:

> Apart from a regimented, rigidly disciplined type of education, which seems to have been [Paul] Schreber's lot from early infancy, he appears to have been forced into complete submission and passive surrender by a father whose sadism may have been but thinly disguised under a veneer of medical, reformatory, religious, and philanthropic ideas. Dr. Schreber invented unusual mechanical devices for coercing his children, presumably his sons more than his daughters, into submission. On the basis of ample evidence in Dr. Schreber's own writings, it is clear that he also used a ''scientifically'' elaborated system of relentless mental and corporeal pressure alternating with occasional indulgence, a methodical sequence of studiously applied terror interrupted by compensatory periods of seductive benevolence and combined with ritual observances that he as a reformer incorporated into his overall missionary scheme of physical education [Niederland, 1974, p. 70].

This passage comes from the writings of the American psychoanalyst W. G. Niederland. He was the first in the psychiatric tradition to claim attention for Paul Schreber's father, principally for his educational work. Niederland's publications on this subject, starting in 1959, are unquestionably still the best, and the significance of his findings was quick to find general recognition in the psychoanalytic world. Outside psychoanalytic circles, however, the educational writings of Paul Schreber's father remained unknown until the early 1970's, when the American psychiatrist Morton Schatzman used Niederland's work for his book *Soul Murder*, which deals with the abominable effect that Schatzman claims the pedagogue Moritz Schreber had on his son.

The "domestic tyrant" literature is chiefly founded on Moritz Schreber's educational writing. However, it also seizes on four details of Paul Schreber's youth.[7] Two of these are found in papers from the psychiatric clinics to which Paul was admitted. In his anamnesis we read: "He was said to have been very gifted and to have been an excellent scholar" (quoted by Baumeyer, 1956, p. 62). And in about 1900 his sister Klara wrote to his psychiatrist: "I do not want to conceal, however, that my brother's hasty, restless, and nervous manner was very noticeable to us, although he had shown this slightly even when he was young" (Krause, quoted by Baumeyer, *ibid.*, p. 67). And then there are two tiny references to his youth in the *Memoirs*. The first is in a passage on sexuality: "Few people have been brought up according to such strict moral principles as I" (D. P. Schreber, 1903, p. 281 = 1955, p. 208). And finally, so he wrote, Paul was "from youth accustomed to enduring both heat and cold" (D. P. Schreber, 1903, p. 172 = 1955, p. 146).

In essence, as I have said, the "domestic tyrant genre" is based on Moritz Schreber's educational publications. These also lend support to the two details from the *Memoirs*: that Paul was accustomed to enduring cold from youth is not surprising in one whose father believed that from the age of two, children should daily be washed all over with cold water (D. G. M. Schreber, 1858a, p. 80). And as regards strict moral principles in upbringing, Moritz Schreber's books are a veritable cornucopia.

For the rest I shall confine myself here to those passages in Moritz Schreber's writing which have justifiably most often been used in the psychiatric literature. Such passages are of two types: those in which Schreber told us something about his own family, and those in which he recommended, and illustrated, mechanical devices to be used in bringing up children which to modern eyes have a certain terrible fascination.

Moritz Schreber referred explicitly in his writing to three incidents in his own family. The first such reference occurs in a passage about bringing up children before the age of one. He gave the urgent recommendation that between mealtimes children should never be given anything to eat, and despite the weaknesses of domestic staff he considered that this is an achievable ideal.

> In this connection, here is just a small example from my own family circle. The nanny of one of my children, a very good person in general, once, despite the express prohibition from giving the child anything at all, however insignificant, outside its mealtimes, gave it a piece of a pear she was eating herself, as the child's subsequent behaviour made plain. . . . Without there being any other grounds she was at once dismissed from our service, since I had now lost the necessary faith in her unconditional conscientiousness. This was effective. One successor told it to the next, and never again since have I ever, either with this or with any of the later children, made such a discovery [D. G. M. Schreber, 1858a, p. 64].

When Schreber is writing on children's illnesses, which are naturally more easily treated "when the patient behaves obediently," he again wrote about his own family:

> One of my children was taken ill at the age of 1 1/2 in such a way that the only treatment which would give hope of saving its life, and which was also quite dangerous, was only possible if the little patient were completely calmly obedient. It was successful, because the child was from the very start used to the most unconditional obedience towards me, whereas otherwise in ordinary human terms the child's life would most probably have been beyond saving [*ibid.*, p. 67].

A third glimpse of the Schreber family is granted us in Schreber's "straightener" (Geradehalter), a device that prevents its wearer from bending forward while writing, which I have already referred to in the introduction (p. 17), where I also quote Schreber's statement that it worked well for his own children. This third and final glimpse of his family which Schreber himself gave us is also the first example of his orthopedic educational apparatus. In the domestic tyrant literature these devices have attracted a great deal of attention, being regarded as having something to do with the delusional experiences of the adult Paul Schreber. In the case of the straightener there appears to be some connection with the "compression-of-the-chest-miracle" experienced by the insane Paul. On account of the same "miracle," attention has been drawn to Moritz Schreber's views on the correct position to be adopted in sleep. Children should sleep on their back, and where other means fail, resort should be taken to the bed-bands of Figure 9 (*ibid.*, pp. 173–175).

In connection with Paul Schreber's later "tearing and pulling" pains in his scalp, attention has been drawn to the "headholder" shown in Figure 10: a leather strap with at one end clip *a*, which is attached to the hair at the back of the head, and at the other end button-hole *b*, which fastens to a button on the child's underpants.[8] This device promotes the "proud bearing" by pulling the wearer's hair as soon as the head is allowed to hang. Finally there is a device which has been associated with Paul's later "head-compressing-machine," the feeling that his head was being compressed, as in a vise, into the shape of a pear. I quote Moritz Schreber:

> Not uncommonly an incongruity develops between the two *jawbones* due to prevailing growth of the lower jawbone. . . . A case from my own observation, relating to an eight-year-old girl, is best suited to illustrate this as the fault in question was here most markedly manifest. . . . I had a chin-strap made from soft leather, as shown in the illustration [Fig. 11]: . . . the device was used only at night for a period of twenty months, was left off only during the troublesomely hot summer nights, and otherwise caused not the slightest complaints [*ibid.*, pp. 219–220].

The essential question to be asked here is, to what extent it is possible on the strength of Moritz Schreber's writings to draw conclusions about the actual life of the Schreber family. In some literature the equation of theory and practice is certainly made extremely easy: Moritz Schreber "wrote eighteen books and booklets; many are about his methods of educating children; he applied them to his own children" (Schatzman, 1973a, p. 7). The most cautious is still Niederland, who wrote that Moritz Schreber's chief work, the *Kallipädie*,

> contains passages that indicate that the methods and rules laid down by Dr. Schreber were not merely theoretical principles for the public, but were also regularly, actively, and personally applied by him in rearing his own children—with telling effect, as he reports with paternal pride. Indeed, he ascribes to his use of these methods a lifesaving influence on one of his offspring [1974, p. 50].

This is true. But the question is whether the reader of this passage is aware that in fact Schreber referred explicitly to only three episodes in the life of his own family.

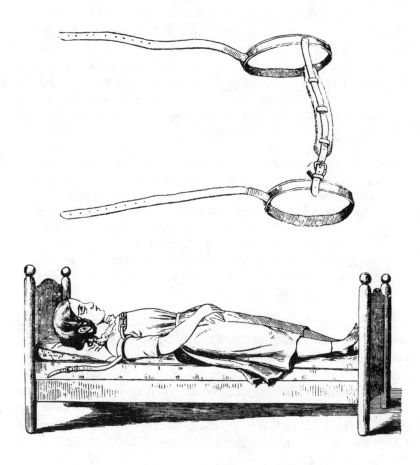

Fig. 9. Bed-bands. From D. G. M. Schreber (1858a, p. 174).

Fig. 10. Head-holder. From D. G. M. Schreber (1858a, p. 199).

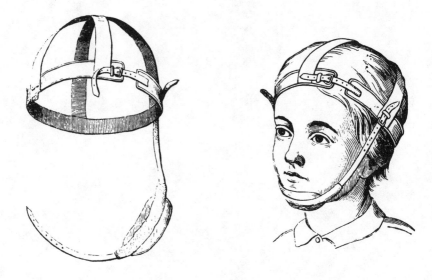

Fig. 11. Chin-strap. From D. G. M. Schreber (1858a, p. 220).

The last of the devices I have described, the chin-strap, illustrates this problem nicely. I have already quoted Schreber himself on the purpose of this device, and it was plain from that quotation that the intention is that it be used in cases in which malformation of the jaw has already taken place. By quoting this passage by Schreber, I have actually departed from the domestic tyrant genre of literature: there, these things are described in much more general terms. For example, we read that Moritz Schreber "had a chin-band made, which was held to the head by a helmet-like device. This was to ensure proper growth of the jaw and teeth" (Schatzman, 1973a, p. 44). A description like this gives the distinct impression that Schreber thought the device should be used on all children, including, therefore, his own.

Now it is important not to be *too* cautious when examining this point—the equation of theory and practice in Moritz Schreber's life. In the case of the chin-strap we have already seen that according to Schreber the malformation for which it was a remedy occurred "not uncommonly." And a closer knowledge of the Schreber family argues in some cases for a close link between theory and family practice in Moritz Schreber's household. For example, the Schreber children as portrayed in the family portrait of 1851 (Fig. 7, p. 50) bear a strong resemblance to the children shown wearing the orthopedic devices: Sidonie and Klara could easily have been models for the "straightener," Anna might be the girl strapped down to her bed, Paul's may be the slightly melancholic face in the chin-strap. The probability that members of the family sat for illustrations in the father's books is all the greater when we consider that it is an established fact that he himself modelled for illustrations in his own works (Schildbach, 1862a, p. 5).

Furthermore, Schreber described occurrences in his own family more often than just the three times he expressly mentioned the fact: there is one instance in which he refers expressly to an anonymous family, but in which it can be demonstrated that in fact he is writing about the Schrebers. I refer to the following passage:

I know of a family in which the children are all well brought-up. The three eldest children, then aged 12, 11 and 9 years, two boys and a girl, decided amongst themselves—it was the beginning of the year—that throughout the year they would go without the butter they customarily received at breakfast, and eventually ask their mother for the trifling sum thus saved, so that at the end of the year they could use it to make poorer children happy at Christmas. It was valiantly carried through, without either their resolution wavering,

despite the long time, or any reminder of it being necessary. Tell
your children of such and similar cases [D. G. M. Schreber, 1861a,
p. 62].

The same story appears in one of the Schreber's other books
(1858a, p. 238), where the children concerned are the three eldest in
"an unpretentious family." The ages and sexes correspond to those
of the three eldest Schreber children. But above all, of course, we
have already come across this story in the recollections of Moritz
Schreber's daughters (see p. 28). There the youngest daughters Sidonie
and Klara included themselves in the heroic deed ascribed by their
father only to the three eldest children. In this regard Moritz Schreber
is undoubtedly the more reliable source: his youngest daughter Klara
was then only three.

So a more intimate knowledge of the Schreber family argues in
favor of the proposition that theory and practice were closely allied
for Moritz Schreber. But not everything points that way. In one respect
Schreber shared in some degree the fate of the many improvers of the
world who have made disasters of their own private lives. In his writing
Schreber argued for the father to have a major responsibility in the
upbringing of his children; in reality his curious head complaint often
meant that for long periods it was impossible for him to put this ideal
into practice.

This discrepancy between theory and practice has never been
remarked in the domestic tyrant literature. This is due first to factual
reasons. The onset of the head complaint is placed far too late in such
writing—a number of years, instead of ten years before his death.
Moreover, in this genre the information we are given about the whole
affair is vague and limited (Niederland, 1968, pp. 741–742; 1974, pp.
101–102). To this low level of information is added a theoretical
approach which has not had the effect of sharpening perception in this
regard. In all this literature, Moritz Schreber's educational ideas are
represented as more or less the most gruesome system imaginable:
"The systematized inhumanity of the senior Schreber's methods of
childrearing represent punitive socialization at its most extreme"
(Scheff, 1975, p. 91). Such an attitude does not take kindly to the idea
that perhaps Schreber did not always, in his own family, achieve the
ideal of his books. The author who paints Moritz Schreber's theories
as the blackest of reactionarism will be incapable of seeing that the
reality may have been even more sombre.

We have already seen that Katan simply transposed present-day Western family structure to the time of the Schrebers. At least the domestic tyrant writers realize that there are large differences between the two periods. Before I go into the degree to which even they are the victims of hodiecentrism[9]—distortion of one's picture of the past by one's modern views—I shall discuss the last genre of psychiatric literature about the Schreber family: that in which Pauline Schreber (née Haase) is the centre of attention.

Pauline Schreber as the will-less victim of her husband

In the third genre of psychiatric writing about the Schreber family's home life, Frau Schreber is the central character. As a genre it is not so detached as those I have so far discussed. In its methods it sometimes reminds one of Katan: it tends to infer from Paul Schreber's *Memoirs of my Nervous Illness* that there was something abnormal about his early relationship with his mother. However, it is less immodest than Katan; here there are no reconstructions of whole scenes between mother and son based on the *Memoirs*. To the extent that the relationship between mother and son is reconstructed, it is done on the basis of the domestic tyrant literature, chiefly the works of Niederland. As a result this "Frau Schreber literature" is closely related to the domestic tyrant literature, though without being able to boast, as that genre can, any spectacular results: it simply *uses* the domestic tyrant literature—chiefly the story about the nanny who was dismissed for giving one of the Schreber children a piece of pear.

That story recurs several times in the chief text in this genre, an article entitled "The mother-conflict in Schreber's psychosis" by the American psychoanalyst R. B. White. It is fascinating to see how deeply White is obsessed with this story:

> Of special importance for a study of [Paul] Schreber's oral conflicts with his mother is the Doctor's [i.e., Moritz Schreber's] insistence that during the first year of life babies must learn "the art of re-nouncing." This "art" was taught in a fiendishly simple way: the child was placed in the lap of his mother, or nanny, who then ate or drank whatever she wished. No matter how much the baby begged or cried he was fed nothing—except of course his usual three meals at the usual time [1961, p. 58].

In more than one respect this is somewhat of an exaggeration, but that is not my present point. What Moritz Schreber is trying to promote here is, in a sense, the same as the maxim that you avoid pets' begging for food by feeding them only at fixed times during the day. White (*ibid.*, pp. 58–59) went on to relate the story of how Schreber dismissed the nanny on account of the piece of pear. Later on he wrote:

> Early in life and long before he was willing to, [Paul] Schreber was forced by his mother, or mother-figures such as nannies, to abandon his early, oral-dependent impulses towards her. She did this under continuous pressure and interference from an intrusive, tyrannical husband who, at least in spirit, stood constantly behind her peering suspiciously over her shoulder lest, during some lapse into maternal love, she give the baby on her lap a bite of the forbidden pear instead of teaching him the "art of renouncing" [*ibid.*, p. 62].

Moritz Schreber's wife

> probably was as thoroughly dominated by the father as were the frightened nannies of Leipzig [*ibid.*, p. 64].

> Although it is purely conjectural, I can well imagine [Paul] Schreber's mother saying, or perhaps only thinking, "let me give little Daniel [i.e., Paul] the pear" only to be restrained by the stern father. Thus she, as well as her husband, may have been highly ambivalent and inconsistent in her behaviour towards her infant [*ibid.*, p. 69].

> In this manner the father invaded and disrupted that special intimacy which a mother shares with the child at her breast. He disturbed whatever mutuality the mother was capable of finding with her baby, and perhaps made her behave ambivalently and inconsistently towards her infant. Of course, it is not known that the actual nursing situation was thus intruded upon by the father, but his description of the proper training in renunciation—especially the emphasis on the forbidden pear—suggests that he was eagerly, perhaps jealously intent upon wresting his children from their mother's breast [*ibid.*, p. 62].

"The emphasis on the forbidden pear"? Is it Moritz Schreber who is doing the emphasizing? No, the emphasis on the pear is put there by White, just as there are other points here which spring from White's imagination rather than from the ideas of Moritz Schreber. For example, there is the idea that Frau Schreber was just as frightened of her husband as the "nannies of Leipzig." The idea of Moritz Schreber trying to tear his children away from their mother's breast is also a figment of White's imagination: Schreber, indeed, argued in quite a contrary sense. He lashed out strongly against those mothers who do *not* feed their own children: "If the mother is in good health she should . . . only nourish the child at her own breast. This is the sacred will of Nature. If she can do so and yet does not, this is the greatest maternal disgrace and sin" (D. G. M. Schreber, 1861a, p. 11).

The picture which White paints of Frau Schreber—the will-less victim of her husband—has continued to taint the subsequent literature about her. "Indeed we have seen that this mother did not exist in her own right" (Chasseguet-Smirgel, 1975, p. 1017). Searles (1965, pp. 431–433) was full of praise for White's findings ("formidable evidence"); he also summarized White's passage about Moritz Schreber's method of bringing up children: "the cruelly stern programme he [Moritz Schreber] had devised for teaching the infant to become stoical in face of oral needs, a programme which included deliberate tantalization of the infant when he was crying from hunger" (*ibid.*, p. 432). And Searles believed that he could give White even more support:

> My own perusal of Schreber's memoirs leaves me in no doubt that Schreber's mother possessed, in reality, strong, repressed cannibalistic strivings towards her infant son, was greatly anxious lest uninhibited closeness with him would destroy him or her or both, and used the powerfully forbidding and intrusive father as the instrument for acting out her own unconscious negative feelings towards her son, as well as for providing a mutually protective barrier between her and the baby [*ibid.*, p. 432].

Searles did not tell us how he arrived at these so confident conclusions on the basis of the *Memoirs,* where there is no mention of this kind of matter. The little factual information known about Frau Schreber is distorted to fit the picture of her given by White. Thus Niederland quoted from what he calls the letter from her daughter Anna: " 'Father discussed with our mother everything and anything; she took part in all his ideas, plans, and projects, she read the galley proofs of his writings with him, and was his faithful, close companion in everything' " (Niederland, 1963, p. 203 = 1974, p. 96). This, in turn, was simply turned into Moritz Schreber usurping the maternal role "with the assent of his wife, who merely concurred with his wishes and managed the secretariat'' (Racamier and Chasseguet-Smirgel, 1966, p. 18).

The only new and useful product of this sort of literature is that it brought to light a photograph of Pauline Schreber (Fig. 12), found by Baumeyer (1970, facing p. 244; 1973, facing p. 365). It was probably taken while her husband was still alive, since Baumeyer also found a photograph of him in the same studio setting (Fig. 13). It is also quite interesting to know how Baumeyer came by these photographs. Moritz Schreber was the family doctor to a lawyer in Leipzig called Schulze, "the two families were also on friendly terms," and the lawyer's daughter was nanny and later companion to an aunt of Baumeyer's.

Less amusing is the way Baumeyer went about interpreting this photograph of Pauline Schreber:

> In the picture . . . Frau Schreber makes a very depressive impression. . . . This physical appearance of Schreber's [Paul's] mother presumably also explains why we know so little about her and why she demonstrably played so slight a role in *Schreber's* life. . . . *Schreber's* mother was evidently a severely depressive and passive woman who was completely downtrodden by her husband, *Schreber's* father [1970, p. 245 = 1973, p. 366].

However, passivity is a feature not of Pauline Schreber but of those authors who ascribe such a characteristic to her. The absence of activity is a fabrication of these writers' imagination: what traces can one *expect* to find a woman who had to look after five children and a sick and exceptionally active husband? The fact that so little was known about her is the result not of *her* passivity, but of that of the authors in question: in what follows (pp. 203 ff.) it will become apparent that there are still plenty of traces of Pauline Schreber in her old age. Incidentally, Baumeyer actually comes out of this rather well compared with almost all other writers, some of whom are capable of writing such depressing statements as Kohut's according to which Paul's "mother was subordinated to, submerged by, and interwoven with the father's overwhelming personality and strivings, thus permitting the son no refuge from the impact of the father's pathology" (1971, p. 255 = 1978, p. 307).

It is scarcely possible at this distance to ascertain quite what sort of relationship existed between Moritz Schreber and his wife. But even in what little material there is, there is enough to point to a certain

Fig. 12. Pauline Schreber.

Fig. 13. Moritz Schreber.

degree of independence in Frau Schreber. The story of the fur coat for Christmas reveals her clearly as someone rather more appreciative of her creature comforts than her husband. Something of the kind also comes through in all her stories about how grand her home had been—stories which also show how conscious she was of her noble background.

Criticism of the psychiatric literature about the Schreber family

In the work of Katan we have observed hodiecentrism in its purest form: there the point of departure for his analysis is the family of father, mother, and children, a structure such as was the prevailing norm when Katan was writing—some three decades ago. Hodiecentrism is also a feature of the domestic tyrant literature, though it is not so immediately apparent. At least here the authors can see that Moritz Schreber's ideas are quite different from those of today. But in the manner in which they react to this "shock of non-recognition"[10] they nevertheless behave with extreme hodiecentricity, in that Moritz Schreber is reduced to that shape which is the next easiest to conceive of after one's own idea of the norm, viz., its diametrical opposite: and that, where the norm is the American conception of equality, is a cruel despotism.

We have already seen how it was possible for White to progress effortlessly from a Schreber who dismissed a nanny because she gave a child a piece of pear to a Schreber who tore the child from its mother's breast.

Another example: In the following story concerning a banana, is it possible to detect anything more than an author's compulsion to paint Moritz Schreber as black as is humanly possible?

Niederland's work (1959a, 1959b, 1960, 1963) on the inhuman, crazy child rearing ideas and practices of Paul Schreber's father has supplied the environmental genesis for the soul murder. The child Schreber was manipulated as if he were a thing. He was purposely, systematically, and, above all, righteously deprived of his own will, and of his capacity for pleasure and joy. And he was not permitted to register what had happened to him.

I shall illustrate this with a clinical example of soul murder (Shengold, 1975). A father entered the dining room. The round table was set for the family meal. Beside each plate was a fresh banana—the dessert. The man made a complete round of the table, stopping at every chair to reach out and squeeze a banana to pulp, but spared his own. The older children and the intimidated mother, used to such happenings, said nothing. But the youngest, a 5-year-old boy, began to cry when he saw the mangled banana at his plate. The father then turned on him viciously, demanding that he be quiet—how dare he make such a fuss about a banana? [Shengold 1975, p. 684].

Rather than by despotism, the Schreber family was governed by a complex hierarchy which was more or less taken for granted. In fact, it ought not to be necessary for me to pay more than passing attention to the stupidity of those who conclude from the powerlessness of a nanny that Frau Schreber herself trembled with fear before her husband's wrath. My flat in Berlin, built approximately in 1890, had a maid's room: the bathroom had a lowered ceiling, and the space above it, where it was not possible to stand upright, was where the maid slept (in the days when the occupants had a maid). In all the other rooms it was possible to stand upright normally—and that includes the rooms originally occupied by the lady of the house and the children.

However much the fictitious despotism which is alleged to have terrorized the Schreber household is no more than the American bugbear, it is still closer to the American ideal than is the reality of the complex and accepted hierarchy, to the extent that, although Moritz Schreber himself no longer meets the criteria of American ideological psychology for a decent democratic person, that psychology does still apply in the case of all the other members of the family groaning under the Moritz Schreber reign of terror. By contrast, a form of society in which a relatively high degree of inequality was accepted as the normal state of things by all its members would shatter the American ideal with far greater thoroughness.

4. MORE FACTUAL DATA

To end this chapter on the family life of the Schrebers, let us look at data which are so factual that they can be treated apart from the idealizing or psychiatric literature: Moritz Schreber's activities as an author and the financial position of the Schreber family.

Moritz Schreber's writing

We have already seen that during the last ten years of his life Moritz Schreber frequently secluded himself on account of his head complaint, and that it was during this period that the major part of his writing was published. Writing not only meant isolation, however: it also brought Schreber new contacts. From 1855 he was one of the four editors of the *Neue Jahrbücher für die Turnkunst* (an annual review of gymnastics), which were published in Dresden. During this period he came into contact with people interested in his ideas and publications on the public education system: "He advised Director Teichmann on the building of his new school house on the Schillerstrasse, he associated with the headmaster of the *Bürgerschule* [higher-grade elementary school], Vogel, and frequently talked to Dr. Hauschild about 'school or parent evenings' " (Siegel, 1909b, p. 208). Schreber not only wrote books and articles, however: the surviving manuscripts also include speeches, talks, and letters. It will also be recalled that he wrote "paternal words" for his children on their Confirmation (see page 69). And finally in 1852 he drew up a Schreber family tree (G. Friedrich, 1932).

The financial situation

Moritz Schreber's financial position is something of a puzzle. We have already seen that as a student he was dependent on external sources of income. Two decades later, in 1847, he had a colossal house built for him "in front of the Zeitzer Gate." I can solve the puzzle only by assuming that, as I surmised above, the death of Pauline Schreber's mother meant a large legacy for the Schrebers, though the house in front of the Zeitzer Gate was in Moritz Schreber's name only. Evidence for this is provided by the "Acta" on Pauline Schreber, which state that following the death of her husband she acquired the property at Zeitzer Strasse 43 and 44, a quarter by inheritance and three-quarters by purchase from the other heirs.

There are also other data on Moritz Schreber's financial affairs. First of all, a story which belongs lock, stock and barrel in the idealizing literature: "Once when he had successfully treated a Russian nobleman, the latter wished to thank him with a number of gold pieces, which he placed on the table. Schreber pushed the major part back, considering this fee far too much. And this happened at a time when his financial position was not exactly glittering" (Fritzsche, 1926, p. 13). This episode was related to Fritzsche by Schreber's daughter Anna.

Finally, there was the "Schreber family scholarship," for which

II. Literatur über Schreber.

1. 1903: Dr. med. Schreber und die Leipziger Schrebervereine mit besonderer Berücksichtigung der Schrebervereine der Nordvorstadt. Fritzsche-Brückner.
2. 1925: Das Buch der Schreberjugendpflege. Gerhard Richter.
3. 1923: Die Entwicklung der Deutschen Kleingartenbewegung bis zum Jahre 1921 und ihr Einfluß auf die Volksernährung. Dissertation Rostock.
4. Schreber. Deutsche Turnerzeitung, 1862, Nr. 1. Schildbach.
5. Ein Vorkämpfer f. v. Jugendspiel. Gartenlaube, 1908, Nr. 42, S. 891/92.
6. Dr. D. G. M. Schreber ein Kämpfer für Volkserziehung. Ed. Mangner.
7. Leipziger Staatsexamensarbeit. Walter Bernhardt.
8. Spielplätze und Erziehungsvereine. Eduard Mangner.
9. Schrebervereine und Schule. Hugo Fritzsche.
10. Bemerkungen über den Wert der Spielplätze. Hugo Fritzsche.
11. Über Entwicklung und Bedeutung der Schrebergärten, insbesondere der Braunschweiger. Friedr. Ott.
12. Der 1. Schreberverein (Cornelia). Gustav Siegert.
13. Die Leipziger Schrebervereine: Entstehung, Wesen, Wirken. Richard Siegel.
14. Die Bedeutung der Kleingärten für Fürsorge und Erziehung. Dissertation von E. Rathje.

Fig. 14. A portion of Ritter's bibliography. (From Ritter, [1936a, p. 94].)

Moritz applied in 1855 for his sons: from 1857 to 1860 for Gustav, and from 1860 to 1863 for Paul. The pertinent correspondence is brief. The municipal authorities in Oschatz replied to Schreber that the scholarship had been awarded to Wilhelm Martin Spitz, son of Friedrich Wilhelm Spitz, a Leipzig schoolmaster and would not terminate until 1858. To this Schreber answered that it would be easy for him to prove that his sons had a better entitlement than Herr Spitz, but that he was withdrawing his application, partly because he was "personally acquainted with the Spitz family" (D. G. M. Schreber, 1855b). Anyone who can so readily give up applying for a scholarship can hardly be very short of cash.

Schreber applied for the scholarship to finance his sons' university education. Naturally enough, they had had some formal education. Indeed, the daughters also had attended school, if we may judge by a passing reference in the eldest daughter Anna's recollections of her childhood: "Frau Jung can also remember the Year of Storm, 1848, and she relates how one afternoon she was fetched from school and her father was wearing the uniform of the Civil Guard" (*Neue Leipziger Zeitung*, 1939). All the information about money that we have considered so far corresponds closely with something Anna once said about her father: "Dr. Schreber, who left quite a substantial fortune, was not wealthy by birth" (Fritzsche, 1926, p. 13).

A last financial detail: the substantial fees paid for treatment will be discussed in the next chapter, which deals with daily practice at the clinic.

NOTES TO CHAPTER 6

[1] I have already criticized the way in which Ritter deals with detail (see Notes 4 and 7 to Chapter 1, note 8 to Chapter 2, notes 13 and 17 to Chapter 4, and note 1 to Chapter 5). In fact, however, the whole of his thesis is of mediocre quality. To prove this, let us look at the second part of Ritter's bibliography (Fig. 14)
In every case Ritter gave the name of the author last. For example, title 4: "Schreber. Deutsche Turnerzeitung, 1862, Nr. 1. Schildbach" means: C. H. Schildbach, "Schreber," in: *Deutsche Turnzeitung* (not *Turnerzeitung*) (1862), pp. 4–6. But this is only the beginning of the problems with identifying authors. For example, in title 1 it is not Ritter's intention to say that the author has a double-barrelled name, "Fritzsche-Brückner," but that there are two authors, that is, H. Fritzsche and G. A. Brückner. Author statements can be reduced to infinite brevity: in title 3 Ritter has completely omitted to tell us the author's name. The only way of finding this title is to wade through the lists of dissertations in Rostock from 1923 onward; it turns up in the list for 1926 and proves to be by Kurt Heilbrunn. Incidentally, it is dated 1922, not 1923.
It is not only the way the authors are identified that is often peculiar: the rest of the title is also frequently reproduced in an idiosyncratic manner. For example, title

9, "Schrebervereine und Schule. Hugo Fritzsche," is undoubtedly an article by Hugo Fritzsche, "Schrebervereine und Schule," which appeared in *Der Freund der Schreber-Vereine* in 1914 on pages 181–185 and 196–199. But even sloppier references are possible: title 13, "Die Leipziger Schrebervereine: Entstehung, Wesen, Wirken. Richard Siegel," undoubtedly means: Richard Siegel, "Die Leipziger Schrebervereine. Ihre Entstehung, ihr Wesen und Wirken," in *Der Freund der Schreber-Vereine*, 1907, pages 2–10. Title 12, "Der 1. Schreberverein (Cornelia). Gustav Siegert," I have been unable to find. Possibly Ritter meant to say that this is an article which appeared in the magazine *Cornelia*. His way of giving this title does, incidentally, explain how Tabouret-Keller (1973, p. 300) came to be under the impression that the first Schreber Association was called "Cornelia." Title 7 is also curious. I happened to find this *Staatsexamenarbeit* by Walter Bernhardt because I happened to visit the library of the educational establishment for which Bernhardt wrote his paper, namely, the Leipzig sports college, and because the college happens to include such papers in its library catalogue.

It is possible that all my criticism of someone like Kleine (note 9 to Chapter 4) gives the impression of taking a sledgehammer to crack a nut (albeit a professorial nut), but in Ritter's case such severe criticism is certainly justified. Ritter's work is an official German philosophical dissertation, written in order to obtain a doctorate. Moreover, no other authors have ever offered any criticism of the academic standard of this work, and Ritter's account of the life of Moritz Schreber has been taken as gospel by the writers of the psychiatric work about him who are now themselves regarded as authors of gospel, namely Niederland, Schatzman, and Tabouret-Keller. I am hopeful that in the future my own book will be allowed to assume the present functions of Ritter's book.

[2]This article by Siegel of 1909 cannot be found in ordinary libraries. In the only other place where this text was subsequently published, i.e., in Gerhard Richter's book of 1925, the deceptiveness of the "we daughters" form is even greater. Richter headed the text: "Interesting statements by the daughters of Dr. Schreber relating to their father," at the same time adding a footnote in which the true author of these "statements" appears to have been reduced to the status of compiler of the magazine issue in which the text originally appeared: "These recollections have only once previously been published, namely in the compilation by Richard Siegel (Freund der Schrebervereine, V. Jahrgang, October 1909, Heft x)" (G. Richter, 1925, p. 10).

[3]However, it should not be imagined that the whole family drank coffee in the morning: Moritz Schreber was not an advocate of coffee for children.

> During the childhood years . . . the consumption of coffee should be avoided entirely, because at that age it lays the foundations for the currently prevalent condition of over-stimulation of the nervous system and helps promote premature puberty and hence the rapid exhaustion of vitality. Here water, milk, cocoa or simple light beers are the only wholesome beverages [D. G. M. Schreber, 1861e, p. 144].

To modern eyes the curious thing here is the approbation of beer. This is a general tendency in Schreber's works. For example, he writes of "spirituous beverages" that "They are to be regarded (with the exception of beers, which are also nutritious and are otherwise generally of a milder nature) as stimulants pure and simple" (D. G. M. Schreber, 1861e, p. 145). In the main text I shall quote Anna, who in 1935 recalled that her father never drank beer. I suspect that since Moritz Schreber's day coffee has risen and beer fallen in the public estimation. In both cases—the twentieth-century reports that coffee was drunk and that beer was not—I am inclined to leave open the possibility that to some extent memories have been colored by changes in attitudes to the two beverages during the intervening years.

[4]This mention of meat-eating in the Schreber family has suffered rather the same fate as the story about occasionally having the ice broken for a quick invigorating dip—a story which, it will be recalled, has been blown up into bathing in the icy water for the entire family. A similar mechanism is at work here. Sidonie and Klara reported that once a week no meat was set on the table for the midday meal, and that meat was seldom served in the evenings. This means that the Schrebers ate meat at least seven times a week, including the evening meal on Sunday but not counting any holidays or feast-days. However, in Ritter (1936a, p. 13), Schütze (1936b, p. 1889), and G. Richter (1939b, p. 18) this emphasis on a certain degree of moderation has already become "eating meat was a rarity." The same thing happens in the psychiatric literature: "meat was only eaten on rare occasions" (Tabouret-Keller, 1973, p. 299). According to Bankhofer (1977, p. 15), Moritz Schreber himself "one day" said: "Eating meat must only be a rarity!" In reality Schreber saw meat-eating in quite a different light:

> Taken by and large the right porportion for an active, healthy person in middle life might be about equal quantities of animal and vegetable foods, with a preponderance of the latter in youth and of the former in old age. [D. G. M. Schreber, 1839, p. 111).

[5]This representation of the role played by religion in Schreber family life must not go unaccompanied by a reference to what the psychoanalyst Niederland had to say on the subject. Saying that he was drawing on a letter written by Anna, the eldest daughter, he wrote:

> She describes in it in some detail how everything in the Schreber home was *gottwärts gerichtet* (oriented towards God), how God was present in their childhood world at all times, not merely in their daily prayers, but in all their feeling, thinking, and doings. She concludes the letter with the words: 'All this was finished with the sudden death of our beloved father . . . *unser Kinderparadies war zerstört*' [1963, p. 205].

This passage is important not merely because Niederland accorded religion a much more essential role in Schreber family life than I do, but also because here we have, in the psychiatric literature, some much more interesting material on the life the Schrebers led than we otherwise find in that genre. Niederland wrote, as I say, that this is a letter from Anna. He presented this discovery with a certain justifiable aplomb in his book *The Schreber Case*, first in the summary of his sources: "an unpublished letter of one of Schreber, Jr.'s sisters" (Niederland, 1974, p. xv) and later on in the book: "In the course of my search for authentic background material on the Schreber family, I secured a letter written by the patient's eldest sister, Anna, in 1909—two years before Schreber's death" (*ibid.*, p. 96). Earlier (1963, p. 203) Niederland had called himself "fortunate enough" to have found this letter. He gives no further details: no exact date, no addressee, no information about how he came to find it. This "letter from Anna" is important, as we see from the later Schreber literature: "Little is known of the mother Schreber, née Pauline Haase, who was the third child of a doctor in Leipzig. One of the few documents to have been found is a letter from Anna, the son's eldest sister, written in 1909" (Croufer, 1970, p. 218). A few pages earlier, Croufer had written:

> From a letter written in 1909 by the eldest sister, Anna, we know that everything in the Schreber home was oriented towards God. God was present in the world of their childhood,

at all times, not only in their daily prayers but in all their thoughts and actions [*ibid.*, p. 216]:

Melman managed to make the volume of quotation from this "letter from Anna" expand considerably:

> In the rediscovered correspondence of one of the patient's sisters, Anna, we find this invocation: 'How everything at home was "gottwärts gerichtet" (done in the spirit of God), how God was present at all times in our childhood world, not merely in our daily prayers, but in all our feeling, thinking, and doings. All this was finished with the sudden death of our beloved father . . . our children's paradise was destroyed (unser Kinderparadies war zerstört)' [1980, p. 5].

And Daniels even informs us that: "A sister wrote to Dr. Niederland that everything in the Schreber home was oriented toward God" (1975, p. 1338). This is interesting: In 1909 Niederland was four or five years old. However, Daniels can hardly have guessed that the manner in which Niederland actually came by the "letter from Anna" was scarcely less remarkable—and that is the chief reason for going into the matter of this "letter" in such detail. For the fact is that I doubt whether Niederland ever saw such a letter from Anna; indeed, I even question whether such a letter ever existed. I suspect that in fact Niederland has used, not a letter written by Anna in 1909, but passages from Siegel's article of that year, in which he reproduced the words of Anna's sisters Sidonie and Klara.

I have already quoted one passage from Niederland's quotation from the "letter from Anna": "She concludes the letter with the words: 'All this was finished with the sudden death of our beloved father . . . unser Kinderparadies war zerstört' " (1963, p. 205). Let us compare this with Siegel's closing lines: "Within the space of a few days a rapidly worsening abdominal complaint put an unexpected end to our beloved father's life. A severe blow for us, and our children's paradise was destroyed [unser Kinderparadies war zerstört]——" (1909b, p. 209). The final words correspond; what precedes them, however, is only partly accurate. For this reason I believe that Niederland is not only using a different source from the one he says he is using, but also that he is using it carelessly. I realize that this does not yet sound very convincing. Let us therefore look at another passage from Siegel's article:

> He discussed everything with our mother; she shared in all his ideas, plans and designs, she also read the proofs with him when his writings were published. And when an iron ladder struck our dear father on the head and an enduring chronic head complaint often took him away from his job and the family for hours at a time and banished him to painful silence and loneliness, in these difficult hours too his wife was his faithful helpmeet [1909b, p. 205].

Niederland quoted as follows from the "letter from Anna": " 'Father discussed with our mother everything and anything; she took part in all his ideas, plans, and projects, she read the galley proofs of his writings with him, and was his faithful, close companion in everything" (1963, p. 203 = 1974, p. 96). So Niederland's quotation from the "letter from Anna" is in fact a pretty faithful translation of Siegel's text, except that it omits the part about Schreber's head complaint. Schatzman (1973a, p. 14), Croufer (1970, p. 218), and Schalmey (1977, p. 46) borrow Niederland's quotation.

I can offer no further comparisons between the "letter from Anna" and Siegel's article about Sidonie and Klara for the simple reason that Niederland gives us no other quotations from this "letter." I can imagine that the reader is still unconvinced. True, there are remarkable parallels between the "letter from Anna" and Siegel's article, but there are also differences, and we have yet to explain the fact that Niederland changes the names of Sidonie and Klara into Anna; quite apart from the fact that he does not quote more from the Siegel article.

In my initial enthusiasm at this discovery I thought I could explain why Niederland transforms Sidonie and Klara into Anna. I considered it unlikely that Niederland knew the 1909 article, since it is not to be found in ordinary libraries. True, it was later reprinted in Gerhard Richter's book of 1925, but that work has been little used in the later literature. Much more important is the fact that Schilling (1964) quoted Siegel's article of 1909 at considerable length. All the passages from Siegel's article that Niederland uses for his "letter from Anna" also appear in Schilling's article (which has received none of the attention it deserves). I therefore concluded that Niederland, while not knowing the original article by Siegel, was familiar with the quotations from it in Schilling's article. Moreover, Schilling (1964, pp. 4, 5) suffered under the misapprehension that Siegel reproduced the words not of Sidonie and Klara but of Anna. (That these are indeed the words of Sidonie and Klara is clear from the text itself, where there is mention of "we two youngest sisters" [Siegel, 1909b, p. 207].) This, it seemed to me, was the explanation for Niederland's confusion of Sidonie and Klara with Anna.

However, this reconstruction of Niederland's method fails to stand up to closer examination, for Schilling's article was published in 1964 and Niederland used the "letter from Anna" a year earlier, in his article of 1963. In addition to this, it is naive psychologizing to assume that where violence is done to the truth there is necessarily a deliberate deception; this is a reflection of the tendency to ascribe events in the social world too exclusively to the intentions of individuals. Psychologically, too, this idea is unsatisfying: mankind does not consist solely of liars and speakers of the truth.

It is in fact possible to offer a complete reconstruction of how Niederland's "letter from Anna" came into being; it is, moreover, a reconstruction which shows the degree of deliberate falsification on Niederland's part to have been quite slight. What happened was the unplanned consequence of communication between two people, in this case between Niederland and an informant whose identity he does not reveal at this place in his book. For what do we find elsewhere in Niederland's book (1974, p. xvi), where he lists the sources he has used? "Correspondence with Dr. K. Schilling"—that is, with the author who in 1964 was to quote Siegel's article of 1909, and who mixed up Sidonie and Klara with Anna! Presumably, then, Niederland wrote to Schilling asking whether he knew anything about the family life of the Schrebers, and Schilling, being familiar with Siegel's article on precisely that subject, would have written back with extensive quotations and paraphrases from that article. Moreover, he is very likely to have been rather vague as to his source: he would have been understandably reluctant to divulge the secret of so beautiful a source to another writer. Probably he merely referred to "statements made by Anna and written down" or something equally vague. So Niederland now had a letter containing statements apparently made by Anna, and decided therefore that it would be safe to refer simply to a "letter from Anna." In my opinion no blame should be attached to Schilling here: there is no obligation in a correspondence of this kind to reveal one's plum sources. Nor, in fact, is Niederland liable to any severe censure. It is understandable that, not being aware of the original source, he should have relied on Schilling, for on many points Schilling is extremely well informed. But he ought not to have written that he had seen a letter from Anna; he ought to have confined himself to a statement that in a letter from Schilling he had read statements which Schilling believed to have come from Anna.

There is, incidentally, no particular reason why one should be surprised that Niederland should quote so carelessly from his unpublished source: in note 2 to Chapter

12 I shall discuss similarly slapdash treatment of a source whose identity is only vaguely indicated.

How was it possible for Niederland to make such an error? The answer is that he failed to stick to the cardinal rule of good research that one reports one's sources as fully and as precisely as possible. Of course, there is bound to be a tendency in every researcher to keep his material to himself—and it is then up to the academic community to point out the dangerous aspects of such behavior. Perhaps I have been a little overenthusiastic in my efforts in that regard. I have no doubt that the essentials of Niederland's mistake are as I have outlined them, but I have not actually asked him. If he reads this, perhaps he would like to tell me: it might lead to a nice footnote should this work ever see a second edition. Schilling is not available for questioning: he died in 1970.

Finally let us return to the beginning of this note and the account which Niederland gives, on the basis of "Anna's letter," of the highly religious atmosphere in the Schreber household. The reader would be well advised to consult the original version given by Siegel in 1909: it is true that we find there the words " 'gottwärts' gerichteten Sinn" (p. 207), which Niederland quoted as "gottwärts gerichtet" (1963, p. 205); but in general it does not give a picture of excessive religiosity. One might well speculate as to the origins of this exaggeration by Niederland. Schilling referred to Moritz Schreber's "deep religiosity" (1964, p. 11) and may have passed this kind of overdrawn characterization on to Niederland. He, in turn, had something of a vested interest in laying stress on the role of religion in Schreber family life, in view of the fact that the adult Paul Schreber was later to cast his madness in the mold of a theology in which the Deity clearly displays some of the traits of his father.

⁶Earlier it had appeared in Mangner (1884, p. 24) and Mittenzwey (1896, pp. 49–50). It is also the dramatic nucleus of a short play (Krey, 1913). The story also turns up in *Die Gartenlaube* (F., 1908, p. 892), the work of Gerhard Richter (1914a, p. 8; 1925, p. 9; 1939b, p. 20), in Hänsch (1925, p. 289), in Ritter (1936a, p. 18), in the *Neue Leipziger Zeitung* (H.B., 1940), in Schilling (1964, p.9), in Seidel (1974b), and in the "Deutsche Schreberjugend" (*c.* 1958, pp. 7–8). Above all: the story has more than once been repeated to me in conversation.

⁷It also drew on Niederland's "letter from Anna" (the existence or nonexistence of which is dealt with in note 5 to this chapter). There is also a great deal of "information" such as that Paul Schreber was "a rather melancholic sort of chap" (Meijer and Rijnders, 1977, p. 22). As there is no substance to this kind of remark, I shall pay no further attention to it.

⁸In Schatzman's works the headholder is regularly to be seen upside-down (1973a, p. 43; 1976, p. 43; 1977, p. 53; 1978, p. 48; Schatzman and Freud, 1974, p. 58). One wonders how Schatzman supposed it to have been worn. . . . . Where Niederland referred to the *"Kopfhalter"* (1974, pp. 51, 54, 77, 93) he in fact meant the chinstrap, which I shall describe.

⁹The term comes from Goudsblom (1977, p. 7).

¹⁰The term comes from Goudsblom (1977, p. 35).

7

THE ORTHOPEDIC CLINIC FROM 1847
UNTIL 1861

Closely bound up with the life of the Schreber family was the orthopedic clinic run by Moritz Schreber in the same building as their own apartment. The part of the clinic most closely involved with the family was, of course, the boarding house section for young inpatients.

1. THE BOARDING HOUSE

As we have already seen, the boarding house took in between four and seven children, who probably more or less joined the Schrebers in their family life. Little is known about it. There is a reference to it at a conference held in 1859 in a speech by F. A. Bormann, a teacher at Döbeln, a place about forty miles from Leipzig, on Moritz Schreber's ideas about education. Bormann referred to Schreber himself, "who, if I am correctly informed, has the children entrusted to him for the cure taught in a special class-room in his own house" (1859, p. 2). Whether Bormann was correctly informed, I cannot say: I have not come across this information anywhere else.

Most of the information I have about the boarders stems from problems Schreber had with the Leipzig police concerning their registration. At that time, a person spending long periods outside his established place of residence had to have a *Heimatschein*—a certificate of domicile—from his local authorities. This had to be presented for inspection by the authorities of the district in which he intended to stay. In many cases Moritz Schreber was unable to assure that his inpatients' *Heimatscheine* were presented to the Leipzig police. The many reports drawn up by the police on this matter (fourteen in 1852 alone) are still in the Leipzig city archives. In a report dating from 1859 we read: "And since the year 1856 Herr Dr. Schreber has not registered a single one of the pupils admitted to his orthopaedic clinic." In reply, Schreber declared:

> From 1856 onwards I had handed over the boarding house for my pupils to someone else, and that person had also assumed responsibility for registration; however, the person in question has now left this position again and has left Leipzig, so that there is nothing else I can do but take responsibility for any negligence of which that person may be guilty in respect of registration.

So Schreber ran the boarding house until 1856, and again in 1859. In that year he sold the clinic, with the boarding house, to C. H. Schildbach; more on this below. The boarders unquestionably came from wealthy families: in 1861 they paid—apart from any charges for a single room—75 thalers per person per quarter (Schildbach, 1861, p. 16). The Leipzig carpenter's mate referred to above was now earning 144 thalers per annum (Saalfeld, 1974, p. 421). The fee for the cure alone was between 4 and 36 thalers per quarter; two hour-long sessions of the "hygienic-gymnastic" cure per week cost 4 thalers (Schildbach, 1861, p. 16). So the clinic was equipped not only for inpatients but also for those who came as outpatients.

2. THE ORTHOPEDIC TREATMENT

It is difficult to establish how many outpatients the clinic had. As we have seen, the clinic was never very large. Most of the disorders treated were spinal malformations—between 1844 and 1852 Schreber treated 252 such cases—though muscular paralysis, rheumatism, and other conditions were included. This information comes from Schreber's book, *Kinesiatrik oder die gymnastische Heilmethode*, published in 1852 (1852a, p. 9). From the same work we also learn that he had "trained helpers" for his clinic. The book consists largely of diagrams and instructions for a large number of gymnastic exercises, in addition to details of the disorders which they can cure.

Despite this abundance of exercises, however, we do not have a clear picture of what the clinic itself was actually like. Perhaps we should do better to look at a description of the most important room in the place: the gymnasium. "That the floor is covered with fine earth or pounded tan may perhaps, considering the gymnasts' respiratory organs, be inappropriate, in view of the worsening of the air due to the inevitable dust" (Knorr, 1858, p. 25). Dr. Knorr expressed this view in a report of a tour of "gymnastic institutions." The equipment in the gymnasium was summed up by Schildbach:

> The gymnasium contains 4 sets of parallel bars, 3 horizontal bars, 2 slanting ladders, 1 back-ladder, 1 rope ladder, 1 pair of knotted ropes, 1 pair of rings, 1 turntable (described in *Schreber's* Kinesiatrik), 1 worm screw for cranking, 1 high narrow and 1 low broad upholstered horse. . . 1 *Delpech* spiral ladder, 1 *Glisson* hanger, 1 *Kunde* stretching machine with 8 arms, 1 roundabout with 4 spokes, and a number of dumbells of various weights, as also staves of various lengths. Apart from that there are also, though not of course for orthopaedic purposes, 1 pair of spring bars with cord and 1 vaulting-horse. In the dormitory there are also 1 extra pair of parallel bars and 1 slanting ladder [1861, p. 13].

Figures 15–24 contain the illustrations of the above apparatus.

Moritz Schreber's orthopedic treatment consisted largely of gymnastic exercises. As regards his methods, he stands somewhere between the more traditional orthopedics, which favored a greater emphasis on working with mechanical devices, and "Swedish" gymnastics, a system of therapy whereby each patient exercised with an assistant, so that, it was claimed, there was a wider range of possible movements. The polemic between the German therapeutic gymnastics favored by Schreber and the Swedish gymnastics later resulted in a volume by Schreber and an opponent, *Streitfragen der deutschen und schwedischen Heilgymnastik,* which appeared in 1858.

Schreber's head complaint also had repercussions for the clinic, as Schildbach related:

> In 1851 while practising his profession Schreber sustained an injury and was never again in perfect health. He was thereby obliged to cut back both his work for the clinic and the clinic itself as far as possible [1864, p. 4].

> Being frequently interrupted in his accustomed activities by suffering during the last ten years of his life, he had been obliged to decide to hand over the separate running of the boarding house to someone else. What he achieved in this way was unable to satisfy him in the

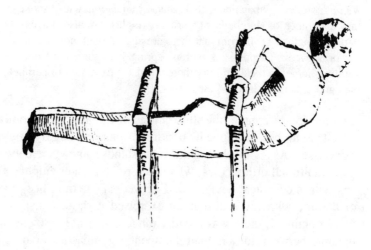

Fig. 15. Illustration taken from D. G. M. Schreber (1852a).

Fig. 16. Illustration taken from D. G. M. Schreber (1852a).

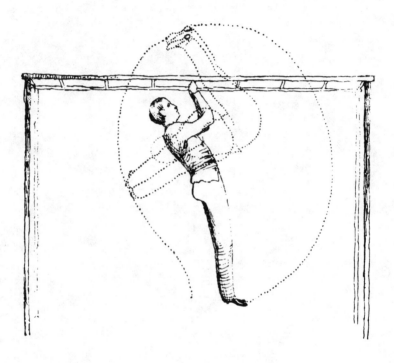

Fig. 17. Illustration taken from D. G. M. Schreber (1852a).

Fig. 18. Illustration taken from D. G. M. Schreber (1852a).

Fig. 19. Illustration taken from D. G. M. Schreber (1852a).

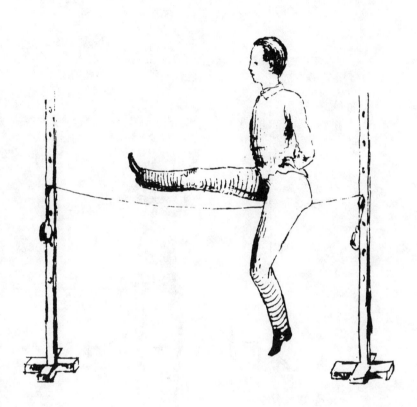

Fig. 20. Illustration taken from D. G. M. Schreber (1852a).

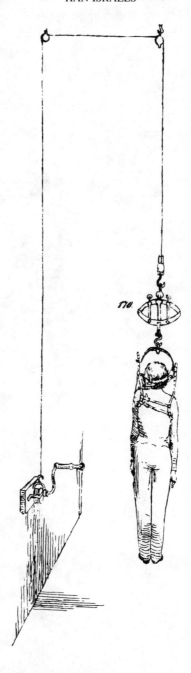

Fig. 21. Illustration taken from D. G. M. Schreber (1852a).

Fig. 22. Illustration taken from D. G. M. Schreber (1852a).

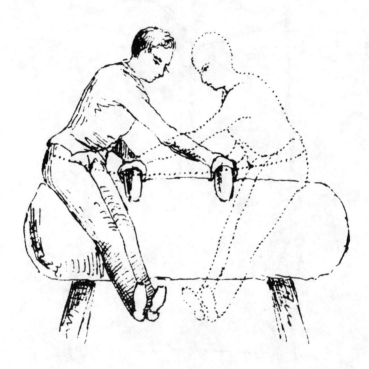

Fig. 23. Illustration taken from D. G. M. Schreber (1852a).

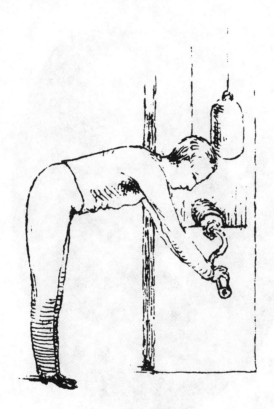

Fig. 24. Illustration taken from D. G. M. Schreber (1852a).

Dr. med. Schildbach, Carl, Arzt.

Fig. 25. Dr. C. H. Schildbach. (From the archives of the *Kleingartensparte Dr. Schreber* in Leipzig.)

long run, and he therefore offered to sell me the clinic in the autumn of 1858 [1877, p. ix].

3. THE TAKEOVER OF THE CLINIC BY C. H. SCHILDBACH

From 1859 onward Dr. C. H. Schildbach (Fig. 25) was officially referred to as the deputy director of the orthopedic clinic. This is therefore the place to say something more about the man, especially as he was one of the most important writers about the life of Moritz Schreber. Carl Hermann Schildbach (1824–88) was Moritz Schreber's junior by sixteen years. Spending his youth in various places in Saxony, he went to secondary school in Leipzig and studied medicine in Leipzig and Heidelberg.[1] He qualified as a doctor in 1847. After a few years in medical practice and a journey as a personal physician he was asked to run "the watering and therapeutic gymnastics clinic at Pelonken, near Danzig, in which post he remained for six years, before in the spring of 1859 going to run the famous gymnastic-orthopaedic clinic in Leipzig as deputy director alongside Dr. Schreber" (Brehme, 1889, p. 10).

Schildbach himself (1864, p. 4) wrote, "So it was that at Easter 1859 I took over the clinic, while Schreber himself continued to act as its representative outside."

True enough, from the outside it looked as though even after 1859 until his death, Moritz Schreber was still in charge of the clinic; see, for example, the Leipzig directory for 1861 (section 4, p. 314):

Orthopaedic therapeutic gymnastic clinic. (Zeitzer-Str. 43) Director: Herr Dr. Daniel Gottlob Moritz Schreber. In the clinic. Surgery 10-11 a.m., 2-3 p.m. Deputy Director: Hr. Dr. C. H. Schildbach. In the clinic. Surgery 8-10 a.m., 2-3 p.m.

Perhaps Moritz Schreber's activities in the clinic during these final years were only for the sake of appearances, to avert such detrimental effects on the numbers of patients as the appointment of a new and unknown director might have.

It is not only unclear who was in charge of the clinic between 1859 and 1861; the reasons for the sale are also somewhat obscure. Schildbach referred to Schreber's illness as the reason but he also quoted a letter from Schreber in 1858 saying that he wished to sell the clinic because he "had made it a very special task of his life to use

all his powers to work towards modern, thoroughly necessary reforms
in our entire system of education and schools, as far as this is possible
for an individual" (D. G. M. Schreber, as quoted by Schildbach [1864,
p. 4]. Probably both motives played a part. We have already examined
Moritz Schreber's health problems in Chapter 5; his ambitious initi-
atives for reforming education will be discussed in the next chapter,
which deals with the last years of his life.

NOTE TO CHAPTER 7

[1]In Paul Schreber's *Memoirs* there is a reference to a "Doctor of medicine S. in
Leipzig" who was a member of the "Corps Saxonia" student society in Leipzig
(1903, p. 50 = 1955, p. 71). This cannot be Dr. Schildbach: in his student days he
belonged to the "*Burschenschaft Germania,*" later becoming an honorary member
(Leonhardt, 1928, p. 194; Hirschfeld and Franke, 1879, p. 75); this was the *Burschenschaft* that Paul Schreber himself was later to join.

8

GUSTAV SCHREBER'S EARLY STUDENT DAYS AND THE LAST YEARS OF MORITZ SCHREBER'S LIFE (d. 1861)

Independent sources describing some of the activities of Moritz Schreber's children date from before his death.

1. GUSTAV SCHREBER'S STUDENT DAYS UP TO 1860

Moritz Schreber's elder son Gustav was enrolled at the University of Leipzig as an undergraduate in the "rerum naturum (chem. et botan. cult.)" from the summer semester of 1857 until the summer semester of 1858. On 4 October 1858, the archives of the university tell us, he took his examination.

During the 1858/9 winter semester and the summer semester of 1859 he studied at Göttingen,[1] the following semester he was in Heidelberg, and for the summer semester of 1860 he was back in Göttingen. All this time he was studying "natural sciences." In Göttingen the emphasis was on chemistry, as his leaving certificate testifies (Göttingen University archives). This *Abgangszeugnis* provides no evidence to show that he completed his studies in Göttingen in any way but merely certifies as to which subjects he studied. It was undoubtedly these studies in the natural sciences at Leipzig, Göttingen, and Heidelberg which a nephew later referred to as a chemistry course (Baumeyer, 1956, p. 69), which is also how it is described in the Schreber family tree drawn up by G. Friedrich (1932).

In the autumn of 1860 Gustav returned to his birthplace, Leipzig, where he enrolled for the philosophy course for the 1860-61 winter semester. On 24 January 1861 he took a doctorate in philosophy. Paul Schreber began his university career in the summer semester of 1860, at Leipzig. I shall discuss this below.

2. MORITZ SCHREBER'S ATTEMPTS AS AN EDUCATOR TO REACH A WIDER PUBLIC

This new phase in the life of the sons more or less coincides with Moritz Schreber's attempts to transform himself from a physician who dabbled in the fields of public health and education into a person of consequence devoting all his attention to these subjects. Schreber's intentions in this regard have already been cited as one of the reasons for selling the clinic to Schildbach. An obituary of Moritz Schreber contains references to his first steps toward ensuring that his books ended up in the right quarters. These references are calculated to show how often he received small thanks for his pains. For example, we read that ''on sending 50 copies of the 'Zimmergymnastik' to the doctors of the two penal institutions at Waldheim and Zwickau (for distribution among the prisoners) only one of them bothered to thank him at all'' (*Illustrierte Zeitung*, 1862, p. 82). The *Ärztliche Zimmergymnastik* (Medical indoor gymnastics) appeared in 1855 (1855a).

However, his lack of success in 1855 did not deter Schreber from planning even bigger campaigns a couple of years later for two other publications. However, ''when he offered to send gratis 500 copies each of the 'Ärztlicher Blick' and the 'Schärfung der Sinnesorgane' [for distribution among the teachers], he had still not received an answer even after a year'' (*Illustrierte Zeitung*, 1862, p. 82). But these efforts were child's play compared with what Schreber must have envisaged in a plan initiated in 1861. In 1858 he published *Kallipädie oder Erziehung zur Schönheit* (Education towards beauty) (1858a), a large and lavishly produced book about child-rearing. Three years later he brought out an abridged and popularized version, entitled *Der Hausfreund als Erzieher und Führer zu Familienglück, Volksgesundheit und Menschenveredlung für Väter und Mütter des deutschen Volkes* (1861a) (The family friend as educator and guide toward family happiness, public health and the ennoblement of man, for fathers and mothers of the German nation). In January 1861 Schreber sent a copy of this little book to all the German governments, together with a printed text of four pages headed ''To a High State Ministry of Culture and Education." In it he offered the various governments his educational booklet at cost, so that it might be distributed among the population through the clergy (to bridal couples), teachers, organizers of relief for the poor, and the like. In the case of the kingdom of Prussia he did not restrict himself to the ministry of culture but also addressed himself directly to the king with the words:

> Even if, as may be seen from the accompanying program, a similar communication has already been made to the Sovereign Royal Prussian State Ministry of Culture, the most humble undersigned, nevertheless, considered that in view of the far-reaching significance of the matter aspired to he owed a direct intimation of the matter in the very highest place, since among the states leading the rest of Germany in such matters the Kingdom of Prussia stands at the head. The second small tract, 'About the Education of the People,' which has no relevance here, the most humble undersigned has nevertheless considered it necessary to append in order the better to make plain the whole of the plan in its entirety.
>
> May Your Majesty deign to accept this bold step solely as the most sincere and all-pervading desire of an insignificant individual to serve the beloved fatherland!
>
> Your Royal Majesty's
>
> most respectful and humble
>
> Leipzig, January 1861   Dr. Moritz Schreber

It is possible that Schreber also addressed himself to the heads of state in the other German states as well, but there is no way of telling: the primary sources to be found on this campaign are confined to a single copy of the leaflet "To a High State Ministry" (originally preserved in the *grossherzogliche Hessische Hofbibliothek*) and the letter to the King of Prussia.

Just as scarce as the primary material itself is information about how the campaign went after that. Schildbach (1864, p. 4) wrote of "The Family Friend": "A general circulation of this book for the people, as he had intended and initiated in the most unselfish fashion, failed only because of the indifference of most German governments." And in an obituary we read of "The Family Friend": "The latter work, written in a thoroughly noble yet popular style, was intended for distribution among the lower classes and was offered by Schreber to the German governments for the price of the technical production." However, as with the earlier similar campaigns, "here again, with one exception the governments came up to his noble expectations to an exceedingly limited extent or not at all'' (*Illustrierte Zeitung*, 1862, p. 82). The question of which government was the exception, and what form that government's reaction took, is an intriguing one but remains unanswered.

The picture Schreber must have seen before him was one of him becoming a sort of Doctor Spock to German fathers and mothers—if I may be permitted such an anachronism—bearing in mind that of course he would have been a typically German version of Doctor Spock, i.e., one initiated by the authorities. This, then, failed; it was not for over a hundred years that Moritz Schreber was to be referred to as the Doctor Spock of the nineteenth century by badly informed American and French authors.

The written word was not the only medium in which Moritz Schreber tried to make his educational ideas better known. At the end of his life we find traces of some talks to the same end, in his involvement with the Pedagogical Society of Leipzig. Founded in 1861, the year of Schreber's death, the society had a few dozen members who met about once a month to discuss new books in the field of education (Leipzig Directory, 1863, p. 94). One of the founders, the teacher E. Mangner (Fritzsche and Brückner, 1903, p. 28), wrote of Schreber:

> In the pedagogical society in Leipzig he found . . . adherents who sadly were too briefly able to listen to the words of the experienced doctor. On the very same evening on which he had intended, in this circle of which he was so fond, to make further communications from the rich treasurehouse of his experiences, death, after a brief illness, called away this tireless champion[2] [Mangner, 1877, p. 14].

3. MORITZ SCHREBER'S INTESTINAL DISORDER AND DEATH (1861)

According to Kloss (1862, p. 10, 11), editor-in-chief of the *Neue Jahrbücher für die Turnkunst*, Moritz Schreber's death was quite sudden:

> When we all marched out of the gates of Berlin with him during the Berlin Jubilee last summer [1861], to help put up a monument to past master Jahn in the Hasenhaide, jointly with the gymnasts of

Germany—we never imagined that we should have to fill the very *first* issue of this year with the obituary of the man who only a few months earlier, full of energy and good cheer, joined in with the gymnasts of Germany and rejoiced at the new life which had been breathed into gymnastics in the fatherland. . . .

Schreber's death was not simply rather unexpected: toward the end of his life his health had actually seemed to be improving. According to his daughter Anna, "the severe head complaint had improved considerably during the last years of his life. Whether his cures at Gastein and Carlsbad and his trip to Heligoland had contributed to this I am unable to say" (Fritzsche, 1926, p. 14). Later Gerhard Richter was to record Anna as relating that "her father became very ill on a Friday. He had previously been in Carlsbad because he had an intestinal disorder" (G. Richter, 1935).

We have a little more information on this stay in Carlsbad: "Only last autumn, during his stay at Carlsbad, he overtook an old gentleman in a race, who, greatly dismayed, said that this was his first defeat in the sprint"[3] (Schildbach, 1862a, p. 5). And according to Siegel his youngest daughters recalled:

Also, a cure at Carlsbad in 1861 did him so much good that at the end of September he had the whole family join him, because it was only with them around him that he could enjoy himself to the full. We spent an incomparably wonderful time there. That autumn he really came to life again, and after returning home he was uncommonly "full of plans". Every week one or two walks were organized, and on 15 October, his birthday, in exceptionally fine weather, we even went on a boat trip to Plagwitz and back. On the way back we all so much loved the marvellous moonlight—and four weeks later the same moon was shining on his grave [1909b, p. 209].

This melodramatic reference to the moonlight seems to me to be a construction typical of the written rather than the spoken language, and hence an indication that Siegel is not reproducing the words of the daughters literally but giving something of a "creative" interpretation. The same passage continues: "Within the space of a few days a rapidly worsening abdominal complaint put an unexpected end to our beloved father's life" (ibid., p. 209).

Moritz Schreber died on 10 November 1861.[4] "At his own request a post-mortem was carried out on Schreber; the intestine was found to have been eaten away by an abscess. The doctors had been treating him for a twisting of the bowel": This is what Anna told the president of a Schreber Association, Gerhard Richter (1935); he included the statement in his next book:

> The doctors thought it was a twisting of the bowel; but section by Prof. Wagner showed an intestinal eruption, so that it would be fairly safe to assume that the cause of death was acute appendicitis.*

> *Oral communication from Frau Anna Jung [1939b, p. 21].

Anna also told Richter (1935) something of the effect her father's death had: "After his death her mother, in her grief, destroyed everything that reminded her of him." This is a detail which Gerhard Richter did *not* include in his next book. Nevertheless it would have been a nice detail for the various genres of writing about the family life of the Schrebers: for an author writing from the point of view of the Schreber Associations it would have symbolized Frau Schreber's deep sorrow at the loss of her husband, whereas to a psychiatrist it would be the final eruption of all the suppressed aggression toward the tyrannical head of the family.

NOTES TO CHAPTER 8

[1]According to his *Abgangszeugnis* (leaving certificate, now in the university archives at Göttingen) he was enrolled as a student only until Michaelmas 1859, though the same certificate shows that he also received instruction in Göttingen during the summer of 1860.

[2]Tabouret-Keller (1973, p. 300) even believed she knew which lecture he had been planning to give:

> Schreber died . . . on 10 November 1861 while preparing to deliver a lecture the same day to the *Pädagogische Gesellschaft* of Leipzig, a lecture entitled *Die Jugendspiele in ihrer gesundheitlichen und pädagogischen Bedeutung und die Notwendigkeit ihrer Beachtung von seiten der Schulerziehung.**

> * *Children's games from the point of view of their importance for hygiene and health* [sic], *and the necessity of their consideration by school education.* The text was to be published after his death, *Gartenlaube*, 1861; No. 26.

It is easy enough to show that there is something wrong here: No. 26 of *Die Gartenlaube* for 1861 appeared before, not after, Moritz Schreber's death. It does not contain the text of his lecture, nor did that text appear in the magazine after his death.

To explain this complicated state of affairs we shall have to return to an episode to which I referred in the chapter on Schreber family life; when Frau Schreber saw how some children who had been playing quite innocently were shooed off by a policeman, she indignantly told her husband about it, whereupon he sat down and wrote an article about children's playgrounds in the city, entitled "Children's games and their significance for health and education." This article appeared in *Die Gartenlaube* and in the *Jahrbuch für Kinderheilkunde und physische Erziehung* (Pediatrics and physical education yearbook), and also, at the end of 1861, shortly after the author's death, in the magazine *Die Erziehung der Gegenwart* (Modern education). The first slight deviation from the facts began with the writer of an obituary of Moritz Schreber, school headmaster Vogel, who evidently only knew of the publication in *Die Erziehung der Gegenwart*. At least, he reported that Schreber wrote the article

shortly before he fell ill, and so that it should be more widely distributed through the medium of print, sent it to the editors of the journal *Die Erziehung der Gegenwart*. It was the same 'die Jugendspiele in ihrer gesundheitlichen und pädagogischen Bedeutung und die Nothwendigkeit ihrer Beachtung von Seiten der Schulerziehung' [Vogel, 1861, p. 38].

These words were later quoted by Ernst Hauschild (1862, p. 218), the founder of the first Schreber Association. In this way the idea that Schreber wrote the article just before his death came to be accepted as gospel truth by many subsequent authors writing in the tradition of the Schreber Associations (Mangner, 1884, p. 24; Mittenzwey, 1896, p. 56; Fritzsche, 1903, pp. 8, 51; C.F., 1908, p. 892; *Der Freund der Schreber-Vereine*, 1908, p. 165; Fritzsche, 1911, p. 197; Hänsch, 1925, p. 289; *Leipziger Neueste Nachrichten*, 1931, p. 9; Schütze, 1936b, p. 1889; K. Pfeiffer, 1937, p. 28; and "Deutsche Schreberjugend," c. 1958, p. 8).

When, as evidently happened, it was later discovered that the article had already appeared in *Die Gartenlaube*—in 1860, so that there was no question of Schreber's having written it just before his death—many authors, rather than correct this erroneous story, so attractive because of its air of tragedy, preferred simply to alter the year in which the *Gartenlaube* article had appeared: 1860 became 1861 in Mangner (1884, p. 24); Mittenzwey (1896, p. 49); Fritzsche (1903, p. 9); Siegel (1907e, p. 253); C.F. (1908, p. 891); Fritzche, (1911, p. 197); G Richter (1914a, p. 8; 1925, pp. 5, 9); Ritter (1936a, p. 19); Schütze (1936b, p. 1889); K. Pfeiffer (1937, p. 32); A. (1943, p. 218); and Ackermann (1943, p. 288).

We now have the ingredients from which Mme. Tabouret-Keller concocted her hodgepodge: Moritz Schreber wrote his article *"Die Jugendspiele"* shortly before his death (not so); it appeared in *Die Gartenlaube* in 1861 (also not so); and Moritz Schreber died on the very day that he was going to give a lecture (this is probably true). So the result is that, as we have seen, on the evening of the day he died Moritz Schreber was due to give a lecture entitled *"Die Jugendspiele"* which was subsequently published in *Die Gartenlabue* in 1861. This (1973–74, p. 14) and Colas (1975, p. 86) perpetuated this mishmash.

Schilling too (1964, pp. 9, 10) provided us with some complicated confusion. He gave the correct year for the first publication of *"Die Jugendspiele,"* i.e., 1860, but did something very curious with the journal *Erziehung der Gegenwart*, in which, as we have seen, the essay was later reprinted.

Thereupon Schreber wrote first of all, in 1860, 'Die Jugendspiele in ihrer gesundheitlichen und pädagogischen Bedeutung und die Notwendigkeit ihrer Beachtung seitens der Schulerziehung', and in 1861, a few weeks before his death, the essay 'Erziehung der Gegenwart'. In both essays he called upon local authorities to set up public playgrounds in sufficient numbers.

And another quite different mélange of approximately the same constituents (in

this case the playgrounds for which Schreber argued in *"Die Jugendspiele,"* approaching death, and the Schreber Associations which later sprang up on the edges
of the city) is provided by the following quotation:

> Just before his death in November 1861 Dr. *Schreber* had himself pushed to Leipzig city
> hall in his wheel-chair so that he could remind the city fathers that the material and
> spiritual dangers of the big city were a particular threat to young people and would best
> be countered by *children's playgrounds at the periphery of the city.* The fact that Dr.
> *Schreber* was a voice crying in the wilderness became clear when his call for joint sports
> for boys and girls was scorned as—immoral [K-d, 1936, pp. 1262–1263].

This "immoral" suggestion, incidentally, is something that appears nowhere and is
the exclusive product of Dr. K-d's imagination.

    [3]It is amusing to see how in the passage of time this story has gradually assumed
more and more heroic proportions. The adjective "old" applied to the gentleman who
declared in dismay that this was his first defeat has already disappeared in Gasch
(1896, p. 50): "Just before his death he overtook a gentleman in a race who gloomily
described it as his first defeat." Ritter went quite a long way further: "Even at the
age of 52 he beat a well-known runner at Carlsbad" (1936a, p. 11). This version was
adopted by Schütze (1936b, p. 1889); Brauchle (1937, p. 244); G. Richter (1939b,
p. 16); Schilling (who referred to "an acknowledged runner of the time" [1961, p.
218] and "a famous runner" [1964, p, 7]); Tabouret-Keller (who wrote of "a celebrated runner") [1973, p. 297]; This (1973–74, p. 10); and Colas (1975, p. 86).
Bankhofer even managed to quote Moritz Schreber's "diary" on the subject: "Later
he wrote in his diary: '. . . I kept myself in good shape and at the age of 52, in
Carlsbad, managed to beat a noted long-distance runner' " (1977, p. 15).

    For the time being this story reached its zenith in Niederland where the original
"old gentleman" has climbed to the status of "much younger competition" (1968,
p. 741) while the health resort of Carlsbad has expanded to cover central Europe:
Moritz Schreber, wrote Niederland, "had been a very active athlete of wide reputation
and had won the championship in a gymnastic contest in Central Europe against much
younger competition."

    [4]The places in the literature where the date of Moritz Schreber's death is quite
manifestly wrong are of scant interest: it appeared as "19 November" in the *Bayerisches Ärzteblatt* (1961, p. 394), where it is simply a matter of careless copying
from K-d (1936, p. 1262,), as "20 November" in Mangner (1877, p. 14), and as
"1862" in White (1963, p. 214). More interesting is the fact that Schreber is frequently
reported as having died a day later than the actual date: 11 instead of 10 November
(Fritzsche, 1903, p. 10, and 1911, p. 197; G. Richter, 1914a, p. 6, and 1940, p. 50;
Macalpine and Hunter, 1955, p. 1). Ritter (1936a, p. 15) explained why 10 and not
11 November is the correct date. Niederland exploited this evident uncertainty about
the date of Moritz Schreber's death to draw a chronological parallel between father
and son Schreber.

> At that time some Leipzig newspapers had erroneously reported November 11, 1861, as
> the day of the father's death. Even this uncertainty seems to be reflected in the son's
> description of his own hospitalization, 32 years later. His otherwise very detailed report
> in the *Memoirs* (Chapter IV) does not make it clear whether he was hospitalized on
> November 10 or 11, 1893 [1974, p. 84].

Here Niederland said more than he can account for. His knowledge of the uncertainty
as to the date of Moritz Schreber's death is almost certainly the result of his having
read Ritter (1936a, p. 15): "The date of his death is erroneously given as 11 No-

vember." *Where* the date is given erroneously, Ritter does not tell us. In this connection Niederland refers to "some Leipzig newspapers." However, in the *Leipziger Tageblatt* the date is stated correctly (J., 1861). As Niederland failed to indicate in *which* Leipzig newspapers the date of death is given wrongly, I assume that he has slightly embellished his data for the benefit of his chronological parallel.

Unfortunately, the other side of this parallel is also rather dubious. According to Niederland, Paul Schreber's own account of the matter failed to make clear whether he was admitted on 10 or 11 November. The fact is that he was admitted on neither date. In contrast to what he has to say about the date, Paul Schreber is quite definite as to the day of the week: it was, he said a Tuesday (1903, pp. 39–41 = 1955, pp. 64–66). By contrast, his statement that he was admitted to the clinic on a Tuesday accords perfectly with the date given in the psychiatric reports (Weber, 1899, p. 379; Baumeyer, 1955, p. 514 = 1973, p. 342), viz. 21 November 1893. (And not 31 or 30 November, as Baumeyer wrote elsewhere (1955, p. 526 = 1973, p. 353; 1956, p. 69 = 1979, p. 190).)

9

THE FIRST YEARS AFTER MORITZ
SCHREBER'S DEATH

After Moritz Schreber's death there is no undisputed chief character in the family history of the Schrebers. Paul Schreber never became the paterfamilias to the extent that his father did, and at this time, of course, he was nothing of the kind at all, being only nineteen years of age when his father died. The elements common to the various sections of this chapter are therefore no more than a period—the beginning of the 1860s—and a place—*Zeitzer Strasse 43*, the building in which the orthopedic clinic was housed and in which Schreber's widow and her children continued to live on the top floor, directly over the new director of the clinic, Dr. Schildbach.

1. THE WIDOW SCHREBER, NÉE HAASE

At the end of 1862 and early in 1863 Pauline Schreber applied for civic rights in Leipzig, having acquired the plots of land and the houses built on them at *Zeitzer Strasse 43* and *44* (see p. 35). Another property remained in the joint possession of all the heirs: the business premises in Brühl, the shopping street in the center of Leipzig (see p. 25), which the Leipzig directories continued to list as owned by "heirs of Dr. Schreber."

The following text is among those contained in the "Acta" (1863) in the city archives:

Leipzig
29th June 1863
Herr Stud. med. Schreber applied at the council chambers on behalf
of his mother Frau Louise Henriette Pauline, widow of Dr. Schreber,
née Haase, of Zeitzer Strasse 43 in this place, presenting a certificate
of baptism, for a certificate of domicile for abroad, for a visit to
Kennenberg i. Würemberg.

"Kennenberg i. Würemberg" undoubtedly refers to Kennenburg, a
hamlet not far from Stuttgart, in Württemberg. I do not know what
took Frau Schreber to Kennenburg. And what about the "medical
student Schreber" who made the application on his mother's behalf?
Paul was then a student of law; Gustav had studied natural sciences
and philosophy, as noted above and was later to become a student of
law, but in 1863 he was not enrolled at the university of Leipzig.

2. GUSTAV

On 18 March 1865 Gustav Schreber applied for civic rights in
Leipzig, as a "chemist" (we shall see why below). It is interesting
to read what he has to say about his life up to then:

> I was at St. Thomas's School for three years until Easter 1857, after
> which I was at the university here until Michaelmas 1858, reading
> chemistry. I was then at Heidelberg and Göttingen universities until
> Michaelmas 1860, since when I have lived here most of the time.
> I am also still single ['Aufnahmeakte' 23050, Leipzig city archives.].

It is still unclear, therefore, what Gustav did with himself between
1861 and 1865. When making this application for citizen's rights he
also brought with him a "certificate of military exemption" dated at
the end of 1859: he had paid money to avoid military service.

3. PAUL AS A STUDENT

From the summer semester of 1860 until the end of November
1863 Paul Schreber was enrolled at Leipzig University to read law.
The president of the faculty of law in Leipzig from 1862 was Professor
(later *Geheimrat,* or privy councillor) C. G. Wächter. I have referred
to him above as one of those who regularly visited Paul's mother's

parents. He was also mentioned by Paul Schreber in the *Memoirs* as one of the dead souls who haunted his head during his "nervous illness," *Geheimrat* Wächter "knew me personally in [his] lifetime and presumably for that reason took a certain interest in me" (D. P. Schreber, 1903, p. 50 = 1955, p. 72). These "dead souls" which inhabited Paul Schreber's head during his "nervous illness" of later years included more than one figure from his student days. There were, for example, all sorts of former members of the Leipzig *Corps Saxonia* and, above all, numerous *Burschenschaftler,* members of another sort of student society. These two groups saw the events inside Paul's ill head as a continuation of the age-old rivalry between *Corps* and *Burschenschaft,* according to Paul Schreber in his *Memoirs of my Nervous Illness* (1903, p. 50 = 1955, pp. 71, 72).

All this is directly linked with the reality of earlier years. The history of the *Corps Saxonia* for the early 1860's records several battles with the *Burschenschaft Wartburg* (Beneke, 1912, p. 118). And at the time in question Paul Schreber was playing a leading role in that *Burschenschaft*—a fact which, incidentally, I should never have discovered had it not been for his own reference to it in connection with the "dead souls."

Among the "dead souls" Paul Schreber also mentioned "my friend of my youth Ernst K., who died young in 1864" (1903, p. 51).[1] It would be reasonable to assume that this name also refers to someone whom Paul knew as a student, viz. Ernst Koch, who joined the Wartburg student society the same month as Schreber and also read law at Leipzig (Hirschfeld and Franke, 1879, p. 62).

Paul Schreber joined "Wartburg" on 4 November 1860. Officially it was a "learned society"; in fact it was a secret *Burschenschaft* (a much more rowdy and political affair) (Hirschfeld and Franke, 1879, pp. 3, 62). In 1861 "Wartburg" officially and openly declared itself to be a *Burschenschaft,* and in the following year, through fusion with another society, the name was changed to "Germania."

At this time "Wartburg" had a few dozen members. The society's honorary members, among whom were Professor Biedermann (see p. 40) and Moritz Schreber's successor Dr. Schildbach, were well known for their nationalist, pro-Prussian attitudes. Obligatory activities for the ordinary members included, besides attendance at the weekly beer-cellar evening, "visits to the gymnastics ground, the fencing hall, and—until *Heinrich von Treitschke*'s lectures became well-attended of their own accord—whichever one of his lectures Treitschke was giving" (Blum, 1907, p. 174). Von Treitschke, who was professor of history and extremely pro-Prussian, was also a regular attender at the "Wartburg" society evenings (*ibid*. p. 216).

I owe this information to the *Lebenserrinnerungen* (Memoirs) of Hans Blum, another member of "Wartburg" and son of the radical politician Robert Blum. The latter had already come up as the great opponent in the Leipzig council of Professor Biedermann, and thus indubitably also of the less prominent councillor Moritz Schreber. In "Wartburg" the positions of the sons paralleled those of the fathers in the city council: the son of Robert Blum was more important than the son of Moritz Schreber. This is not to say that Paul Schreber did not occupy a prominent place in the society: on the contrary, from the summer semester of 1862 until the end of the winter semester of 1863–64 he appears consistently as one of the two or three "speakers"—the most senior function in the society (Hirschfeld and Franke, 1879, p. 76). Moreover, he sat on all sorts of committees: in May 1861, for example, he and Hans Blum were both on a five-man committee established to draw up new statutes because the society was openly going to become a *Burschenschaft*. Ernst Koch—Paul's friend of his youth "Ernst K."—was against the change to a *Burschenschaft* and left the society at this time. Paul Schreber was also on the three-man committee which in 1863 drew up a petition against the stipulation in the university statutes that undergraduates must not be members of societies or clubs involved in "public affairs" (such as those involving politics, religion, and gymnastics).

Now that "Wartburg" had officially become a *Burschenschaft,* the question was whether it would join the north German "Cartel" of *Burschenschaften*. One of the aims of this "Cartel" was to further the cause of German unity under the leadership of Prussia, so that in Saxon terms it was "highly treasonable," according to Hans Blum (1907, pp. 175–176). Blum then made a fiery speech in which—with references to Treitschke—he spelled out why this aim was anything but illegal. The speech was roundly applauded, according to Blum: "Some of the best jurists and speakers of the society, such as Schreber, backed me up" (*ibid*. p. 218). Then two representatives, of whom Paul Schreber was one, presented "Wartburg" to the "Cartel" as a society which, among other things, "has the aim of preserving the principle of morality, including the chastity principle" (Hirschfeld and Franke, 1879, p. 9). At the meeting of the "Cartel" in 1862, "Wartburg" was represented by Paul Schreber and Hans Blum (*ibid*., p. 11).

On one occasion Hans Blum and Paul Schreber gave more direct expression to their sympathies with the Prussian government. At the annual general student beer-drinking evening of 31 October 1861, held in Leipzig, Blum appealed to those present to make a collection for the "German fleet."

> As the presiding student, not a member of a society, wanted to postpone the collection until after the Sovereign [i.e., a later point in the evening's proceedings], Schreber proposed that the collection should take place at once. When he was interrupted from the *Landmannschaften* [another sort of student society] table in a manner as unseemly as it was malicious, members of Wartburg began to challenge *Landmannschafters*. This was the start of a duelling relationship of some duration [*ibid.*, p. 10].

I assume that collecting for the "German fleet" meant siding with the Prussian government, which at this time was engaged in a long-drawn-out conflict with the Prussian parliament concerning approval of the budget for the armed forces—a conflict which Bismarck eventually won for the government.

The pro-Prussian attitude of the *Burschenschaft Wartburg* meant that they were unenthusiastic about taking part in the festivities to welcome the king of Saxony, who was due to visit Leipzig in the summer of 1862. Hans Blum, son of a radical father, argued that they ought not to take part at all.

> Thereupon the Wartburger *Schreber* proposed that participation should be confined to the festivities accompanying the reception. One party considered that they were forced to accept this proposal in order that no danger to the Burschenschaft arise out of a total non-participation [*ibid.*, p. 14].

Blum said that taking part out of fear of reprisals was cowardice. Paul Schreber's faction lost the vote.

When "Wartburg" united with another *Burschenschaft* to form the *Burschenschaft Germania,* negotiations on "Wartburg's" behalf were conducted by three members, two of whom were Hans Blum and Paul Schreber. One of their tasks was to inform the "Convent" (convention) of the other *Burschenschaft,* confidentially, of "Wartburg's" "narrower statutes." The society had two sorts of membership: first one became a member of the *"äussere Verbindung"* (outer society), and only later might one be admitted to the *"innere Verbindung."* The rules regulating this were accompanied by a text drawn up by Paul Schreber and adopted in the winter semester of 1863–64:

> All members may attend the sessions of the inner convention, voting rights in the same are the entitlement only of the members of the inner society. The members of the outer society may not be present at proceedings and votes relating to admission to the inner society. The members of the inner society have the right in secret sessions (to which members of the o.s. have no admittance) to determine matters to be discussed and decided at a meeting only open to the members of the i.s. [(D. P. Schreber, quoted in Hirschfeld and Franke, 1879, p. 18].

A budding lawyer, it appears. And indeed Paul Schreber ended his law studies that semester, passing the faculty examination with an "excellent" ('Personalakte' fo.2). On 7 December 1863 he was entered in the books as having ended his membership of the *Burschenschaft Germania* (Hirschfeld and Franke, 1879, p. 64). Later he was to be made an honorary member.

4. ANNA, SIDONIE, AND KLARA

Anna's marriage in 1864 will be discussed in the following chapter. Unmarried, Sidonie remained with her mother in the *Zeitzer Strasse,* leaving virtually no traces.

The youngest of the sisters, Klara, once wrote about an event which took place about eighteen months after their father's death. The beginning of this text was quoted in the chapter on Schreber family life.

> On their Confirmation day my father had presented my brothers and my eldest sister with his "paternal words," with the recipient's full name. Sadly he did not live to see the Confirmation of my sister Sidonie and me (Easter 1863). Our mourning for our beloved father was therefore now joined by the painful thought that we two youngest children would not receive such a "paternal word." That is why it was an unforgettable moment of the most profound inner emotion, when on our return from the Confirmation ceremony our dear mother presented each of us with just such a familiar and longed-for envelope and contents, written for each of us by father in his own hand, and

identified with our names; so while he was alive even in this respect he had lovingly taken care of us [Klara, quoted by Siegel, 1909a, p. 75].

Another matter I have already mentioned is a drawing done by Klara in February 1865, when she was seventeen, of the street as seen from the flat in the Zeitzer Strasse; see page 50. This was certainly more than an isolated artistic exercise: several paintings by Klara are also in existence.

NOTE TO CHAPTER 9

[1]The English translators have for some reason anglicized the name (D. P. Schreber, 1955, p. 72).

10

EVENTS FROM 1864 UNTIL GUSTAV SCHREBER'S SUICIDE IN 1877

As the 1860's progressed, so the three eldest Schreber children, Gustav, Anna and Paul, left the family home and embarked upon lives of their own. The careers chosen by the eldest child, Gustav, were clearly inspired by the events and circumstances of the lives of Anna and Paul. I shall therefore deal with Gustav last, not only for that reason but also because his suicide terminated the period covered by this chapter. The first Schreber Association and Anna's mother will also be discussed.

1. PAUL SCHREBER'S CAREER FROM 1864 UNTIL 1877

On 3 December 1863, immediately after taking his finals, Paul Schreber joined the Leipzig lawyer Moritz Hennig's "dispatching department" as a "staff member" (Mitarbeiter). A year later he wrote to the Saxony ministry of justice asking to be allowed to take the "examination for legal practice." This letter marks the start of the *Personalakte*, the personal file which the ministry then opened on him, which has been published by Devreese (1981). It is from this personal file that I have taken information about Schreber's career in the judiciary of Saxony. As part of the examination, at the end of 1864 he was given the documents in two court cases to take home; the idea was that he should write a report on them within the next three months. At the end of March 1865 he wrote asking for an extension of the time allowed:

Impediments of various kinds, but chiefly the circumstance that it has been possible for me only to a very limited extent to exempt myself for a time from the obligations imposed upon me by my business relations with a lawyer's dispatching department here, have made it impossible for me to complete working out the relations within the period originally set me [D. P. Schreber, 1865].

In June 1865 he had a *viva voce* examination on his essay, completed a month earlier. He passed, being assessed "particularly good."

At the end of 1865 he embarked upon a long career with the judiciary, chiefly within the kingdom of Saxony—a career which was later to be characterized as follows in a psychiatric report: "He was regarded as brilliant, and made a comparatively rapid career" (quoted in Baumeyer, 1956, p. 62).

On 10 October 1865 he took the *Richtereid* (judicial oath), and from 1 November was employed at the district court at Chemnitz, the present Karl-Marx-Stadt, about sixty miles south of Leipzig. He started there as a *Hilfsaktuar* (deputy or assistant actuary) at a salary of 1050 marks annually—about twice the average German worker's income (cf. W. G. Hoffmann [1965, pp. 91, 461]).

On 1 January 1867 he was promoted to *Referendar* (the title for a junior qualified lawyer still undergoing practical training; something like being apprenticed), and was paid 1350 marks per annum; in the second half of 1869 he became an *Assessor* (the next rank up), and his salary rose to 1650 marks per annum, later rising to 1800 marks. In addition, from 1 October 1868 until 31 March 1870, he was *Auditor beim Appellationsgericht Leipzig* (judge at Leipzig court of appeal), according to his *Personalakte*. In 1869 he therefore appears in the directories of both Leipzig and Chemnitz. In Leipzig he lived at home with his mother in the *Zeitzer Strasse*. According to the *Polizei-Amt der Stadt Leipzig 105*, he left for Meissen on 9 March 1869 as a *Referendar*. Beyond this somewhat contradictory information I have nothing further to offer regarding this period of Paul Schreber's life.

On 2 October 1869 he took his doctorate in law at Leipzig (Leipzig University archives), and on 22 January 1870 he passed the state law examination, again with a "particularly good" rating.

According to his *Personalakte* he was *Assessor* at the district court in Leipzig starting on 1 February 1871 and as of 1 June 1872 at the local court. In fact, however, during and after the war of 1870–71 against the French he was working in Strasburg.

After the outbreak of the German-French [i.e., Franco-Prussian] War he considered it his duty to place himself at the disposal of the fatherland; during the campaign and for some time afterwards he worked with the civil administration in Alsace-Lorraine, first at the prefecture, then as investigating magistrate at the standing court martial in Strasburg [*Chemnitzer Tageblatt*, 26 October 1884, second supplement, p. 1].

Thirty years later Schreber was to refer to this war in his *Memoirs* (1903, p. 9 = 1955, p. 47). It appears as though something of his war experiences in Alsace comes through in some of his hallucinatory experiences during the most severely psychotic phase of his second "nervous illness." "I had visions according to which Professor Flechsig had shot himself either in Weissenburg in Alsace or in the police prison in Leipzig"[1] (D. P. Schreber, 1903, p. 82 = 1955, p. 91). He also heard from a supernatural source what was to become of him after a future transmigration of souls. There was also the part played by "an Alsatian girl who had to defend her honour against a victorious French officer" (*ibid.*, p. 85 = 1955, p. 93). Unfortunately there is nothing else to be found about Schreber's actual experiences in Alsace. According to the *Polizeiamt der Stadt Leipzig 105*, Schreber was transferred from Strasburg to Leipzig in September 1872. There, as I have already said, he became *Assessor* at the local court II for 2310 marks per annum, this salary being raised to 2700 marks on 1 January 1874. From 1 September 1874 he was working at the appeal court in Leipzig, at a salary of 4500 marks per annum. On 30 November 1875 he was granted civic rights in Leipzig (*Polizeiamt der Stadt Leipzig 105*), and on 1 November 1877 he became "judge with the status of a lord of appeal" at the Leipzig district court, where his salary was again raised, to 5400 marks annually. All these years he lived at home with his mother in the Zeitzer Strasse.

2. ANNA, THE FIRST SCHREBER ASSOCIATION, AND PAULINE SCHREBER AROUND 1870

Anna was the first of the children to leave home for good. On 26 July 1864 she married, at the age of twenty-three, the twenty-five-year-old businessman Carl Jung of Leipzig. He worked for his father's factory; some years later he would become co-owner of the firm, Friedrich Jung & Co., which made toilet soaps and perfumes. The firm was founded by his father, Friedrich, and his father's brother-in-law, the "chemist and pharmacist" Heinrich Mengerssen (G. Friedrich, 1933).

Of the five Schreber children Anna was the only one to have children of her own: Heinrich (1865–68), Friedrich, named Fritz (born in 1867), who would play a role as owner of a manorial estate), Helene (born in 1868), Paula (born in 1870), who when her parents had been married 25 years would recite a poem written by her uncle Paul for the occasion, and whose husband Paul Friedrich, professor of medicine in Kiel, would be mentioned in passing in the *Memoirs* (D. P. Schreber, 1903, p. 89 = 1955, p. 96) as "Professor Dr. F. in K."), Wilhelm (born in 1872), and Felix (born in 1882), whose statements about his uncle Paul dating from the 1950's will be quoted in what follows.

In 1871 the Jung family moved to *Zeitzer Strasse* 44, where they had a flat on the first floor, so that Anna had her mother as her neighbor and landlord.

A year earlier on 1 April 1870, Anna had joined the Schreber Association of Leipzig (G. Richter, 1939b, p. 58). The Association had been founded in 1864; the Schreber family was not directly involved, though their downstairs neighbor, the clinic director Dr. Schildbach, was on the first committee and also gave the Association's first talk, entitled "Schreber's Merits" (Schreiber, 1894, p. 62).

In the Introduction (p. xv) I outlined how this Schreber Association soon developed from an educational club with a gymnastics ground to an association of what may be loosely described as allotment-holders, people who had "Schreber gardens." By 1870 the Schreber Association had already become so much of a gardening club that the connection with the doctor-educator Moritz Schreber was evidently in need of explanation: on 15 November 1870 the teacher Karl Gesell gave the Association a talk on "Schreber the orthopedist and his connection with the aims of the Schreber Association" (Schreiber, 1894, p. 63). On the same date—unquestionably on the same occasion—Moritz Schreber's widow was made an honorary member of the Association (G. Richter, 1939b, p. 17).

I have been able to find only one more link between the Schreber Association and the Schrebers at this time, and that was at the Association's ninth anniversary in 1873, when a prominent member of the committee was presented with "1 album of pictures of Schreber, his sons and various members of the Association" (Schreiber, 1894, pp. 53–54). An enviable possession. The only picture I know of Gustav Schreber is the family portrait of 1851, in which Paul is an eight- or nine-year-old. Other photographs of Paul show him between the ages of sixty and sixty-five, and finally there is one undated photograph which must date from about this time or a little later; see Figure 26. Baumeyer (1970, p. 244 = 1973, p. 365), who discovered this photograph, estimated the subject to be "a man of between thirty and at the most forty years of age."

To return to the honorary member of the Schreber Association, Pauline Schreber: Little else is known about her in these years. From 1874 her address was no longer *Zeitzer Strasse* 43, Third Floor, but *Zeitzer Strasse* 43 Garden Building or Rear Building. Figure 27 shows this house in the garden of the *Zeitzer Strasse* as it looked thirty years later. Before 1874 it did not appear in the directories, and I assume it was built in the early 1870's by Frau Schreber for herself and her children. The children still at home at this time were Sidonie and Klara, about whom there is no record for this period, and occasionally Gustav and Paul; the last child, Anna, was living next door, as we have seen. There were also doubtless domestic servants living in.

For a while during 1866 Frau Schreber had some extra lodgers. In that year Prussia defeated Austria in a lightning war, occupying Saxony *en passant*. According to a statement drawn up in Leipzig on 8 July 1866, Frau Schreber had "at her kind request, two wounded Prussian soldiers" billeted on her.

3. GUSTAV SCHREBER'S FACTORY, LEGAL CAREER, AND SUICIDE (1866–77)

Gustav Schreber also had personal experience of the Prussian occupation of 1866: at the time he was living at home in the *Zeitzer Strasse*. The Prussian attack meant the end of the longstanding disunity over the political future of Germany. Prussia favored a "little German" solution, a Germany without Austria in which Prussia would have undisputed hegemony, and Austria wanted a "greater German" solution, a federation of German states to which Austria would belong. The military defeat of Austria by Prussia in 1866 abruptly decided this debate in Prussia's favor.

When Saxony was suddenly and violently obliged to choose the Prussian solution, both pens and printing-presses were set in motion. Gustav owned a book containing eight pamphlets written in 1866 about Saxony's political future, presenting both pro- and anti-Prussian viewpoints (Fig. 28). Among these pamphlets was "Treitschke's notorious

Fig. 26. Paul Schreber. (From Heiligenthal and Volk, 1973, facing page iii.)

Fig. 27. Garden of *Zeitzer Strasse* 43.

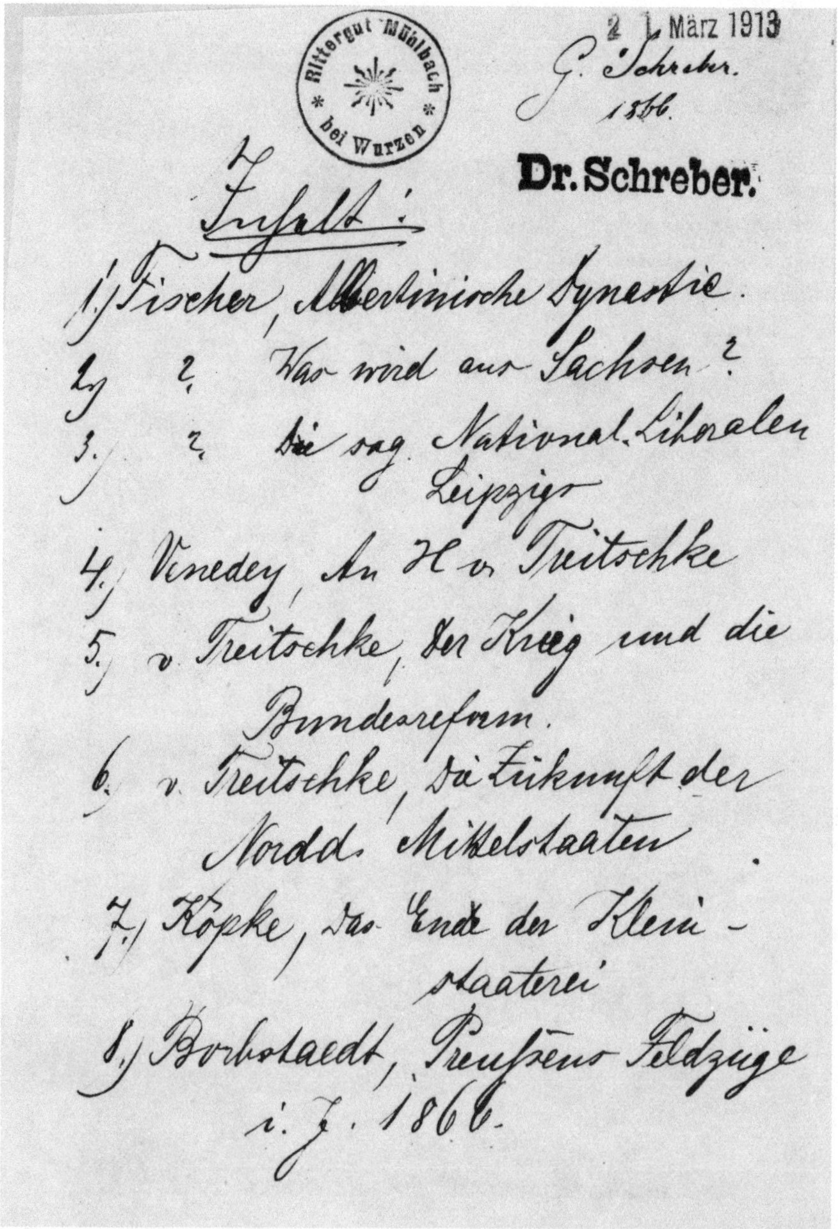
Rittergut Mühlbach bei Wurzen

21 März 1913

G. Schreber.
1866.

Dr. Schreber.

Inhalt:

1.) Fischer, Albertinische Dynastie.
2.) ?, Was wird aus Sachsen?
3.) ?, Die sog. National-Liberalen Leipzigs
4.) Venedey, An H. v. Treitschke
5.) v. Treitschke, der Krieg und die Bundesreform.
6.) v. Treitschke, die Zukunft der Nordd. Mittelstaaten.
7.) Köpke, das Ende der Klein-staaterei
8.) Borbstaedt, Preußens Feldzüge i. J. 1866.

Fig. 28. Title page of a book from the library of Gustav Schreber.

war-cry *'Die Zukunft der norddeutschen Mittelstaaten'* '' (Kötzschke
and Kretzschmar, 1965, p. 360). Reference has already been made to
the admiration in which the pro-Prussian Von Treitschke was held by
Paul Schreber's *Burschenschaft*. It is not surprising, then, that the
book later came into Paul's possession. Gustav's interest in the pro-
Prussian viewpoint may at first sight appear somewhat curious in the
light of the fact that in 1866 the vast majority of the Saxon population
was anti-Prussian; however, there were exceptions in certain commercial circles in Leipzig (*ibid.*, p. 363), and Gustav moved in such
circles.

In 1866 Gustav appears in the Leipzig directory as "Schreber,
Dan. Gstv., B. [= Bürger, i.e. he had civic rights], Dr. phil and
owner of the firm: Gustav Schreber u. Comp. Chem. Fabrikate [Chem-
ical products]. [address:] Brühl 54–55. Private address: Zeitz. Str. 43.
III [3rd floor]." This company cannot have been very large. The
ground floor of Brühl 54–55—the premises owned by "Dr. Schreber's
heirs"—is listed as the address not only of "Schreber, Gustav, u. Co.
Chemische Fabrik" but also of a plumber's business, a *Schlosser-
meister* (master locksmith or mechanic), and a Hebrew bookshop. The
factory is still mentioned in the directory for 1867 but then disappears.
In the centuries-old family tree of the Schrebers this sort of commercial
activity was something quite new. We may suppose that Gustav got
the idea from the factory of Anna's husband—a factory which, after
all, also had a chemist as one of its founders.

If the factory was inspired by the circumstances of his younger
sister Anna, Gustav's next choice of career clearly followed in the
footsteps of his brother Paul, three years his junior. From the summer
semester of 1867 until the summer semester of 1869 Gustav was enrolled as an undergraduate of the law faculty at Leipzig university.[2]
The university archives show that he took his finals on 3 June 1869.
The archive card referring to Gustav's legal studies records his address
as "Mockau bei Leipzig," a small place a few miles north of the city.
However, according to the Leipzig directories at this time, he was still
living with his mother in the Zeitzer Strasse.

In 1869 or 1870 Gustav embarked upon the same sort of career
as his brother.[3] Until November 1872 he worked in Leipzig, first at
the first local court and about a year later as a *Referendar* with the
district court, later still as *Assessor* there. His address in Leipzig is
given as *"Zeitzer Strasse* 43, third floor." In the second half of 1872,
therefore—by now Gustav was thirty-three—the two brothers were

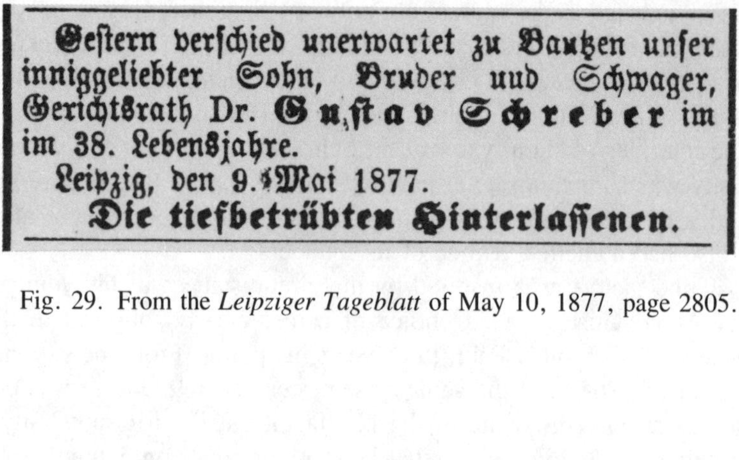

Gestern verschied unerwartet zu Bautzen unser
inniggeliebter Sohn, Bruder uud Schwager,
Gerichtsrath Dr. Gustav Schreber im
im 38. Lebensjahre.
        Leipzig, ben 9. Mai 1877.
        Die tiefbetrübten Hinterlassenen.

Fig. 29. From the *Leipziger Tageblatt* of May 10, 1877, page 2805.

together at home with their mother and their two youngest sisters, while their eldest sister and her family lived next door.

From November 1872 until 30 September 1874 (*Polizeiamt der Stadt Leipzig* 105) Gustav was employed at Zwickau, some forty-five miles south of Leipzig, first as an *Assessor* with the district court and later as *Appellationsrath* ("lord of appeal") at the court of appeal.

On 1 October 1874 he returned to Leipzig and again took up residence at *Zeitzer Strasse* 43, now in the garden house with his mother, brother, and two youngest sisters. He again became an *Assessor* at the Leipzig district court.

In 1877 we find a reference to Gustav as an "appeal judge at Dresden district court and for the time being at Bautzen district court" (letter from Bautzen municipal archives). Bautzen is about thirty miles east of Dresden. On 7 May 1877 he wrote a postcard to his mother:

> L.M.! [Liebe Mutter = Dear Mother]
> I assume the intended party [or match in the marriage sense] has been abandoned, to which I am quite agreeable, and therefore go to Leipzig on Wednesday evening. As I may not arrive till late, please send the front-door key.   Best wishes
> Bautzen
> 7/5 1877   your G.

That same night he shot himself through the head.

Niederland (1974, p. 97) quoted the municipal archives of Bautzen: "Schreber, Daniel Gustav, Doctor of Law, Royal Judge in Bautzen, according to church register St. Peter, Bautzen, died on 8 May, in the morning, 38 years old, unmarried. Suicide by gunshot." The *Chemnitzer Tageblatt* of 10 May 1877 carried a brief mention of the affair "Bautzen. On May 7 the recently appointed appeal judge at the district court, Dr. Schr., put an end to his own life by a shot through the head. It is to be assumed that a strong tendency to melancholy is the cause of the sad event" (p. 4). There is not much else to be found about Gustav's suicide:

> The reasons behind the fatal resolve are shrouded in obscurity. The church book of the parish of St. Peter in Bautzen records merely 'took his own life', and the daily newspapers in Bautzen, Dresden and Leipzig [Fig. 29], in a family notice, announce only the decease. Only a Chemnitz newspaper observes: 'from melancholy' [Schilling, 1964, p. 4].[4]

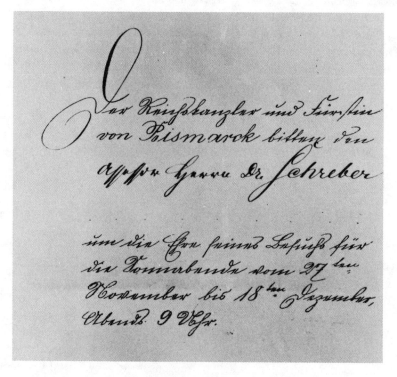

Fig. 30. Invitation for Dr. Schreber.

The text of the notice in the papers reads as follows: "Suddenly, yesterday at Bautzen, our dearly beloved son, brother and brother-in-law, appeal judge Dr. Gustav Schreber passed away in his 38th year. Leipzig, 9 May 1877. His deeply grieved relatives." According to the Bautzen town archives, Gustav's body was taken to Leipzig and buried there (G. Friedrich, 1932).

Some information relating to this affair is to be gleaned from the subsequent illness of Gustav's brother Paul. A report on Paul's hereditary background states: "One brother paralytic, committed suicide" (quoted by Baumeyer, 1956, p. 62). And in 1900 Klara wrote in a letter to her brother's psychiatrist "that the progressive psychosis of our dear eldest brother had already been recognized at that time, but that the doctor, who had already thought of placing him an in asylum, did not then consider the poor man to be ill enough"[5] (quoted by Baumeyer, 1956, p. 68).

To end this section, an item of information for whose accuracy I cannot vouch: According to Herr Troitzsch (see page xxiii), who was born in 1888, "Pauline Schreber told my mother that Gustav, who like his younger brother was a first-class lawyer, had been on the point of being appointed to some high office in Berlin shortly before his suicide" (Troitzsch, 1974, p. 2). Herr Troitzsch told me that there were even rumors of contacts with Bismarck—something I should not have mentioned had I not found invitations addressed to "Assessor Dr. Schreber" for a number of Saturday evenings with Bismarck and his wife, viz., Saturdays from 27 November until 18 December, and from 22 January until 5 February (see Fig. 30). The first years with Saturdays on these dates to which the invitations can refer are 1875–76. By this time Paul was no longer an *Assessor,* and I conclude that these were invitations addressed to Gustav at the end of 1875 and beginning of 1876.

NOTES TO CHAPTER 10

[1]Of course it is also possible to see this vision as a sort of late visual echo of the shot with which Gustav ended his life in 1877 (Kitay, 1963, p. 207).

[2]According to the psychiatric literature on the Schrebers, Gustav read first law and then chemistry. This incorrect order was derived from Baumeyer (1956, p. 69). He had it from a nephew of Gustav who had written to him "There was also a brother, Gustav Schreber. I never knew him, since he committed suicide, sometime at the end of the seventies, I believe. Studied law, then chemistry, I believe." Sometimes Gustav was granted the title 'dr. iur.' (doctor of law) (G. Friedrich, 1932; Niederland, 1963, p. 204 [quoting from the Bautzen municipal archives]; Schilling, 1964, p. 4). This

is an understandable mistake to make with someone who held a doctorate and—as we shall see—embarked on a legal career. Gustav's doctorate, however, was not in law.

[3]The dates of Gustav's legal career are known less precisely than those of his brother. A "personal file" still exists on Paul Schreber; Gustav's legal career had to be reconstructed chiefly from *Staats-Handbücher für das Königreich Sachsen,* volumes published annually or biennially in which the entire government apparatus of Saxony was set out in detail, and from directories and address-books. Such sources, of course, lag behind the actual situation.

[4]This reference to "melancholy" in the *Chemnitzer Tageblatt* was also recorded by Niederland (1963, p. 204; 1974, p. 97). In the work of later authors this melancholy sometimes became Gustav's chief characteristic, despite its origins as a speculation in a minute item on his suicide in a newspaper published some sixty miles from the fatal spot. Calasso (1974b, p. 63) referred to "Gustav Schreber the melancholic," and Meijer and Rijnders summarized his entire life as follows: "The elder son, Gustav, suffered from melancholy and committed suicide" (1977, p. 24).

[5]White (1961, p. 59; 1963, p. 214) made of this that Gustav from the age of about 20 onward suffered from a progressive psychosis. This was carried over by Masson (1973, p. 3).

11

PAUL SCHREBER: MARRIAGE IN 1878 AND CAREER UP TO 1884

1. MARRIAGE BETWEEN PAUL SCHREBER AND SABINE BEHR (1878)

On 5 February 1878 Dr. jur. Daniel Paul Schreber married Ottilie Sabine Behr at Leipzig ("Polizeimeldebuch Chemnitz"). Paul Schreber "at the time of his marriage in 1878 expressed hypochondriacal ideas" according to a later psychiatric report (quoted by Baumeyer, 1956, p. 62).

Sabine Behr (Fig. 31 and probably also Fig. 32) was born on 19 June 1857 (*ibid.*, p. 69); she was therefore twenty years of age when she married Paul Schreber and fifteen years younger than him. In 1954 her nephew Felix Jung wrote of her background:

As far as I know, my aunt Sabine Schreber, née Behr, was born in Leipzig, where her father [Heinrich Behr] was artistic director (*Oberregisseur*) at the municipal theatre. He had himself once been an operatic singer (bass) and had married a daughter of the comic dramatist Roderich Benedix.

So Sabine Behr came from quite a different background from her husband. She seems never to have been really accepted into her husband's family, and (as Herr Troitzsch told me) she was not among the later circle of "cousins" who used to meet regularly. When I asked a granddaughter of Paul's sister Anna about his wife's antecedents, she expressed the belief that Sabine came from a circus background.

153

Fig. 31. Sabine Behr. From Baumeyer (1970, facing page 244).

Fig. 32. Probably Sabine Behr.

Until his marriage Paul had lived with his mother in the Zeitzer
Strasse. Now, with his bride, he moved to *Flossplatz* 9, third floor
(*Leipziger Addressbuch*, 1878, p. 251), no more than a few hundred
yards from his mother's address.

Nothing more is known of the first years of this marriage except
that by 1884 Sabine Schreber had had two miscarriages (Baumeyer,
1956, p. 61).[1]

2. PAUL SCHREBER'S CAREER FROM 1878 UNTIL 1884

In the same year that he married, Paul Schreber was transferred
to Berlin: "In 1878 Schreber was sent as an assistant to the ministry
of justice in Berlin, where he was employed on secondment until 1
October 1879" (*Chemnitzer Tageblatt*, 26 November 1884, second
supplement, p. 1). His *Personalakte* does not record his working in
Berlin, nor for that matter, his earlier period in Strasburg; evidently
the *Personalakte* compiled on him by the Saxon ministry of justice
only covered his appointments in Saxony itself. Nevertheless, there
is no doubt that Paul Schreber did work in Berlin at this time: in the
Festschrift of his *Burschenschaft* of 1879 his entry reads: "Honorary
member. Dr. of law, privy government counsellor in Berlin" (Hirschfeld and Franke, 1879, p. 64).

There can be little doubt that Schreber's work in Berlin was
concerned with the integration of the formerly independent judicial
apparatuses of the various German lands into a single
judiciary—something which was bound to come, of course, after the
absorption of Saxony in 1866 into a wider political federation under
Prussian leadership. On 1 October 1879 the "unified German organization of courts" was introduced (Kötzschke and Kretzschmar,
1965, p. 369). On the same day Paul Schreber's task in Berlin came
to an end, and he returned to Saxony to become, for the next five
years, *Landgerichts-director* (the rank below president of the district
court) at Chemnitz, the place where he had first embarked on his legal
career. On 6 October 1879 he registered, with his wife, with the police
in Chemnitz, and on 2 November 1881 he was granted local citizen's
rights. His income was now 6000 marks per annum; on 1 January
1883 this was raised to 6600 marks, thus putting him in the top one
per cent of the population of Chemnitz with regard to income (Böhmert,
1898, p. 16).

In 1888 Paul's sister Klara married "Landgerichtsdirektor Theodor Krause in Chemnitz'' (G. Friedrich, 1932). Krause worked at the same court as Paul Schreber during the period covered by this chapter, so that it may be assumed that Klara met her husband through her brother. She was forty when she married; the marriage was childless.

NOTE TO CHAPTER 11

¹Schultz-Hencke wrote of Sabine Schreber as follows: "So now I should certainly also be inclined to place strong emphasis on the statement that in sexual matters Schreber's wife evidently displayed severe disturbances and aversion symptoms" (1952, p. 262). Schultz-Hencke omitted to maintain where he found this "statement." The only thing I can think of is the miscarriages, though this would certainly be a rather free interpretation of them. (Although the miscarriages were first mentioned in an article by Baumeyer of 1955, i.e., three years after Schultz-Hencke's observation, at this time Baumeyer was working as a psychiatrist under Schultz-Hencke and had brought with him transcripts of the psychiatric reports mentioning the miscarriages.)

12

PAUL SCHREBER'S CANDIDACY FOR THE REICHSTAG AND FIRST PERIOD OF ILLNESS (1884–85)

1. PAUL SCHREBER'S CANDIDACY FOR THE REICHSTAG (1884)

In 1884 Paul Schreber stood as a candidate for the Imperial Diet, or Reichstag. He referred to this himself in his *Memoirs* (1903, p. 34 = 1955, p. 61); it is confirmed by the psychiatric reports found by Baumeyer ("In October, 1884, he took a very active interest in the elections"); and it is to Niederland's credit that he closely examined this election campaign (1963, pp. 205–206 = 1974, p. 99). However, Niederland's account contains so many errors that I shall leave a discussion of it to the notes to this section.

Schreber was one of three candidates for the Chemnitz constituency, the favorite being the socialist Bruno Geiser.

> This time Geiser's opponents were Schreber, a conservative Landgerichtsdirektor [judge], and the liberal barrister Wilh. Harnisch, . . . having politically liberal ideas, was just as foreign and rejecting in his attitude to socialism as the former [Heilmann, 1911, p. 183].

The course of the campaign is easily followed in the *Chemnitzer Tageblatt*. On 19 October 1884 (second supplement, p. 1) the paper carried an extensive preview of the elections: "Of the 23 Reichstag constituencies in Saxony there can scarcely be one more exposed to the danger of again being represented by an adherent of social democracy than ours. This has been its lot more than once." The nonsocialists in Chemnitz had tried to put up a joint candidate to oppose the socialist, but that had failed. It was true that the conservatives and national liberals, again according to the *Chemnitzer Tageblatt,* had "in the person of the local Landgerichtsdirektor, Dr. Schreber, a candidate who, it is universally agreed, is eminently suitable and indeed excels others in uprightness of character, richness of knowledge and an uncommon talent for public speaking," but the German Liberal Movement declined to cooperate and was not even prepared to enter into new negotiations, even though "Herr *Landgerichtsdirektor* Dr. Schreber, in a free decision dictated solely by patriotism, had declared himself willing to withdraw in favor of the joint candidate." The outcome was that all the Conservatives and National Liberals could do was to

> stick to the candidate they have put forward, Herr Landgerichtsdirektor Dr. Schreber, and this they are doing in the ever cherished and firm conviction that precisely in him a man has been found who, if his election could be brought about, would not only represent the constituency most excellently but would also be a veritable adornment to the Reichstag. In the days to come Herr Dr. Schreber will on several further occasions, some of them in the city, though not at election meetings open to the general public, present himself to the electorate [*Chemnitzer Tageblatt,* 19 October 1884, second supplement, p. 1].

Two days before the elections the newspaper again wrote at length about Dr. Paul Schreber:

> [A]lthough he has always taken part with a lively interest in the public life of our city, in wider circles he had nevertheless until now remained relatively unknown. Now that the confidence of numerous respected citizens of our city has chosen him to be a candidate, it can therefore only be welcomed by our readers that we should, on the basis of notes on his life hitherto, made available to us from a friendly quarter, relate, in brief, the following [p.1].

There follows what is, as far as I know, the first account of Paul Schreber's life. I have already quoted from it on more than one occasion, but here is the text in its entirety:

Dr. iur. Paul Schreber was born in Leipzig in 1842, the son of the doctor widely known as author of *Ärztliche Zimmergymnastik* and other medical educational works and as director of an orthopaedic clinic. After studying law he entered the civil service, being employed in Chemnitz as early as 1865–9 in the former office of the district court. After the outbreak of the German-French War he considered it his duty to place himself at the disposal of the fatherland; during the campaign and for some time afterwards he worked with the civil administration in Alsace-Lorraine, first at the prefecture, then as investigating magistrate at the standing court-martial in Strasburg. This was followed by appointments first as assistant, then as a judge in the former court of appeal at Leipzig. In 1878 Schreber was sent as an assistant to the ministry of justice in Berlin, where he was employed on secondment until 1 October 1879; on the introduction of the new judicial system on 1 October 1879 he returned to his more immediate homeland, ever since when, as president of civil court No. 1 in the royal *Landgericht* here, he has again made his home in our city [*Chemnitzer Tageblatt*, 26 October 1884, second supplement, p. 1]

The election campaign did not confine itself to the editorial columns of the *Chemnitzer Tageblatt:* the advertisements, too, were full of it. Geiser, the socialist, was nowhere named: to this evidently strictly bourgeois daily the only contenders were Schreber and Harnisch. On 12 October a large pro-Schreber advertisement appeared:

The united National Liberals of the XVIth constituency hereby commend for the forthcoming Reichstag elections HERR LAND-GERICHTSDIRECTOR DR. PAUL SCHREBER IN CHEMNITZ, a man who equally by his outstanding qualifications and knowledge and by his patriotic devotion to duty and firmness of character offers the total guarantee that he would represent us worthily and successfully [*ibid.*, 12 October 1884, p. 19].

The advertisement went on to outline Schreber's political program, from which I quote the following passages:

Having been put forward by the Conservative and National Liberal Union as a candidate for the election for the Reichstag in the XVIth constituency, I set out below the outlines of my political confession of faith:

Unshakeable fidelity to Emperor and Empire, as also to the

constitutional independence of our more immediate Fatherland [i.e., Saxony].

. . . neither limitation of the constitutional rights of the people, nor support for the efforts, which have revealed themselves more or less overtly in recent times, directed towards the introduction of the so-called parliamentary form of government [*ibid.*, p. 19].

During the early sixties the Prussian parliament had fought in vain for a parliamentary form of government: by repeatedly voting down the war budget, parliament hoped to bring down the government. In the end Bismarck prevailed. In the next point on Schreber's program he returned to this affair:

Unweakened maintenance of the fighting strength of our nation despite every economy in particulars; the retention of relatively long periods for approval of the military estimates, in order not to put the state of our armies at the mercy of party politicking, and diminish the guarantee of peace preserved in Germany's military strength.

The rest of the Schreber program also conformed exactly to Bismarck's political line,[1] that mixture of elements seeming conservative (support for manual workers), progressive (the beginnings of health insurance), or colonialist:

Furthering efforts aimed at maintaining a strong artisan class through corporate strengthening. . . .

Vigorous advocacy of the imperial government's colonial policy and its attempts, brought down by the opposition parties in the last Reichstag, to further overseas trade.

Continuation of social reform work along the lines of the correct principles upon which the Health Insurance Act and Accident Insurance Act are based, first by widening health and accident insurance to include those groups of workers at present excluded from them, support for all further measures for improving the situation of the working classes, in so far as they are within the bounds of practicallity and are founded on the existing economic order.

Recognition of the necessity of provisional retention of the Socialists Act, the dispensability of which, however, may be expected in the not too distant future as feelings are gradually reconciled.

Chemnitz, 2 October 1884

DR. JUR. PAUL SCHREBER, Landgerichtsdirector.

[*Chemnitzer Tageblatt,* 12 October 1884, p. 19]

The party of the liberal democrat candidate, Harnisch, attacked Schreber directly in a later advertisement:

DO NOT VOTE FOR THE UNKNOWN SCHREBER![2] Who has ever heard of Herr Schreber's services for the common good? Nobody. Barrister Harnisch has been in public life for decades, as city councillor and as alderman. Herr Harnisch has proved his worth. It is men who have proved their worth who belong in the Reichstag. That is why we vote Herr RECHTSANWALT HARNISCH! [*Chemnitzer Tageblatt*, 28 October 1884, p. 11].

The result of the election was a gigantic victory for the socialist candidate, who gained nearly sixty per cent of the vote. Paul Schreber received just under twenty-five per cent, and Harnisch almost seventeen per cent of the votes cast. According to Heilman, "the election campaign and turnout in Chemnitz in 1884 were lukewarm because it was not possible to have serious doubts about Geiser's victory, and indeed he won with the formidable total of 14512 votes over 5762 conservative and 4123 liberal votes" (1911, p. 184). The *Chemnitzer Tageblatt* for 29 October 1884 (p. 6) gave the voting figures for the individual polling stations. It did not, however, offer any comment on the result: could it have been too depressing? It was certainly a disappointment to Paul Schreber; very soon afterward his first period of illness began.

2. PAUL SCHREBER'S FIRST PERIOD OF ILLNESS (1884-85)

The elections in Chemnitz took place on 28 October 1884. After they were over, Paul Schreber went for a cure to Sonneberg, some eighty miles to the east of Chemnitz, and on 8 December he was admitted to the "nerve clinic" of Professor P. E. Flechsig at Leipzig.[3]

He remained in Leipzig for just under six months. Baumeyer reproduced an extract from the psychiatric reports on him at this time: Schreber made two attempts at suicide, wanted to be carried, believed that he was about to die at any moment, and so on. The report ended on 1 June 1885 with these words: "Departure for Ilmenau. He imagines that he has lost thirty to forty pounds in weight. Has in fact gained two kilogrammes. Complains that he is being purposely deceived about his weight" (1956, pp. 61–62). Ilmenau is not far from Sonneberg.[4]

Paul Schreber's *Memoirs* deal with his second period of illness and refer only very briefly to this first period of mental disorder; the

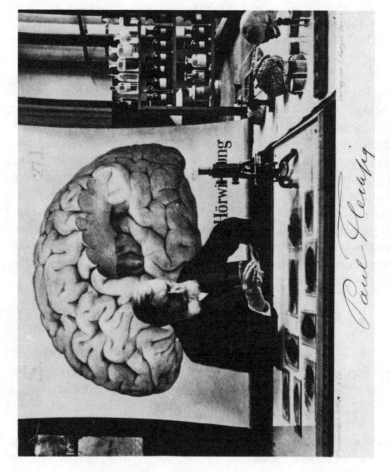

Fig. 33. Professor Flechsig. From *Festschrift für Paul Flechsig* (1909, facing p. i).

only subject to which he paid any real attention was his psychiatrist, Flechsig (Fig. 33). At this time Schreber's impression of Flechsig's method of treatment was generally favorable, though he expressed the view that even in the case of psychiatric patients, white lies ought to be avoided as far as possible, and "were hardly ever appropriate in my case, for he must soon have realized that in me he was dealing with a human being of high intellect, of uncommon keenness of understanding and acute powers of observation" (D. P. Schreber, 1903, p. 35 = 1955, p. 62). My purpose in quoting this is not to pour scorn on Schreber. In those days people were less reluctant to come out into the open about their own merits. "Yet I could only consider it a white lie when, for instance, Professor Flechsig wanted to put down my illness solely to poisoning with potassium bromide, for which Dr. R. in S., in whose care I had been before, was to be blamed" (*ibid.*, p. 35 = 1955, p. 62). He was also of the opinion that he might have been more quickly rid of his hypochondriacal delusion that he was losing weight if he had been allowed to operate the scales himself. But these, he says, are irrelevancies:

> The main point was that I was eventually cured (after a prolonged convalescence), and therefore I had at the time no reason to be other than most grateful to Professor Flechsig; I gave this special expression by a subsequent visit and in my opinion an adequate honorarium. My wife felt even more sincere gratitude and worshipped Professor Flechsig as the man who had restored her husband to her; for this reason she kept his picture on her desk for many years [*ibid.*, pp. 35, 36 = 1955, pp. 62, 63].[5]

NOTES TO CHAPTER 12

[1]The text makes it quite clear that it is scarcely possible to imagine a more faithful supporter of Bismarck than Paul Schreber. Niederland, however, has quite different ideas on this: He tried to explain Paul Schreber's first period of illness, which began shortly after the elections, on the basis of anxiety about rebellion against a father-figure, i.e., Bismarck. It is worth the effort to have a look at the way reality—Paul Schreber's admiration for Bismarck—is distorted into the situation of a son rebelling against a threatening father: "running for the Reichstag signified in a way running against Bismarck, the most powerful man in Germany, who all his life was sternly opposed to parliamentary ("filial") intrusion: (1951, p. 580).

That it was also possible to become a member of the Reichstag in order to *support* Bismarck does not appear to have occurred to Niederland. In 1974 he put his point of view even more simply and with even greater emphasis: *"running for the Reichstag meant running against Bismarck"* (p. 86). On the election of Paul Schreber Niederland wrote: "When called upon to become a member of the Reichstag as a rebellious son in opposition to the awe-inspiring Bismarck, he fell ill the first time" (1951, pp. 582, 583).

At the time he wrote this, Niederland did not know that Paul Schreber lost the election and only then fell ill. In this connection Schalmey stated, in a book about the psychoanalytic method of reasoning:

> We now know (through Niederland 1963) that Schreber lost the elections by miles. According to Niederland's specific assertion, Schreber ought to have felt unconscious joy at this outcome, since after all it spared him from having to meet Bismarck face to face. So why did he have to take refuge in a psychotic condition? Niederland (1963) does not correct his specific assertion, though there are of course several conceivable reasons for that, e.g. the quite trivial one that his specific assertion no longer interested him. My observation is therefore not susceptible of systematic evaluation [1977, p. 69].

However, Niederland considered the idea interesting enough for him to include it unchanged in his book of 1974 (p. 41). My view is therefore that Schalmey's criticism is very definitely "susceptible of systematic evaluation" in the terms of his book, which is entitled *Die Bewährung psychoanalytischer Hypothesen* (The confirmation of psychoanalytical hypotheses). Niederland's behavior demonstrates that a psychoanalyst's hypothesis can only be "confirmed," never weakened or refuted, by newly discovered facts. Even when Niederland realized that Schreber was a candidate for the National Liberal Party, i.e., the party which generally supported Bismarck, he managed to fit this new fact into his own theory, simply by writing that the party was part of the opposition against Bismarck: "Schreber was then running for the Reichstag as the avowed candidate of the *Nationalliberale Partei* (National Liberal party) which was in opposition to Bismarck's autocratic and reactionary *régime* in Germany" (1963, pp. 205, 206 = 1974, p. 99). Nonsense. Let us look at an advertisement for Paul Schreber: "We want to go FORWARD, FORWARD WITH BISMARCK, and that is why DR. SCHREBER is our MAN" (*Chemnitzer Tageblatt*, 28 October 1884, p.11). Almost everyone has blindly accepted Niederland's view of National Liberal politics. Paul Schreber, we read,

> had put himself forward to the parliamentary elections as a representative of the liberal party, in opposition to the reactionary party of Bismarck (the perfect authoritarian father-figure) [Racamier and Chasseguet-Smirgel, 1966, p. 14].

> At this time, as he had already been for over twenty years, Bismarck was a Prussian minister. His autocratic and reactionary régime was opposed to the national liberal party for which Schreber was an official candidate for the Reichstag [Croufer, 1970, p. 220].

> 1884 Daniel-Paul Schreber stands in the elections for the Reichstag in opposition to Bismarck [Colas, 1975, p. 90]

Only the appendix in the French translation of the *Memoirs* gives a more accurate picture of the National Liberals: "Contrary to what has been advanced apropos of Schreber's candidature, their opposition to Bismarck was very intermittent" (D. P. Schreber, 1975, p. 387).

²Niederland wrote: ". . . a local newspaper in his election district—Chemnitz in Saxony—carried the somewhat scornful headline about his candidature: *Wer kennt schon den Dr. Schreber*—who after all knows Dr. Schreber?" (1963, p. 206, 1974, p. 99). This has been taken over into all sorts of later literature (Croufer, 1970, p. 220; S. M. Weber, 1973, p. 5; appendix in D. P. Schreber, 1975, p. 385; London, 1976, p. 697; Meijer and Rijnders, 1976, p. 36, 1977, p. 22; Rabant, 1978, p. 180;

Melman, 1980, p. 7). It is my belief, however, that Niederland's headline *"Wer kennt schon den Dr. Schreber?"* never existed but is merely a corruption of the advertisement quoted in my main text from the *Chemnitzer Tageblatt: "Wählt nicht den unbekannten Schreber!,"* "Do not vote for the unknown Schreber!" It is practically impossible to show that Niederland's text does *not* exist, since the source is identified simply as "a local newspaper in his election district." However, there is no doubt that Niederland used the newspaper in which the advertisement appeared, the *Chemnitzer Tageblatt* (1963, p. 204; 1974, p. 97). I have searched through the editions of this paper that appeared during the weeks preceding and following the elections, looking in vain for Niederland's headline. Moreover, Niederland's text is made all the more unlikely by the fact that in those days the newspapers had headlines of quite a different kind. The biographical item on Paul Schreber, for example, appeared under the heading of "Local and Saxon affairs." This kind of headline, indicating the sort of subject-matter that followed, was certainly not a monopoly of the *Chemnitzer Tageblatt.*

[3]See Baumeyer (1956, p. 61), where Sonneberg was erroneously translated as Sonnenstein. The mistake has been retained in the French translation (Baumeyer, 1979, p. 172).

[4]Meijer and Rijnders reported, with regard to Paul Schreber's first period of illness, that

> He is transferred to Leipzig (1884) and shortly afterwards, at his own initiative, pays his first visit to Dr. Paul Theodor Flechsig, director of the psychiatric department of the University Clinic in Leipzig. He is overworked, sleeps badly, hears strange noises ("hundreds of mice behind the wallpaper") and makes a suicide attempt. . . . After a stay of two months in Flechsig's clinic he is sent home again, apparently cured [1977, p. 22].

Paul Schreber was transferred to Leipzig not in 1884 but in 1885; see the next chapter. His visit to Flechsig took place *before* his transfer. His complaints of insomnia and the strange noises date from before his second, not his first, illness (see D. P. Schreber, 1903, pp. 37, 38 = 1955, p. 64). He stayed in Flechsig's clinic not for two months but for almost six, after which he did not go home but to Ilmenau.

[5]Stone (1972, p. 774) stated that "The reverence of the Schreber family for Dr. Flechsig was so great that Frau Schreber kept a framed photograph of Dr. Flechsig in their bedroom." Why did Stone move the photograph from the desk to the bedroom? On various occasions during his second illness Paul Schreber had nocturnal emissions. Freud speculated that these were accompanied by homosexual fantasies involving Flechsig which were forgotten by morning. Evidently Stone thought this speculation required some sort of support: Paul Schreber, he declared, "had seen his [Flechsig's] picture every night when he went to bed!" (*ibid.,* p. 746). As it happens, I can tell Stone which photograph stood in the bedroom. This was tied up with the illegitimate girl whom Paul and Sabine Schreber later adopted (see page 189). Paul Schreber's nephew Felix Jung wrote of her: "Her father was . . . an opera singer in Cologne by the name of Petter, who must also in some way have been related to my aunt, for I can remember well that a small photograph of him had a place on my aunt's bedside table."

13

PAUL SCHREBER BETWEEN HIS FIRST AND SECOND PERIODS OF ILLNESS (1886–93)

Gradually we are approaching the second period of illness, the period described by Schreber in his *Memoirs*. The years between the two periods can largely be described by drawing on what Schreber himself wrote about them in his book. "The first of the two illnesses . . . was fully cured at the end of 1885, so that I was able to resume work as Chairman of the County Court at Leipzig to which I had in the meantime been transferred on 1st January 1886" (D. P. Schreber, 1903, p. 34 = 1955, p. 62).

In Leipzig Schreber lived in the *Harkortstrasse*, which was again close to the *Zeitzer Strasse* and thus also close to his mother. In 1886, i.e., shortly after his first illness, Schreber and his wife drew up a will which included a clause whereby Schreber undertook to provide for his wife during his lifetime (see D. P. Schreber, 1903, p. 512 = 1955, p. 353): Was this perhaps a precaution in case he were again to become mentally ill?

On 1 October 1889 Schreber became president of the district court at Freiberg, a place between Dresden and Chemnitz. By this time his income stood at 7800 marks a year. In 1891 and 1892 he was elected "to membership of the district assembly by the highest taxpayers of the district of the Freiberg district president," according to a letter in which he applied to the ministry of justice for permission to accept his election (D. P. Schreber 1892). His name also appeared among the signatories to an advertisement in the *Freiberger Anzeiger und Tageblatt* of 31 December 1892 (p. 6), headed "A New Year's Greetings Card," in which the signatories state that they have for the benefit of the worthy poor of this place paid the sum of 1 to 5 marks into the funds of the Society for the Prevention of Begging, in return forgoing the receipt of personal and written good wishes and abstaining from sending New Year's cards.

Schreber himself did not mention his work in Freiberg in his *Memoirs*;[1] this period is referred to only in very general terms:

After recovering from my first illness I spent eight years with my wife, on the whole quite happy ones, rich also in outward honours and marred only from time to time by the repeated disappointment of our hope of being blessed with children [D. P. Schreber, 1903, p. 36 = 1955, p. 63].

One of these outward honors was certainly the "Knighthood of the Order of Merit, 1st Class" of Saxony, which he was awarded on 23 April 1888 "in recognition of his many years of faithful and beneficial services" (Sächsische Ordenskanzlei 61, ff. 120–121). The mention of repeated disappointment of their hope of having children refers to the fact that during this period Sabine Schreber had possibly as many as four miscarriages.[2]

In the *Memoirs* (1903, p. 36f. = 1955, p. 63f.) Schreber himself described his appointment in 1893 to the presidency of a senate of the *Oberlandesgericht* at Dresden,[3] the highest court in Saxony. He was then fifty-one years of age, young for so high an office. His nephew Felix Jung, born in 1882 and later himself a lawyer, wrote in 1955: "Professionally too my uncle was held in high regard, and more than one of his colleagues saw in him the future minister of justice in Saxony. However, that was not to be, on account of the outbreak of his illness."

I shall not embark on my account of this second period of illness at once; instead, I want to pay some attention to what Schreber himself tells us about his own personality in the period which preceded it. "I have from my youth been anything but inclined towards religious fanaticism. . . . I was by no means what one might call a *poet*, although I have occasionally attempted a few verses on family occasions" (D. P. Schreber, 1903, p. 63 = 1955, p. 80). One poem from this period has survived. Entitled "den 26. Juli 1889," it was written for his sister Anna's silver wedding, on which occasion it was recited by Anna's daughter Paula. Here I shall merely quote a few pertinent lines from this long and conventional poem.

> Yes, dear parents, more richly and beautifully than for many
>   others
> The succession of the years gone by has passed;
> Not to all who walk Life's pilgrim's paths
> Is Fortune's horn of plenty poured out as to you.

Those who care to do so may read into this a degree of jealousy on the part of the childless heir of his sister with her many children.

> So let us first, united with you, direct our gaze
> Upwards and, hands devoutly folded,
> Praise God with thanks for the gracious gifts
> With which he has mercifully governed over you.

Conventional lines like these seem to accord well with Schreber's own testimony that when he was in good health he was anything but a religious fanatic:

> I had occupied myself too much with the natural sciences, particularly with works based on the so-called modern doctrine of evolution, not to have begun to doubt, to say the least, the literal truth of all Christian religious teachings [D. P. Schreber, 1903, p. 64 = 1955, p. 80].

In a footnote he then gave a brief list of the chiefly Darwinist literature he read in the ten years before his second illness, including Häckel's *Natürliche Schöpfungsgeschichte* (1868) (Natural history of creation), a book "whose very title should be noted as being opposed to the Biblical story of creation" (Buchheim, 1966, p. 187). In taking an interest in the theory of evolution, Schreber was by no means alone in Germany: "Charles Darwin's theory of natural selection was a British phenomenon, but Darwinism was German" (Buchheim, 1966, p. 183). Closer study of the Darwinist literature named by Schreber lies outside the scope of the quite narrow biographical task which I have set myself and may perhaps better be left to Schreber interpreters, since "allusions to ideas contained in these works" may be found throughout the *Memoirs*, as Schreber himself justly observed (1903, p. 64 = 1955, p. 80).

NOTES TO CHAPTER 13

[1]According to Niederland (1974, p. 7), S. M. Weber (1973, p. ix), and Heiligenthal and Volk (1973, p. ix), Paul Schreber was *Landgerichtsdirektor* in Leipzig from 1886 until 1893. In other words, they do not mention his post in Freiberg. Both Leipzig and Freiberg are absent from Meijer and Rijnders account, where, following his first period of illness, we read that "After his discharge, Schreber was in October 1931 [*sic*] given the prestigious post of 'president of a senate' of the Court of Appeal in Dresden" (1977, p. 22).

[2]My statement that Sabine Schreber may have had as many as four miscarriages by this time is based on the following facts: In all, she had six miscarriages (Baumeyer, 1970, p. 243 = 1973, p. 364). Two of these were before her husband's first period of illness (see p. 156). By the time he returned home after his second period in psychiatric clinics she was forty-five. So probably the miscarriages took place before his second period of illness.

On this point the literature tends to be rather careless. According to Baumeyer (1970, p. 243 = 1973, p. 364), who is otherwise usually reliable, Paul Schreber referred to two miscarriages suffered by his wife between 1885 and 1893; in fact, however, he merely referred to more than one thwarting of their hope for children. In the appendix to the French version of the *Memoirs*, the entry for Frau Schreber tells us that "From 1878 to 1884 she had six miscarriages (wrongly reported by Schreber as having taken place between 1885 and 1893)" (D. P. Schreber, 1975, p. 387). Green (1977, p. 36) accepted this. This wrote without a shred of evidence that one of the miscarriages took place in 1884 (1973–74, p. 14). Colas "dated" even more miscarriages: in 1880, 1884, and 1892 (1975, p. 90).

[3]*Senatspräsident* in Dresden, not Leipzig, as Fritzsche wrote (1926, p. 14), Ritter carried over (1936a, p. 11), Gerhard Richter borrowed from Ritter (1939b, p. 18), and Tabouret-Keller assumes from the two last: "Daniel Paul, whom the biographers never mention without his title of *Senatspräsident am Oberlandesgericht Leipzig*" (1973, p. 297).

Paul Schreber was not given the most senior of all the posts at this most senior court in Saxony, despite what Niederland (1974, p. xiv) and Shulman (1959, p. 180) wrote. Baumeyer gave a correct assessment of Paul Schreber's new position: "A further promotion would have brought him to the highest post in the judiciary of his country" (1956, p. 71).

14

PAUL SCHREBER'S SECOND PERIOD OF ILLNESS (1893–1902)

1. THE VICISSITUDES OF PAUL SCHREBER

In his new post as president of a senate of the *Oberlandesgericht* in Dresden, Schreber soon became overworked. Then he began to suffer from insomnia. In November 1893 he took what was supposed to be a brief holiday in order to go to Leipzig—where he and his wife stayed with his mother—to consult Professor Flechsig, the psychiatrist who had treated him in 1884–85. A sleeping cure failed, Schreber tried to hang himself in the bedroom, and he was admitted to Flechsig's clinic as an emergency case.[1] His holiday was extended, initially until the end of 1893, then for an indefinite period ("Personalakte," folios 16, 18).

He remained in the Leipzig clinic for over six months, after which, in June 1894, he was taken for a fortnight to the Lindenhof clinic at Coswig, some 30 miles to the north (Fig. 34). The final eight years and more of his second illness were spent at Pirna, near Dresden, in the Sonnenstein clinic run by Dr. Weber (Fig. 35).

Initially, in the clinic in Leipzig, Schreber was prey to all-enveloping delusions:

he thought he was dead and putrefying, sick of the plague, imagined that his body was being manipulated in a great many hideous ways, that they had turned him into a woman. The patient was absorbed with these sick suggestions to such an extent that he would sit for hours, totally rigid and motionless, shut off from every other impres-

173

Herrenhaus.

Fig. 34. Lindenhof. From F. Lehmann (1910, p. 626).

Sonnenstein, innere Männerabteilung.

Fig. 35. Sonnenstein. From Weber (1910, p. 427).

sion; on the other hand he was so much tormented by them that he
called death down upon himself, tried repeatedly to drown himself
in his bath, and demanded "the cyanide meant for him." Gradually
the delusions assumed the nature of mystic religiosity, he commu-
nicated directly with God, the devils played games with him, he saw
"miraculous apparitions," heard "holy music," and finally even
believed that he was in another world [Weber, 1894, ff. 24–25].

This is how the situation was summed up at the end of 1894 by Dr.
Weber, the director of the Sonnenstein clinic, in his medical report on
his patient for the *Oberlandesgericht,* when they wanted to know
whether there was any likelihood that Schreber would ever be able to
resume his work as president of a senate. At this stage Weber did not
exclude the possibility of a complete recovery:

> The prognosis for this type of illness is problematical, it is true, but
> as long as, as in the present case, the symptoms are still in a state
> of complete flux and maintain their acute nature, and as long as they
> are accompanied by vivid effects, and in particular as long as the
> delusions have not yet become fixated and been worked into a closed
> system, it remains possible to cling to the hope that the progress of
> the illness will take a favourable turn; in any event, at the present
> time it would be wrong to say that in Herr Senatspräsident Dr.
> Schreber's case the return of complete fitness for duty is absolutely
> excluded [*ibid.,* folio 26].

Partly as a result of this report, at the end of 1894 Schreber was
placed under guardianship at the request of the *Oberlandesgericht.*
This was done in accordance with his wife's wish "that the chairman
of the local court at Leipzig, Oberjustizrath Clemens Schmidt, should
be appointed her husband's guardian and that the management of the
guardianship should be put in the hands of the local court at Leipzig."
(Werner, 1894, folio 22) On the grounds of the same medical report
Schreber was provisionally retired as of 1 January 1895, according to
a letter to Schmidt, his guardian, from the ministry of justice ("Personalakte," folio 31).
About a year later Dr. Weber again wrote a medical report for the
Oberlandesgericht:

> Over the year which has since passed, though the patient's general
> condition has undergone some improvement in certain

particulars . . . he is more sociable and forthcoming, enjoys chess and, in particular, music, to a lesser extent reading, and is more surely orientated with regard to places and persons, unfortunately, however, in essence the features of the picture of his illness have displayed no change, having rather fixated themselves in an alarming manner.

Consequently Weber now arrived at a more gloomy conclusion than a year previously:

As the delusions have become increasingly fixated and interwoven with his personality as a whole, although we may still hope to bring about an improvement of the condition to the extent that life in the outside world, with the appropriate care and nursing, becomes possible, we may not reasonably suppose that Herr Präsident Dr. Schreber will recover total mental intactness and become capable of carrying out the duties of his office [1895, folios 34–35].

On the basis of this report Schreber was retired permanently as of 1 January 1896; his pension amounted to almost 7000 marks annually ("Personalakte," folios 32–33).

2. REFERENCES TO MATERIAL ON THIS PERIOD

Dr. Weber's medical reports of 1894 and 1895 are the only new material I have been able to find on Paul Schreber's condition at this time. And even this discovery had little to reveal, since Weber reused his outline account of Schreber's initial symptoms when he was again called upon in 1899 to draw up a medical report on him (1899). This report was necessary for a court case in which Schreber was contesting his guardianship, an action which he eventually won at the highest level and which I do not have to describe here because Schreber himself included the most important documents in the case, among them Weber's medical reports, in his book *Memoirs of my Nervous Illness*.

In essence the *Memoirs* consist of a detailed account of Schreber's second illness, i.e., his experience in psychiatric clinics and the conclusions which he drew from those experiences regarding a supersensory world. The reader wishing to know what course this illness took should therefore read not this book but the *Memoirs;* he would do best to start at Chapter 4 (D. P. Schreber, 1903, pp. 34 ff. = 1955, pp. 61 ff.).

Further information about Schreber's life at this time is found in material published by Baumeyer (1956). The most important part of this material is a number of psychiatric reports on Schreber which are still in the psychiatric hospital at Leipzig-Dösen, and which Baumeyer quoted in their entirety. He also quoted from letters about Schreber written to the Sonnenstein management by his wife and other relatives. All I can do here is refer the reader to Baumeyer's excellent work; the only new thing left for me to do in this chapter is to make one or two observations regarding his publications.

3. OBSERVATIONS ON BAUMEYER: CONCERNING PAUL SCHREBER'S WIFE AND OTHER RELATIVES

I shall begin by taking some sentences from the psychiatric reports on Paul Schreber. Under the heading "heredity" we read: "The father (originator of the 'Schreber garden allotments' in Leipzig) suffered from obsessional ideas with homicidal tendencies. Mother: quick changes of mood, nervous. One sister hysterical" (quoted by Baumeyer, 1956, p. 62). These words have been quoted interminably in the literature, as though these were factual characterizations of members of Paul Schreber's family: "His celebrated father suffered from an obsessional neurosis with homicidal impulses . . . Schreber's mother was described as nervous with quick changes of mood, a sister was hysterical" (p. 70).

Doubts as to the objectivity of these characterizations were first expressed by the psychiatrist G. Friedrich, a great-grandson of Moritz Schreber, who in a letter to Ullstein Taschenbuchverlag of 28 April 1980 wrote as follows:

> The cited entry in the Sonnenstein file (according to Domeyer [read: Baumeyer]) about the family anamnesis fails to give an indication of its source. One is inclined to suspect that this assertion springs from the delusions of the sick Senatspräsident Paul Schreber, which were recorded in the file by the doctor who examined him.

This possibility, which at first seemed to me to be extremely improbable, is nevertheless kept emphatically open by the medical director of the psychiatric hospital at Leipzig-Dösen, where the case record is still kept, and by his secretary, who has worked there for several decades. The most curious aspect is that this is an interpretation which

Baumeyer has never suggested, despite the fact that he too was once director of a psychiatric clinic. Niederland had this to say on the subject:

> In a personal communication, Dr. Baumeyer has expressed his agreement with my opinion that this illuminating statement contained in the medical report of the Sonnenstein Asylum, where the son was confined after his second breakdown, must have been based on information given to an attending psychiatrist in the Asylum by some close member of the Schreber family, because the father had died more than thirty years before the entry was made.

However, it seems to me that we can exclude any likelihood of these negative remarks about members of the Schreber family having emanated from a member of that family other than Paul; for example, I have never come across anything that might be taken to point to the existence of a "hysterical" sister,[2] nor have I ever observed anything like a breach in the family solidarity. It therefore appears to me most likely that these observations do indeed relate to remarks passed by the sick Paul Schreber himself. However, I should also like to leave open the possibility that the original remarks were made by his wife: negative sentiments would be understandable coming from her, considering the fact that, as we have already seen (p. 153), she was never able to get on with her husband's family; this is also illustrated by the following passage from a letter which she wrote about her husband: "I have no notion whether my mother-in-law wishes him to come. I shall pay no attention to that because I am always credited with wrong motives" (Sabine Schreber, 1902, quoted by Baumeyer [1956, p. 68]).

Baumeyer rightly observed that Sabine's letters reflect helpless anxiety about her husband's illness.[3] Less impressive, to my mind, are various other conclusions which he drew from the letters to the Sonnenstein management about Paul Schreber. On the basis of this material he characterized Schreber's sister Klara as "the one who during the years 1893 to 1902 was most concerned with Schreber" (Baumeyer, 1956, p. 69). In 1956 objections were raised to this by Felix Jung, the youngest son, born in 1882, of Paul's sister Anna:

> whether she herself [i.e. Klara] ever went so far as to write him [Paul] large numbers of letters appears doubtful to me, since she was herself in poor health and had a seriously ill husband to look after. From my own recollection I know that the closest person to my uncle

> Paul was his unmarried sister Sidonie Schreber, whose constant concern for him was touching and who used to visit him at least once a month when he was at Sonnenstein. On one occasion I even went with her myself. My aunt Sidonie was a very charitable, selfless person whom I remember fondly as an aunt who always greatly spoiled me with presents.

Felix Jung was in a position to know: the Jung family, it will be recalled, lived next door to Sidonie and her mother in the *Zeitzer Strasse*.

> For decades my parents and my grandmother were neighbors on our own plot of land, and so it was that aunt Sidonie was always the good aunt to my brothers and sisters, and myself in particular, always lending a hand and putting herself at our disposal. She sacrificed herself greatly for her brother Paul, which cannot be said of aunt Klara, simply because she was not so dispensable.

Almost all Paul Schreber's relatives lived close together: his sister Sidonie with his mother, and his other sister Anna and her family in the house next door; only Klara lived at some distance, in Chemnitz. Moreover, because of her husband's ill health she was probably unable to visit her brother with any degree of frequency, so it is not especially surprising that she most often addressed herself to the management of the clinic in writing. This is better accounted for as a sign of isolation than—as Baumeyer claims—as a reflection of a particular interest in her brother's welfare.

Baumeyer also observed, in connection with the letters to the clinic about Paul Schreber: "It is noteworthy that his mother never wrote to the Asylum Board to enquire about her son's condition" (1956, p. 68). Baumeyer attached great importance to this:

> I have already pointed out in my earlier work that between 1894 and 1902, i.e. during his long stay in the clinic, Schreber's mother never wrote to enquire after her son's health. Schreber's mother was evidently a severely depressive and passive woman . . . [1970, p. 245 = 1973, p. 366].

But so much importance ought not to be attached to the absence of letters from her to the clinic management: She had a daughter living with her who visited her son regularly, and she was approaching eighty when he was admitted to Sonnenstein. Nor was her passivity quite as severe as Baumeyer would have it: below (p. 230ff) we shall see that, on the contrary, she was an active and enterprising woman until well into her eighties.

Not that Frau Schreber went to any great lengths for her son's benefit: according to Herr Troitzsch she did not visit him at Sonnenstein for many years:

In the report of 5 April 1902 drawn up by Geh. Rat Dr. Weber [reprinted in D. P. Schreber, 1903, pp. 464 ff = 1955, p. 452 ff], it is mentioned that D. P. Schreber's mother and sister visited him in the summer of 1901. Pauline Schreber told my mother of it with much emotion. She was living with her daughter Sidonie in Wehlen and drove up to Sonnenstein from there. On the way, her son came to meet her, already waving from a distance and then greeting her. The first meeting since his illness, a year and a half before his release from the asylum [Troitzsch, 1974, pp. 2–3].

Wehlen is close to Pirna, and thus close to Sonnenstein, in the Sächsische Schweiz. I assume that Pauline Schreber was staying there for the summer.

With this meeting between Paul Schreber and his mother we are already nearly at the end of his second illness, when he was allowed to leave the clinic every now and then and was engaged both in legal proceedings to bring about his release from guardianship and in writing *Memoirs of my Nervous Illness*. The following chapter is concerned with the publication of the book and the reception it was accorded.

NOTES TO CHAPTER 14

[1]The onset of his second illness is described in considerable detail by Paul Schreber himself (1903, pp. 37–40 = 1955, pp. 63–65). Anyone wishing to know what did *not* happen should consult Stone (1972, p. 744).

[2]It might be thought that the adjective "hysterical" applied to Sidonie, who was rightly described by Baymeyer as "at the end mentally no longer quite right" (1956, p. 69). However, these two references were quite divorced from one another: the term "hysterical" dates back to 1893 or 1894, whereas Sidonie's decline really only began in about 1917.

[3]There is one detail of the picture of Paul Schreber's wife given by Baumeyer which requires amplification. He wrote: "A letter from Schreber's sister (March, 1900) mentions his wife's recurring infirmity; 'her usual ailments are at present ag-

gravated by the effects of influenza.[5] '' (1956, p. 68). She was in fact diabetic. However, she was not "sickly": her nephew Felix Jung, who was born in 1882, wrote in 1954: "Aunt Sabine was a person of very sunny disposition, physically very strong."

15

THE MEMOIRS OF MY NERVOUS ILLNESS

There is no need for me to give an account of how the *Memoirs* came to be written, since Paul Schreber himself wrote about it in the book—how it began with a few brief notes in 1896, which were already an initial attempt at shaping a draft version of his memoirs. "This sketch is contained in a little brown book, entitled 'From my life' (D. P. Schreber, 1903, p. 195 = 1955, p. 160). These notes were followed, after 1897, by diaries. Work on the *Memoirs* themselves began in 1900. At first he wrote with a view to the near future, in the hope that he would soon be able to lead a normal life outside the clinic: His intention in writing the book was to give those close to him, his wife in particular, some idea of his thoughts on religion. Later he decided his work might be of interest to a wider public, and he therefore cast around for a publisher for his curious manuscript.

In 1900 Schreber's psychiatrist Weber could still refer to his patient's efforts to find a publisher as "of course without success" (quoted in D. P. Schreber, 1955, p. 282), but by 1902 Schreber had reached preliminary agreement with the Leipzig publishing house of Nauhardt (see D. P. Schreber, 1903, p. 493 = 1955, pp. 341–342). In the event, the book was published in 1903 by another Leipzig publisher, Mutze, a company characterized by Benjamin (1972, p. 616) as a "focus of the most ludicrous products of spiritist literature."

For the printed edition Schreber made quite a few changes in his original text in order not to cause offense to various persons named in the manuscript. It is for this reason that many of the names in the *Memoirs* are reduced to initials, a number of footnotes left out, and an entire chapter omitted: This was originally the third chapter and dealt with some enigmatic events concerning Paul Schreber's relatives.[1] Unfortunately the manuscript appears to have been lost.

The book received generally fair comment from the specialist literature.[2] Its theological pretensions were nowhere taken seriously; with equal justice, the psychiatric journals at once recognized its considerable importance as a superb description, from the inside, of what was then known as "paranoia." "No thinking person would agree with the author that he is mentally normal; they would, however, concur that he is a man of considerable gifts and of decent sensibilities" (Pelman, 1903, p. 659). There were also some unfavorable reviews: R. Pfeiffer (1904) opined that the book "has nothing new to offer the informed medical man" and that circulation among laymen might cause confusion. Aschaffenburg also saw nothing of merit in the book: "It seems to me that publication does very serious damage, both actual and mental, to the family's interests" (1903, p. 500).

This is probably what the family thought about it too: "It is even said that they bought up and destroyed most copies of the Memoirs" (Macalpine and Hunter, 1955, p. 2). This story is probably true[3]: Mrs. Macalpine spoke to Paul Schreber's adopted daughter, and the story is also current among descendants of his sister Anna. They suspect that Anna's husband Carl Jung was probably the person who did the buying. This is a suggestion to which I can lend some support, since there is an indication that Carl Jung more or less regarded himself as the head of the Schreber family, feeling that he was responsible for family affairs. In about 1900 the publishers of Moritz Schreber's books received a request for details about him, and the letter was forwarded to the family. It was Carl Jung who in 1901 replied to it: "That you should hear from me and not from a [illegible] of the deceased is due to the fact there are only female descendants still alive, apart from a son who is unfortunately not responsible for his actions and has no children" (C. Jung, 1901, p. 2).

NOTES TO CHAPTER 15

[1]It has often been said that the *Memoirs* were censored before publication (see, e.g., Katan [1959, pp. 350, 373]). But this was self-censorship (see also D. P. Schreber, 1903, p. 486 = 1955, p. 337).

[2]I have found the following reviews: Aschaffenburg (1903), Möbius (1903), Kron (1903), Pelman (1903 and 1904), Windscheid (1904), R. Pfeiffer (1904), *Friedreichs Blätter* (1904), Schultze (1904 and 1905), Infeld (1905), R. (1905), and Arnemann (1905). Stone (1972, p. 745) summarized the reviews: the *Memoirs*

had been reviewed as a classical case of paranoia based on religious obsessions, for Schreber had ultimately gone through the phase of being Jesus Christ's redeemer, before he went on to the role of being Mother to the World.

The psychiatrists of Europe had decided that the core of Schreber's paranoia was his religious delusions.

Paul Schreber never believed that he was Christ's redeemer. Not did "the psychiatrists of Europe," or even the reviewers of the *Memoirs,* declare that his religious delusions were the core of his paranoia. I have already referred to one embellishment which Stone added to Freud's theory about Paul Schreber (see note 5 to Chapter 12). These remarks about the reviews were calculated to serve the same purpose: The more stupid you paint Freud's predecessors, the greater Freud's own genius becomes.

³"It is even said that" the family bought up as many copies as possible, according to Macalpine and Hunter. This reappears in subsequent literature—naturally without the "It is even said that": See, e.g., White (1961, p. 55); S. M. Weber (1973, p. 12); Heiligenthal and Volk (1973, p. ix); Calasso (1974a, p. 503); Meijer and Rijinders (1977, p. 23); O. Mannoni (1979, p. 22). Canetti (1976a, p. 132) wrote in 1949 that Paul Schreber's book "was bought up by his relatives, withdrawn from sale and destroyed, so that only a few numbered copies remained" (1976a, p. 132). I fail to see how Canetti can have known this in 1949. I suspect that he added it to the subsequent publication of his notes from 1949. As for "numbered copies": in neither my own copy nor those I have seen in libraries is there any sort of number apart from library shelf-marks.

16

PAUL SCHREBER'S LAST YEARS OUTSIDE PSYCHIATRIC CLINICS (1902–07)

1. PAUL SCHREBER'S RETURN TO NORMAL LIFE (1902–03)

Schreber left Sonnenstein in December 1902. At first he went to live with his mother, where he occupied himself with "property management" ('Häuserverwaltung'; see Baumeyer, 1955, p. 519 = 1973, pp. 346–347). This probably refers to the disposal of the business premises in the Brühl—the premises in which Gustav had once had his chemicals factory. According to the Leipzig directory—which would naturally tend to be behind—these premises still belonged to the heirs of Moritz Schreber in 1905; in the same year Paul referred to the property in his poem for his mother's ninetieth birthday:

> For sixty years it belonged to you and yours,
> And one thing may in retrospect be said in its favor:
> When it was no longer ours, it was a loss
> That we mourn less than other things.
> [D. P. Schreber, 1905, p. 41]

These verses about the Brühl, the street full of Jewish fur-dealers, also contain a slightly anti-Semitic passage:

> And if your heart is scarcely set on furs and skins,
> You may perhaps have only moderate sympathy
> For those that eat kosher, and Poland's Jews.
> [*ibid.*]

Schreber was not only engaged in property management at this time:

187

Fig. 36. Paul Schreber with his adopted daughter around 1905. Photograph in the possession of descendants of Moritz Schreber.

Then it caused a great sensation among the whole family when word went round that Paul Schreber was paying everybody "introductory visits" as a cured man. I can still picture him, a tall man, standing in our "best room," engaged in friendly conversation which included his small eleven or twelve-year-old nephew [Troitzsch, 1963–68, p. 29].

This is what that distant nephew, Herr Troitzsch, wrote at a time when he was still unaware of the existence of Paul Schreber's *Memoirs*. Schreber's fame—that is, the story that he was conducting his own case in the action to have his guardianship rescinded—had preceded him, Herr Troitzsch told me.

In 1903 Schreber returned to his wife in Dresden. In the meantime she had taken into her home a young girl, aged thirteen, who was later formally adopted by the couple (Fig. 36). In later years she was traced by various authors. Baumeyer (1970, p. 244 = 1973, p. 365) managed to extract a few items of information regarding her adoptive father. As she has a great fear of publicity, I shall, like my predecessors, refrain from mentioning her name. I am grateful to her for her confirmation that the photograph is of her with Paul Schreber.

The information given by Baumeyer (1956, p. 65, and 1970, pp. 243–44 = 1973, p. 365) provides an impression of Schreber's life in Dresden. He tried in vain to work for the ministry of justice, spent much time at chess and playing the piano, and got on well with his adopted daughter, helping her with her homework and going for long walks with her, in the *Sächsische Schweiz*—perhaps while staying at his mother's summer residence at Wehlen—and "also in the Tyrol, where we once stayed in the Geiserhof, close to the Schlern. On one occasion at the same time as King August of Saxony and his family, whom Father welcomed with a poem" (unpublished letter). I have been unable to find this poem, though other occasional texts by Paul Schreber dating from this period are still in existence.

2. OCCASIONAL TEXTS BY PAUL SCHREBER FROM ABOUT 1904–05

One of the texts to have survived is that of a speech written by Schreber for the christening of one of his sister Anna's granddaughters at Christmas 1904. For the particular benefit of Wilden (1972), who

Fig. 37. Swans on the estate of Mühlbach. Photograph in the possession of descendants of Moritz Schreber.

has acclaimed Paul Schreber as a radical feminist philosopher, I shall quote a few lines:

> If perhaps [crossed out] the pugnacious element would be strongly represented in her brothers, if perhaps they should one day even be called to go to battle as fighters for the fatherland, it will be her task to work more in the narrower circle of home and family, to reconcile in love existing or newly arising conflicts [D. P. Schreber, 1904, p. 4].

The fact that barely two years after being discharged from a psychiatric clinic Schreber was being entrusted with the job of making a speech at a christening seems to me an indication that he had now been fully accepted by the family, or at least by the child's parents, Friedrich Jung and his wife. Friedrich Jung was Paul's sister Anna's eldest son; he managed his father's manorial estate at Mühlbach, some twenty miles east of Leipzig.

It was at about this time that Pauline Schreber gave her grandson at Mühlbach two swans; see Figure 37. Paul wrote a poem to mark the occasion. He has the male swan saying that he is not, like Lohengrin, a man bewitched.

> Neither do I think I shall transform myself;
> I would rather always wander as a swan.
>
> [D. P. Schreber, n.d.]

At this time the Lohengrin saga was popular on account of the opera by Wagner. I shall refer to another Wagner opera below in this chapter. I have more than once referred to, and quoted from, Paul Schreber's poem for his mother's ninetieth birthday. Entitled "Zum 29. Juni 1905," the poem made a considerable impression when it was recited. Fifty years later Felix Jung, who had been twenty-three years old at the time, wrote:

> My uncle Paul Schreber wrote very beautiful poems, for example. I remember the ninetieth birthday of his mother, my grandmother (29.6.1905), for which he wrote a long poem which was also printed and made a great impression at the birthday celebrations [unpublished letter].

Schreber's poem was in fact the rhyming commentary which accompanied Frau Schreber's actual present, which was an album, since lost,

Fig. 38. *Angelikastrasse* 15a, Dresden.

of photographs of places which had played some part in her life. The only lines of topical relevance were the following:

Finally you behold a modest house,
Not long since built, with your help,
In many ways it still looks unfinished,
Not even the windows are there yet.
But once it has been moved into by your son,
Why should the hope at once depart entirely,
That *she* should one day live in it as a guest,
Who helped him find the path over hill and dale to home?
[D. P. Schreber, 1905, p. 4]

This "modest house" is doubtless the quite substantial property which Schreber was having built for himself and his family in Dresden. In the final lines the poet expressed the hope that his mother will be able to stay with him there—the mother he stayed with at the end of 1902, before he returned to his own house in Dresden.

3. THE NEW HOUSE IN DRESDEN (1905)

Baumeyer (1956, p. 69) pointed out that Schreber had a house built for himself in Dresden at about this time; later the adopted daughter told Baumeyer that "During the building he was interested and involved in everything that went on" (1970, p. 244 = 1973, p. 365). The house, at *Angelikastrasse* 15a, still exists, a large building of three stories, the small rooms on the third floor were presumably for domestic staff. My credibility with the astonished occupants, after I had rung the front-door bell in 1977, rose considerably when, by the gas meter in the cellar, we discovered a yellowed piece of paper on which it was still possible to read that on 12 August 1905 the gas installation in the house of P. Schreber, Doctor of Law, had been found to be in order.

The architecture of the house as a whole is no different from that of the surrounding properties (Figs. 38 and 39). Some aspects which may surprise the modern foreign visitor were probably quite normal for the time and place: for example, the gap of several centimeters between the door to the bathroom/W.C. and the wallpaper surrounding it points to the door and its frame having once been covered with carpeting in order to camouflage them; the tiles on the hall floor bear the text *Grüss Gott,* but there is no need to seek some religious interpretation of this: *Grüss Gott* (literally, "greet God") is a perfectly

Fig. 39. Detail of *Angelikastrasse* 15a, Dresden.

ordinary greeting in everyday German, at least in the southern parts of the country.

The only really unusual feature is the melody the musical notes of which are inscribed in the concrete beam over the front door (Figure 39). A letter written on behalf of the adopted daughter informed me that "the notes over the entrance are the Siegfried motif from a Wagner opera. It was doubtless put there on the initiative of Frau Schreber. [i.e. Sabine], who came from a very musical family" (unpublished letter). Paul Schreber, too, was familiar with Wagner's operas (see D. P. Schreber, 1903, pp. 17, 168 = 1955, p. 55, 143). The motif illustrated comes from the opera *Siegfried;* it is played just before fight scenes in which the hero Siegfried vanquishes monsters.

4. PHOTOGRAPHS TAKEN AROUND 1905

As I have said, the album of photographs given to Pauline Schreber on her ninetieth birthday in 1905 cannot be found. On her next birthday she was given another album. This has survived, and it contains some superb photographs taken around 1905. Photographs from the same period are also to be found in an album which came from the estate of Felix Jung. I have already presented photographs from both of these albums; the most interesting of the remainder are reproduced in this section.

Until now there have been no known photographs or paintings of Paul Schreber, except for a portrait of him as a man between thirty and forty (see p. 144). This meant that any reader of the *Memoirs* was at liberty to form his own picture of the mentally ill, intelligent, misjudged author: a picture described verbally by O. Mannoni (1978, p. 165) with the term "mince" (thin, slight). Figure 40, taken in the Rosental Park in Leipzig, shows this image to be inaccurate. Figure 41 also shows Paul Schreber, and Figures 42 and 43, some of his relatives.

5. A POEM OF 1907 BY PAUL SCHREBER: WAS HE STILL MAD?

The final occasional text by Paul Schreber that I have to offer is a poem written for his wife's fiftieth birthday: "Dedicated to his beloved Sabbie ["Sabchen"] for the nineteenth of June 1907 by her Paul." Here are the final lines of the poem:

Fig. 40. Paul Schreber with his adopted daughter and a grandson of his sister Anna.

Fig. 41. Paul Schreber.

1 2 3 4 5
6—7—8

Fig. 42. 1 = Helene, daughter of Anna; 2 = Anna Jung; 3 = Klara Krause; 4 = Sabine Schreber; 5 = Carl Jung; 6 = son of Helene; 7 = Sidonie Schreber; 8 = Theodor Krause(?).

Fig. 43. Pauline and Sidonie Schreber.

And as autumn, reviving with mild warmth,
Still pleases with many a sunny day,
So may on our path in the evening of our lives
From time to time a tiny grain of joy be strewn.
But should nothing otherwise remain according to our desires,
One thing shall always stand *above* all time:
Keep for me your old love,
As I do truly consecrate it to you.

[D. P. Schreber, 1907a]

Perhaps Niederland was thinking of lines like these when he wrote that "Schreber's letters and poetry discloses his personal sensitivity and a quality of genuine tenderness" (1974, p. 32). Niederland also stated (*ibid.*, pp. 31–32) that the adopted daughter gave him "letters and poems" by Paul Schreber—on condition that he not publish them, as he wrote to me. The adopted daughter also told him that her adoptive father "was 'more of a mother to me than my mother' " (*ibid.*, p. 31). On the following page Niederland commented as follows: "That Schreber as a father displayed more maternal feeling and behavior than the mother rounds out our picture of the subjectively desired self-transformation into a woman" (*ibid.*, p. 32). Niederland made a similar observation regarding Paul Schreber between 1902 and 1907: "one serious vestige of his illness remained: his conviction that he was a woman with female breasts and other feminine attributes" (*ibid.*, p. 7).

This, quite simply, is rubbish. Even when Schreber was writing his *Memoirs,* he no longer thought he was a woman: all he thought was that he could detect the first signs of what might eventually prove to be a change of sex. Niederland's only evidence for saying that after his second illness Schreber still thought he was a woman is his adopted daughter's innocent remark that he was more of a mother to her than her mother. From psychiatric reports (quoted by Baumeyer, 1956, p. 65) we learn that during these years Schreber himself never talked about his illness, and that the auditory hallucinations never disappeared entirely. There is no way of establishing what he thought or desired during those years—but in his overt behavior there is nothing to point in the direction suggested by Niederland. How, for example, does Niederland reconcile Schreber's moustache with his desire to be, or belief that he was, a woman? Schreber's poem for his wife would also seem to confirm that he himself now considered his period in the asylums as a period in which he had been mentally ill:

          disturbed for the second time,
My mind was in the bonds of severe illness;
The bitter cup of separation and of affliction,
Full of worry and sorrow, was again your lot.
So passed nine heavy years.

                              [D. P. Schreber, 1907a, p. 2]

17

PAULINE SCHREBER: FINAL YEARS, DEATH (1907), AND SUBSEQUENT QARRELS CONCERNING HER ESTATE

Paul Schreber's mother was undoubtedly important enough to him for me to devote a separate chapter to her final years. When referring in this way to her importance to him, I am not thinking in terms of any "oral impulses" felt by her son, or of other vague psychoanalytical matters (see p. 89f). I am merely considering, for example, the simple fact that when in Leipzig he always chose to live in her immediate vicinity. Until his marriage, which is to say, until the age of thirty-five, he lived at home with her whenever his posting brought him to Leipzig. Thereafter, both the houses he occupied in the city were barely a stone's throw from her own. And when, at the age of sixty, he left the clinic in 1902 to return to normal life, his first move was to his mother, then aged eighty-seven.[1] His brother and sisters behaved in similar fashion: whenever his juridical career took him to Leipzig, Gustav too always lived with his mother. Up to her mother's death the eldest daughter Anna had spent only seven years not living with her or next-door. Klara, who stayed at home until she was forty, returned there following her husband's death in 1906, thus rejoining her sister Sidonie, who had spent her entire life in the same house.

1. PAULINE SCHREBER'S FINAL YEARS

Pauline Schreber remained an active woman until well into her eighties. Shortly after the turn of the century a Leipzig newspaper

Fig. 44. Sidonie Schreber with bust of Moritz Schreber. Photograph in the possession of descendants of Moritz Schreber.

printed a letter from her complaining that a series of performances of German music in the United States gave too little attention to Mendelssohn.[2] In 1904 she was unable to be present at the christening of her first great-granddaughter (for which her son Paul wrote the speech to which I referred in the last chapter). She did, however, write a poem of over twenty lines to commemorate the occasion.

> Great-grand*sons* have given me pleasure, 6 dear boys,
> But I had not yet managed to look upon a great-grand*daughter*.
> [L. H. P. Schreber, 1904]

The official history of the first Schreber Association also contained references to Moritz Schreber's widow:

> On 15 November 1895 twenty-five years had passed since we first had the honor of calling Dr. Schreber's widow an honorary member. The two presidents expressed most hearty congratulations to the dear lady and presented her with a tribute of flowers [G. Richter, 1939b, p. 103].

A year later "Frau Dr. Schreber visited the new home" of the first Schreber Association (*ibid.*, p. 49). In 1903 the Schreber Association of North Leipzig commissioned a bust of Moritz Schreber for an exhibition (Fritzsche, 1903, p. iv) and at that time enlisted the old lady's help:

> The bust of Dr. Schreber modelled by Prof. Adolf Lehnert in 1903 from some pictures we had was altered by him according to the directions given by the old lady, so that in the judgment of the widow and the children it has become truly lifelike [Fritzsche, 1926, p. 14].

Approximately in 1905 this bust stood in Pauline Schreber's house, or at least it appears in numerous photographs of the time (see Figure 44). On her ninetieth birthday Frau Schreber also received the congratulations of the first Schreber Association (G. Richter, 1939b, p. 104).

I am unable to give any clear picture of her character: the information available to me gives somewhat contradictory impressions. For example, according to the priest speaking at her grave-side, "she probably concurred with the occasional reprimand that she regarded life so absolutely seriously and with such absolute heaviness that it

seemed as if she had eyes especially for what was sombre about her"
(Hartung, 1907, p. 3). Yet at the age of eighty-four she wrote in a
thank-you letter following a visit to her grandson at Mühlbach: "The
journey was very pleasant. I spent the night more in drinking than in
sleeping" (L. H. P. Schreber, 1899, p. 1).

In her last year there was a decline:

> On 29 June 1905 she was able in relative robustness of body and in
> complete freshness of mind to celebrate her ninetieth birthday and
> enjoy the many expressions of respectful interest. In her last year,
> however, the weakness of age became apparent, in part rising to
> agonizing suffering, from which a gentle death has now released her
> [Siegel, 1907c, p. 127].

She died on 14 May 1907. On 17 May the *Leipziger Tageblatt*
published an obituary, and on the same day and the day following, the
paper carried mourning advertisements from Schreber Associations in
Leipzig. The president of the Federation of a number of Schreber
Associations in Leipzig, Richard Siegel, wrote an obituary (1907c,
pp. 126–128) in the Federation's magazine, *Der Freund der Schreber-
Vereine*. He also spoke at her grave on 17 May, after the funeral
oration by the priest, D. Hartung. Both addresses were printed.

Hartung gave a brief and vague account of her life and the situation
during the last years, relating

> how she was able to spend her old age being cared for by her beloved
> daughter [Sidonie], how she was again able to offer maternal help
> and comfort to her severely afflicted daughter [Klara, presumably],
> how she was able to welcome back her son in freshly granted strength,
> then to have about her the blossoming family of her daughter [Anna]
> as it were under the same roof, itself a widely branching tree of
> children and grandchildren [Hartung, 1907, p. 4].

It was then the turn of Herr Siegel to speak. He noted that the deceased
had "for over forty years followed all the endeavors of the Schreber
Associations with the keenest interest, and unobtrusively supported
their work" (1907b, p. 8). Frau Schreber's final deed in support of
the Schreber Associations, yet to come, was to cause so much quar-
reling that the following section is devoted to it.

2. MATTER FOR DISPUTE IN LEGACIES: PAUL SCHREBER CAUGHT BETWEEN QUARRELING SCHREBER ASSOCIATIONS

Not much is known about the effect that his mother's death had on Paul Schreber. "After his mother's death he made many calculations concerning numerous legacies, over-worked himself somewhat and slept badly some nights" (quoted by Baumeyer, 1956, p. 65). This is the account given by one of his sisters when he was again taken off to a psychiatric clinic six months later. In Baumeyer's view, "We do not know whether particular matters for dispute lay behind these calculations" (1955, p. 532 = 1973, p. 359). However, there were matters for dispute concerning the will. Though it is unlikely that a legacy of a thousand marks for the *"Schutzleute Alt-Leipzigs"* (the police of the old city) ("Polizeiamt der Stadt Leipzig 11") would have caused much trouble, some fierce quarrels did result from legacies to a number of Schreber Associations.

The *Freund der Schreber-Vereine*, the magazine of the federation of certain Leipzig Schreber Associations, carried a "vote of thanks" to Pauline Schreber in 1907 (p. 175), who had left each of the Associations the sum of five hundred marks. The condition under which the bequest had been made was

that at their joint federation parents' evening in the autumn these Schreber Associations should "at all times remember Dr. Daniel Gottlob Moritz Schreber's services to education." Just as the ideas and aims of the unforgettable philanthropist's high-minded widow were concerned chiefly with, besides her children, her departed husband and everything connected with his works, so now she has seen to it even after her death that that noble man shall not be forgotten. The noble lady's wish shall be granted [*Freund der Schreber-Vereine*, 1907, p. 194].

This passage is signed "-l," which undoubtedly means that it is the work of Siegel, the president of the Leipzig Federation. A report of the autumn meeting referred to here is also to be found in the same magazine. After the singing of various songs by Schreber Association choirs,

the Federation President [i.e. Siegel] welcomed the large gathering, particularly the large number of guests of honour, among whom were

also . . . the family of Dr. Schreber, paid warm tribute to Dr. Schreber's widow Pauline, who died on 14 May this year in her ninety-
first [actually ninety-second] year, after which he invited those present to stand in memory of Dr. Schreber and his noble wife, then
furnishing, from Dr. Schreber's writings and from the history of the
formation of the Schreber Associations, proof of the fact that the
Schreber Associations are not gardening clubs but parents' and educational societies [*ibid.*, pp. 264–265].

Siegel also referred to Moritz Schreber's descendants:

Misuse of the name "Schreber" is nowadays so widespread that
wherever allotments are established they are called Schreber gardens,
and the association of garden owners Schreber Associations, even
though in such circles no one ever thinks of the endeavors of Dr.
Schreber and Dr. Hauschild, let alone working in the spirit they
intended. Unfortunately we cannot prevent this misuse: only Dr.
Schreber's family might be able to do that; but so long as this misuse
exists, the true Schreber Associations—and this they owe to the
memory of Dr. Schreber and the dignity of the Schreber Associations—must make sharp distinction between genuine and false Schreber associations [Siegel, 1907f, p. 291].

Of those members of the Schreber family present, Paul Schreber, both
as a male descendant and as a lawyer, probably felt most directly
appealed to by Siegel's remarks about taking steps against "false"
Schreber Associations.[3] Why did Siegel want him to take resolute
action against such associations, which "up till a few months ago had
taken an interest in horticulture and animal breeding, but not in the
essential endeavors of a man like Schreber" (*ibid.*, p. 291), as he put
it? Another question: why was it that, as this observation clearly implies, in recent months such associations *had* taken an interest in Dr.
Schreber and his work? Most of all: why was it that, just when one
might have expected a favorable reaction, the *Freund der Schreber-
Vereine* came out so vehemently against these "false" Schreber Associations? (This campaign will be described in detail in the chapter
on the history of the Schreber Associations.)

The answer is that behind the question of which societies might
call themselves the true heirs to Dr. Schreber's spiritual legacy there
was a struggle for the very tangible legacy left by his widow. Leipzig
Schreber Associations which did not belong to Siegel's Federation,

and which had not been remembered with a legacy, protested against this to the heirs. Paul Schreber undertook to see to the matter on behalf of the heirs, and the other societies also received sums of money. This is the state of affairs as recorded in a "statement" drawn up by Schreber on 1 November 1907 after a text had come to his attention in which the Schreber Associations concerned had interpreted his references to the Federation rather more unfavorably than was strictly accurate.

"I must therefore object to the thoroughly partisan hue attributed to my statements" (D. P. Schreber, 1907b, p. 293). This highly correct and formal-sounding statement was printed in the December issue of the *Freund der Schreber-Vereine* (1907, pp. 292–293). By then he had again been admitted, for what was to be the rest of his life, to a psychiatric clinic.

NOTES TO CHAPTER 17

[1]In Paul Schreber's addresses outside Leipzig one might even be persuaded that one can see references to his parental home in Leipzig—in particular, to his father, the gymnastics ("turning") enthusiast Moritz Schreber. In Chemnitz Paul Schreber lived until 1890 in the Leipziger Strasse. In Freiberg (1889–93) he lived in the *Turnerstrasse*. And when he returned to his wife in Dresden in 1903, he moved to the *Moritzstrasse*. However, this final example is in itself a clear indication that the limits of healthy speculation have long since been exceeded: it was Sabine Schreber who moved to the *Moritzstrasse*, not her husband. He was at Sonnenstein.

[2]I am grateful to Herr R. Troitzsch for this information. I have not attempted to find this text, which is probably in the *Leipziger Tageblatt* or the *Leipziger Neueste Nachrichten*. However, I have learned from experience that a high degree of faith in information provided by Herr Troitzsch is not misplaced.

[3]The suggestion made to the Schreber family after the death of Pauline Schreber, that they ought to do something about allotment associations which illegitimately called themselves "Schreber Associations," would appear, some twenty years later, to have been projected back to Frau Schreber herself: "She would very much have liked to patent or copyright the name [i.e., "Schreberverein"], so that gardening clubs would not be able to use it if they were not engaged in educating the young" (Fritzsche, 1926, p. 14).

18

Paul Schreber's Third and Final Period of Illness (1907–11)

The events described at the close of the last chapter are open to interpretation along Schatzmanian lines: Paul Schreber is still being pursued by the shade of his father; the rival Schreber Associations would be bound to call upon the son to act in the spirit of his magnificent father, and Paul Schreber must have had the feeling that whatever he did, he would be getting it wrong—that he would never be able to satisfy all the associations; and the consequence was again a flight into insanity.

I do not know whether such an interpretation is sensible. Certainly, however, these quarrels about the inheritance were not the only, or even the most important, cause of his admission to the clinic on 27 November 1907. One of his sisters recorded the events of the preceding weeks in her brother's life: "Wife ill, 14 November. Apoplectic fit. Was speechless for four days. He immediately had sleepless nights, was very upset, felt that he would relapse, head the 'noises' again and more strongly. He now became quickly worse" (quoted by Baumeyer, 1956, p. 65).

And in 1954 his adopted daughter wrote of him:

At this time he was fully aware of his condition, a fact which was particularly evident when my mother [i.e., Schreber's wife] lost the power of speech for a while as the result of a slight stroke. He was extremely agitated and anxious and was in fear of again becoming ill as a result of his agitation. He therefore charged me, if he should tell me he was in danger, at once to inform the doctor that he should

211

without delay come and fetch him with an attendant, and take him first of all to his sisters in Leipzig. And that is what happened.

Paul Schreber spent the last three and a half years of his life in the clinic at Dösen, a suburb of Leipzig (see Figure 45). In 1968 his adopted daughter wrote: ''Mother and I visited him there twice. However, he would not let us come close to him because he was afraid we might be harmed if we did. Always full of consideration'' (unpublished letter).

The psychiatric reports on this third period of illness are still kept in the clinic archives. They have been published by Baumeyer (1956, pp. 65–67). Baumeyer did not mention that this case history also contains an envelope with eight notes written by Schreber during this period. Some two weeks after his readmission, for example, he wrote (Figure 46):

I am willing with a firm hand to sign a declaration which, as has in some manner become known to me, is to be required of me by the governing body set over the Dösen clinic, with regard to an intended special manner of burial in respect of me, and therefore request that I be shown, or be informed of the essential content of, an order made on that account. D. Schreber, *Senatspräsident*, retd.

Another note, which is undated, is more difficult to read: as Figure 47 shows, only some scraps of the text are decipherable:

Habe doch recht . . . war immer *ehrlich* . . . *rechtschaffen* . . . habe mit meinen Schwestern nicht sprechen können weil mir . . . sehe ein dass ich mit diesen . . . *unschuldig* ['Am right, after all . . . was always *honest* . . . *upright* . . . have been unable to speak to my sisters because I have been . . . realize that with these . . . I . . . *innocent*].

In later years hardly anything of these notes can be deciphered: see Figures 48 and 49, two notes of 13 November 1910. Some imaginative mind has succeeded in unravelling some of the scribbles to make *bin ewig verdammt* (am forever damned).

In the spring of 1911 Schreber's physical health began to decline. In a letter of 14 April a Leipzig doctor who examined him recorded in a note that a disease of the lungs was far advanced. ''The only measure which might be effective here would be an operation. How-

Fig. 45. Leipzig-Dösen. From *Deutsche Heil- und Pflegeanstalten*, 1910, facing page 464.

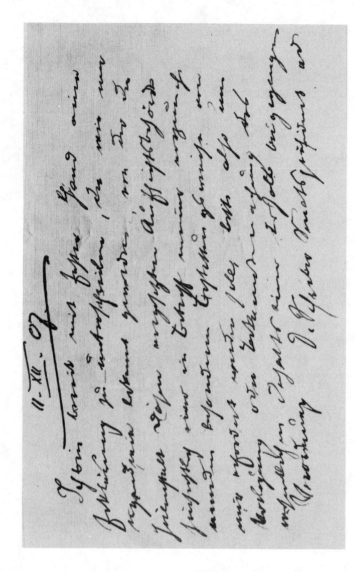

Fig. 46. Note written by Paul Schreber. Archives, Clinic Leipzig-Dösen.

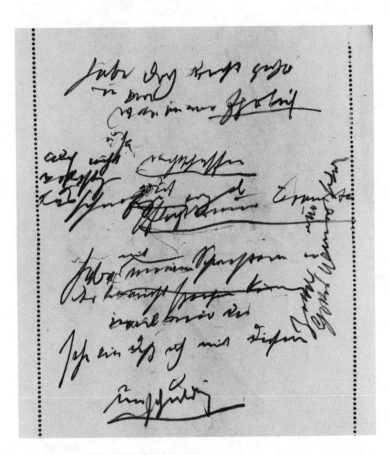

Fig. 47. Note written by Paul Schreber. Archives, Clinic Leipzig-Dösen.

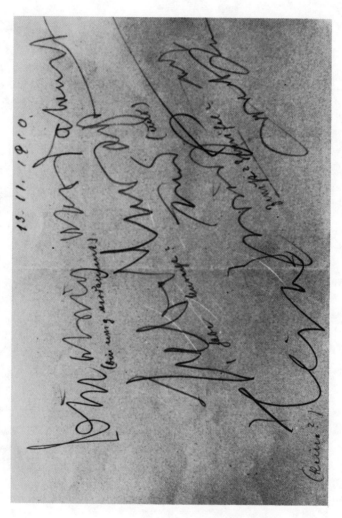

Fig. 48. Note written by Paul Schreber. Archives, Clinic Leipzig-Dösen.

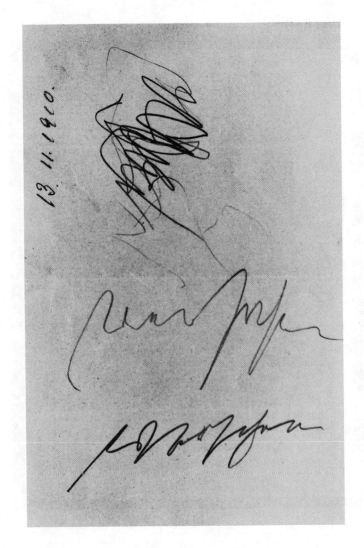

Fig. 49. Note written by Paul Schreber. Archives, Clinic Leipzig-Dösen.

Nachruf!

Am Karfreitag verschied in Dresden

Herr Dr. jur. Paul Schreber

Senatspräsident a. D. am Kgl. S. Oberlandesgericht

ein Sohn Dr. Moritz Schrebers, des Vaters der Schreber-
vereine.

Dem Sohn war es beschieden, die Saat seines Vaters
aufgehen und Frucht tragen zu sehen; er hat es erlebt, wie
sich die volksfreundlichen Ideen seines Vaters weiter und weiter
ausbreiteten und immer mehr realisierten.

Allzeit war der Verstorbene ein warmer Freund und
Förderer der echten Schrebervereinsbestrebungen. Dafür folgt
ihm unser Dank in die Ewigkeit nach. Sein Andenken sei
unter uns in Ehren!

Leipzig, den 19. April 1911.

Der Verband Leipziger Schrebervereine.

Fig. 50. From the *Freund der Schreber-Vereine*, 1911, page 65.

ever, in view of the patient's wretched condition I believe that that would be pointless, and that it may therefore be dismissed with a clear conscience'' (Rösler, 1911).

The same day, not in Dresden (Figure 50) but in the Dösen clinic, Paul Schreber died: ''14 April. Death with symptoms of dyspnoea and cardiac failure'' (quoted by Baumeyer, 1956, p. 67).

19

AFTER THE DEATH OF PAUL SCHREBER

In this final biographical chapter I shall give a brief account of what became of Paul Schreber's wife and his three sisters after his death.

1. SABINE SCHREBER: THE LAST YEAR OF HER LIFE (d. 1912)

On 10 May 1911 Sabine Schreber wrote to the ministry of justice informing them of her husband's death on 14 April and applying for a pension. This was granted her, amounting to 2258 marks per annum, something over a fifth of her husband's last salary ("Personalakte," fo. 39). On May 11 she fulfilled her statutory duty by taking her husband's Iron Cross, First Class, back to the *Ordenskanzlei* (chancellery for orders and decorations) in Dresden. About a year after this, in May 1912, she died.

2. KLARA (d. 1917) AND SIDONIE (d. 1924)

After the death of their mother in 1907 Klara and Sidonie continued to live at *Zeitzer Strasse* 43 until the house was demolished in 1915. In the chapter on the Schreber Associations (p. 269) I shall discuss contacts between Sidonie and Klara and the president of the Federation in about 1909. Here Klara displayed more initiative than her elder sister. The same impression is also gained from stories told by granddaughters of her sister Anna: it is known, for example, that she was something of a painter. The same granddaughters found it a puzzle to account for how their great-aunt Sidonie used to occupy her time.

After Klara's death in 1917 Sidonie's health deteriorated severely; she died in 1924.

3. ANNA JUNG (d. 1944)

Paul Schreber's eldest sister, Anna Jung, was a most remarkable person and not just for having reached the age of 103. However, her exceptional longevity does mean that there is a great deal of written material about her, quite apart from the fact, of course, that there are still many people alive today who knew her at first hand. In 1926 Hugo Fritzsche, Richard Siegel's successor as president of the Federation of Schreber Associations in Leipzig, published an informative article about Moritz Schreber based on conversations with Anna Jung. Gerhard Richter, who was president of the oldest Schreber Association in the years before the Second World War, visited her several times in the thirties to talk about her father; he wrote brief reports of these visits which have survived, and which I have drawn on repeatedly in preceding chapters. I have also found newspaper articles about her, written when she reached the ages of ninety-eight, ninety-nine, and one hundred (A. L., 1938; *Neue Leipziger Zeitung*, 1939; A. L., 1940; H. B., 1940). In addition, her descendants, realizing her exceptional stature as a person, kept texts by her.

The predominant character trait to emerge from all this material is her deep religious feeling. At ninety-eight she read St. Thomas Aquinas; a card she wrote to a grandson at the Russian front in 1943 consisted solely of religious passages.

The divinity who appeared to Paul Schreber during his illness has many characteristics in common with his father. With this in mind, it might also be interesting to consider Anna Jung's singular religiosity. At the same time, however, it is important to stress that she was in no way mentally disturbed: All who know her testified that right up to her death she was perfectly lucid, and everyone stressed her extremely forceful personality.

20

THE HISTORY OF THE SCHREBER FAMILY:

A BRIEF RECAPITULATION

It is my intention in this chapter to summarize the history of the Schreber family as I have told it. A summary of this kind is a perilous undertaking: how am I to decide what to include in and what to leave out? In the case of the Schrebers there is a further problem: in virtually every biography of Paul Schreber his life is described as a series of events all tending to predispose him to his mental illness. This is a tendency to which I do not intend to subscribe: I do not know whether his illness had social causes at all, let alone what those causes may have been. I am apprehensive, however, that my lengthy biography of the Schreber family may be too long for many readers who are not interested in all the details. And however problematical I may find the job of writing a summary, I nevertheless believe that I can offfer a better short biography than has been available hitherto.

Then again, the problem of selection when preparing a summary must not be exaggerated. In most cases it is possible to condense a multitude of details into a single common denominator. In this way, for example, I shall write that Moritz Schreber played an important part in the Leipzig *Turnverein*. The reader wishing to know the details of his part therein may turn to the section dealing particularly with that aspect of Schreber history. This chapter may thus be used as a narrative table of contents for the preceding nineteen chapters. The numbering in this chapter corresponds to that of the preceding chapters, generally followed by the section number.

1. The Schreber family knew their genealogy back as far as the

seventeenth century. It is one of which a family might well be proud: the Schrebers belonged to the uppermost stratum of the bourgoisie of the kingdom of Saxony. (1.1.) Moritz Schreber's grandfather, for example, was a professor. (1.2.) His father did not quite come up to family expectations: Only late in life did he establish himself as an independent advocate, and he married late. He left an autobiography in which he bemoaned his many physical complaints.

2.1. Moritz Schreber was born in 1808. In 1812 a brother followed but died four years later. In 1813 Leipzig witnessed the battle against Napoleon; typhoid fever also broke out; there was also a death in the Schreber household. (2.2.) From 1826 until 1831 Moritz Schreber studied medicine in Leipzig, receiving financial support for his studies from various quarters. In 1833 he took his doctorate, for which he wrote a curriculum vitae. (2.3.) For some years after this he was personal physician to a travelling Russian nobleman. (2.4.) From 1836 he was a general practitioner and *Privatdozent* in Leipzig.

3.1. In 1838 he married Pauline Haase. She was born in 1815, daughter of a rich and prominent family. As a professor of medicine her father had taught Moritz Schreber. In the long run Moritz Schreber probably failed to come up to his wife's social expectations. (3.2.) Over the next few years the family expanded: Gustav was born in 1839, Anna in 1840, Paul in 1842, Sidonie in 1844, and Klara in 1848. Pauline Schreber's mother died in 1841; this probably meant a considerable legacy for the Schrebers. It also meant that Pauline's youngest sister Fanny Haase went to live with them.

4.1. From 1844 on Moritz Schreber was head of an orthopedic clinic. (4.2.) From 1847 the clinic was housed in a building built by Moritz Schreber at the edge of Leipzig at a spot which later became part of the *Zeitzer Strasse*. Until it was demolished in 1915, this house remained the focal point of the Schreber family. (4.3.) Moritz Schreber was a keen gymnast from his undergraduate days onwards; in 1843 he published a book propagandizing gymnastics and in 1845 he was a founding member of the Leipzig *Turnverein* (gymnastic club); until 1851 he fulfilled various functions in the club. (4.4.) He also held various public offices, including that of city councillor. Politically he was probably a moderate left-winger and pro-Prussian. As a member of the *Communalgarde* (civil guard) he was concerned with rioting in 1848; three years previously Leipzig had witnessed more serious unrest, in which anti-Catholic sentiments played a major part. (4.5.) A large family portrait of the Schrebers, painted in 1851 by August

Richter, is still in existence. In 1851 the artist was a patient at the Sonnenstein psychiatric clinic, at which Paul Schreber was later to write his *Memoirs*.

5. In 1851 a ladder fell on Moritz Schreber's head. Some months after this he began to suffer from a "head complaint" which was to trouble him for the next ten years until his death.

6.1. The family life of the Schrebers has led to the writing of two sorts of literature: idealizing accounts by authors connected with the Schreber Associations named after Moritz Schreber, and "demonizing" accounts in modern psychiatric writing. (6.2.) Paul Schreber's sisters on more than one occasion described family life in their youth to officers of various Schreber Associations: much physical exercise, a somewhat ascetic life-style, and a father who often, sometimes for long periods, refused to see his children on account of his head complaint. (6.3.) Accounts of Schreber family life by the psychoanalyst M. Katan cannot be taken seriously. Niederland, Schatzman, and others, drawing on Schreber's educational publications, paint him as a domestic tyrant. The supposition underlying this, that to Moritz Schreber theory and practice lay close together, is not implausible. In much psychiatric literature Pauline Schreber is portrayed as her husband's will-less victim; this picture of her is not founded on accurate information.

7.1. The inpatients at the orthopedic clinic—between five and seven boys and girls aged between ten and eighteen—lived more or less with the Schreber children. (7.2.) The most common complaint treated by Moritz Schreber in his clinic was malformation of the spine. (7.3.) In 1859 he sold the clinic to C. H. Schildbach. Thereafter they were officially in joint control of the clinic's administration.

8.1. From 1857 until 1860 Moritz Schreber's elder son Gustav read natural science at Leipzig, Göttingen, and Heidelberg. In 1861 he took a doctorate in philosophy at Leipzig. (8.2.) At the same time Moritz Schreber was concentrating more on his educational mission in life. An ambitious plan to distribute on a national scale an educational book he had written met with little success. (8.3.) Moritz Schreber died suddenly in 1861 of appendicitis.

9.3. Paul Schreber studied law at Leipzig from 1860 until 1863. He held various offices in the pro-Prussian *Burschenschaft* (a kind of student society), initially called "Wartburg," and later, "Germania." This *Burschenschaft* was involved in repeated quarrels with the "Corps Saxonia" of Leipzig. (9.4.) Sidonie, remaining a spinster, continued to live with her mother in the *Zeitzer Strasse,* as did Klara until her marriage at the age of forty.

10.1. In 1865 Paul Schreber embarked upon a sucessful career in the judiciary of Saxony which may be followed exactly in the 'Personalakte' (personal file) kept on him at the Saxon ministry of justice. Initially he worked in Chemnitz (modern Karl-Marx-Stadt), Leipzig, and Meissen. In 1869 he took a doctorate in law. During and after the war of 1870–71 he worked in Alsace, after which he returned to Leipzig; whenever he was there, he lived with his mother. (10.2.) In 1864 his eldest sister Anna married the Leipzig factory owner Carl Jung. The Jung family, from 1871 on, also lived in the *Zeitzer Strasse.* (10.3.) In 1866 Gustav Schreber had a chemicals factory in Leipzig. From 1867 until 1869 he read law at Leipzig, then beginning a career similar to his younger brother's. For most of the time, Gustav was posted in Leipzig, where he lived with his mother. There is evidence that toward the end of his life he had contact with Bismarck. In 1877 he shot himself.

11.1. A year after Gustav's suicide, in 1878, Paul Schreber, then thirty-five years of age, married Sabine Behr. She was fifteen years younger than he, was the daughter of a stage director, and was never really accepted by the Schreber family. The marriage remained child-less, Sabine suffering six miscarriages. (11.2.) In 1878 and 1879 Paul Schreber worked in Berlin on the integration of the Saxon judiciary into the national legal system. He was then appointed to an important position in the regional court at Chemnitz. In 1888 his sister Klara married Theodor Krause, who worked at the same court.

12.1. In 1884 Paul Schreber stood for the *Reichstag* as a candidate for the National Liberal and Conservative Parties. He supported Bismarck's policies. As expected, the seat was won by a socialist candidate. (12.2.) Shortly afterward Paul Schreber was admitted to the psychiatric clinic in Leipzig for six months.

13. He then resumed his legal career in Leipzig, Freiberg, and finally Dresden. A poem he wrote during this period for his sister Anna's silver wedding anniversary has survived.

14.1. Paul Schreber's second illness, which lasted from 1893 until 1902, is described in detail in his *Memoirs.* (14.2.) Additional material on this period has been published by Baumeyer: It includes psychiatric reports in which his father Moritz Schreber is described as someone who "suffered from obsessional ideas with homicidal tendencies," his mother as nervous and having quick changes of mood, and one of his sisters as "hysterical." When considering these character-sketches, it should be borne in mind that they may be based on accounts originally given by the sick Paul Schreber himself. During these years in the Sonnenstein clinic Paul Schreber was visited regularly by his sister Sidonie; his mother did not visit him there until 1901.

15. During his last years at Sonnenstein Paul Schreber worked at his *Denkwürdigkeiten eines Nervenkranken* (Memoirs of my Nervous Illness); this book appeared shortly after he was released from the clinic following legal proceedings which he conducted himself. Most of the copies were bought up by the family; nevertheless, reviews soon appeared in the psychiatric press.

16.1. After his release Paul Schreber, then sixty, went first to live with his mother. He paid official "introductory visits" to other members of the family and returned to his wife in Dresden in 1903. In the meantime she had taken a young girl into her home who was later adopted by the couple. (16.2.) Various writings by Paul Schreber survive from this period, including a christening speech and a poem for his wife. Most interesting is a long poem about the life of his mother, written for her ninetieth birthday in 1905. None of these texts contains anything reminiscent of delusions. (16.3.) In 1905 the house which Paul Schreber had caused to be built was completed. It still stands, and has some curious architectural details such as a bar of music over the front door: This is a theme from Wagner's *Siegfried*. (16.4.) Many family photographs have also been preserved from this period. Of these many show Paul Schreber as a somewhat corpulent, kindly, and thoughtful-looking man with a moustache.

17.1. Paul Schreber's mother remained active to a great age. Among other things she was an honorary member of the first Schreber Association. The president of the Leipzig Schreber Associations spoke at the graveside at her funeral in 1907. (17.2.) In her will she left money to some of the Schreber Associations, a provision which led to conflicts with associations which had not been remembered in this way. As the representative of the heirs, Paul Schreber stood at the focus of these quarrels.

18. While the matter of the inheritance was still unresolved, his wife suffered a slight stroke. This was followed a few days later by the onset of Paul Schreber's third period of illness. He spent the last four years of his life in the clinic in Dösen, a Leipzig suburb. Notes written by him there show how his handwriting gradually became totally illegible. He died in 1911.

19.1. A year later his wife died. (19.2.) His sister Klara, who displayed something of a talent for painting, died in 1917, Sidonie in 1924. (19.3.) The eldest sister, the deeply religious Anna, lived to be 103, dying in 1944.

PART II

THE REPUTATION
OF
MORITZ SCHREBER

21

MORITZ SCHREBER'S "ORDINARY" REPUTATION

Moritz Schreber is chiefly known on account of the allotment gardens which he never founded and through the writings of American psychiatrists about his mentally ill son. Both types of sources will provide subjects for subsequent chapters in this second part of my study, but this first chapter will be concerned with the reputation that Moritz Schreber acquired by reason of his own, ordinary work—that is, the reputation which he gained independently of the allotments and the work of later psychiatrists.

This "ordinary" reputation cannot always be divorced entirely from the fame which he acquired through the Schreber Associations and the Schreber gardens: through them his name remained in the public eye, and this undoubtedly helped to increase the sales of his books. Nevertheless, it can be considered separately from the reputation he since gained through the writings of psychiatrists: His psychiatric reputation was not founded until long after his "ordinary" reputation was dead and buried.

In what I call the "allotment" literature, and to an even greater degree in the psychiatric literature, Moritz Schreber's "ordinary" reputation was always grossly exaggerated. This exaggeration has formed part of the basis upon which theories have been founded. Thus the psychiatrist Morton Schatzman believes that the God by whom Paul Schreber thought he was being persecuted was in fact his father. The question is then: Why did Paul Schreber transform his father into God? According to Schatzman, Moritz Schreber was, in his day, quite widely deified: "The views of a large network of people may have influenced the operation whereby he substituted God for father. But why did they esteem the father so highly?'' (1973a, p. 142). To answer this question, Schatzman took an obituary of Moritz Schreber (Politzer, 1862), the only one known to him. He correctly quoted this piece as saying that Moritz Schreber's books "went through many editions and translations in almost all languages in a short time" (Politzer, 1862, quoted in Schatzman, 1973a, p. 142). But this obituary by Politzer, written in distant Vienna, is far from reliable. When Politzer wrote it there was as yet no question of there being "many editions": Of the sixteen books which he mentioned, fourteen had not gone beyond their first edition. The fifteenth had seen a second edition twenty-two years after its first appearance. It is also nonsense to talk of "translations in almost all languages": only *Zimmergymnastik* had been translated extensively; otherwise the only translations of Moritz Schreber's books were a number in Dutch.

    Moritz Schreber's supposed fame is also a constituent of a macrosociological theory which Schatzman formed, viz., that Moritz Schreber's educational ideas had much in common with Nazism: *"Remember:* Hitler and his peers were raised when Dr. Schreber's books, preaching household totalitarianism, were popular" *(ibid.,* p. 151). Schatzman's most important theoretical opponent, the psychoanalyst Niederland, tried to refute this assertion as follows:

> Superficially and chronologically speaking, this may appear accurate, but it is not. Franklin Delano Roosevelt, Winston Churchill, Lloyd George, Bertrand Russell and Harry Truman were also reared when Dr. Schreber's writings—published in translation and numerous editions in America and England—were popular in the latter countries [Niederland, 1972, p. 83].

Here, however, Niederland suggested something that is simply not true: No educational work by Moritz Schreber was ever translated into English. But also Schatzman's assertion itself shows that it is important to examine Moritz Schreber's "ordinary" reputation: Schreber's educational work in fact had relatively little influence.

    This is not to say that in his lifetime Moritz Schreber was a totally obscure figure: If that were so, I should be unable to devote an entire chapter to his "ordinary" reputation. On the other hand, it is a relatively short chapter. Then again, I have almost certainly not found everything that Moritz Schreber ever wrote, nor everything that was ever written about him or his work, and that naturally helps to make this chapter a short one. To give one example of my ignorance: there is a very short book by him in Swedish, an *"Öfversättning"* published in 1845, but I am unable to say of which text this is a translation.

In the following sections I shall examine the several fields in which Moritz Schreber was active.

1. ORTHOPEDICS AND REMEDIAL GYMNASTICS

Moritz Schreber was not a particularly important orthopedist. There is only one competent author who has repeatedly referred to Moritz Schreber's great significance in orthopedics, and that is C. H. Schildbach—not the most disinterested observer in view of the fact that he was Schreber's successor as director of the orthopedic clinic (Schildbach, 1864, p. 3; 1867, p. 98; 1872, p. v; 1877, p. ix). Elsewhere in the orthopedic literature, his opinions in this regard are not shared. In his *Geschichte der Orthopädie* (History of orthopedics) Valentin devoted a bibliographically excellent passage to Moritz Schreber. In it he dismissed Schreber's only truly orthopedic book as "a popular tome" (1961, p. 246); he was interested in Schreber only as the director of a clinic with a long tradition. For with a little goodwill it is possible to see the orthopedic clinic of the University of Leipzig as the continuation of Schreber's clinic. This is also why a *Festschrift* of that clinic (Loeffler, 1955, p. 8) referred to Moritz Schreber. Moreover, a doctor from the clinic, P. Uibe, wrote on Moritz Schreber as an orthopedist (Kilian and Uibe, 1958; Uibe, 1959). Dr. Uibe wrote to me that ". . . I also made Schreber the subject of my speech when I was chairman of the annual congress of the *Medizinisch-wissenschaftliche Gesellschaft für Orthopädie der DDR* [the GDR's society of orthopedics] in 1972." Uibe told me that he drew attention to Moritz Schreber because although everyone is familiar with the name because of the allotments, very few people know that he was in fact an orthopedist.

The "allotment literature" on Moritz Schreber is full of remarks about his great importance for orthopedics and remedial gymnastics: "pioneering innovations" and "world renown" (Brauchle, 1937, p. 243) or "Founder of remedial gymnastics" (G. Richter, 1925, p. 7). I could go on, but instead I shall confine myself to just one lengthy example which is a nice illustration of how authors of this kind go about their work.

In the *Illustrierte Zeitung* we read, on the subject of Moritz Schreber's orthopedic clinic:

> Anything that was superfluous and all the instruments of torture that used to be common in such clinics were thrown out, and at the earliest opportunity; but so simple as, for example, the contrivance for countering lateral deformation of the spine is, which he introduced and which is still commonly used in his clinic, so excellently has it proved itself [1862, p. 81].

I have been unable to discover to which orthopedic instrument this is a reference, but it is quite possible that Moritz Schreber introduced a device to cure sideways deformation of the spine and that it was still perfectly satisfactory in 1862. It was probably this passage which led Mangner, fifteen years later, to write: "All the instruments of torture that used to be common in such clinics were thrown out, the simple device which he introduced to counter lateral deformation of the spine is still perfectly satisfactory today" (1877, p. 6). The assertion that a particular piece of equipment is "still" perfectly satisfactory ought not, of course, to be repeated fifteen years later: All that can be said is that it was still perfectly satisfactory fifteen years ago—unless, of course, one has further information at one's disposal. But certainly neither Mangner nor anyone after him ever knew which piece of equipment was the subject of the passage in the *Illustrierte Zeitung:* yet a whole tradition has grown up around it; and all the time it is "still" perfectly satisfactory. Seven years later, for example, Mangner wrote, "Even today the device he invented for lateral deformation of the spine is still the best" (1884, p. 13). Twelve years after this, Mittenzwey wrote: "All the instruments of torture that used to be common in such clinics were thrown out; the simple device which he introduced to counter lateral deformation of the spine is today still considered the best (1896, p. 45). At the beginning of this century Fritzsche wrote: "All the instruments of torture that used to be used by orthopedists disappeared from his clinic; instead he invented, for example, a device to counter lateral deformation of the spine which is still extremely valuable today" (1903, p. 3 = 1911, p. 180).

Another ten years, and Gerhard Richter was writing, "The instruments of torture formerly used by orthopedists disappeared from his clinic. A device invented by Schreber to counter lateral deformation of the spine is still extremely valuable today" (1914a, p. 6 = 1925, p. 7). According to Hänsch, Moritz Schreber tried in his clinic to replace the various instruments of torture hitherto used in orthopaedics with rational appliances. Thus, for example, a 'device introduced by him to counter lateral deformation of the spine' is still considered the best even today [1925, p. 289].

A decade later Ritter introduced a new element:

. . . All the instruments of torture that used to be used by orthopedists disappeared from his clinic; instead he invented, for example, a device to counter lateral deformation of the spine which is still extremely valuable today [1936a, pp. 16–17].

Ritter claimed that this is a quotation from *"Deutsche Turnerzeitung 1862*, Nr. 7 (Leipzig, Keil-Verlag): 'Dr. Schildbach über Schreber.' " In fact the periodical is called, not *Turnerzeitung,* but *Turnzeitung;* in addition, the passage quoted appears nowhere in the article by Schildbach. Presumably Ritter reconstructed his "quotation" from what Fritzsche had written thirty years or so previously. Through Ritter, however, Schildbach acquired a place in this kind of literature:

In the Deutsche Turnerzeitung Dr. *Schildbach* wrote . . . : "All the instruments of torture that used to be used by orthopedists disappeared from his clinic; instead he invented, for example, a device to counter lateral deformation of the spine which is still extremely valuable today . . ." [Schütze, 1936, p. 1889].

Thus Schütze quoted not Schildbach but Ritter.

Dr. Schildbach reports: "All the instruments of murder that used to be used by orthopedists disappeared from his clinic; instead he invented, for example, a device to counter lateral deformation of the spine which is still extremely valuable today" [Brauchle, 1937, pp. 246–247].

So Brauchle too quoted not Schildbach but Ritter, with the sole exception of the instruments of torture, which have now evolved into instruments of murder.

"The instruments of torture formerly used by orthopedists disappeared from Schreber's clinic. . . . A device invented by Schreber to counter lateral deformation of the spine is still extremely valuable today" (G. Richter, 1939b, p. 17). This one contraption then multiplies: "The exercise and appliances developed by him for the purpose, which replaced the 'instruments of torture' employed by earlier orthopedists, are still extremely valuable today" (Gmelin, 1961, p. 341). This device of Schreber's invention is likely to continue to "be extremely valuable" in the future—perhaps in a fifth edition of Brauchle's book of 1937? Certainly the fourth edition, published in 1971, still asserts that: "All the instruments that used to be used by orthopedists disappeared from his clinic; instead he invented, for example, a device to counter lateral deformation of the spine which is still extremely valuable today" (Brauchle, 1971, p. 74).

The attentive reader will have noticed that the "instruments of murder" of 1937 have now become simply "instruments"—even though this 1971 version is still supposed to be a quotation (from Schildbach, according to Brauchle, but, as we have seen, in reality from Ritter). As time passes, the Schreber expert will be called upon to exert greater and greater effort to create some order out of the increasingly complex conglomerations of a little truth, many errors in quotation, and much lazy thinking which go to make up such passages.

2. MORITZ SCHREBER'S PUBLIC LIFE

Moritz Schreber was a prominent member of Leipzig society not solely as the director of an orthopedic clinic but also, from 1846 until 1851, as a member of the city council, and by virtue of the important part he played in the large Leipzig *Turnverein* or gymnastics club: as one of the founders, a member of the committee, and a public speaker. Not surprisingly, then, his name appeared in the history of gymnastics in Leipzig (Gasch, 1896, pp. 50–51; *Festschrift*, 1895, pp. 2–11; Striegler, 1904, p. 93); he is even mentioned in the occasional general work about gymnastics (Euler, 1895, pp. 504–505; Rühl, 1901, pp. 224–225; Gasch, 1920, p. 605, 1928, pp. 176–177). His name also appeared in connection with the two other founders of the Leipzig *Turnverein,* Professor Biedermann (1886, p. 209, and 1896, pp. 34–35) and Bock (H. E. Richter, 1863, p. 487). Three papers about Moritz Schreber in final examinations at the Leipzig sports college would doubtless not have been written if the word *Schrebergarten* had not existed; they may therefore be disregarded here (Bernhardt, 1929; Finke, 1975, Juhnke, 1975). On the national scale Schreber's sporting activities were not in fact of great importance, even though the literature is not devoid of such highly exaggerated assertions as this:

Schreber's services to the development, application and propagation of German gymnastics were so considerable that he has rightly been described as the apostle of the noble art of gymnastics and the champion of German, and particularly Leipzig gymnastics [Mangner, 1884, p. 13; also quoted in G. Richter, 1925, p. 7].

3. NEWSPAPERS AND PERIODICALS

I have found two periodicals with which Moritz Schreber was closely connected, viz., the *Jahrbuch für Kinderheilkunde und physische Erziehung* (Pediatrics and physical education yearbook) and the *Neue Jahrbücher für die Turnkunst* (New gymnastics annuals). The *Jahrbuch für Kinderheilkunde* is a medical journal published in Vienna. Each volume ends with a survey of achievements in the field during the past year. From 1858 until 1861 these included references to Moritz Schreber as "working tirelessly." This is a special reference to his articles for the *Jahrbuch* itself, e.g., one of the benefits of sunbathing (under glass) for children (1858b). The same journal contains summaries and reviews of books by Schreber,[1] and in 1862 it carried an obituary by L. M. Politzer which is exceedingly full of praise.

Politzer's exaggerated encomiums have also found their way into the psychiatric literature: I have already mentioned, for example, his demonstrably inaccurate remark concerning the many translations and editions of Moritz Schreber's books (see p. 232). They are also quoted in places in the allotment literature: Below (pp. 264–267) we shall also see that Freud must have seen them. Politzer called Schreber the "father of remedial gymnastics," placing him among the ranks of "martyrs" and "heroes"; he also wrote: "What the German nation and mankind at large have lost in him has been proclaimed to the world in eloquent words in every class of journal" (1862, p. 1). Whether it is Politzer who is ignorant here or I, I cannot say. All I can say is that the journals in which I myself have found obituaries of Moritz Schreber are mostly medical and gymnastics journals.

The other periodical with which Schreber had close ties, the *Neue Jahrbücher für die Turnkunst*, was published in Dresden by M. Kloss. From its beginning until his death Schreber was a member of the editorial board, also often writing for the journal (e.g., "Macht nicht das Turnen grosse Hände?"—Does gymnastics give you big hands? [1857a]). It also carried reviews of his books.[2] And in 1861 and 1862 no fewer than three obituaries of him appeared, plus a full-page portrait.

The first was published at the end of 1861—a short piece by E. Friedrich—and a further two memorial articles appeared early in the following year. The first of these, by Kloss himself, is interesting chiefly
because it included an autobiographical note of sixty lines by Schreber
himself. Kloss's piece was followed by one of Schreber's associate
and successor Schildbach, who kept it short, having already promised
a proper obituary to another periodical, the *Deutsche Turnzeitung*.

Moritz Schreber himself never published in the *Deutsche Turn-
zeitung*, though it does contain reviews of his works.[3] These reviews—like all reviews of Schreber's work—are largely favorable.
However, I shall mention here one critical observation concerning his
chief work, *Kallipädie*. Over a century later, psychiatrists were writing
about this work in such phrases as: "The absolute conviction with
which Schreber's father upheld his central ideas, the unquestioning
fanaticism with which he pursued his messianic health goals" (Kohut,
1971, p. 256). This passage is all the more regrettable because Kohut
had probably never even seen the book.[4] But something of the same
kind of criticism seemed to be implied in the *Deutsche Turnzeitung*
when a reviewer observed that in *Kallipädie* the "didacticism . . .
occasionally impinges more categorically" than necessary: "but as we
all know, in everything they are consulted about, doctors have the
privilege of behaving slightly dictatorially" (Lion, 1857, p. 112).

At the end of 1861 (p. 249) the *Deutsche Turnzeitung* carried a
brief, black-bordered text about Schreber's death, and early in 1862
it published the obituary by Schildbach referred to above.

Moritz Schreber's activities are reflected, not solely by periodicals
specializing in his own fields, but also by some more general, though
more local, publications. In 1845 the *Leipziger Tageblatt* printed a
message from his booklet about gymnastics, and the paper also has
references to him as a city councillor. It published an obituary notice
(J., 1861) consisting chiefly of a list of his books. I do not know if
Moritz Schreber himself ever published anything in the Leipzig *Illustrierte Zeitung*, but it did carry reviews—brief and favorable—of books
by him, and an informative obituary. The *Illustrierte Zeitung* may be
characterized as the small and more sedate counterpart of the then
exceedingly successful family magazine *Die Gartenlaube* (The summerhouse), which was also published in Leipzig. Two articles by
Moritz Schreber appeared in *Die Gartenlaube:* too few for him to
achieve the nationwide celebrity which Professor Bock was to enjoy
as its regular correspondent on medical matters.

The last obituary of Moritz Schreber that I have found appears in the *Mittheilungen der allgemeinen Bürgerschule zu Leipzig,* a school bulletin (Vogel, 1861). The editor, the school's headmaster Dr. Vogel, devoted almost an entire issue to Schreber in December 1861. Vogel knew Schreber personally; doubtless Schreber's name appeared quite often in the school magazine. Unfortunately I have been unable to trace any other issues of the *Mittheilungen.*

I suspect that these pages on Moritz Schreber's role in newspapers and periodicals contain some of the least well-informed passages in this entire study.[5] This is chiefly because existing literature on the Schrebers tells us next to nothing in this regard. Reviews of Schreber's work have never previously been mentioned in the literature, and virtually the only article by him to be mentioned by other writers is *"Die Jugendspiele,"* an article which its author managed to place in three different periodicals: *Die Gartenlaube,* the *Jahrbuch für Kinderheilkunde,* and *Die Erziehung der Gegenwart.* This last, an educational magazine, was published in Berlin and edited by K. Schmidt, a man who was later to write a bulky history of education in which, however, there is no mention of Moritz Schreber (Schmidt, 1867). This article on children's playgrounds was later reprinted many times in the allotment literature, where it is mentioned so often that one gains the impression that it must have been Schreber's most important and influential work. In it he argued for the establishing of children's playgrounds by local authorities. It is the only argument in Schreber's voluminous oeuvre that can legitimately, with a little goodwill, be linked with the later Schreber Associations, whose allotment gardens were grouped around a playground. This explains why the article was later to be referred to so often. But if the allotment literature claims that the article had a great deal of influence, this is open to doubt. By far its widest circulation was in *Die Gartenlaube,* and most authors who claimed it to be influential did not even know when it was published, citing the year incorrectly (see also note 2 to chapter 8).

4. BOOKS

Where later literature tells us that Moritz Schreber had great influence, it is assumed that that influence was exercised chiefly through his books, "mid-nineteenth century best sellers" (Bregman, 1977, p. 124). Similar claims, unfortunately, were also made by writers who certainly should have known better. Ritter, for example, in his thesis on Schreber cried rhetorically: "Have not many of his writings been printed in downright unbelievable numbers?" (1936a, p. 92). The answer is no. Only one of Moritz Schreber's books was a best-seller, namely *Ärztliche Zimmergymnastik (Medical indoor gymnastics)* (1855a).

Schreber's Indoor Gymnastics

When *Indoor Gymnastics* first went to the press, Moritz Schreber bore part of the financial risk.[6] This does not argue strongly for the success of the eight books which preceded it. However, *Indoor Gymnastics* sold like hot cakes: in all, some three hundred thousand copies must have been printed.[7] For those days this is a very large number (cf. Engelsing, 1973, p. 120), even though it is only a fraction of the number reached by a book on the same subject written fifty years later by the Dane J. P. Müller. The figures for that work can be compared only with those for books like F. E. Bilz's tome on natural healing of 1888: Both works went to several million copies, if we are to believe the figures given in the books themselves (see Müller [1906, p. 5] and Bilz [1927–28, vol. ii, titlepage]). I mention Bilz's book because under the heading "remedial gymnastics" it contains several dozen pages based on *Indoor Gymnastics,* "a book to be warmly recommended" (Bilz, 1895, p. 473).[8] There are several other books which contain passages from *Indoor Gymnastics.* These vary from some twenty pages in a respectable work such as Hirth, *Das gesammte Turnwesen* (1865), through two little volumes by Kochendorf (selections from *Indoor Gymnastics:* one volume of lung exercises and one of exercises to relieve nervousness), to L. Wulff, who in 1929 brought out at his own expense a little book entitled *Was können Schreber's Zimmergymnas-tick-Übungen, auch teils abgeändert, für Alte, Schwache und Kranke leisten?* (What can Schreber's indoor gymnastics exercises, including modifications thereof, do for the old, weak and ill?)—a work which is perhaps best characterized by means of a quotation concerning an arm-swinging exercise calculated to promote healthy bowel movements: "I owe this exercise complete success if I use it sitting during the movement itself, placing my feet sideways so as not to fall over" (Wulff, 1929, p. 8).

The books on child-rearing

Moritz Schreber published three books about bringing up children. The first, published in 1852, had only one printing. At this time a first

impression would normally be fewer than a thousand copies (Engelsing, 1973, pp. 120–121). Schreber's other two books on the subject,
Kallipädie (1858a) and *Der Hausfreund* (1861a), each ran to four
impressions in the course of four decades. This long period can probably be explained by the fact that Schreber only very gradually came
to be known to the public as a result of the associations and allotments
named after him. For example, *Kallipädie* started off very quietly. The
book was also very expensive: over three thalers, more than three times
the weekly wages of the Leipzig carpenter's mate referred to above
(Saalfeld, 1974, p. 421). When the book was revamped for a second
edition in 1882, "it had almost been forgotten," according to the
reviser (Hennig, 1882, p. ix).

Translations

In Holland, the success of Moritz Schreber's books was at first
scarcely less than that which they enjoyed in Germany. The first educational booklet, only one edition of which ever appeared in Germany,
was published in three Dutch translations (1853b, 1857b, and 1864),
with titles such as "Our children. Their bad habits and injurious pos-
tures." The influence of Schreber's books in Holland is also clear from
the catalogue which the pedagogical library of the Netherlands Society
of Teachers published in 1891 (Catalogues, 1891): Of the two thousand
or so authors listed there, only seventeen are represented by more titles
than Moritz Schreber.

My assertion that Moritz Schreber's last two books on child-
rearing would not have been reprinted so often over a period of several
decades if his name had not become something of a household word
on account of the Schreber Associations and the Schreber allotments
is confirmed by the subsequent course of his reception in Holland:
Here his success was not prolonged by Schreber neologisms, and the
last Dutch translation of his work—apart from *Indoor Gymnastics*,
which was a big sales success in translation as in the original—appeared
as early as 1864.

Indoor Gymnastics appeared in at least seven translations. Schreber's second book on gymnastics, the *Pangymnastikon* (1862a), was
also translated. As part of an American compilation, indeed, this work
was reprinted at least twenty-five times, namely in D. Lewis, *The new
gymnastics for men, women, and children. With a translation of Prof.
Kloss's Dumb-bell instructor and Prof. Schreber's Pangymnastikon,*

which first came out in 1862. But, as I have said, none of Schreber's works on *education* was ever translated into English.

Other books

We have now looked at *Indoor Gymnastics* and the three books on education. All Schreber's other books were printed only once or twice and may therefore be assumed not to have made much of an impression.

5. APPLIANCES

Anybody familiar with the modern psychiatric literature about father and son Schreber is likely to think first, on hearing the name Moritz Schreber, of his remarkable child-rearing contrivances. These are not merely one of the constituents of the strongest parallels between Paul Schreber's education and his madness: They are in themselves so curious that it is worth the effort to try to discover how widely they were used.

Apart from the "straightener" (Geradehalter) the position is simple: I know of no reference to the other devices beyond the context of "the Schreber case." Similar educational devices are almost equally rare.[9] Seeking Schreber's appliances, one naturally thinks of the Victorian contrivances for preventing masturbation: contrivances which are eagerly discussed in modern stories of the "horrors" of those times, but which are totally absent from anything connected with Moritz Schreber.[10]

The "straightener"

The situation is more complicated when it comes to the *Geradehalter,* the iron bar fixed to the table in front of a child to prevent it from leaning forward while writing. This is the only device about which Schreber tells us where it is to be bought: in Leipzig. The readers of the Dutch translation had to be content with the address in Leipzig. Even so the fame of the "straightener" did penetrate as far as Holland[11]; witness the following passage on the correct posture for writing: "Successful use is being made by educationalists and others, both in Germany and here, of a simple piece of equipment known by the name of straightener" (Lubach and Coronel, 1870, p. 145).

On one occasion when I was leafing through my paper of 1977 on Moritz Schreber with a lady born in Leipzig in 1909, the picture of the *Geradehalter* elicited a shock of recognition. She had not herself had actual experience of the thing, but she had been threatened with its introduction if she did not sit up straight when writing. According to the East Germans Uibe (Kilian and Uibe, 1958, p. 339) and Kilian (1958a), contraptions designed by Moritz Schreber such as the *Geradehalter* "have now celebrated their resurrection." However, a Leipzig orthopedist assured me that this is certainly no longer the case.

In Schreber's own day and afterward whole libraries were written about one "contrivance," namely the school bench (Baginsky, 1883, p. 253). This literature also contains an occasional reference to Schreber's "straightener." In every case, however, the reference is made in passing (Eulenberg and Bach, 1891, p. 228) or is disparaging: Buchner considered "that these straighteners do not help at all, but can only do harm" (1869, p. 9); Baginsky wrote that the device "gives rise to pain when used for longer periods" (1883, pp. 264–265), and Fahrner wondered whether it is necessary "to harness children with bridle and bit in this way, for that is what the straightener involuntarily reminds me of" (1865, p. 14). Not surprisingly, in later editions of *Kallipädie* the reviser, Carl Hennig, made considerable changes in the "straightener" (D. G. M. Schreber, 1891, pp. 155–157).

6. MORITZ SCHREBER'S PLACE IN THE HISTORY OF EDUCATION

The reader who is in any degree familiar with modern literature about the Schrebers will probably be somewhat surprised, when reading this chapter, at the slight influence which I ascribe to Moritz Schreber's educational works. After all, in all the modern writing about the Schrebers, father and son, the suggestion is that in his day Moritz Schreber was a celebrated educator. If, armed with this kind of information, one looks for references to Moritz Schreber in books about the history of education, one is in for something of a surprise: they contain no mention of him at all.

Not, at least, until recent years. But that is another story: His reputation in connection with education was one acquired not by way of his educational work, but by way of Schatzman's work—that is, by the devious route of his mentally sick son and the literature about him. I shall therefore discuss this more recent role of Moritz Schreber in the history of education in my final chapter, where I examine Schatz-man's contribution and the response to it.

To some extent Moritz Schreber's absence from books about the history of education is quite justified, since as an educator he was never a particular success: All the more recent assertions that he was "the Dr. Spock of the nineteenth century" are founded merely on inadequate knowledge of the facts. However, it is true that Schreber's failure to figure in histories of education also has something to do with the implicit premises upon which those histories are based.

In the ordinary historical description of "genuine" sciences, the chief purpose is to point out the most important discoveries and inventions which have over the years contributed to the branch of knowledge in question in its evolution to the state existing in the historian's own times. In other words, what we are left with is a history of progress. And the criterion for selection is thus not the popularity enjoyed by any given scholar or scientist in his own day, but the extent to which his discoveries or inventions have influenced, in the historian's view, the subsequent course of events within his discipline.

The history of education follows the same pattern. The gallery of heroes is not selected according to the popularity of individual educators in their own day: on the contrary, popularity, real influence, and so on are matters in which this kind of historical writing is scarcely interested at all—all the emphasis is on the educators' *theories*. The criterion by which a theory is or is not included in the history of education as the historian writes it generally remains implicit but appears in the main to be the extent to which the theory was in advance of educational ideas which gained common currency only at a later stage.[12] Thus the highest praise which Rattner could bestow in his book *Grosse Pädagogen* is that the educator in question was "astonishingly modern" (1956, p. 31). And in his *Inleiding in de historische pedagogiek* Noordam "only included the ideas of the small number of educators discussed in so far as they were not only important at the time but also remain so today" (1968, p. viii). However, Noordam immediately followed this with the statement "That some educators have been discussed and others not is ultimately the result of a subjective choice." This would appear to be a totally different principle of selection. Curiously enough this evidently does not lead to contradictory selections, nor does the "ultimate subjectivity" in making a selection lead to radically different selections in the work of different historians of education. Most writing on the history of education is pervaded both by the idea of progress in the way we bring up our children and by the notion that ultimately the choice of particular educators is subjective; and in my view both ideas are uncomprehended expressions of what is really going on in the history of education.

In the history of education in western Europe it is possible to discern certain more or less continuous developments: for example, the age at which adulthood is attained rises steadily, whereas corporal punishment gradually declines. These changes in upbringing are part of more general developments in human relationships and in the concomitant attitudes toward those relationships. Because attitudes toward the relationship between parents and children develop more or less in one direction, each new generation will generally see history as a change for the better, since, of course, it appears to be a development toward the individual's own ideas of good and evil. This is how the history of education appears to be both progress and development in the direction of the individual's own subjective convictions. In reality, however, the history of education develops more or less in a straight line; so that one can only speak of progress from the point of view of the scale of values applied by the most recent adult generation.

The writer who abandons the idea of progress in the history of education will write that history quite differently. Ideas from the past which are clearly quite different from those of today then become just as interesting as ideas which anticipate what has since become more generally accepted. Not only are revolutionaries like Rousseau then interesting; so too are those educators who put into words the ideas which were prevalent at the time, such as Moritz Schreber. And in the search for what was widely accepted in the past, one of the first places one should look is books written for use within the home rather than for other educators. Here, too, Schreber is an example.

7. THE INFLUENCE OF THE ALLOTMENT GARDENS ON MORITZ SCHREBER'S SUBSEQUENT REPUTATION

In this last section I shall examine, more or less chronologically, Moritz Schreber's reputation in later years. It will become apparent that we can no longer ignore the influence of the allotment gardens.

Until 1864 things are quite simple: until, that is, the founding of the first Schreber Association. That a conference of teachers in Saxony in 1859 should be treated to a speech by the schoolmaster F. A. Bormann on the subject of a book by Moritz Schreber cannot yet have

Fig. 51. The Schreber Street in Leipzig.

anything to do with the allotments, nor can Schreber's inclusions in a work of reference containing several hundred persons and entitled *Galerie berühmter Pädagogen, verdienter Schulmänner, Jugend- und Volksschriftsteller und Componisten aus der Gegenwart* (Gallery of famous educators, meritorious teachers, writers for young people, popular authors, and composers of today), published in the same year. (In a letter, Moritz Schreber had himself provided the compiler of the *Galerie*, J. B. Heindl, with his personal data.)

In 1870 Leipzig acquired a *Schreberstrasse* (G. Richter, 1925, p. 10). The present street name-plate (Fig. 51) is certainly of more recent date. The street itself is close to the grounds originally owned by the first Schreber Association. Subsequently the city acquired a Schreber Lane (Schrebergässchen), a Schreber Bridge (Schreberbrücke), and a Schreber Baths (Schreberbad).

Where Moritz Schreber is included in encyclopedias, the influence of the Associations and allotments is not at first very clear. For example, he already had an entry in *Pierer's Jahrbücher* in 1873 (p. 480). In *The Brockhaus Encyclopedia*, on the other hand, he did not appear until the early years of this century, and when he did, it was in connection with the Associations and gardens. Nowadays he appears in most German encyclopedias, generally simply as the "founder" of the Schreber allotments.

In other works of reference the influence of the allotments is more difficult to establish. In the *Biographisches Lexikon der hervorragenden Ärzte aller Zeiten und Völker* (Biographical dictionary of the great doctors of all areas and nations) (1887) he is given an entry which makes no mention of the Associations or allotments, and the same is true of the *Allgemeine deutsche Biographie* (General German biographical dictionary) of 1891. There is no way of telling whether the existence of the Associations and allotments influenced the decision to include Schreber in these works.

The successive editions of the *Handbuch des gesamten Turnwesens* (Comprehensive gymnastic handbook) provide an illustration of the later influence of the Associations and allotments. In 1895 the article on Schreber in the *Handbuch* was based on an obituary in the *Deutsche Turnzeitung* by his colleague Schildbach, so that Schreber was discussed solely as a gymnast and orthopedist (Euler, 1895, pp. 504–505). In the 1920 edition a sentence was added to the entry: "The Schreber gardens named after him were founded by his son-in-law Dr. Hauschild" (Gasch, 1920, p. 605). In the next edition, which appeared in 1928, there was a completely new entry after "Schreber," viz., *"Schrebervereine"* (Schreber Associations). In the style of this article (which uses, for example, as a word the expression *"Schreberge-danke"* [Schreber idea]), I detect the pen of Gerhard Richter, a prolific writer and officer of the first Schreber Association, to whom I shall refer again, in more detail, in the following chapter on the Schreber Associations.

There are other cases in which Moritz Schreber turns up in texts which at first sight appear to have nothing whatever to do with the Schreber gardens but in which it is nevertheless possible to detect the direct influence of officers of Schreber associations. For example, generally speaking, Schreber does not appear in books about Leipzig, but he does turn up, together with the gardens, in a chapter by W. Lange (1927, pp. 233, 276–277) on nineteenth-century Leipzig in a book edited by K. Reumuth entitled *Heimatgeschichte für Leipzig* (literally: Homeland history for Leipzig). In the previous year Reumuth had published the text of a lecture in the series *Schriften des Landes-verbandes Sachsen der Schreber- und Gartenvereine* (Papers of the federation of Schreber and garden Associations of the Land of Saxony): from the same text it is apparent that the speaker was also an officer of the East Leipzig Schreber Association.

Sometimes I have been unable to find the link with the allotments despite being sure that there is one. For example, Moritz Schreber made a brief and erroneous appearance in K. Buchheim's *Deutsche Kultur zwischen 1830 und 1870* (1966, p. 180). Buchheim's data clearly originate from the more extensive and excellent remarks about Moritz Schreber in the earlier edition of the book (Bauer, 1937, p. 235), but I have not yet been able to establish how Bauer came by his text on Schreber.

In 1942 H. O. Kleine published *Ärzte kämpfen für Deutschland* (Doctors fight for Germany). Each chapter in this work takes one fighting doctor, and one of these is Moritz Schreber. Here the central theme is Schreber's booklet promoting the sport of gymnastics, so that it would appear as if Kleine's book belongs in this chapter. Never-theless, what Kleine has to say about Schreber is more properly seen as a product of the allotments. It appears that he came across Moritz Schreber in a medical journal, in a memorial article in the tradition of the allotments (Schütze, 1936a). Besides, the atmosphere of Kleine's chapter on the gymnastics booklet is heavily laden with the perfume of the Schreber gardens (see note 9 to Chapter 4).

Another book by Moritz Schreber, *Die Kaltwasser-Heilmethode* (The cold water cure) of 1842, was quoted at length in a book compiled by Groh (1960) on the cold water therapy of Priessnitz. I do not know why Groh should have attached so much importance to Schreber's book in particular, but the link may lie in the fourth edition of Brauchle's *Naturheilkunde in Lebensbildern* (Natural cures in biographical sketches): for this fourth edition the book was revised by Groh in 1971; it contains a biography of Moritz Schreber.

Schreber also turned up in Van Ussel's *Geschiedenis van het seksuele probleem* (History of the sexual problem) of 1968 (pp. 318–319). I regard this as having neither much connection with Schreber's "ordinary" reputation nor any link with the allotments; instead, I believe Van Ussel probably just happened across a Dutch translation of *Der Hausfreund* (1862b). There is another way in which Van Ussel differs from all the other authors I have so far mentioned: he is extremely disparaging about this "German vulgarizing work." In what follows I shall be returning to the shift in appreciation of Moritz Schreber: initially, in the allotment literature, admiration, and in the more recent psychiatric literature about father and son, general revulsion. With his disparaging attitude to Moritz Schreber, Van Ussel, who evidently knew nothing of Paul Schreber, showed that the present low opinion of him has much more general causes than knowledge of Paul Schreber's illness.

Looking back on Moritz Schreber's "ordinary" reputation, I believe that he was not so well known in his own day that his fame could have contributed to the repression of feelings of hatred in Paul Schreber, as Schatzman suggested. An exception to this, perhaps, is the influence of *Indoor Gymnastics,* which sold well until after the turn of the century. Moreover, Paul Schreber's *Memoirs* testify to the great importance which *Indoor Gymnastics* had in his life (D. P. Schreber, 1903, pp. 166, 493, 510 − 1955, pp. 142, 342, 352). But if Moritz Schreber's fame really weighed heavily on his son, then it must have been the fame which he acquired as a consequence of the Schreber Associations and the Schreber gardens.

That an educational association should be named after Moritz Schreber in Leipzig in 1864, three years after his death, deserves mention. But the fact that from these beginnings the name "Schreber" came eventually to be associated first and foremost with the German word for an allotment garden, *Schrebergarten,* is a development that has so little to do with Moritz Schreber's own work that I shall devote a separate chapter to it.

NOTES TO CHAPTER 21

[1]In order not to make my main text too boring I shall give references to reviews and the like in the notes. The following summaries appeared in the *Jahrbuch für Kinderheilkunde:* 1859, Auszüge (extracts), pp. 17–22 (from *Kallipädie*); 1859, Auszüge, pp. 65–69 (from *Ein ärztlicher Blick);* a review of *Anthropos* is to be found in 1859, Notizen, p. 47, and in 1860 Widerhofer wrote something between an extract and a review (pp. 10–11) of *Die planmässige Schärfung der Sinnesorgane.*

[2]The *Neue Jahrbücher für die Turnkunst* published the following reviews of books by Moritz Schreber: E. Friedrich, 1855, pp. 166–169, on *Ärztliche Zimmergymnastik;* Kloss, 1858, pp. 208–212, on *Ein ärztlicher Blick;* E. Friedrich, 1859, pp. 143–152, on *Anthropos;* Kloss, 1860, pp. 50–54, on *Die planmässige Schärfung;* E. Friedrich, 1860, pp. 125–134, on *Über Volkserziehung,* and Kloss, 1862, pp. 300–302, on *Das Pangymnastikon.*

[3]The *Deutsche Turnzeitung* published the following reviews of books by Moritz Schreber: Lion, 1857, pp. 111–112, on *Kallipädie;* and in 1858, p. 83, an anonymous review of the *Streitfragen.* The magazine also published (1857, p. 112, and 1858, pp. 16, 56, 111) reviews of the *Neue Jahrbücher für die Turnkunst* where Moritz Schreber's contributions to the *Jahrbücher* were also mentioned.

[4]Kohut wrote this because of *Das Buch der Erziehung,* as the later editions of *Kallipädie* were titled. Kohut (1971, p. 256) expressly referred his readers to this work, but his reference made it perfectly clear that he himself had not actually seen the book: The erroneous year of publication that he gave (1865) was no mere mistake but was almost certainly taken from an article by Niederland (1960, p. 499). All this does not prevent Kohut from arriving at some highly detailed psychiatric diagnoses with regard to the author Moritz Schreber, such as:

> profoundly narcissistic and prenarcissistic . . . hypochondriacal tensions . . . a hidden psychotic system . . . a special kind of psychotic character structure in which reality testing remains broadly intact even though it is in the service of the psychosis, of a central *idée fixe.* It is probably a kind of healed-over psychosis [1971, pp. 255, 256].

[5]One pointer to this: Just as I was putting the final touches to this book, I found another article by Moritz Schreber: a long review in Schmidt's *Jahrbücher der in- und ausländischen gesammten Medicin* (1848, vol. lix, pp. 207–211).

[6]According to Graefe (1902, p. 3), the reviser of *Zimmergymnastik,* the first edition of the book was "self-published." This is incorrect as the first edition was published in the normal way by Fleischer in Leipzig: See the title-page (D. G. M. Schreber, 1855). There was however, a *Kommissionsvertrag* (commission contract), whereby the author bore a certain amount of the financial risk (see D. P. Schreber, 1955, p. 342).

[7]This estimate of about three hundred thousand copies for all editions of *Zimmergymnastik* is based on the following figures: The edition published by Fleischer went to something more than 32 impressions and thus totalled at least 205,000 copies—a figure taken from the book itself, quoted by S. M. Weber (1973, p. 5). Around 1900 the book was also published by four other publishers. One of these editions, published by Radestock, also went to at least nine impressions.

Tabouret-Keller (1973, p. 303) used false reasoning to arrive at the correct conclusion that the book was popular:

The popularity of this work may be judged from the fact that the university library at Strasburg bought a further two copies of this last edition when it already had five copies of preceding editions, including one of the second edition (1855), and, in addition, a copy of the English edition.

However, all these copies of *Zimmergymnastik* cannot have found their way into the university library because of a deliberate purchasing policy. In almost all cases they would have been bequeathed or otherwise donated. Such numbers of such books in university libraries merely say something about the nature of the reading public that uses them, i.e., that there are intellectuals among them.

[8]Through the medium of Bilz, fragments of *Zimmergymnastik* (without reference to Schreber) found their way into a popular Dutch book of amusing illustrations and anecdotes concerning nineteenth-century medical practice, de Vries's *Ha doktor, ho dokter. Knotsgekke geneeskunde uit grootvaders tijd* (1976, pp. 91, 93).

[9]Here I call on the authority of someone who has a better view than I, namely, K. Rutschky. It was she, incidentally, who drew my attention to the Herder brothers, who in 1788, when they were about ten years of age, wrote to their father: "We have all been given belts to make us walk and sit straight and properly" (Quoted in Mencken [1965, p. 70; see also p. 73]). Deleuze and Guattari wrote regarding Moritz Schreber's appliances, that "very similar instruments of pedagogical torture are to be found in the countess de Ségur: thus 'the good posture belt', 'with iron plate at the back and iron branch to take the chin' " (1972, p. 353). However, an essential difference from Moritz Schreber is that in de Ségur (1866, pp. 165ff.) everyone expressed his horror at the nasty man with his dreadful belt.

[10]According to a review of a radio programme in *The Listener* (1973), Schatzman said something about Paul Schreber which he almost certainly did not say in quite the way stated.

Schatzman said: "The point after which Schreber was considered mad followed a night in which he had an unusual manner of, as he puts it, 'pollutions'. His father had an obsession about preventing pollutions. There was one piece of apparatus he invented, a dogtoothed clip to fit around a boy's penis while he slept, so that if the penis became erect it would bite into it and wake him up."

[11]I have heard of several Dutch people of the older generation who were brought up with a "straightener." However, the appliance to which they refer is not something designed by Moritz Schreber but a sort of corset (see, e.g., Hemelrijk [1965, p. 162].

[12]Sometimes the self-assurance of educators is so great that they quite openly mention this mechanism behind the historiography of education: "A study of the great educational authors of the past reveals that everything that is laid conclusively bare by modern scientific research has already been anticipated by poets and thinkers since ancient times" (Liebling, 1956, p. 9).

22

MORITZ SCHREBER'S REPUTATION AS
ACQUIRED THROUGH THE SCHREBER
ASSOCIATIONS AND SCHREBER GARDENS

1. SCHREBER ASSOCIATIONS, SCHREBER GARDENS, AND THE *DEUTSCHE SCHREBERJUGEND*

I shall devote this section to an examination of the words which have made the name "Schreber" a household word even in present-day Germany: *Schreberverein* (Schreber Association), *Schrebergarten* (Schreber garden) and the *Deutsche Schreberjugend* (literally: German Schreber Youth [organization]).

The origins of the first Schreber Association

The first Schreber Association was founded in Leipzig by Ernst Hauschild in 1864, three years after Moritz Schreber's death. Hauschild was a school headmaster with progressive ideas who introduced such new subjects to the school curriculum as drill, shorthand, and gymnastics for girls. In Chapter 21 I mentioned headmaster Vogel, who devoted almost an entire issue of his school magazine to Moritz Schreber after the latter's death. Hauschild did something similar (1862, pp. 210-219): in one of his "Educational letters from the school to its pupils' parental home" he followed Vogel's example by printing Moritz Schreber's essay on children's playgrounds, concluding with a call to the local authority to donate a playground and gymnastics ground to the Fourth Secondary School (Vierte Bürgerschule)—that is, his own school. This playground, he suggested, might be called the *"Schreberplatz."*

Two years after this, Hauschild was the prime mover in the foundation of an educational association which took as its aims the organization of lectures, the establishment of a library, and the setting up of a playground (see also Hauschild [1865, pp. 108-117]). This association was called the *"Schreberverein"* after Moritz Schreber. Why, exactly, this should have been the name chosen I cannot say.[1]

The Schreber gardens

I have already given a brief account (p. xv) of how the Schreber Associations soon evolved into an allotment gardening association. A year after its foundation, in 1865, the association acquired a piece of ground, and this recreation ground was called the *"Schreberplatz."* On the edges of the *Schreberplatz*, children's gardens were later laid out; and these in turn were eventually taken over by the parents. As early as 1869 only owners of these gardens were eligible for membership of the Schreber Association (G. Richter, 1925, pp. 48-49). And gradually the gardens on the *Schreberplatz* came to be known as "Schreber gardens"—*Schrebergärten.*

Unfortunately there is no documentary evidence of the origins of this word: it must have been exclusively a coinage of the spoken language. One of the first texts in which the word *"Schrebergarten"* appears—in fact a plea that the word should *not* be used—did not appear until 1907: "The term *Schrebergärten* is erroneous, because Dr. Schreber neither created such family gardens nor encouraged them to be established" (Siegel, 1907e, p. 254). Whether the word *Schrebergarten* itself—the word to which Moritz Schreber owes most of his fame—only became current at about this time, I cannot say. Certainly the Schreber Associations took some time to gather momentum: the second successful Schreber Association was not formed until 1874, ten years after the first. There were six Schreber Associations in Leipzig in 1891.

By 1907, however, there were already so many Schreber Associations in Leipzig that a quarrel broke out over which of them were actually entitled to call themselves Schreber Associations. In the subsequent decades the terminological difference between the various sorts of allotments (*Familiengärten, Arbeitergärten* [family gardens, workers' gardens] and *Schrebergärten*) was officially abolished, only the term *Kleingärten* (literally: small gardens) being officially approved. However, the word *"Schrebergarten"* survived undaunted in colloquial speech. (Should the non-German-reader be confused: the plural of *Garten* is *Gärten*.)

Psychiatrists on the Schreber Associations and Schreber gardens

It is thus perfectly possible to call all the allotment gardens in Germany *Schrebergärten*. What cannot be said, however, is that all owners of German allotments are members of Schreber Associations, as implied by the psychoanalyst Niederland:

> according to my latest information (1958) from Germany, there are today over two million members in the so-called *Schreber Vereine*, associations dedicated to the propagation of physical culture, calisthenics, gardening, fresh-air activities, and the like [1960, p. 492].

Stranger yet is what we read in Niederland's book about "the Schreber case," where he wrote about Moritz Schreber as the man

> who created the *Schreber movement* and whose teachings inspired the development of the Schreber gardens as well as the *Schreber Vereine*, associations devoted to the methodical cultivation of activities in fresh air, gymnastics, gardening, calisthenics, and sport [Niederland, 1974, p. 3].

Where did Niederland get this high-flown language—"methodical cultivation of activities in fresh air"—for the perfectly ordinary business of owning or running an allotment? I think he probably borrowed it from the officers of allotment associations with whom he corresponded (Niederland, 1974, p. xvi); it is understandable that such people should wish to invest their activities with a certain style; they live in a linguistic climate in which the word *"Schrebergärtner"* (Schreber gardener) also has the figurative meaning of "a person of limited intellect and narrow mind" (Wahrig, 1973, p. 3170).

In the psychiatric literature there is only one known text written in the allotment tradition: Ritter's thesis on Moritz Schreber as an educator. Ritter cunningly managed to suggest that Moritz Schreber was closely involved with the associations and gardens: "Enthusiastic supporters saw to his success even after his death. Schreber Associations were founded and Schreber gardens laid out everywhere . . ."

(Ritter, 1936a, p. 22). Evidently Ritter thought that his plea for the educator Moritz Schreber would lose force if he were to tell his readers that Moritz Schreber himself had nothing to do with the thing that made his name a household word, the Schreber gardens.

Apart from Ritter's thesis, nothing of the allotments tradition has penetrated the psychiatric literature on the Schrebers. True, Niederland (1974, p. 117) did mention an article by K. Schilling in a bibliography; but if he had actually read that article he would never have written that Moritz Schreber himself founded the associations and gardens. Schatzman clearly took his information from Niederland: "The Schreber Associations . . . are societies for callisthenics, gardening, and fresh air activities. . . . Dr. Schreber also began the Schreber Gardens, small plots of land near the outskirts of cities" (Schatzman, 1973a, p. 13). One wonders exactly what such an author has in his mind's eye when he talks of the "Schreber Associations." I quote some psychiatric fantasies:

> Dr. Daniel Gottlieb Schreber was a doctor widely known in his day; even today more than two million Germans are organized into Schreber clubs to apply and propagate his doctrine and authoritarian methods of education [*Le Coq-Heron*, June/July, 1973, p. 8].

> The father, Dr. Daniel Gottlieb Schreber, is still revered as one of Germany's great educationists. His doctrines, which taught blind obedience to superiors as well as rigorous discipline for children, were immensely influential in forcing the German character into its authoritarian mould (two million Germans still belong to Schreber associations) [Gillie, 1973].[2]

And Moritz Schreber's works "were so widely read that there were numerous Schreber Associations devoted to studying his methods" (Storr, 1973, p. 4). Do people like Gillie and Storr actually visualize anything when they use all these words? Study clubs where hierarchical thinking and strict discipline are practiced? Psychiatric thinking on the Schreber Associations has some more striking developments to show us: whereas in 1958 Niederland was talking about over *two million* Schreber Association members, "in 1958 [the "Schreber movement"] still counted two-and-a-half million adherents" (Appendix to D. P. Schreber, 1975, p. 385). Neither did the mental illness of Mortiz Schreber's son "prevent Schreberian educational ideas from having a great reputation: numerous Schreber associations were founded to apply them . . . and it appears that even today they count almost three million members" [Moreau, 1974, p. 45].

The Deutsche Schreberjugend

Yet it would be unwise to laugh too soon at these psychiatrists' imaginings about Moritz Schreber,

> whose educational theories were unbelievably repressive and were widespread throughout Germany, and undoubtedly anticipated the creation of the Nazi spirit—it is said that even today these methods have three million adepts [Schatzman, 1974c, dustjacket text].

There is in fact in West Germany an educational organization named after Moritz Schreber, the *Deutsche Schreberjugend*, which, according to its own presentation of itself "within the framework of leisure education pursues both youth-educating and youth-promoting aims" (*Deutsche Schreberjugend*, n.d., p. 1). An organization that wraps its aims in such woolly language does indeed appear somewhat suspect. What sort of organization might the *Deutsche Schreberjugend* be?

Here we have a surprise: the *Deutsche Schreberjugend* is a dyed-in-the-wool progressive organization! "To fight uncompromisingly against the spectre of fascism" is the aim expressed in the organization's bulletin *Wir* (March, 1979). No wonder such an organization was able to write of itself: "From 1933 to 1945 the Schreber youth Organization had to practise illegaly [*sic*]" (*Deutsche Schreberjugend*, c. 1979, p. 2). The *Deutsche Schreberjugend* was founded in 1951 (Leucker, 1979). (But why should not Germans too be allowed to derive a sense of moral uplift from their imaginary activities in the Hitler era?)

The nature and size of the *Deutsche Schreberjugend* are somewhat obscure to me; even a conversation with the organization's national chairman was unable to remedy this situation. In any event: Their name is to be seen below many an expression of antinuclear-power sentiment, they run a number of youth hostels, they organize summer camps, and they build playgrounds, and of course I applied for membership.

2. TRIBUTES TO MORITZ SCHREBER FROM WITHIN THE SCHREBER ASSOCIATIONS

In Part I we have seen that the quarrelling among Schreber Associations about legacies from Moritz Schreber's widow certainly did nothing to increase Paul Schreber's peace of mind: His last psychotic phase began shortly afterward. At this time he had control over the booty over which the Associations were fighting. What effect the Associations had on his life prior to this is difficult to say. I do not think that he himself was a member of a Schreber Association, like his sister Anna; ownership of an allotment is not a very practical proposition for one whose job means that he is continually moving from house to house. However, it is curious in this connection to find the following note in the summary of his career in his personal file: "Use of a garden on the farm premises of the Landgericht building at Freiberg, for an annual rent of 12 marks. Order of 9 October 1889" (Personalakte, fo. 2).

Schreber Association texts about Moritz Schreber are of interest not only because of their effect on Paul Schreber but also from a bibliographical point of view: The tradition produced several works which are of considerable documentary value for the study of Moritz Schreber's life.

The reader of this section may gain the impression that the Schreber Associations, especially the first one, spent all their time going on about how important Moritz Schreber was. If so, it will of course be the result of the fact that comments of that kind are gathered together in this section. In fact, I assume that Moritz Schreber's name only came to the fore on anniversaries and similar official functions. In most Schreber Associations there was one member who predominated in keeping the memory of Moritz Schreber alive. By and large, then, this section will be devoted to a study of the periods in which those authors published their works.

The early years: chiefly lectures (from 1864)

During the early years of the Schreber Associations the tributes paid to Moritz Schreber generally took the form of lectures. The first Schreber Association organized about five lectures every year. As we saw in Part I, the first lecture was given in 1864 by Dr. Schildbach, his title being "Schreber's Merits." Later themes worthy of mention are: "Schreber the orthopedist and his connection with the work and aims of the Schreber Association" in 1870 and 1871, "Schreber's aspirations and work" in 1876, and "Dr. Schreber's principles of education" in 1883 (Schreiber, 1894, pp. 62-67). When the first Schreber association celebrated its fifteenth anniversary a wreath was laid on Moritz Schreber's grave (*ibid.*, p. 54).

The South Leipzig Schreber Association: three books (1877, 1884, and 1896)

The lecture given in 1876 on the subject of "Schreber's aspirations and work" was delivered to the members of the two associations then in existence; the speaker was the schoolmaster E. Mangner, president of the second Schreber Association, that of South Leipzig. It was printed in the magazine *Cornelia* in 1876; in the following year it also appeared separately as a brochure of fifteen pages under the title *Dr. D. G. M. Schreber, ein Kämpfer für Volkserziehung* (Dr. D. G. M. Schreber, a fighter for the education of the people). This is the first example of a genre that was to become a solid tradition between the two World Wars. This firstling of 1877, however, did not yet show many signs of promise: It was full of uninformative praise for Schreber and contained, by way of news, not much more than erroneous dates of Schreber's birth and death (Mangner, 1877, pp. 4, 14). Mangner's second little book, dating from 1884, was an improvement: *Spielplätze und Erziehungsvereine. Praktische Winke zur Förderung harmonischer Jugenderziehung nach dem Vorbilde der Leipziger Schrebervereine* (Playgrounds and educational associations. Practical hints for the furtherance of harmonious education of young people according to the example set by the Schreber Associations of Leipzig). Considering its title, the purpose of this little book was surprising: Mangner hoped to prove

> that all, *almost all the efforts* which today mobilize wide circles of our nation for a *better* and above all *more natural education* for young people, *are to be traced back to the philanthropic, child-loving doctor Dr. Schreber* [Mangner, 1884, pp. 9-10].

In 1896 Mangner's successor as president of the South Leipzig Schreber Association, the headmaster L. Mittenzwey, published *Die Pflege des Bewegungsspieles insbesondere durch die Schrebervereine* (The cultivation of outdoor games, particularly by the Schreber Associations). "The goal of this little book is that the merits are remembered of the important man, whose name is remembered in the Schreber Associations" (Mittenzwey, 1896, p. VII). This book was a more elaborate version of the book by Mangner that had appeared twelve years before. It contained a description of the life and work of Moritz Schreber, quotes from his article on "Children's games," and a short history of the Schreber Associations.

The Schreiber years: anniversaries and a monument (1889–1902)

At the end of the nineteenth century the preservation of the historical legacy of the Schreber Associations was dominated strongly by the schoolmaster E. Schreiber, president of the first Schreber Association. His presidency of the Association was marked by celebrations of anniversaries. In 1889 the first Schreber Association was 25 years old, and Schreiber made a speech about "the life and work of Dr. Schreber and Dr. Hauschild" (G. Richter, 1914a, p. 62), while a tree on the "*Schreberplatz*" was named after Moritz Schreber (G. Richter, 1914b, p. 109). A few months later, during the "*Nachfeier*" of (celebration after) the jubilee, Schreiber spoke again, this time on "Dr. Schreber's life and work" (Schreiber, 1894, p. 68). On 28 February 1893 the oldest Schreber Association held a "memorial celebration for Dr. Schreber and Dr. Hauschild, a biographical sketch of the same being drawn by Schoolmaster Emil Schreiber" (Schreiber, 1894, p. 69).

The next year the Association celebrated its thirtieth anniversary. As 15 years previously, a wreath was laid on Moritz Schreber's grave. Schreiber produced a "*Festschrift*" to mark the occasion, an informative little book about the Association's history. It began with a brief biography of Moritz Schreber. The next year again provided occasion for celebration: Moritz Schreber's widow had been an honorary member for twenty-five years, in recognition of which she was presented with flowers (G. Richter, 1939b, p. 103). In the same year Schreiber published an article about Moritz Schreber and the Leipzig Schreber Associations in the *Jahrbuch für deutsche Jugend- und Volksspiele*. In 1900 Moritz Schreber was again remembered, and Schreiber gave a lecture on "The child in the first years of life. Memorial celebration for Dr. Schreber and Dr. Hauschld" (G. Richter, 1914a, p. 91).

A memorial plaque to Moritz Schreber had already been put up in the first Schreber Association in 1887. In 1901 the Association erected a "Hauschild-Schreber Monument," which Eschner (1910, pp. 194-195) included in his *Leipziger Denkmäler* (Monuments of

Leipzig). The centerpiece of this monument, with the portraits of Hauschild and Schreber, is still to be seen in Leipzig.

The North Leipzig Schreber Association: exhibition (1903)

In 1903 the Schreber Association in North Leipzig participated in the German cities' exhibition in Dresden. Part of their entry was a bust of Moritz Schreber (Fritzsche, 1903, p. iv) to which I have already referred in connection with the fact that it shortly afterward turned up in the Schreber family (see p. 205). To mark the occasion of this exhibition, the schoolmaster H. Fritzsche wrote a booklet entitled *Dr. med. Schreber und die Leipziger Schreber-Vereine mit besonderer Berücksichtigung des Schreber-Vereins der Nordvorstadt* (Dr. Schreber and the Leipzig Schreber Associations, with special reference to the Schreber Association of the Northern suburb).

The Siegel years: quarrels (1907), reading-matter for Freud (1908), and important texts (1909)

In the period during which the chief protagonist was the schoolmaster R. Siegel, 1907 to 1909, every year was important: 1907 was marked by the quarrels over the legacy of Moritz Schreber's widow, 1908, by an issue of a magazine to which Freud owed his knowledge of Moritz Schreber, and 1909, by two truly important articles, one by, and the other about, Moritz Schreber.

Richard Siegel was the president of the coordinating Federation of Leipzig Schreber Associations. The Federation had its own magazine, *Der Freund der Schreber-Vereine*. The first two volumes of this publication are also significant here, for they too carried extracts from works by Moritz Schreber (1906, pp. 125-129; unfortunately, I have been unable to find any copies of the 1905 issues).

In the January number of 1907 Siegel wrote about the founding of the first Schreber Association and, at the same time, about Moritz Schreber. "Through his numerous writings *Dr. Schreber* had acquired significant influence over his contemporaries" (Siegel, 1907a, p. 5). He also called Schreber's article on *"Die Jugendspiele"* such a superb text "that even in our own times it is frequently reprinted" (*ibid.*, p. 5).

In May 1907 Pauline Schreber died. I have already given an outline of the problems that surrounded her legacy to the Schreber

Associations in Part I, the salient points being that the will referred only to the Associations belonging to Siegel's Federation and that the Schreber Associations thus excluded lodged a protest with the heirs. Siegel must have heard about this quite soon: I can think of no other explanation for the fact that during the months immediately following Pauline Schreber's death *Der Freund der Schreber-Vereine* was filled with vituperations directed at the Associations outside the Federation and their magazine, *Der Schrebergärtner*. Siegel accused these other Associations of not being genuine Schreber Associations, since they were mere gardening clubs, whereas the chief aims of a proper Schreber Association were educational. To try to prove his point, Siegel found himself obliged to go back to the origins of the first Schreber Association and the work of Moritz Schreber himself, so that the number of references to Moritz Schreber reached a maximum during these months. For example, most of these objectionable Associations, wrote Herr Siegel,

> promote horticulture and small animal husbandry, according to their statutes, and are not even acquainted with the efforts of Drs. Schreber and Hauschild. The very title of the organ of their federation, *"Der Schrebergärtner,"* shows all too clearly the nature of these associations [Siegel, 1908a, p. 6].

Wisely, in the circumstances, Siegel forebore to quote the full title of this magazine: *Der Schrebergärtner. Wochenschrift für Volksbelehrung und Kindererziehung im Sinne Fröbels, Schrebers und Hauschilds* (The Schreber gardener. A weekly magazine for the enlightenment of the people and the education of children according to the ideas of Fröbel, Schreber and Hauschild).[3]

The August 1907 issue of *Der Freund der Schreber-Vereine* contained an expression of gratitude to Pauline Schreber, who had left a number of Schreber Associations the sum of five hundred marks each. In the following issue Siegel quoted the owner of a meeting-hall as saying "that the Schreber gardens were not irreproachable in the matter of morals either." Siegel replied: "we protest against the fact that garden complexes are being linked with the Schreber name when their owners have nothing to do with the efforts and aspirations of Dr. Schreber" (Siegel, 1907d, p. 218).

The October issue contained a nice portrait of Moritz Schreber (which over 60 years later Baumeyer [1970, facing p. 244] was to "discover" elsewhere) and a vehement attack on the heretical associations:

> since until now the majority of the associations that are at issue here *have concerned themselves neither with Dr. Schreber* (for example, none of these associations was represented at Frau Schreber's funeral) *and Dr. Hauschild and their efforts and aspirations, nor with genuine Schreber work* [*Der Freund der Schreber-Vereine*, 1907, p. 243].

The November issue contained a long article by Siegel, beginning:

> *Dr. Schreber and the Schreber Associations.* (Copyright.) Only a few years ago the name *"Schreber"* was seldom heard outside the Schreber Associations, but now it is on everyone's lips. Unfortunately the depressing experience is that Dr. Schreber's name is being applied to institutions and associations that are quite unconnected with his efforts and aspirations. These appearances [of the name] give repeated cause to ask the searching question: *"What did Dr. Schreber really desire and work for?"* [Siegel, 1907e, p. 251].

And Siegel proceeded to quote at length from Moritz Schreber's works. In fact, this article was a slightly abridged version of the speech Siegel made at the autumn meeting of his Federation—a meeting which, since the Schreber family was present, I have discussed in Part I (p. 208).

This quarrelling reached its height in the December issue of *Der Freund der Schreber-Vereine*, where once again, with the help of Moritz Schreber, an attack was launched on the false Schreber Associations: "What in the world has such a garden complex to do with Dr. Schreber, with his work for a sensible upbringing for our young people, for whose benefit he applied all his considerable energy?" (Fritzsche, 1907, p. 280). And Siegel addressed himself directly to the Federation's competitors' journal, *Der Schrebergärtner*, which had had the effrontery to describe the work of a Schreber Association as a children's party, an outing, a flower show, and so on:

> So these are the examples by which the *Schrebergärtner* wishes to typify a Leipzig Schreber Association. But this beginning is nothing less than a slap in the face for all those associations and all those men who until this day have with all their strength and selflessness worked for the aspirations of Drs. Schreber and Hauschild and have continuously extended their work. . . . It is only right to speak of

genuine Schreber Association work where . . . in every institution
and enterprise the hygienic-educational spirit of Drs. Schreber and
Hauschild is at work. . . . There are no cosy outings with music and
the pleasures of the hostelry, but joyful walks in the open air [Siegel,
1907f, pp. 289-290].

This article was followed by Paul Schreber's "Statement" about the
trouble involving the distribution of the legacy to the various Schreber
Associations (p. 209).

Henceforth, the reader will want to know, quotation will be
briefer, since we have now arrived at 1908 and all further tributes to
Moritz Scheber can have had no effect on his son Paul.

Extracts from the work of Moritz Schreber were also published
in *Der Freund der Schreber-Vereine* during 1908 (pp. 165-169, 185-
186, 249-251); in addition, headmaster Vogel's obituary of him was
reprinted, and Siegel exclaimed, "Let a monument to Dr. Schreber
now be erected in Leipzig in bronze or stone!" (1908b, p. 26). Nor
was Moritz Schreber forgotten at the children's summer party:

On 5 July 1908 the children's party was combined with a special
memorial celebration to mark the hundredth anniversary of the birth
of our founders [i.e., Schreber and Hauschild]. Every child joining
in the games was given a picture postcard bearing the portraits of
the founders of our Association [G. Richter, 1939b, p.104].

The October number of *Der Freund der Schreber-Vereine* deserves particular attention on account of a link with Sigmund Freud.
In his article about Paul Schreber's illness Freud (1911, p. 46 = 1958,
p. 51) gave, more or less in passing, a brief sketch of Paul Schreber's
father that is full of praise for him. This character-sketch appears to
present something of a problem for the psychoanalysts of today: At
least, they treat it rather curiously. Often it is conspicuous by its
absence in their publications, and sometimes there is a suggestion that
Freud actually thought the opposite of what he was writing. I shall
discuss these modern psychoanalysts' problems at length in the chapter
on the psychiatric literature about the Schrebers. The later psychoanalysts do not use one means of escape open to them, viz., saying that
Freud was poorly informed on the subject of Moritz Schreber. One of
the reasons why this escape route is left unused is that nobody knew
of the magazine from which Freud derived his knowledge of Moritz
Schreber, namely, *Der Freund der Schreber-Vereine* for October

1908.[4] This may be some justification for taking a closer look at what Freud might have read about Moritz Schreber.

The following brief account of what was in the October issue of *Der Freund der Schreber-Vereine* is to some extent tendentious: I shall be drawing attention chiefly to passages at which many a modern reader will shake his head, and in the reading of which one may well be surprised that Freud nevertheless arrived at such a positive impression of Paul Schreber's father.

The issue opens with an article entitled "On the hundredth anniversary of the birth of Dr. Schreber and Dr. Hauschild." Here Freud might have read, among other things, quotations from Moritz Schreber's books such as: "Wrong education, mollycoddling, laziness, coarse sensuality, the fetters of multifarious circumstances etc. have dulled the natural urge to fulfil the conditions for physical development" (D. G. M. Schreber, as quoted in Siegel, 1908c, p. 207). There follows an article entitled "Dr. Daniel Gottlieb Moritz Schreber," which contains an almost exhaustive survey of Moritz Schreber's books and a biography from which I quote:

> The majority and the best of his writings appeared in the last ten years of his life, though it was precisely during that period that he suffered severely from the consequences of a concussion caused by an iron ladder falling on his head. During this most difficult period of his life, when he always had to fear mental derangement, Dr. Schreber was only able to keep himself going by his iron energy, by incessant appropriate physical exercises [*Der Freund der Schreber-Vereine*, 1908, p. 211].

The article ends with a lengthy quotation from an obituary:

> The times of increasingly deep corporal and moral decay, which characterize the generation of our century, demanded and created a man like Schreber. In times . . . when a restless haste and passionate searching after the pleasures of life have seized hold of all strata of society . . . ; in such times the unilaterally theoretical and dogmatizing warning cry of the pedagogue, educator and dietitian was unable to find an audience—a man had to come who combined with the sharp eye of the observer and teacher the most exhaustive insights of the physician, and with the most extensive physiological knowledge the insight of the practical psychologist, who in a single person was doctor, teacher, dietitian, anthropologist, gymnast and gymnastic therapist, and in addition to and above all this was a man of

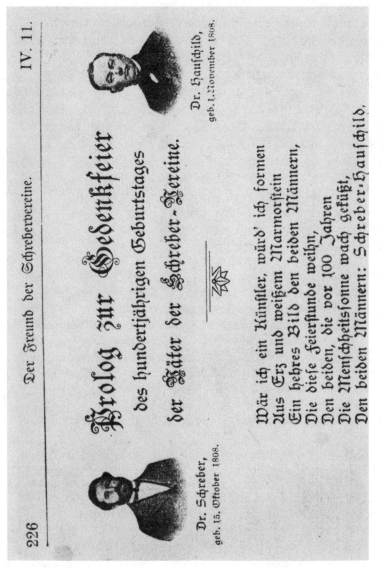

Fig. 52. Schreber poem. From *Freund der Schreber-Vereine* (1908, p. 226).

action, a man of impassioned aspirations, of the most unresting endurance, a man with a head filled with the clearest insights and a heart filled with the most selfless devotion, ready to live and to die for his mission, a man who in himself presented the most vivid model and example and the clearest illustration of all that he endeavours to realize for others—such a man had to be created for such times, and *such a man was Schreber* [Politzer, 1862, quoted in *Der Freund der Schreber-Vereine*, 1908, pp. 211-212].

At the end of the issue Freud could read Siegel's invitation to everyone to be present at a "memorial celebration of the hundredth anniversary of the birth of Dr. Schreber and Dr. Hauschild (Siegel, 1908d, p. 220). *Der Freund der Schreber-Vereine* of November 1908 (pp. 238-240) carried a report of this celebration. Schreber's bust, crowned with laurel, stood on the stage. In his opening speech Siegel extended a welcome to "the many members of the Schreber family" who were present. A poem was then recited (Fig. 52), followed by a "commemorative lecture on Dr. Schreber and Dr. Hauschild" by "Sanitätsrat Dr. med. Brückner" (*Sanitätsrat* was an honorary title bestowed on distinguished medical men). The celebration ended with lantern slides,

> starting with the excellent pictures of the spiritual father of the Schreber Associations, Dr. Schreber. . . . But to end with there followed Dr. Schreber's noble widow (who only last year went to her eternal rest at the God-given age of 91), Herr Sanitätsrat Dr. med. Brückner, and finally our revered, never resting, energetic, overworked Federation president, Herr schoolmaster Richard Siegel.

Considering the role that the "revered" Herr Siegel must have played in the life of Paul Schreber, his portrait also deserves a place here (Fig. 53).

During the last year of his presidency of the Federation, 1909, Siegel produced two texts which are of considerably more than curiosity value in relation to this study. In April 1909 *Der Freund der Schreber-Vereine* contained "Paternal words to my dear Anna" by Moritz Schreber—the piece written by Schreber in 1856 for the confirmation of his eldest daughter (see page 69). Siegel appended a brief wish: "May in the lives of families that spirit return which prevailed in that family, and in which alone the new generation can find the strength for victory in the struggle of life!" (Siegel, 1909a, p. 75). The second of these

Fig. 53. Portrait of Moritz Schreber, Ernst Hauschild, and Richard Siegel. From *Freund der Schreber-Vereine* (1913, p. 73).

important texts is entitled "Memories of Dr. Moritz Schreber. Compiled from accounts given by his daughters by R. Siegel" (Siegel, 1909b, p. 205). I have made much use of these recollections by Sidonie and Klara, as recorded by Siegel, in part I.

The years 1911 and 1912

Siegel's successor as president of the Federation of Leipzig Schreber Associations was the schoolmaster Hugo Fritzsche, to whom I referred on page 26 as the author of a small book on Moritz Schreber published in 1903. Later Fritzsche was more than once to excel in paying expansive tribute to Moritz Schreber, as in his long article in *Der Freund der Schreber-Vereine* in 1911 on "Dr. Daniel Gottlieb Moritz Schreber, a fighter for the education of the people. On the 50th anniversary of his death," (p. 179) and, above all, in an article published in 1926 entitled "Aus Dr. Schrebers Leben" (From the life of Dr. Schreber), based on a conversation with Schreber's daughter Anna Jung. Like the early volumes of *Der Freund der Schreber-Vereine*, this informative article by Fritzsche is no longer to be found in any normal library. But this does not mean that it was a rare publication in 1926: The periodical in which it appeared, *Garten und Kind* (Garden and Child) then had a circulation of 68,000 (G. Richter and Dietze, 1928, p. 15).

Paul Schreber died in 1911. In *Der Freund der Schreber-Vereine* a brief, black-edged text appeared, referring to him as "a dear friend and furtherer of the genuine efforts and aspirations of the Schreber Associations" (*Der Freund der Schreber-Vereine*, 1911, p. 65); see also page 268 above. The same year saw the fiftieth anniversary of Moritz Schreber's death: "On 10 November 1911, at a special memorial gathering, the *fiftieth anniversary of the death of Dr. Schreber* was remembered" (G. Richter, 1939b, p. 104).

At the autumn gathering of the Leipzig Schreber Associations in 1912 Fritzsche spoke "grateful words remembering Schreber, Hauschild and Siegel" (Volhard, 1912, pp. 169-70). (Siegel had died in 1910.) There was also a performance of a playlet entitled "Schreber's dream." The play begins with Moritz Schreber, fatigued by all his work, nevertheless wanting to write a little more, about "children's games." He asks his wife to fetch the lamp. When she has gone, however, he falls asleep. The stage goes dark. When the lights go up again, the audience see little girls dancing and singing of the sleeping beauty. Then the stage empties again. Frau Schreber returns with the lamp and says softly: "He's dreaming."

The Richter years (1913–40)

The last, most prolific, and in many way best writer from the Schreber Associations was Gerhard Richter, who held various posts in the original Schreber Association. His words eclipse everything else published during the last successful decades of the Schreber Associations.

In 1913 the text of the playlet "Schreber's dream" was published in *Der Freund der Schreber-Vereine* (Krey, 1913). Richter continued on the same theme with an article entitled "A dream fulfilled": Schreber's dream, he wrote, had been fulfilled by the Schreber Associations and by such groups as the *"Wandervögel"* (Rovers, a youth group).

> Yea, when the grateful eye of a child catcheth us, when children's shouts and children's joy peal in our ears during games or on a walk, then do the bells of thy resurrection peal, thou true children's friend, Schreber. Then livest thou again among us, and rejoicest with us at the joyful flourishing of thy work.
>
> He is not dead! He has risen again! Into the bitter cup of death there fell a comforting droplet of eternity.
>
> May it be ever more and ever more perfectly fulfilled:
> "Schreber's dream!"
>
> [G. Richter, 1913, p. 41].

In short, it is not only in the theological insanity of Paul Schreber, but even later, in the semireligious pathetics of Gerhard Richter, that Moritz Schreber rises from the dead.

In 1914 the first Schreber Association celebrated its fiftieth anniversary. Moritz Schreber received a new wreath on his grave; a Schreber lime was planted on the recreation ground; members of the Association received a portrait of him (Volhard, 1914, pp. 116–118); Richter wrote a *Festschrift* and an article about the history of the oldest Schreber Association (1914a,b), and of course there was a celebratory meeting attended by members of the Schreber family, at which Moritz Schreber's work was surveyed (Lehmann, 1914, p. 159). Also, poems were recited, such as the following:

Come, come and let our *children* live!
So taught us Schreber, Hauschild;
Through games in youth to raise the people's *strength*,
That was their wish—and we did hear it.

[Thierfelder, quoted in Volhard, 1914, p. 116].

Ten years later, to mark "sixty years of Schreberdom" (*Der Schre-bergärtner*, 1924, p. 33) a "giant children's procession" took place; see Figures 54 and 55. Figure 55 is taken from *Das Buch der Schreber-Jugendpflege* (The book of Schreber youth work) by Gerhard Richter, published in 1925—a book that is of interest not only on acount of these and other marvellous pictures, or the comprehensive biography of Moritz Schreber, but also for the peculiar Schreber language which Richter uses. Figure 56 reproduces words from the book.

That these are not merely new coinings by an individual will, I hope, become clear from references to a number of brochures from the series *Schriften den Landesverbandes Sachsen der Schreber- und Gartenvereine* (Writings of the Federation of Schreber and Garden Associations of the Land of Saxony). In Book 3 of the series K. Reumuth referred to "Schreber activities," "Schreber movement," "Schreber duty," "Schreber youth," "Schreberdom," and so on (1926). Book 5 records a speech made by K. Ringpfeil in 1927 entitled "What do we offer our Schreber children for their bodies and minds?" Book 7 consists of a "Memorandum of the Schreber youth work in the free state of Saxony for the purpose of obtaining state funds," a text full of praise for Moritz Schreber's ideas on educating the people: "Unfortunately in his day there was but little sympathy for such progressive ideas" (G. Richter and Dietze, 1928, p. 4). It also gave a survey of the wonderful activities of all sorts of Schreber Associations. For example: "*Schreber greeting*: On 26 September we again gave 38 old age pensioners a little Schreber pleasure" (*ibid.*, p. 13).

In later years Richter published several works on Moritz Schreber (G. Richter, 1930, 1936a, 1939b, 1940), his book of 1939 deserving special mention because it not only gave the best survey of the history of the first Schreber Association, but also revealed the political leanings of its author, whose name appears on the title-page as "Pg. Gerhard Richter." "*Pg.*" stands for *Parteigenosse*—comrade. The entire book is politically colored. For example, here is a passage on the method of upbringing in the Schreber family:

Familie Regentrop u. Pötzsch als, Familie Schreber."

Fig. 54. From the archives of the "Dr. Schreber" allotment branch. The text reads: "The Regentrop and Pötzsch families as 'The Schreber family.'"

Sinniger Festwagen: Der Schreberbrunnen.

Bild Schrebers und Hauschilds an der Seite. Unten Spruch: „Kommt, laßt uns
unsern Kindern leben." Oben Blumenkorb. Rings herum Kinder, die sich am
frischen Quell des Schreberbrunnens laben.

Fig. 55. The text reads: "An appropriate float: the Schreber fount. Pictures of Schreber and Hauschild on the side. Under, the motto: 'Come, let our children live.' On top, flower basket. All round, children refreshing themselves at the fresh source of the Schreber fount." From G. Richter (1925, p. 150).

Schreberziel
Schrebertum
Schreberheim
Schrebergemüse
Schreberliebe
Schreberplatz
Schreberfeste
Schreberspiel

Schrebersache
Schreberfälen!
Schreber=Idee
Schreberwagen
Schreberbetrieb
Schreberfrüchte
Schreberwesens
Schrebergärtner

Schrebermädels
Schrebervereine
Schreberblumen
Schreberfreundel
Schrebergedanke
Schrebererzieher
Schrebertätigkeit
Schrebermädchen

Schreber-Reigen
Schrebervereinler
Schreberwandern
Schreberhausbau
Schrebererziehung
Schreberbäumchen
Schreberjugendpflege
Schreberpflegschaften

Schreber=Ideal
Schreberabwanderungen
Ein Blick in das Schreberpara-
dies. (Stimmungsbilder aus der
Schreberspielzeit.)

Schrebergeist und Schrebertat
Schreberspielplatz
Schrebererziehungsfragen
Schrebergeschichte
Schrebervereinsmitglied

Schreberfamilie mit Schreberkind im Schrebergarten.

Fig. 56. G. Richter's words (1925).

The children also had to learn early how to make sacrifices. For instance, for a while they did without butter at breakfast, and with the pennies thus saved bought Christmas gifts for poor children.

Are these not all genuinely national socialist methods of upbringing? [G. Richter, 1939b, p. 18].

Richter's contributions to Schreber history went beyond publishing books and articles. He also maintained contact with Moritz Schreber's eldest daughter, Anna Jung. Short reports of four visits he paid her still exist and have been quoted in Part I; Figure 57 shows the most informative of these.

After the Second World War

After the Second World War another sort of "comrade" came to power in Leipzig. Gerhard Richter was obliged to relinquish all his official functions, though he was allowed to keep his allotment. In the G.D.R. *Festschrifte* of Schreber Associations are clearly not one of the higher priorities. In the case of West Germany it would be misleading to speak of Schreber Associations, though there are a number of West German phenomena that belong in this section. The most significant of these are the publications of Kurt Schilling.

Before the war Schilling worked in Dresden as a horticultural adviser to the Schreber Associations; in his booklet on *Das Kleingartenwesen in Sachsen* (Allotment gardening in Saxony), published in 1924, he made brief mention of Moritz Schreber (pp. 6–7). After the war three articles by him on Moritz Schreber appeared in West German allotment-holders' magazines (1950, 1961, 1964), the last of which is particularly informative.

Schilling is the only author in the allotment tradition who knows anything about "the Schreber case" in psychiatry: He corresponded with the American psychoanalyst W. G. Niederland (see note 5 to Chapter 6 and Niederland, 1974, p. xvi). His view of Moritz Schreber was unshaken by his knowledge of the tragic lives of Gustav and Paul. Through a study of Moritz Schreber's ancestors Schilling believed he could demonstrate "that time and again the intellectual talents were brought out from all the collateral lines, providing the conditions in which Dr. Schreber could rouse himself to the peak of performance on the intellectual plane" (1964, p. 4). However, Schilling continued, Moritz Schreber's son Gustav committed suicide.

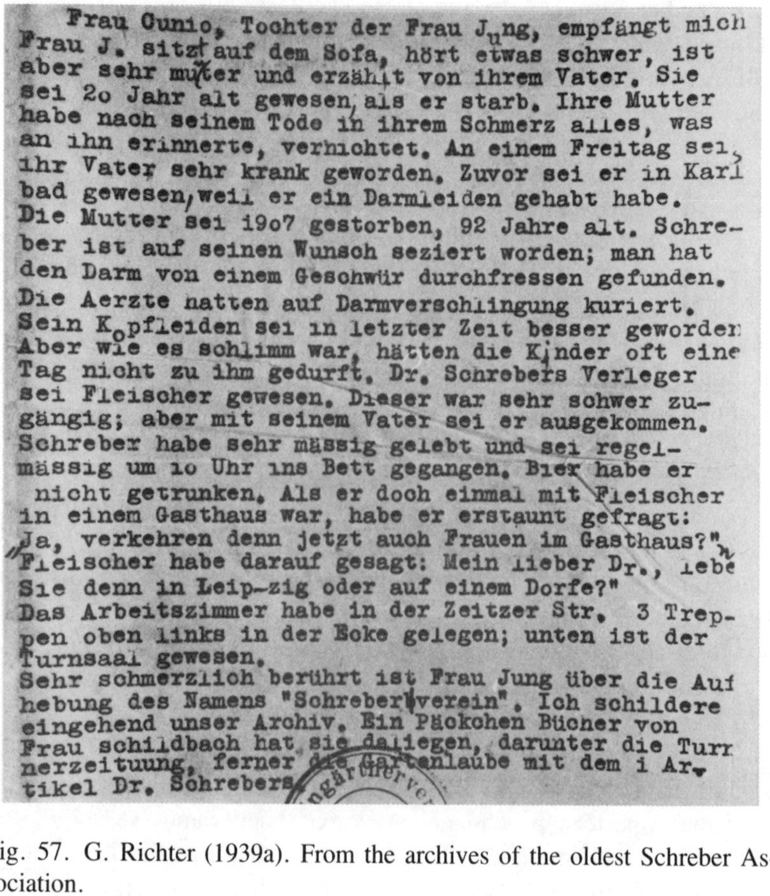

Frau Cunio, Tochter der Frau J$_u$ng, empfängt mich
Frau J. sitzt auf dem Sofa, hört etwas schwer, ist
aber sehr mütter und erzählt von ihrem Vater. Sie
sei 2o Jahr alt gewesen, als er starb. Ihre Mutter
habe nach seinem Tode in ihrem Schmerz alles, was
an ihn erinnerte, vernichtet. An einem Freitag sei
ihr Vater sehr krank geworden. Zuvor sei er in Karl
bad gewesen, weil er ein Darmleiden gehabt habe.
Die Mutter sei 19o7 gestorben, 92 Jahre alt. Schreber ist auf seinen Wunsch seziert worden; man hat
den Darm von einem Geschwür durchfressen gefunden.
Die Aerzte hatten auf Darmverschlingung kuriert.
Sein K$_o$pfleiden sei in letzter Zeit besser geworden.
Aber wie es schlimm war, hätten die Kinder oft eine
Tag nicht zu ihm gedurft. Dr. Schrebers Verleger
sei Fleischer gewesen. Dieser war sehr schwer zu-
gängig; aber mit seinem Vater sei er ausgekommen.
Schreber habe sehr mässig gelebt und sei regel-
mässig um 1o Uhr ins Bett gegangen. Bier habe er
nicht getrunken. Als er doch einmal mit Fleischer
in einem Gasthaus war, habe er erstaunt gefragt:
Ja, verkehren denn jetzt auch Frauen im Gasthaus?"
Fleischer habe darauf gesagt: Mein lieber D$_r$., lebe
Sie denn in Leip-zig oder auf einem Dorfe?"
Das Arbeitszimmer habe in der Zeitzer Str. 3 Trep-
pen oben links in der Eoke gelegen; unten ist der
Turnsaal gewesen.
Sehr schmerzlich berührt ist Frau Jung über die Auf
hebung des Namens "Schrebertverein". Ich schildere
eingehend unser Archiv. Ein Päckchen Bücher von
Frau schildbach hat, sie daliegen, darunter die Turr
nerzeituung, ferner die Gartenlaube mit dem i Ar-
tikel Dr. Schrebers

Fig. 57. G. Richter (1939a). From the archives of the oldest Schreber Association.

If it is already logical here to think of oversensitivity of the nerves due to one-sided overtaxing of the intellectual legacy, in the case of the second son, Daniel *Paul*, it becomes a certainty that no ability can be pushed past the absolute peak of performance into infinity [p. 4].

Schilling then gave a brief account of the life of Paul Schreber. After Paul became *Senatspräsident* in Dresden Schilling wrote,

. . . he contracted a nervous illness, and died in the asylum at Leipzig-Dösen on 14 November [should be April] 1911, an incurable lunatic. The derangement of his genetic material is also evident from the fact that his marriage to Ottilie *Sabine* Behr—daughter of the actor and singer at the Leipzig city theatre Heinrich Behr—only resulted in two [should be six] still-born children [p. 5].

It would be an exaggeration to say that the memory of Moritz Schreber is kept alive by the only organization officially to bear his name today: the *Deutsche Schreberjugend*. Nevertheless, something of it does still remain there. Two manuals on group work contain a brief account of his life (Deutsche Schreberjugend, c. 1958, pp. 6-9; Brocke, 1977), and in the information which the organization put out about itself there are also references to the activities of "Dr. Gottlieb Schreber" *(Deutsche Schreberjugend, n.d., p. 1; c. 1979, p. 1). A text by Gerhard Richter was reprinted in the organization's bulletin in 1973, though the occasional sentence has been omitted. For example: "In visionary enthusiasm Schreber worked undaunted at strengthening national sentiment" (G. Richter, 1914a, p. 5; omitted from G. Richter and Wahl, 1973).

3. MEMORIAL ARTICLES ABOUT MORITZ SCHREBER

In this section, which continues my discussion of Moritz Schreber's more general reputation acquired through the allotments named after him, I shall confine myself almost exlusively to one aspect, articles about him in newspapers and periodicals, most of which appeared on the more important anniversaries of his birth or death. I have no doubt that I have found only a fraction of all these texts. Even to say that what I have found is the tip of the iceberg would be wrong: from an examination of the tip of the iceberg it is possible to calculate the size of the whole, but I have no idea how much remains hidden. Articles from specialist journals, chiefly medical, are greatly overrepresented, because there are reference works to guide one in such publications. By contrast, there are no library aids to help one find such minor items in ordinary newspapers.[5] In many cases, then, such articles reached me by quite indirect routes. For instance, Bankhofer's text (1977) in an Austrian newspaper was sent to me by one of Moritz Schreber's descendants living in the German Democratic Republic; it had been sent to her by relatives in the United States.

My survey of such articles will be brief, since this aspect of Moritz Schreber's influence is of no great significance. With the exception of W.'s article in the *Leipziger Tageblatt* in 1908, these texts tell us nothing new about Moritz Schreber. Nor can they be of any real use in documenting a widespread and approving public image of Moritz Schreber, which might have been able to reinforce the suppression of feelings of hatred for him in his son, for before 1907, i.e., before the onset of Paul Schreber's final period of illness, I have only been able to find one article. This section may be seen as a study of how a person acquires fame, and, in particular, how he acquires fame through something that he did not do. The emphasis will be on the way the accent shifts with the changing periods. In addition, this section complements the psychiatric literature. There, a link is often made between admiration of Moritz Schreber and national socialism: "... Dr. Moritz Schreber (1808–61), who was long considered, notably by the Nazis, one of the most eminent and influential educationalists of his times" (Jaccard, 1979). This accords well with the vilification of Moritz Schreber that is quite general in the psychiatric literature. However, it will become clear as this section proceeds that approving texts are much more common and that, for example, they even appear in East Germany.

Most memorial articles about Moritz Schreber are constructed more or less according to a fixed pattern. Starting from the Schreber gardens, one soon arrives at Schreber the man. There then follows a brief biography, and the occasional remark about his work: here the emphasis is usually on his article on children's playgrounds, "*Die Jugendspiele.*" Eventually the writer reaches the subject of the Schreber Associations. Here some writers are sufficiently well informed to know that the first Schreber Association was founded not by Schreber but by Hauschild; others invent ingenious links between Moritz Schreber and the gardens named after him: for example, that he left some money to the city of Leipzig for the purchase of allotments which were to be rented to "modest citizens" (K-d, 1936, p. 1262), or that he went on journeys "to France, Belgium and England, where he lectured energetically on behalf of public health. Everywhere he made propaganda for his idea of small gardens at the edges of towns" (Bankhofer, 1977). Schreber's influence is often exaggerated in these articles:

> Three creative areas have made the doctor Moritz Schreber famous throughout the world: his work as an orthopaedist, his writing as a medical educationalist, and his activities on behalf of the allotment garden movement associated with his name [Kilian, 1958a].

This is the beginning of one of the articles to appear in East Germany. It is, however, the most extreme example of its kind: The exaggeration found in these texts does not assume the proportions that we shall see in the psychiatric literature.

A feature common to all these articles is their admiration for Moritz Schreber, which is just as unanimous as the antipathy to him in psychiatric writing. In discussing the latter, I shall attempt to give some explanation of this shift in attitudes. It is largely a matter of changing epoch: Nowadays it is difficult for those with a knowledge of Moritz Schreber's work to have much admiration for him.

Before 1907

Before the end of 1907, i.e., during the period in which Paul Schreber might have taken "conscious" notice, I have been able to find only one article: *"Auf Leipzigs Schreber-Plätzen"* (On Leipzig's Schreber grounds) in the popular family magazine *Die Gartenlaube* (Stötzner, 1883). The article gives extensive attention to Moritz Schreber's life and work.

1908–33

Despite my inability to find any more articles predating Paul Schreber's hospital admission in 1907, Moritz Schreber must still have been fairly well known at the beginning of the century as the man after whom the Schreber Associations were named, for I have found four articles published in 1908, one in *Die Gartenlaube* and three in local newspapers in Saxony.[6] 1908, of course, was the hundredth anniversary of Schreber's birth. In two of the articles (Lipsius, 1908a, 1908b) the word *"Schrebergarten"* was still in quotation marks, thus indicating that it was not yet fully accepted.

Despite this sudden rush of four articles in 1908, the stream of articles about Moritz Schreber did not really get under way until the 1920s: in 1925 there was an article in the monthly *Leipzig*, in 1927 an extract from Schreber's *Kallipädie* in the *Deutsche Turn-Zeitung*, and in 1929 two major newspaper articles.[7] These appeared on the occasion of the "general Saxon Schreber Day," on which old people's homes and hospitals were to receive gifts of flowers. I have found no other references to this annual Schreber Day whatsoever. In 1931 virtually identical articles appeared in two medical journals: one written by Dr. Karl Bornstein, the other by "K. B." In the same year the *Leipziger Neueste Nachrichten* carried a short article headed "70th anniversary of the death of Dr. Moritz Schreber."

1933–45

During the national socialist era many of the articles on Moritz Schreber bore the stamp of the regime. He was often praised as the man who had first recognized the tie with "the soil," and one also comes across such phrases as *"Blut und Boden"* (blood and soil) and *"Verwurzelung in Vaterland, Volk und Boden"* (being rooted in father, nation and soil). However, phrases of this kind always appear only in the first paragraph or the final lines of the article. Does this mean that they are mere lip-service to the regime? I am not, in fact, particularly happy with the term "lip-service" because it suggests that verbal servitude is less important than other forms of servitude. Other changes were taking place at this time. For example: the street on which the orthopedic clinic was located, the *Zeitzer Strasse*, was renamed the *"Adolf-Hitler-Strasse."* And is it coincidence that the great family trees of the Schrebers and the Haases were drawn up in the years 1932 and 1933? I have never dared asked the person who drew them up. In any event, several articles on Moritz Schreber appeared during the same period without any sign of ideological coloring.

The year 1933 was the one hundred and twenty-fifth anniversary of Moritz Schreber's birth, and that produced two articles. The one in the *Allgemeine deutsche Lehrerzeitung* (General German teachers journal) begins as follows: "The old longing for one's own soil has now taken hold of broad strata of our nation" (Foerster, 1933, p. 680).

The other, in the *Sächsische Kurier*, contains in its opening sentence the terms "German spirit" and "German national community." The year 1936 saw the appearance of Alfons Ritter's thesis *Schreber, das Bildungssystem eines Arztes* (1936a). This is the only text from the allotment tradition that has become known in the psychiatric literature, and it is due solely to Ritter's book that Moritz Schreber has ever been linked with Nazism (see, e.g., Niederland [1960, p. 496] and Schatzman [1973a, p. 152]). To make that link, to be sure, one only has to read the first sentence of Ritter's preface: "The path to the renewal of the German spirit and of German strength leads necessarily to an avowal of blood and soil" (Ritter, 1936a, p. 3). However—apart from a racist remark on page 35—Ritter's book is tainted with ideology only in its brief preface. It is a bow in the direction of the authorities before saying what one actually has to say. Ritter's dissertation also appeared in a commercial edition with the title *Schreber, Künder und Streiter für wahre Volkserziehung* (Schreber, proclaimer and fighter for real education for the people) (1936b).

After this Moritz Schreber also made appearances in various other books. In 1937 K. Pfeiffer received a doctorate for his thesis, *Daniel Gottlob Moritz Schreber und sein Wirken für die Volksgesundheit* (Daniel Gottlob Moritz Schreber and his work for the public health), a text devoid of ideology and also totally lacking even a single remark of any noteworthiness at all. Pfeiffer's subject had been selected for him by W. Haberling, one of the revisers of the *Biographisches Lexikon der hervorragenden Ärzte aller Zeiten und Völker* of 1934, which contains an entry on Moritz Schreber (see page 247). In his *Naturheilkunde in Lebensbildern* of 1937 (see page 249) A. Brauchle devoted a chapter to Moritz Schreber; Kleine did the same in 1942 in *Ärzte kämpfen für Deutschland* (page 248 above and note 9 to chapter 4).

In 1936 not only did Ritter receive his doctorate: it was also the seventy-fifth anniversary of Schreber's death. This prompted a further five articles, three of them in medical journals.[8] Several articles also appeared at the end of the 1930's.[9] Schreber also turned up (not surprisingly) in pieces on Hauschild, the true founder of the first Schreber Association,[10] and in articles on his daughter Anna Jung which appeared in the press on the occasions of her ninety-eighth, ninety-ninth, and hundredth birthdays and when she died.[11]

In the 1940's the articles at first continued as usual: quotations from Moritz Schreber's *Das Buch der Gesundheit* in *Der Landarzt* (The country doctor; Hoffmann, 1940); in 1942 little text and many pictures in *Die neue Gartenlaube* under the heading "Who was Dr. Schreber?"; and in 1943 two almost identical articles in medical journals, one written by Dr. med. W. Ackermann, the other by "Dr. A." In the same year articles on Moritz Schreber also appeared in two Austrian newspapers.[12]

After the Second World War

The effect of the war on the flow of articles only really became apparent after 1945. Earlier there had been no evidence of any obstruction; afterward, ten years were to intervene before the stream started moving again. I shall discuss the articles appearing in East and West Germany separately.

East Germany

According to one East German writer, Moritz Schreber's ideas anticipate "the realization of the principle of dialectic materialism of the unity of theory and practice" (Gr. 1958). Yet there is a difference between the German Democratic Republic and the Third Reich. Once Moritz Schreber had been called a "man full of ideas for social reform" (Loeffler, 1955, p. 8), the words "full of ideas for social reform" more or less became the East German epithet for Moritz Schreber—often appearing in quotation marks. This kind of shying away from political partisanship did not occur during the period of national socialist rule.

It took until 1958 for the first article on Moritz Schreber to appear in East Germany; it was the hundred-and-fiftieth anniversary of his birth. I have already referred to the publications of the Leipzig orthopedist Uibe of 1958 and 1959 (see page 233). The 1958 aritcle was written in collaboration with his patient W. G. Kilian. Kilian characterized Schreber in quotation marks as a "man full of ideas for social reform" (Kilian and Uibe, 1958, p. 335). In the same year Kilian also wrote about Moritz Schreber in two newspapers (1958a, 1958b), and I have quoted from another article printed in that year (the passage about the unity of theory and practice). In 1960 Kilian published an article in an orthopedic journal under the heading "Is Moritz Schreber still close to the present?" Answer: Yes; moreover, he is a man "full of ideas for social reform" (1960, p. 2). The early 1960's produced several more articles,[13] including one with the sentence, "Above all,

Schreber supported the idea of making gardens available to the workers" (Quoted in Schilling, 1964, p. 2).

In the 1970's two Leipzig newspapers carried a series about allotment gardens. In the *Leipziger Abendzeitung* the sixth instalment of the series was devoted to "Dr. Schreber's idea"; here Schreber was characterized as a man "full of ideas for social reform" whose books are "full or revolutionary ideas" (Keilman, 1973). And the *Mitteldeutsche Neueste Nachrichten* ran a "series about Dr. Schreber" that contained the statement that "The authorities were not impressed by his ideas for social reform" (Seidel, 1974b).

Recent years have seen an article on the "Fathers of the Schreber gardens" in a Leipzig newspaper (Starke, 1976) and an interview in the *Mitteldeutsche Neueste Nachrichten* with a Dutch researcher whose thesis is on the subject of Moritz and Paul Schreber (Seidel, 1977), while at 9 o'clock in the evening on 16 October 1978 the radio station "Voice of the G.D.R." (broadcasting in German) devoted a program to Moritz Schreber, "a man full of ideas and revolutionary plans" according to the program announcement.

West Germany

In West Germany too, writers have adapted to the changed political circumstances, and texts about Moritz Schreber have lost their political color. In 1937 Schreber was still a "fiery patriot" in Brauchle's eyes (page 281); by 1951 those words had disappeared. And Kleine changed the title of his book from "Doctors fight for Germany" (1942) to "Doctors in the storms of time" (1958; see also note 9 to Chapter 4).

The only exception is an article of 1968 in the *Leipziger Neueste Nachrichten*—not an East German newspaper but an '*émigré*' periodical—which even in a piece on Moritz Schreber managed to get in a little anti socialist propaganda:

> Daniel Gottlieb Moritz Schreber was born in Leipzig in 1808. He was a distinguished doctor of the people, though not in the sense of the present system, which has never been particularly keen on the little garden for the small man, since a man who likes gardening is a man who does not go to meetings in the evening. He is a functionary within his own fence-posts [Lange, 1968, p. 3].

In the West it took nearly ten years for the flow of Schreber articles to get going after the war. After that, articles began to appear in various quarters, including a magazine for schoolteachers and one on natural healing.[14] There would be little point in discussing them all here.

More interesting is a radio program broadcast of the sixties about Litfass and Schreber, the men whose names are embodied in the words *Litfaßsäule* (advertising pillar) and *Schrebergarten*. In view of the positive attitude to Moritz Schreber which emerged, this program can be placed firmly in the tradition of the allotment literature. However, the writer, Renate Milczewsky, took the trouble to find more documentation on Moritz Schreber than the majority of authors,[15] so that her text shows signs of the problems facing someone wishing today to combine a knowledge of Schreber's work with enthusiasm for his ideas. In fact, such a combination is no longer really possible. This is not a value-judgment: all I am saying is that a century after the death of Moritz Schreber, ideas on educating children have changed. The manner of, and reasons for, this change will be discussed below.

Milczewsky did not say that Schreber is out of date. In her amiable view of him, he was a man of solid, somewhat old-fashioned ideas. For example, to a gathering of schoolmasters she had him say: "Give instructions that on every school day the children must spend some minutes sitting straight to attention!" (Milczewsky, n.d., p. 24). And the old-fashionedness of these words becomes apparent when they rouse "laughter" among his audience, and a shout that "Children aren't soldiers!"

Clearly, Frau Milczewsky invented this scene herself; and that, of itself, is no problem. But the question is whether the scene would have been possible at all, considering Moritz Schreber's work and the nature of his public. The answer is no, on two counts. First, Schreber never argued in favor of sitting up straight at attention in school: on the contrary, as an orthopedist he warned against school benches without backs because they led to spinal overstrain in pupils. Thus Schreber was by no means more soldierly than his times; his advice, indeed, was closer to modern attitudes. On the other hand it would be quite wrong to give the impression that Milczewsky simply invented this sitting at attention for "some minutes." Both concepts appear in Schreber's work, but in a very different form: rather than wanting the children to sit at attention for some minutes every day, he recommended that they should be allowed to use the backs of their benches for "two or three minutes" in every lesson. "If one grants the children these breaks for relaxation, when they are sitting free one may demand that they always sit upright, as they should" (D. G. M. Schreber, 1858e, p. 17). In short, the standpoint by virtue of which Moritz Schreber was ahead of his times had become so out of date a hundred years later that it first had to be extensively "modernized," and can even then be presented only as old-fashioned. This is the result of benevolent hodiecentrism.

In the early 1960's articles appeared in three medical journals to mark the hundredth anniversary of Moritz Schreber's death.[16] Schreber was also referred to in a talk on "unknown ancestors of Werner Siemens" during the "Siemens family gathering" (Siemens, 1966), but this kind of thing falls somewhat outside the scope of this section.

During the 1970's it proved possible to see in Moritz Schreber a forerunner of another new ideology, namely that of concern for the environment.

> Hats off to the physician Dr. Schreber, born in Leipzig in 1808! He foresaw the atrophying and degeneration of the body through the atrophying of the senses. . . . We stand, in our dark glasses, motorized, destitute of all pleasure in the sense of smell, before a pile of atrophied and dead senses. . . . Dr. Schreber foresaw the whole deterioration of health. He is modern and contemporary [*Gesundheitswesen und Desinfektion*, 1972, p. 161].

In 1976 the *Kneipp-Blätter* devoted three pages to Schreber in a series entitled "Significant figures in medicine" (Kuppe, 1976).

Comparison of the Schreber articles in East and West Germany shows that there are not many fewer articles in the East than in the West. This means, since there are very many more periodicals in the West, that as regards this kind of article the German Democratic Republic is far more strongly represented. The relative dearth of articles that approve of Moritz Schreber in the Federal Republic may have something to do with the psychiatric "Schreber case," which is practically unknown in the East. However, I do not feel that this plays a very significant role. In 1973 the excellent magazine *Der Spiegel* carried a long article on the psychiatric case of father and son Schreber. "People's educator Gottlob Moritz Schreber: Sadism under the veil," it said under his portrait (*Der Spiegel*, 1973, No. 36, p. 130). And as if there had never been a psychiatric "Schreber case," six years later Moritz Schreber reappeared in the same magazine in an article about allotment gardens. Now, underneath the same portrait, we read "Orthopedist Schreber: fun with spade and hoe" (*Der Spiegel*, 1979, No.

45, p. 91).[17] Moritz Schreber's more enduring popularity in East Germany seems to me to be more a consequence of the general backwardness of that country, and of the apparent innocence which makes the subject of Moritz Schreber attractive to East German writers.

NOTES TO CHAPTER 22

[1]The Schreber Associations themselves apparently know very well why they are named after Moritz Schreber. The canonical reading of the story is as follows: When the new association had to find a name for itself, suggestions such as "Parent-Teacher Association" or "School Association" met with little general acclaim. Someone then suggested the name "Hauschild Association." "Only too modestly"—so goes the ritual turn of phrase—Hauschild rejected this out of hand and put forward the name "Schreber Association," "in reverent memory of that admirable medical educator, the man from whose so admirable writings they had hitherto drawn their chief strength and comfort, and in whose spirit the enterprise was wholly and entirely conceived." In short, a noble gesture and a beautiful piece of syntax from Dr. Hauschild. Not surprising, therefore, that this utterance appears so frequently in the literature: Mittenzwey (1896, pp. 67-68), Fritzsche and Brückner (1903, p. 14), G. Richter (1914a, p. 4; 1925, pp. 3-4; 1936a, p. 5; 1939b, p. 12; 1940, p. 49), Kilian and Uibe (1958, p. 337), Kilian (1960, p. 418), Seidel (1974a), Kilian (1977, p. 29), and with slight variations in Siegel (1907a, p. 4; 1914, p. 17), Foerster (1933, p. 681), Schilling (1961, p. 218; 1964, p. 14), and Milczewsky (n.d., p. 31).

Nevertheless, I fear the entire story is apocryphal. Hauschild's words are first quoted over thirty years after the event (Mittenzwey, 1896, pp. 67-68); there are no minutes of the meeting (G. Richter, 1925, p. 3); and the quotation does not appear in the work of those writers who might have been actually present (Mangner and Schildbach).

[2]In its next edition the newspaper in which this passage appeared, the *Sunday Times*, printed a letter in which Moritz Schreber and the Schreber Associations were brought back to their true proportions (Janssen, 1973).

[3]The magazine *Der Schrebergärtner* completed two volumes (1907 and 1908, after which the title was changed to *Der Arbeiter und Schrebergärtner*). I have never been able to find a copy of it; a reward to anyone who succeeds. The same goes for the first volume (1905) of *Der Freund der Schreber-Vereine*.

[4]I have no proof, of course, that after Freud no author from the psychiatric tradition ever saw this issue of *Der Freund der Schreber-Vereine*. However, I believe I have good reason for believing it: There is not a single edition of Freud's text about Schreber in which the erroneous volume ("ii" instead of "iv") ascribed to this issue by Freud has been corrected, not even the version in the *Standard Edition* (Freud, 1911b, p. 51), which is always highly praised precisely on account of its accuracy and references.

[5]There is one important exception: the fiches on Moritz Schreber in the biographical section of the history of Saxony catalogue in the Sächsische Landesbibliothek in Dresden.

[6]Viz.: F., 1908, Lipsius,1908a, and 1908b, and W., 1908. On the last of these, see also note 11 to Chapter 3.

[7]Viz.: Hänsch, 1925, Wehlitz, 1927, and Von dem Hagen, 1929a, 1929b. There is also a third article by Von dem Hagen about Moritz Schreber in *Der Volksstaat* (vol. iv, No. 198, p. 6), but I have not seen it myself.

[8]Viz.: Schütze, 1936a, 1936b, and 1936c, Jahn, 1936, and K-d, 1936.

[9]Viz.: in 1937, an article by Kempe that I have never seen, in *Der neue Weg* (vol. vi, 1937, p. 182), in 1938 Schwatlo's, in the *Neue Leipziger Zeitung*, and in 1939 an article by Weinmeister.

[10]Articles on "Ernst Hauschild: From Schreber's Ideal World to Reality" appeared in 1941 in the *Nossener Anzeiger*, 1941, No. 183, the *Thalheimer Zeitung*, 1941, No. 183, the *Grosshartmannsdorfer Landbote*, 1941, No. 183, and in various other dailies, according to the catalogue of the history of Saxony in the Sächsische Landesbibliothek in Dresden. According to the same catalogue there also appeared in the same year articles on Hauschild in the *Wurzener Tageblatt*, 1941, No. 188, p. 5, and 1941, No. 191, in a "supplement" (Beiblatt).

[11]Viz.: A. L., 1938, *Neue Leipziger Zeitung*, 1939, A. L., 1940, H. B., 1940, *Der Freiheitskampf*, 1944, *Neue Leipziger Tageszeitung*, 1944, and the *Dresdner Zeitung*, 1944.

[12]Viz.: in the *Wiener neueste Nachrichten* of 1943 and in the *Neues Wiener Tagblatt* of 23 November 1944, p. 3.

[13]Viz.: in 1961 Niemann and an article from the "Eastern Zone" from which Schilling (1964, p. 2) quoted, and in 1964 an article in *Die Union*.

[14]Viz.: *Berliner Lehrerzeitung*, 1954, Mette, 1955, Friedrich, 1956, G., 1958, Diem, 1958, and K.F.H., 1959.

[15]Frau Milczewsky wrote to me that her documentation came from Leipzig. This is why even in West Germany we find a reference to Moritz Schreber's "ideas for social reform" (Milczewsky, n.d., p. 3).

[16]Viz.: Gmelin, 1961, *Der Landarzt*, 1962, p. 589, and the *Bayerisches Ärzteblatt* of 1961. This last publication wrote of Moritz Schreber, who had died a hundred years previously, that he had "settled as a general practitioner and *Privatdozent* in his home town exactly a hundred years ago" (*ibid.*, p. 394). Most of the journal's readers would have missed this curious dating; possibly it crossed some minds that it was a printing error. However, it is not; for this centennial year the *Bayerisches Ärzteblatt* took over, word for word, passages from the article that had appeared twenty-five years earlier in the *Wiener Medizinische Wochenschrift* (K-d, 1936). Even the period that had elapsed was not adjusted: from 100 to 125 years.

[17]Exactly the same sort of thing happens in *Stern*, which in 1974 published a review of Schatzman's book: "The inventor of the Schreber garden brought up his children so brutally that the sons landed up in the madhouse" (Randschau, 1974, p. 198). And in 1980 the same magazine carried a lengthy piece of reporting on allotment gardens, with a fine color photograph of the name "Dr. Schreber" done in flowers, and statements like: "Dr. Schreber invented the allotment in Magdeburg in 1852, as a garden for children. His son-in-law Hausschild then reshaped them into workers' gardens" (Stephani, 1980, p. 54). This quotation also illustrates the wholesale manner in which mistakes creep into this kind of historical writing. Moritz Schreber did not invent the allotment garden. How the author arrives at Magdeburg or 1852 I cannot even guess. Hauschild's name was not Hausschild, he was not Moritz Schreber's son-in-law, and like him he had no connection with allotments.

23

PSYCHOANALYSTS ON MORITZ SCHREBER

In the preceding two chapters we have looked at the slight "ordinary" reputation which Moritz Schreber enjoyed and at the reputation which he gained through the allotment gardens he never founded. We have seen that in the allotment literature Moritz Schreber is credited with a fame as an educator equal to that which he tried in vain to achieve during his lifetime. In the final two chapters the central theme will be Moritz Schreber's third kind of fame, namely, the notoriety he acquired during the past few decades as the father of "the most frequently quoted patient in psychiatry." We shall see that here the alleged influence of Moritz Schreber the educator—in demonic reversal—far outdoes even the fantasies of the allotment literature.

The significance of the educator Moritz Schreber for the psychiatric "Schreber case" was discovered by the psychoanalyst W. G. Niederland. Since 1959, he has pointed out in a succession of articles certain striking parallels between delusions experienced by Paul Schreber and child-rearing methods advocated by his father which now appear abominable. Following Niederland's work, in the psychiatric literature Moritz Schreber has achieved a certain notoriety as an "inhuman" pedagogue. Outside psychiatric literature, Moritz Schreber did not become known in this role until the early seventies, when Morton Schatzman published his interpretation of the links between delusions and upbringing: According to Schatzman, Paul Schreber's persecution mania was the consequence of the way he had been persecuted by his father as a child. With this new interpretation Schatzman also criticized Freud's interpretation of the Schreber case, and that in turn led to a defense of Freud by psychoanalysts.

In this chapter I shall pay particular attention to the problems which Freud's favorable opinion of Moritz Schreber caused modern psychoanalysts—who do not share it and who therefore tie themselves in knots trying to deal both with Freud's remarks on Moritz Schreber and with Schatzman's work, which criticized Freud's study of the Schreber case.

In section 1 of this chapter I discuss what Freud has to say about Moritz Schreber. Section 2 deals with the work of Niederland, Section 3, with its reception in psychoanalytic literature; in Section 4 I examine the psychoanalysts' reactions to Schatzman's work.

1. FREUD ON MORITZ SCHREBER

Freud explained Paul Schreber's persecution mania in terms of repressed homosexuality. Paul Schreber, he said, had secret homosexual feelings about his father, which he repressed: "I do not love him, I *hate* him"; subsequently he projected this hate onto his father: "I hate him because he persecutes me"; and finally he raised his father into a God who persecuted him. His homosexuality also explained, said Freud, why Paul Schreber first feared, and later accepted, that he was to change into a woman, subsequently to be impregnated by God. I do not propose to go into the details of Freud's theory concerning Paul Schreber's persecution mania. It is a theory that makes pronouncements almost exclusively about transformations supposed to have taken place inside Paul Schreber's head; and with my new biographical material I have nothing to offer that might either support or undermine that theory.[1]

Freud's theory is concerned with the transformations which Paul Schreber's love for his father underwent in his psychic apparatus. Thus Moritz Schreber played an essential role in it—though in a highly specific sense. Freud took as his point of departure Paul Schreber's love for his father; the actual qualities of that father played a relatively minor role. I shall now take Freud's remarks about Moritz Schreber and submit them to close scrutiny—not because they are essential to Freud's theory (they are not, as we have seen) but because they serve as material for the following sections in which I shall show how curiously they have been treated by later psychoanalysts.

There can be no doubt about Freud's favorable opinion of Moritz Schreber:

Now the father of Senatspräsident Dr. Schreber was no insignificant person. He was the Dr. Daniel Gottlob Moritz Schreber whose memory is kept green to this day by the numerous Schreber Associations which flourish especially in Saxony; and, moreover, he was a *physician*. His activities in favour of promoting the harmonious upbringing of the young, of securing co-ordination between education in the home and in the school, of introducing physical culture and manual work with a view to raising the standards of health—all this exerted a lasting influence upon his contemporaries. His great reputation as the founder of therapeutic gymnastics in Germany is still shown by the wide circulation of his *Ärztliche Zimmergymnastik* in medical circles and the numerous editions through which it has passed.

Such a father as this was by no means unsuitable for transfiguration into a God in the affectionate memory of the son from whom he had been so early separated by death [Freud, 1911a, p. 46 = 1911b, p. 51].

Elsewhere, too, Freud referred to Moritz Schreber in similar vein: "a distinguished doctor" (Freud, 1973, p. 306), or "a most eminent physician, and one who was no doubt highly respected by his patients" (Freud, 1911a, p. 47 = 1911b, p. 52).

Although Freud's theory about Paul Schreber's mental illness is chiefly concerned with intrapsychic processes, he nevertheless attributed a favorable influence to the real role that Moritz Schreber played in his son's life: Freud did not exclude the possibility

that what enabled Schreber to reconcile himself to his homosexual phantasy, and so made it possible for his illness to terminate in something approximating to a recovery, may have been the fact that his father-complex was in the main positively toned and that in real life the later years of his relationship with an excellent father had probably been unclouded [Freud, 1911a, p. 68 = 1911b, p. 78].[2]

I have quoted these passages at such length not because they appear to me to be particularly brilliant or so terribly wide of the mark, but because they indicate quite a different appreciation of Moritz Schreber from what we find in the work of later psychoanalysts, and because in later sections I shall demonstrate that it is a difference which places those psychoanalysts in a quandary: and their best way of solving their problem is apparently to be conspicuously silent about these passages. Instead, in order to avoid the hint of any discrepancy between their own negative attitude of Moritz Schreber and the work of Freud, they make copious use of certain other passages in Freud taken out of context. Before I turn to the work of later psychoanalysts on Moritz Schreber, let us look at the passages in Freud which are later so frequently quoted.

Freud wrote that he would exercise "tact and restraint" in his interpretation, so that even the reader unfamiliar with psychoanalysis will be prepared to following his reasoning. And:

> In working upon the case of Schreber I have had a policy of restraint forced on me by the circumstance that the opposition to his publishing the *Denkwürdigkeiten* was so far effective as to withhold a considerable portion of the material from our knowledge—the portion, too, which would in all probability have thrown the most important light upon the case [*ibid.*, p. 33 = 1911b, p. 37].

In short, Freud would have been able to produce a better analysis if all sorts of interesting passages, particularly about Paul Schreber's family, had not been excised from the *Memoirs*. This spelling out of the facts would not be necessary were it not for the circumstance that in the later psychoanalytical literature we are told that Freud exercised "restraint" in his Schreber analysis, but not what that restraint related to. It is also implied that the restraint applied to Moritz Schreber, and that Freud would not dare say anything derogatory about a man who—according to the later psychoanalysts—was then held in high esteem. But as we have seen, the "restraint" in question has nothing to do with that.

In order to reinforce the suggestion that Freud wrote nothing unfavorable about Moritz Schreber for considerations of discretion, references to this "restraint" are sometimes accompanied by the statement that Freud asked himself whether Paul Schreber would not be offended by a discussion of the *Memoirs* (*ibid.*, p. 10 = 1911b, p. 10). However, Freud then expressly followed the lead given by the *Memoirs* themselves, and allowed the interests of scholarship to prevail unambiguously over personal sensibilities.

Later authors, writing on the cruelty of Moritz Schreber, were also fond of quoting Freud when he stressed Paul Schreber's curious attitude towards his God:

> It will be recalled that Schreber's God and his relations to Him exhibited the most curious features: how they showed the strangest mixture of blasphemous criticism and mutinous insubordination on

the one hand and of reverent devotion on the other [*ibid.*, p. 45 = 1911b, p. 51].

Freud traced this back to the earlier relationship with the father:

> We are perfectly familiar with the infantile attitude of boys towards their father; it is composed of the same mixture of reverent submission and mutinous insubordination that we have found in Schreber's relation to his God, and is the unmistakable prototype of that relation, which is faithfully copied from it [*ibid.*, pp. 46, 47 = 1911b, p. 52].

But this says nothing disparaging about Moritz Schreber: The reference is to sons in general; every son is insubordinate toward his father. Freud's chief point was to explain the subsequently hated God in terms of the previously loved father: "The person who is now hated and feared for being a persecutor was at one time loved and honoured" (*ibid.*, p. 37 = 1911b, p. 41).

Later psychoanalysts were also given to quoting Freud's sentence, "Thus in the case of Schreber we find ourselves once again on the familiar ground of the father-complex" (*ibid.*, p. 49 = 1911b, p. 55). As long as one omits to mention what Freud means by this, namely, that the basis for the insanity lies in the love for the father, this statement of Freud seems not to contradict the arguments by later writers whose central theme is Moritz Schreber's inhuman stance with regard to his son.

2. NIEDERLAND ON MORITZ SCHREBER AND ON FREUD

In a succession of publications beginning in 1959, the psychoanalyst W. G. Niederland (1959a, 1959b, 1960, 1963, 1974) pointed to the importance of Moritz Schreber's educational ideas for "the Schreber case." He is undoubtedly the best of the psychoanalyst writers on father and son Schreber. He showed convincingly that in Paul Schreber's psychotic system there are traces left by his previous life. Thus in the *Memoirs* we find mentions of "Frederick the Great" (Friedrich der Grosse) and a certain Julius Emil Haase. Paul Schreber's grandmothers were named Friderique Grosse and Juliana Emilia Haase.[3] And change of gender played a major role in Paul Schreber's psychosis (Niederland, 1963, p. 204 = 1974, p. 97).

Most of the parallels found by Niederland, and the most striking ones, are connected with Moritz Schreber's system of bringing up children. I mentioned an example of this in my introduction: the "compression-of-the-chest miracle" in which the sick Paul Schreber on several occasions felt that his chest was being compressed by "divine miracles" to the point of suffocation—a sensation allegedly connected with child-rearing contraptions of his father's invention such as the "straightener"—the iron bar preventing the child from leaning forward while writing—or the bed straps over the chest to ensure that the child slept on its back.

Another example relates to Paul Schreber's feeling that his head was being compressed as in a vise—a sensation referred to as the "head-compressing machine" by the supersensory voices he could hear. Niederland linked this experience to the chin-strap, the helmet-like device mentioned on pp. 86–87. The sick Paul Schreber also complained that his eyes were being "miracled on," that is, being forced to look at particular objects. His father described eye exercises for children which sharpen the eyesight by making them look at various objects. Moreover, he recommended regular eyewashes: and the sick Paul Schreber complained that his eyes are regularly closed by "divine miracles."

In his publications Niederland gave a multiplicity of such links between insanity and method of upbringing. There is no point in going over all of them here: The interested reader may read Niederland's works for himself. But Niederland did more than simply point out parallels between insanity and upbringing. Now that it has become apparent that the method of upbringing has left traces in the psychotic illness, one cannot avoid asking what was the nature of the influence which Moritz Schreber's method of upbringing evidently had on his son.

Niederland was remarkably reticent when it came to drawing conclusions from the parallels he found, however striking they might be. His judgment of Moritz Schreber the educator was unambiguously negative: "a father whose sadism may have been but thinly disguised under a veneer of medical, reformatory, religious, and philanthropic ideas" (Niederland, 1959b, p. 386). Niederland believed, furthermore, that Moritz Schreber's method of upbringing had a deleterious effect on Paul Schreber. On Moritz Schreber's campaign against masturbation he wrote:

That the violent, sadistically tinged methods used by him in this fight prevented at least one of his children from establishing an identity for himself, particularly a sexual identity, is recorded throughout the *Denkwürdigkeiten* [Niederland, 1959a, p. 161].

Niederland opined that as a result of this upbringing Paul Schreber "had already undergone a notable degree of traumatization when he entered his third or fourth year of life" (Niederland, 1959b, p. 389). But despite all such pronouncements, Niederland nowhere wrote that Moritz Schreber's methods of educating children caused or helped cause his son's mental illness. On the contrary, discussing the parallels between upbringing and psychosis, he stated that he did "not claim that the data so far accumulated throw light on the nature of Schreber's psychosis" (Niederland, 1963, p. 206). This conclusion is, of course, incorrect: There are all sorts of elements in Paul Schreber's psychosis, such as the "compression-of-the-chest miracle" and the "head-compressing machine," which before Niederland's discoveries were simply incomprehensible nonsense, but, as a result of his studies have most certainly been clarified.

There are other curious features in Niederland's work. For instance, he described Moritz Schreber's educational ideas as: "a 'scientifically' elaborated system of relentless mental and corporeal pressure alternating with occasional indulgence, a methodical sequence of studiously applied terror interrupted by compensatory periods of seductive benevolence" (Niederland, 1959b, p. 386). Yet I am unable to find any trace in Moritz Schreber's writings of any such alternation of terror and benevolence.

The solution of these peculiarities in the work of Niederland must be sought, it seems to me, in his relation to Freud. In a moment we shall see that Niederland emphatically stated that his work fits into the Freudian tradition, and we have already seen how differently Freud and Niederland looked at Moritz Schreber and his qualities as a father. If Niederland wished to remain faithful to Freud, he was precluded from drawing the obvious conclusion that Moritz Schreber's educational methods contributed to the onset of mental illness in his son, since according to Freud the underlying factor in that illness was not a father acting to the detriment of the son, but the son's love for his father. I presume that this must be how Niederland arrived at his otherwise still inexplicable conclusion that his work sheds no light on the nature of Paul Schreber's psychosis.

Similarly, I am unable to comprehend the supposed alternation of terror and benevolence in Moritz Schreber save as an attempt on Niederland's part to find some sort of compromise between his own unfavorable opinion of Moritz Schreber's idea of education and Freud's remark quoted on page 291 to the effect that Paul Schreber's relationship with his "excellent" father may have had a beneficial effect on his illness—a remark which, incidentally, is mentioned nowhere in Niederland's work.

This brings us to the principal theme of this chapter: the dogmatism of the psychoanalysts, and their "solidarity" with Freud. In the remainder of this section I shall show that Niederland did some peculiar things with Freud in order to present his own work as orthodox psychoanalysis. In his first article on father and son Schreber, for example, he quoted at length from the passage in which Freud referred to Moritz Schreber's enduring influence in the field of education and the success of *Indoor Gymnastics*. Directly after this quotation Niederland continued:

> It is evident that in describing the father's fame and work, Freud refrained from saying more about the man's personality; nor did he mention any of the other books published by Dr. Schreber. This was in conformity with Freud's "policy of restraint" explicitly stated in his monograph, a policy to which Freud both wisely and deliberately adhered while writing about the memoirs of the younger Schreber. It is most likely due to this rule of restraint that Freud spoke of Schreber senior in the general terms that he did. Several of Dr. Schreber's children and members of his family, Professor Paul Flechsig, and others were still alive at the time of Freud's publication. It could hardly have escaped Freud's attention that there was more to this remarkable man, his character, influence, and work [Niederland, 1959a, p. 153].

This is a curious passage. Freud's "policy of restraint" has nothing to do with observing moral discretion, but, as we have seen, only with the fact that the most interesting passages in the *Memoirs* have been left out. And even supposing Freud to have had moral scruples, then he ought to have applied his "policy of restraint" to the matter of accusing a possibly still living *Senatspräsident* of homosexuality, rather than to a closer examination of books by an educator who had already been dead for half a century. The same applies with respect to Paul Schreber's family. And why, when discussing Moritz Schreber, should Freud have had to exercise restraint in consideration of the psychiatrist Professor Flechsig, not to mention those persons so neatly characterized as "others"?

Niederland himself placed his approach firmly within the tradition of Freud's work; thus he found looking for parallels between upbrining and psychosis "a legitimate approach, since it is based on the only childhood material at present available to us as well as on Freud's main thesis in this case: 'Here we find ourselves . . . on the familiar ground of the father-complex' " (Niederland, 1959b, p. 384). But that Paul Schreber's father-complex looks quite different in Freud's work is something that Niederland does not tell us.

In some cases Niederland indicated that his findings confirm Freud's theory. Thus he recorded that Moritz Schreber experimented more with his sons than with his daughters, and that the sons came to stickier ends than the daughters. This is immediately followed by the claim that "This outcome, completely unknown to Freud, essentially corroborates Freud's main thesis about the case" (Niederland, 1959a, p. 168). This sentence is meaningless—apart from the fact that it is an expression of solidarity. A later article concluded as follows:

> It is finally worth noting that of Dr. Schreber's five children the two sons succumbed, the first to suicide and the second to a psychosis, whereas the three daughters, to our knowledge, remained healthy. I am inclined to regard this outcome as a striking, if indirect proof of Freud's main thesis in this famous case [Niederland, 1960, p. 499].

In short, powerful though Niederland's new discoveries may be, their presentation as support for Freud's work is decidedly shaky. Now the reader may ask whether all this is really so terrible, whether Niederland's false position with regard to Freud really has to be the catalyst for discrediting the whole of psychoanalysis. But that is not the point. The point is that Niederland's curious attitude to Freud has never been rectified in the later psychoanalytic literature: Indeed, even more curious defenses of Freud sometimes crop up there, and I shall deal with these in the next section on psychoanalysts' reaction to the work of Niederland.

3. PSYCHOANALYSTS ON NIEDERLAND

We have seen that Freud and Niederland have quite different ways of looking at Moritz Schreber. Niederland's was to become the accepted view; and here I shall show how psychoanalysts have tried to play down this incongruity with Freud. This is not a simple matter of personal whims in the way the two men look at things: It is a question of the much more general change of opinion. Freud's opinion closely matched other opinions of Moritz Schreber as we see them in the allotment literature which flourished at the same time. Niederland's work likewise fit into a much more general pattern. In many respects his thoughts since 1959 about Moritz Schreber the domestic tyrant were anticipated by ideas which, in retrospect, can easily be interpreted as their precursors.

Niederland's work is an expression of interest in the abominable father of a paranoiac; we find something similar in the theoretical field in Knight's work of 1940. Knight wondered whether the homosexual love regarded by Freud as the foundation for the persecution mania was not created chiefly "by the intense need to neutralize and erotize a tremendous unconscious hate" (1940, p. 153). Two years later Menninger and Menninger came to a somewhat similar conclusion: "The man who feels himself persecuted is obviously defending himself not against his love of someone so much as against his hate for someone, someone whom the persecutor represents" (1942, p. 262).

Thus the paranoia theory implicit in Niederland's work need not occasion surprise, but this is also true of his turnabout in his appreciation of Moritz Schreber. A few years previously Baumeyer had adopted an attitude that was clearly a half-way stage between Freud and the later psychoanalysts: in the psychiatric reports on Paul Schreber Baumeyer discovered the statement that Moritz Schreber had suffered from "obsessional ideas with homicidal tendencies." On the other hand Baumeyer also clung to what had always been written about Moritz Schreber in the past: "His father [Paul's] was a doctor with philanthropic inclinations, who, at the same time, suffered from homicidal impulses" (Baumeyer, 1956, p. 70).

In the same period the English translators of the *Memoirs* adopted an unambiguously unfavorable attitude with regard to Moritz Schreber: He "published a number of books of which the titles alone, quite apart from their text, show that he was eccentric, not to say a crank" (Macalpine and Hunter, 1955, p. i).[3]

At the time when Niederland began writing on Paul Schreber's father, not only was attention already being paid to the feelings of hatred in paranoiacs and to the negative attitude to Moritz Schreber, but there was also a gathering interest in the family in which Paul Schreber had grown up. For example, in 1959 Shulman lamented the fact that an Adlerian interpretation of the Schreber case was not really possible because "the familiar material used by Adlerians to arrive at an understanding of a person, the family constellation and early recollections, are unavailable" (1959, p. 187). And the psychoanalyst M. Katan tried to fill this gap by reconstructing scenes which supposedly took place in the family in which Paul Schreber grew up; I have already discussed these (see pp. 75ff.).

An article by A. Tabouret-Keller of 1973 on the educational thinking of Moritz Schreber can serve as an even clearer illustration. A psychologist of the school of the French Freudianist Jacques Lacan, Tabouret-Keller evidently did not know the work of Niederland. This reprehensible omission helps to illustrate the degree to which the time was ripe for an approach such as Niederland's. For Tabouret-Keller too looked at Moritz Schreber's educational ideas in the hope of finding something that would shed light on Paul Schreber's illness, and she too subscribed spontaneously to the exceedingly unfavorable view of Moritz Schreber the pedagogue (1973, p. 318). The fact that the time was ripe for Niederland's approach in no way detracts from his individual achievement: However much such parallels as that between the chin-strap and the "head-compressing machine" appear obvious now, there is no trace of any such discovery in the work of Tabouret-Keller.

This failure to be acquainted with Niederland's work is, incidentally, fairly unusual in a French author on the Schreber case. In general Niederland cannot complain of a lack of interest in and appreciation of his work in France, either among authors who, like Tabouret-Keller, first became familiar with the Schreber case through the work of Lacan (e.g., Deleuze and Guattari, 1972, p. 353; M. Mannoni, 1973, pp. 28-29, 31; Elliott-Smith, 1973, p. 4), or among the official French psychoanalysts (e.g., Racamier and Chasseguet-Smirgel, 1966, pp. 5-24; Chazaud, 1966, pp. 100-101; Prado de Oliveira, 1979a, pp. 227-259, 330-355, 419-431).

Even more rapidly forthcoming was praise in the American literature for Niederland's work on Moritz Schreber (see, e.g., Donadeo [1960] and Kitay [1963, p. 192]).[4]

Moritz Schreber, who tried in vain to become an influential educator during his lifetime, and who was erroneously invested with the influence on account of his reputation for having founded allotment gardens which he did not found: This Moritz Schreber the educator finally achieved a late third fame through the work of Niederland. In the psychoanalytic literature about Moritz Schreber, as it came into being through Niederland's work, the exaggeration of Moritz Schreber's educational influence was taken yet another step further than in the allotment literature. Psychoanalysts characterize him as "the leading expert in all Germany on childrearing" (White, 1963, p. 217) or "the authority on childrearing in the Germany of that day" (Kitay, 1963, p. 191); Chasseguet-Smirgel wrote about "the whole of Germany observing the precepts of the celebrated Dr. Schreber" (1975, p. 1018). And according to Calasso the "cruel and famous educationalist" Moritz Schreber had "enormous influence in Germany as a proponent of hygiene, gymnastics and a strictly moralistic education throughout the nineteenth century, and, in an underground sort of way, down to the present day" (1974b, pp. 524-525). Such overdrawn characterizations are not found in Niederland's articles. However, it looks as if even he eventually began to believe the exaggerations which grew up in his wake: In his book about the Schreber case in 1974 he referred to the "enormous popular appeal" and the "numerous subsequent editions" of Moritz Schreber's "more voluminous writings" (Niederland, 1974, p. 79).

I do not propose to go into such mistakes more deeply but shall return to the criticism that is the central theme of this chapter, i.e., my criticism of the psychoanalysts' attitude toward the work of Freud. In the foregoing sections on the work of Freud and Niederland we have seen that the two have widely diverging opinions of Moritz Schreber and of the effect he may have had on the mental health of his son. We have also observed the contortions Niederland went through to give the impression that his work latches directly onto Freud's. I shall demonstrate that this is not, alas, a blind spot in a single individual psychoanalyst.

Racamier and Chasseguet-Smirgel begin their summary of Niederland's work with the sentence: "Freud perfectly grasped the overwhelming importance of the father. Documents acquired later have confirmed and more closely identified it" (1966, p. 15). Kitay concluded: "Niederland, continuing his documentation of the Schreber case, had demonstrated convincingly that there is much factual support for the Freudian interpretation of the case" (1963, p. 223). Eickhoff had this to say about the book in which Niederland brought together his studies of father and son Schreber: "Freud's conclusions from his analysis of the 'Memoirs of my Nervous Illness' by Daniel Paul Schreber have been profoundly confirmed and deepened by Niederland's book" (1979, p. 1062).

Neither has Niederland's incorrect interpretation of Freud's "policy of restraint" ever been challenged. On the contrary: ". . . it has to be remembered that Freud himself, as Niederland repeatedly reminded us, spoke of his "policy of restraint" in interpreting the Schreber case and accordingly refrained consciously from interpreting all its aspects" (Kitay, 1963, p. 222).

The psychoanalysts' attitude to Freud corresponds to the manner in which they reacted to the work of Schatzman, who, with the aid of Niederland's discoveries, himself challenged Freud's theory: Might not the persecution mania actually be the product of persecution, rather than of repressed homosexuality?

Here again, the time was ripe for this approach. As long ago as 1960, Kohut suggested such an interpretation of Niederland's work, only to reject it outright:

What is the relation between the anamnestic data from childhood and the delusions of the adult psychotic? The temptation to tacitly accept a simplified cause and effect sequence is great: the early trauma "caused" the later symptom, somewhat like the "imprinting" of the ethologists. Yet, we know that the relation between adult symptom and childhood experience is more complex [Kohut, 1978, p. 306].

Another psychoanalyst, Ehrenwald, anticipated Schatzman's ideas far more directly. In many cases of persecution mania he saw it as a product of a very domineering mother's upbringing. He then wondered how these "schizophrenogenic mothers" are to be reconciled with the best-known case of persecution mania, the Schreber case. He found the solution in "a fascinating study entitled *Schreber: Father and Son*, recently published by William Niederland" (1960, p. 54). In Moritz Schreber, Ehrenwald saw

. . . the paternal counterpart of these "schizophrenogenic mothers"—a "schizophrenogenic father," as it were [*ibid.*, p. 55].

the son's paranoid trend is the direct continuation of his early symbiotic bondage to an omnipotent parent figure, elevated to the status of an all-powerful divine agency [*ibid.*].

Ehrenwald went so far as to say that such ideas do not coincide with Freud's theory of persecution mania:

> Freud's hypothesis of an underlying bisexual or latent homosexual orientation with the tendency to denial, reaction formation, or projection need not necessarily be the only, nor even the principal determining factor [*ibid.*, p. 56].

Nevertheless, his own argument is couched in extremely pro-Freudian terms: "One is reminded of Freud's statement: 'Delusion owes its convincing power to the element of historic truth which it inserts in the place of rejected reality" (*ibid.*, p. 55). Perhaps such genuflections in Freud's direction are the reason why these thoughts, even though they were later repeated in book form (Ehrenwald, 1963, pp. 43-48), attracted little attention. As far as I know, Schatzman was not even aware of Ehrenwald's work when, some ten years later, he formed his own theory about the Schreber case.

4. PSYCHOANALYSTS ON SCHATZMAN

At the beginning of the 1970's Morton Schatzman propounded a new theory about "the Schreber case": Paul Schreber's persecution mania must be accounted for in terms of the manner in which as a child he had been persecuted by his father. In this section I shall concentrate on the reactions of psychoanalysts to Schatzman's work; because they have never actually paid much serious attention to Schatzman's theory itself, I prefer to delay my discussion of it until the next chapter. Schatzman also offered theoretical criticism of Freud, and that too will not be discussed here because the psychoanalysts have never given it any serious attention. They have, however, taken exception to a perfectly innocent remark of Schatzman's, in which he expressed surprise at the fact that Freud, a person who believed that the roots of many psychological problems are to be found in childhood and who knew that Paul Schreber's father was the author of works on education and upbringing, nevertheless never read any of Moritz Schreber's educational works.

The reasons for Freud's omission are not hard to find: His theory of paranoia was already present in outline when he first studied the case of Paul Schreber; in the *Memoirs* he found all sorts of things to confirm it; and he therefore had no need of Moritz Schreber to achieve what he wanted to achieve. It should also be remembered that Freud wrote his study of the Schreber case in a matter of months, alongside all his other day-to-day work.

Modern psychoanalysts have all reacted quite differently to Schatzman's remark. I begin with a long tirade from the first reaction to Schatzman's work, namely Niederland's.

Schatzman in his opening paragraph writes that "Freud . . . neglected an important source of data—the writings of Schreber's father about child-rearing." Such remarks are not only incorrect but also disparaging. They reveal an almost complete absence of factual and historical perspective. The statement, indeed, must be categorically rejected as unjustified and misleading. It ignores, wittingly or unwittingly, . . . many of Freud's original comments. . . . The criticism which Dr. Schatzman levels against Freud is particularly objectionable, since he himself neglects certain important facts to which Freud referred in his text, *expressis verbis*—namely, that "Dr. Schreber may still be alive" (which he was, when Freud began his work on the *Memoirs*) and "may be pained by these notes upon his book," that "in working upon the case of Schreber I have had a *policy of restraint*," and similar clarifying comments. It is also well to remember that at the time of the publication of Freud's monograph, other close members of the Schreber family as well as his psychiatrist, Paul Theodor Flechsig, were still living and that therefore Freud's self-imposed "rule of restraint" was more than justified [Niederland, 1972, p. 80].

This reasoning is worth closer attention. Niederland started with a whole barrage of value-judgments: incorrect, disparaging, almost complete absence of factual and historical perspective, unjustified, misleading. These were followed by arguments calculated to justify them: Schatzman ignored "many of Freud's original comments" (which Niederland did not specify, and I do not know to which comments he refers). Then we have the arguments I have already referred to: the "policy of restraint" and the question of whether Paul Schreber might not be pained by a discussion of the *Memoirs*; observations, as we have seen, that have nothing to do with Moritz Schreber. The "similar clarifying comments" are just as enlightening as the "many of Freud's original comments" just mentioned. It remains unclear why Flechsig should be shocked by remarks about Moritz Schreber, and why Paul Schreber's family should prefer a member of the family possibly still living to be accused of homosexuality to having anything said about books by Moritz Schreber fifty years after his death. Niederland continued: "In other words, the very ethical and professional considerations to which Freud refers in his text are now held against him" (*ibid.*, p. 80). In other words, Niederland drew attention to "ethical and professional considerations" on the part of Freud which never existed. He went on to state that

> Any attentive reader of Freud's monograph will readily understand that Freud must have been aware of various special features and personal attributes which were characteristic of Schreber's father. This awareness was also indicated in a personal letter written by Freud to Ferenczi, a letter known to me as to content and tenor [*ibid.*, p. 80].

To which "various special features and personal attributes which were characteristic of Schreber's father" does Niederland refer, and what have they to do with Schatzman's criticisms of Freud? Or does it become apparent from these questions that by asking them I disqualify myself from the status of "attentive reader"? In the last sentence Niederland added to his statement about Freud's knowledge of the unspecified "various special features and personal attributes" of Moritz Schreber by referring to an unpublished letter from which he chose not to quote. Such an argument is not particularly convincing in a polemic.[5]

In 1974 Niederland published his book *The Schreber Case: Psychoanalytic Profile of a Paranoid Personality*. It consists of three parts, the middle one of which is the most important: In it Niederland assembled his earlier studies, chiefly concerned with father and son Schreber. He wrote of the chapters in the book: "All but one have appeared as contributions to various scientific journals. . . . In order to avoid inevitable redundancies, some articles have been amended, others abridged, and still others expanded" (1974, p. 37). Then, for "all but one" of the subsequent chapters, Niederland gave references to where the texts previously appeared. The exception is the final chapter, "The Schreber Case, Sixty Years Later," where there is no indication that it previously appeared elsewhere. Yet it certainly did appear earlier: It is the attack on Schatzman just referred to (Niederland, 1972). True, Niederland thoroughly revised the text for his book, to the extent that Schatzman's name disappeared completely, so that it is now an attack on a totally anonymous "conspirational theory of psychosis" (1974, p. 109). This deletion of Schatzman's name and omission of a reference to a text in which Schatzman's name does appear has nothing to do with avoiding "redundancies": In this entire book there is not one mention of Schatzman, not even in the extensive bibliography.

In his first article about father and son Schreber Niederland quoted Freud at length on the subject of Moritz Schreber (1959a, p. 153); in the revised text for his book he omitted this quotation (1974, p. 50). This again has nothing to do with avoiding "redundancies": Despite the fact that there is even an entire chapter devoted to Freud's analysis of the Schreber case, there is no record anywhere in the book of Freud's favorable opinion of Moritz Schreber.

So the recipe of Niederland's book seems to be: Keep quiet about any deviant opinions which Freud may have had, and leave out entirely the name of the man who attacked Freud's analysis.[6]

Nobody, apart from Schatzman, ever exposed these practices of Niederland's.[7] And this is a new mistake: This is not a polemic between Niederland and Schatzman, but an infringement of the rules of scholarship by Niederland. In the minds of almost all its readers, Schatzman's comments on Niederland's book must have come over as a reviewer complaining that his own work has received too little attention in the book he is reviewing (Schatzman, 1974b). This is where the academic community ought to have stepped in but failed to do so.

To the contrary: Subsequent psychoanalytic publications on the Schreber case contain even more curious remarks about the work of Niederland and Schatzman. Let us look at a few examples:

> Dr. Niederland should be congratulated for clarifying the complex circumstances surrounding the case and continuing the work Freud foreshadowed in his own conclusion of the case when he wrote, "it remains for the future to decide whether there is more delusion in my theory (of paranoia) than I should like to admit, or whether there is more truth in Schreber's delusion than other people are yet prepared to believe" [Shraberg, 1975, p. 346].

This is a mysterious sentence. Did Niederland show that Freud's analysis is partly delusion? Or did Freud already suspect that the horror of Paul Schreber's God pointed to the horror of his father? No—this is simply a quotation from Freud taken out of context in order to give the impression that Freud already knew a great deal.

One lengthy review by a psychoanalyst of the books of Niederland and Schatzman began with praise for Freud's analysis of the Schreber case. Then the reviewer, Rosenkötter, said of Niederland's work: "By it, the work began by Sigmund Freud is significantly perfected and extended" (1975, p. 185). Rosenkötter went on to write that he is surprised

at Schatzman's casual assertion in his book of 1973 that Niederland only tried to "confirm Freud's conclusions about why Schreber became paranoid," whereas Schatzman himself has "linked Schreber's curious experiences . . . to specific procedures of the father. . . ." Here Schatzman has shifted the balance of the scholarly contributions in his own favour to such an extent that it can only be called dishonesty, for he presents all the historical and biographical facts adduced by Niederland as his own cognitions [*ibid.*, p. 185].

The dishonesty here is not in Schatzman but in Rosenkötter: Schatzman did refer to Niederland's work (Schatzman, 1973a, especially p. 8). But in theoretical terms, too, Rosenkötter's attack on Schatzman is pitiful:

Basically Schatzman's reasoning amounts to saying that the persecution mania comes from persecution by the father and society. To the psychoanalyst this appears as a tautology in which there is no inherent power of explanation and which represents a relapse to the state of knowledge existing *before* psychoanalysis [1975, p. 186].

This last sentence raises all sorts of queries: Why is the assertion that persecution mania is the result of actual persecution tautologous? (And now we are using difficult words: a "tautology in which there is no inherent power of explanation"—that is called a pleonasm.) If this is a tautology, is not then every other theory, e.g., Freud's, a logical contradiction? And did psychiatry before Freud consist entirely of tautologies? Where has Rosenkötter read that before Freud, psychiatry explained paranoia in terms of actual persecution?

Rosenkötter himself was spared criticism. On the contrary, Eickhoff wrote that in this article Rosenkötter "adopts a clarifying position" (1979, p. 1058) with regard to the confusion created by Schatzman's book.

Schatzman caused other psychoanalysts a certain amount of irritation too. Chasseguet-Smirgel, for example, described him as someone who "shamelessly exploits documentation gathered by other authors, particularly Niederland" (1975, p. 1018). She did not say why it is "shameless" to use material collected by others; indeed the whole point of what Schatzman did is that he took facts which had been known for years and used them to give a new twist to theoretical thinking. Shengold missed in Schatzman an

> awareness of what it means that Freud was writing in 1911, only eight years after the publication of Schreber's widely read *Memoirs*, when children of the elder Schreber were still alive and potentially in the public eye. The utmost tact on the subject of the father and the family was necessary, especially on the part of one like Freud [1974, pp. 368, 369].

Accusing Freud of paying too little attention to Moritz Schreber has hitherto been countered chiefly by a moral argument: Freud, so his supporters will have it, was too discreet to venture into such an area. It is also possible to put forward an argument that is a stage more orthodox and say that in fact Freud already held similar views on Moritz Schreber to those which were later to be expounded by Niederland and others. Niederland seems once to have applied this strategy: According to Donadeo he once said:

> Freud's "restraint" in dealing with the material, a point he himself made explicit in the monograph, was probably due to the fact that many of the principals connected with the case were still alive. He, too, had for a while thought Schreber's father to be psychotic [1960, pp. 303-304].

I have not come across Niederland's use of this strategy anywhere else. Katan, by contrast, employed it consistently. In his view any reader who is not *too* stupid will see straight away that in fact Freud was expressing the same unfavorable opinion of Moritz Schreber as Niederland and Schatzman. Freud

> quoted [Paul] Schreber's belief that God did not understand living human beings and was used to having contact only with cadavers. This makes it very easy for the reader to conclude that the father required a *Cadavergehorsam* (the type of obedience demanded in the German army) from his children [Katan, 1975, p. 359].

Yet I find it a pity that Freud did not say this himself, that he took no account of readers such as myself, who would never arrive at such a "very easy" conclusion. In any event, according to Katan, Freud, without knowing Moritz Schreber's work, made a much better job of it than Niederland and Schatzman:

> I ask: Did Freud really need any information provided by an outside source? Was he not building a construction of Schreber's childhood which in no way is contradictory to but is even more informative than what the father's books might have brought to light? My answer is: Freud demonstrated that a construction can provide more complete insight into Schreber's childhood development than all the books written by the older Schreber could do! [*ibid.*, p. 360].

Furthermore, according to Katan Freud deliberately decided against using Moritz Schreber's books:

> There are of course [sic] compelling reasons why Freud presumably had never thought of consulting the father's books. . . . How can one find out in what ways and to what extent the father's influence left its marks on Schreber's mind? How did the son conceive of his father's treatment? *All this we can learn only from the son and not from the father* [*ibid.*, p. 358, 359].

That goes without saying: Of course we can see the eventual effect on the son only by looking at the son. But that such an end-product as the "head-compressing machine" could have anything to do with Moritz Schreber's method of child-rearing—*that* is an idea which will occur to no one who does not know the books of the father. But Katan had yet more arguments up his sleeve:

> There may be an even more important reason why Freud would not have wished to read a book by Schreber's father, assuming he had known of its existence. In my opinion, Freud had no incentive to read statements made by the father, for he did not want to be influenced by any material that did not come from Daniel Paul Schreber himself [*ibid.*, p. 359].

The facts are against this: For example, I have already referred (page 264) to the magazine issue on Moritz Schreber that Freud read. Theoretically, too, it is nonsense: After all, surely Freud could first have read the *Memoirs*, then write down his findings, and finally look at work by Moritz Schreber, could he not?

This article of Katan's is not merely a curiosity that has somehow accidentally reached a printing press: It is a text that has also been translated, included in a French collection of psychoanalytic essays, and characterized as "one of the most important" texts on the Schreber case (Prado de Oliveira, 1979a, p. 12).

The reader who has read this far in this chapter may perhaps accuse me of a strong bias, namely, in that I have virtually passed by any interesting theoretical speculation and have done little but exhibit a downright petty concentration on the attitude to Freud. However, it is my view that the lip-service which psychoanalysts pay Freud and which I observe here is not a matter of individual mistakes but a general, more or less deliberate, policy. It is all the more necessary to point up this dogmatism because it is precisely Niederland's fascinating discoveries that prove that the psychoanalytic literature cannot simply be dismissed as nothing more than gullibility to be quietly ignored. The isolation of psychoanalysis has already progressed to a dangerous degree, when we see that it took over ten years before anyone noticed that the parallels found by Niederland were perfectly capable of being interpreted so as to show that Paul Schreber's persecution mania was an expression more of hatred than of love for his father. It is this conclusion arrived at by Schatzman that is the subject of the final chapter.

NOTES TO CHAPTER 23

[1]The immunity of this psychoanalytic theory to certain facts seems to point in the direction of Popper's objection that psychoanalysis cannot be refuted. However, that is not true: A theory which explains persecution mania in terms of repressed homosexuality is perfectly capable of being refuted, namely by finding homosexuals who suffer from persecution mania. It is only in the way in which this refutation is later parried that the psychoanalysts appear after all to have made Popper's objection of irrefutability the cornerstone of their argument, namely by arguing (e g , Carr [1974, p. 160]) that conscious homosexuality and unconscious repressed homosexuality can easily go together in one and the same person.

[2]In all the subsequent psychoanalytic literature about the Scheber case, in which Moritz Schreber is presented as an evil genius, this remark by Freud is conspicuous by its absence. But it is also absent from the work of his critic Schatzman, the reason being that Schatzman accused Freud of concentrating exclusively on Paul Schreber's desires for his father and their suppression, and of considering that the father's actual behavior is of no relevance:

The father, in Freud's analysis of Schreber, is not an agent. He is, for Freud, an object towards which the son's desire is directed. But he (or it) in no way governs, determines, limits, opposes, suppresses, fears, desires, rouses, inflames, sustains, acknowledges, or even knows of his son's alleged desire for him [Schatzman, 1973a, pp. 95, 96].

Freud's remark about the favorable effect that Moritz Schreber may have had on the course of his son's illness shows that Schatzman is not entirely right here. Schatzman's exaggeration is a pity, because there is no doubt that he does have a valid point which touches an essentially weak spot in psychoanalysis. As I have said more than once: Schatzman wanted to explain Paul Schreber's persecution mania in terms of actual persecution. The psychoanalyst Niederland wrote that actual persecution and persecution mania are sometimes extremely difficult to tell apart. He cited the example of a woman patient who complained of her husband's behavior in a manner which appeared thoroughly plausible—it was only on taking her leave that she added in a whisper that her husband had placed twelve detectives round the house to watch her. "This, of course, solved the diagnostic problem" (Niederland, 1974, p. 111). But here Niederland made the very same mistake that Schatman accused psychoanalysis of making: As soon as Niederland detected mental disorder, any attention he may have been ready to give to real complaints flew out of the window.

[3]In a note Macalpine and Hunter justify their contention that even the titles of Moritz Schreber's books, quite apart from their text, are enough to show "that he was eccentric, not to say a crank" (1955, p. i). This note reads as follows: "For instance, one of his books is called GLÜCKSELIGKEITSLEHRE FÜR DAS PHYS-ISCHE LEBEN DES MENSCHEN" (How to achieve happiness and bliss by physical culture) (Macalpine and Hunter, 1955, p. i). Now the genius of psychiatrists who can determine the character of a person from the title of a book must surely command respect; in this case the feat is all the more superhuman because the diagnosis of monomania in Moritz Schreber is based on the title of a book which he did not write. Schreber was nothing more than the reviser of this book by P. K. Hartmann—a book which had this title even before he revised it. Apart from that, I do not believe such a title was all that strange for those days.

[4]Katan enjoys the unique distinction of being the only person who is not enthusiastic about Niederland's work. He objected to the use of other sources besides Paul Schreber's own text:

> Katan objected to the speculative rather than deductive approach in attempting to explain the psychosis. As in any analysis where the patient is practically the only source of material used, in Schreber's case too the deductive approach should be followed. As in other analyses, we are no better informed about the inner experiences when we take recourse to material from outside sources [Donadeo, 1960, p. 302].

For such a deductive approach by Katan, see pages 75ff above. Niederland did, however, give Katan a good answer: He believed that his findings "do disprove a point made by Dr. Katan in a previous paper (1954): "Psychotic symptoms do not have a direct connection with infancy' " (Donadeo, 1960, p. 303).

[5]J. M. Masson quoted from this unpublished personal letter in an unpublished paper called "Schreber and Freud" (1982). This quote was published in Israels (1984, p. 139). See the latter paper for a discussion of problems arising from using unpublished texts as arguments in a polemic.

[6]To keep quiet about one's opponents does not need to be the end; one might also try and silence them: Niederland once made it a condition for his work to be included in a collection of essays on the Schreber case that no work by Schatzman be included: So I am informed by a letter from the publisher concerned.

[7]There is one exception: In 1975 T. Lidz wrote an excellent review of Niederland's

The Schreber Case in *The Psychoanalytic Quarterly*. He gave highest praise for Niederland's discoveries, but could not understand why they did not bring Niederland to a revision of Freud's theory, so that the religious delusion is the result not of suppressed and projected homosexuality, but of repressed feelings of hatred. Lidz also expressed surprise at the absence of any mention of Schatzman. Now Lidz is certainly not an orthodox psychoanalyst. Even so, it is still gratifying, of course, that a review of this kind can appear in a recognized psychoanalytic journal.

24

SCHATZMAN ON MORITZ SCHREBER

In this chapter I shall be discussing Morton Schatzman's work on Moritz Schreber and the wider fame which Schreber thus eventually achieved in the history of education. My attitude towards Schatzman's work is nothing like as unfavorable as to the psychoanalytic writing discussed in the previous chapter. The psychoanalysts' wounded reactions would seem to suggest that Schatzman's aim was accurate. I hope in this chapter to show that this is not the case—however, Schatzman's view of the Schreber case is so lucid, so obvious, that his book *Soul Murder*, did it not exist already, would have to be written without delay.

First, I shall deal with the various stages in Schatzman's reasoning, in which he tried to show that Paul Schreber's persecution mania was the logical product of the manner in which he was "persecuted" by his father when he was a child. My criticisms will be levelled chiefly against the moral indignation and the ideal of freedom in Schatzman's argument. Second, and finally, I shall show that my objections to moralizing scholarship also apply to the manner in which Moritz Schreber's work, thanks to Schatzman, has become a part of the modern history of education.

1. SCHATZMAN'S PSYCHIATRIC THEORY

Schatzman gave a good summing up of *Soul Murder* in the book itself:

> I propose that experiences he [Paul Schreber] thought were super-
> natural revelations and doctors have seen as symptoms of mental

313

illness can be regarded as *transforms* of his father's treatment of
him. I also suggest that his father had taught him as a child patterns
of operating upon his experience such that later on he felt forbidden
(or forbade himself) to see that his strange relation to God was a re-
experience of his childhood relation to his father. This book illustrates
and embodies this thesis [1973a, p. xiii].

It is important here to note Schatzman's phrasing. If we disregard the
opening sentence of his book, which is perhaps calculated to shock,
he does not say that Paul Schreber was mad or insane. Indeed, he tries
to show that on closer inspection that "madness" is quite understandable. My use of words is somewhat blunter: I simply use words like
"madness" or "insanity," and people can then read "a madman,"
for example, as meaning "someone who is regarded as mad."

Schatzman's thesis is composed of two stages. First: The madness
had something to do with the method of upbringing, is a re-experience
of it. Second: The re-experience took the form of a religious mania
because the method of his upbringing made is impossible for Paul
Schreber to see the true nature of his relationship with his father. In
my treatment of Schatzman's thesis I shall follow these two stages.
I shall begin, therefore, with the interpretation of the parallels between
upbringing and madness; the second half of the section will be concerned with the procedures in Moritz Schreber's educational system
which are supposed to have prevented Paul Schreber from seeing who
was the underlying character behind his God.

The parallels between upbringing and madness

According to Schatzman, Paul Schreber's persecution mania is
to be seen as a logical consequence of the manner in which he was
"persecuted" by his father during his childhood. Schatzman words
his argument in a highly suggestive manner; thus every summary of
his work inevitably implies a thorough rephrasing. For example,
Schatzman often presents his own assertions only in the form of an
appeal to his readers: "Some of you may have begun to see Dr Schreber
as laying the basis for a system of child *persecution*, not child education" (*ibid.*, p. 25). But this is surely Schatzman's own opinion:
The subtitle of his book is *Persecution in the Family*. I shall therefore
present such remarks as assertions by Schatzman himself. This, of
course, is somewhat risky, but I see no alternative. The above quotation

about "child *persecution*" reveals another feature of Schatzman's argument. He leaves no doubt whatever about the revulsion which Moritz Schreber's educational thinking arouses in him, and inherent in his indignation is also the argument that such a dreadful way of bringing up children can never be a good thing. This implicit yet ever-present argument hardly needs discussion here: Schatzman's dismay is an indication of the extent to which ideas of the relationship between parents and children have changed during the past century—nothing more. As an argument for a causal relationship between upbringing and subsequent schizophrenia, this indignation is, of course, valueless.

The strongest argument in *Soul Murder* lies in the parallels between the apparently gruesome methods of child-rearing and the horrifying "divine miracles" later experienced by Paul Schreber in the psychiatric clinics of which he was an inmate. Schatzman demonstrated that there is method in this madness: the method devised by the father. He presented the parallels discovered by Niederland in easily understood form and made one or two other comparisons himself. For example, in the clinics Paul Schreber suffered from curious headaches, as if someone were pulling his hair or tearing out pieces of his scalp. This recalls the "head-holder" (see pages 83, 85): the strap designed to pull a child's hair if it lets its head hang (*ibid.*, pp. 44–45).

All these parallels show convincingly that elements of Paul Schreber's upbringing return in his gruesome delusions. This would appear to prove that Moritz Schreber and his educational methods were the evil genius behind the madness—and most of the reviewers of *Soul Murder* are so convinced. In the best reviews, however, the parallels nevertheless raise a problem:

> Dr Schatzman exclaims at his good fortune in being able to spot how Schreber's suffering could be linked with his father's behaviour. Very often, however, the transformation gives insight only into the *content* of the delusions, hallucinations, or other morbid phenomena, and leaves the question of their cause unanswered [*Times Literary Supplement*, 1973].

Clare raised the same objection, and then rightly went on to observe:

> If the discussion on the concept of mental illness is to proceed, rather than stagnate, such an argument needs to be met. It is made all the more pointed by this absorbing and provocative study [1974, p. 27].

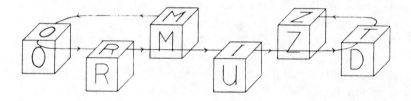

Fig. 58. Moritz-Ormuzd.

Another reviewer wrote:

whether one believes that they [the methods of upbringing] did any more than colour the delusion of schizophrenia, and actually form the primary cause of the illness, depends on the psychiatric sect to which one belongs [*Medical History*, 1974, p. 381].

I am not so sure that discussion of this point is out of the question; I shall try to say something about this problem with the help of some new material.

It is possible to find a further parallel to add to the material adduced by Schatzman. In the psychiatric clinics Paul Schreber's lungs were also the scene of "divine miracles." He feared that he was going to die of phthisis; sometimes he had the feeling that there was only a tiny residue left over of his lungs, with which he was barely able to breathe (D. P. Schreber, 1903, p. 150 = 1955, pp. 132, 133). On other occasions his breathing was excessively accelerated by "miracles" (*ibid.*, 1903, pp. 323, 352 = 1955, pp. 232, 248). Here he seemed in his psychosis to be repeating warnings issued by his father: Moritz Schreber pointed out that many people die of phthisis because they have "weak, unformed lungs." Most people, according to him, breathe far too shallowly, "so that to a large part of their lungs remains almost always inactive, and thus shrinks and becomes a sick, useless part of the body which destroys health and life" (D. G. M. Schreber, 1861a, p. 76). Moritz Schreber therefore recommended "deliberate breathing exercises," which, he said, are particularly important for young people.

According to Schatzman—and the psychoanalysts—the God whom Paul Schreber encountered in the psychiatric clinics was actually his father. According to Paul Schreber's own complicated theology there are two gods: an upper god named Ormuzd, and a lower god called Ariman. There are certain other links to be made between the senior god Ormuzd and Moritz Schreber. For example, G. Rijnders has drawn my attention to the similarity of the two names: See Figure 58. Ormuzd had a preference for nations of originally blonde race (D. P. Schreber, 1903, p. 19 = 1955, p. 53); Moritz Schreber (1859a, p. 2) referred to the superiority of the Caucasian race. The mentally sick Paul Schreber has indications that "the sun is not really a power in itself and separate from God—in a certain sense she is even to be identified with God: in other words she is the instrument nearest to earth of God's power of miracles" (D. P. Schreber, 1903, p. 247

= 1955, p. 189). Here we have the sun as the instrument of God: and Moritz Schreber was an advocate of sunbathing. In particular, weak and "glandular" children ought to be exposed to the sun for a short while every day, either in the open air or, if the weather is chilly, in a sunny room (D. G. M. Schreber, 1861b, p. 90). Paul Schreber often referred to

> the language spoken by God Himself, the so-called 'basic language', a somewhat antiquated but nevertheless powerful German, characterized particularly by a wealth of euphemisms (for instance, reward in the reverse sense for punishment . . .) [D. P. Schreber, 1903, p. 13 = 1955, pp. 49, 50].

It is of course tempting, when reading of this "antiquated but nevertheless powerful German," to think of the German used by Moritz Schreber. The "euphemistic" use of the word "reward" can also be easily imagined in Moritz Schreber's vocabulary. For instance, he advised parents to let a child know "that despite the punishment it has received it still has something to make up to you" (D. G. M. Schreber, 1861a, p. 38). If one takes this attitude it is easy to imagine how Moritz Schreber might explain to a child that punishment is good for it.

These parallels seem to tie up well with Schatzman's thesis that the god by whom Paul Schreber was persecuted was actually his father. However, this material may be equally well adduced in support of Freud, to whom Moritz Schreber was no evil genius. Here the parallels are differently loaded emotionally from the parallels given by Schatzman. He confined himself to gruesome delusions and methods of education, but without saying that he was only giving examples of gruesome elements. But the links between god and father just mentioned are all emotionally more or less neutral. Is this an argument against Schatzman's thesis? I shall postpone answering that question until I have examined some parallels which depart even more radically from Schatzman's material.

As I have said: when considering Paul Schreber's delusions, Schatzman confined himself to unpleasant experiences. This is not a particularly drastic restriction, since almost all Paul Schreber's experiences during his illness were unpleasant. But it is interesting that the influence of Moritz Schreber may also be seen in the few "supersensible" influences which Paul Schreber tells us were pleasant or instructive. Let us look at a few examples.

Paul Schreber suffered in the clinics from "heat and cold miracles," unpleasant sensations which consisted of parts of his body suddenly being "miracled" very hot or very cold. Schatzman—following Niederland—related this to the cold baths in Moritz Schreber's plan for child-rearing.[1] Those baths, however, can also be related to an experience in the psychiatric clinics which Paul Schreber described as pleasant:

> the effect of the one cold shower I was allowed to take in the bathroom was almost miraculous. All at once I felt perfectly well and free from all the threatening manifestations of miracles by which my head and other parts of my body had been visited—although only for a short time [D. P. Schreber, 1903, pp. 172, 173 = 1955, p. 146].

Another instance of Schatzman pointing out a link between father and delusion but tacitly leaving out those elements of the psychosis which were described as pleasurable has to do with the "rays." Now in his books Moritz Schreber often referred to "rays" ("in prayers the child must let the pure rays of God penetrate to it"); in the delusion the word appears to have turned into reality: Paul Schreber was afraid that he would be emasculated by "divine rays." However, Schatzman omitted mentioning the chief characteristic of these "divine rays," namely their healing effect. On several occasions Paul Schreber thought he owed his life to these healing "divine rays," when all kinds of internal organs had been damaged by "miracles" (D. P. Schreber, 1903, pp. 93, 149, 152 = 1955, pp. 98, 132, 134). Here Paul Schreber's psychosis would appear to be not a disguised protest but a disguised tribute to his father as a doctor.

There are quite a few instances of Moritz Schreber's words reappearing in the delusions in a positive light. During his illness Paul Schreber heard all sorts of interesting remarks made by "dead souls": "I have thus gained insight into the nature of human thought processes and human feelings for which any a psychologist might envy me" (D. P. Schreber, 1903, p. 167 = 1955, p. 142). Here is an example: " 'A job started must be finished' was the formula expressing that man should pursue to its ultimate goal what he starts, without being distracted by adverse influences, etc." (D. P. Schreber, 1903, pp. 164, 165 = 1955, p. 141). A similar thought is to be found in the work of Moritz Schreber: "What has been promised or decided must be carried out as far as possible, if only *because* it has been promised or decided" (1861a, p. 64).

The sick Paul Schreber suffered from "compulsive thinking": supersensible voices would challenge his every thought with "why?" This was naturally tiresome, but it also had its useful points, as Paul Schreber said: It

> forced me to ponder many things usually passed over by human beings, which made me think more deeply. . . . As one of many examples: while writing these lines a new house is being built in the Asylum garden. . . . Watching this work the idea automatically arises: that man or various workmen are now occupied in doing this or that; if simultaneously with this thought a "And why" or "Why because" is spoken into my nerves, I am unavoidably forced to give myself an account of the reason and purpose of every single job [D. P. Schreber, 1903, pp. 228, 229 = 1955, p. 179].

Moritz Schreber argued that children's understanding should be sharpened by outings

> because there at every step everything presents itself for an unforced cheerful conversation naturally and in the most easily assimilated form.
>   Here, for example, one would observe a house, in the process of being built, in its construction. On somewhat closer inspection one would observe the different ways of joining the individual bricks to each other, depending on their purposes, along with the preparation and application of the mortar. One could ascertain that wherever an open space is to be covered by masonry (cellars, windows etc.) this can only be done by means of building arches, that a pointed arch throws the load vertically downwards, a flat arch sideways, that the resisting power of the pillars must be constituted accordingly [D. G. M. Schreber, 1859b, pp. 10-11].

And so on. Evidently the "unforced cheerful conversation" between father and son was continued thirty years after the father's death. And here again Paul Schreber, full of praise for the "mentally stimulating effect" of this compulsive thinking, seemed to be praising his father.

All these "positive" parallels are absent from Schatzman's work. His primarily moralizing attitude and his indignation at Moritz Schreber's educational ideas led him only to see the more horrific effects of those ideas in Paul Schreber's psychosis. With this "positive" material now lacking in Schatzman it would be possible to build up an even more extreme version of Schatzman's theory: It would then emerge from the psychosis that more than thirty years after his death Moritz Schreber was still exerting a much more total influence on the feelings of his son—not only on the unpleasant but also on the pleasant sensations. Schatzman was unable to come to such a conclusion because his modern aversion to powerful authority blinded him to the insight that an all-powerful despot can be the source not only of misery but also, of course, of joy.

I do not believe in such a "totalitarian" Schatzmanian theory. This is because there is a third type of parallel between Paul Schreber's psychosis and his ordinary life. So far all the emphasis has been on the role played by Moritz Schreber in his son's delusions, the tacit implication being that this is a measure of the extent to which the father was responsible for the son's illness. However, one of the things Schatzman omitted mentioning is that in Paul Schreber's psychosis there are all sorts of signs of things that have nothing whatever to do with Moritz Schreber. For example, there is a passage in the *Memoirs* where Paul Schreber related that at one time "*almost all the patients in the Asylum*, that is to say at least several dozen human beings, looked like persons who had been more or less close to me in my life" (D. P. Schreber, 1903, pp. 103, 104 = 1955, p. 194). In the literature, other such links had already been established before Schatzman appeared on the scene. For instance: one of Paul Schreber's ancestors (J. C. D. Schreber, 1760) wrote a book called *Novae species insectorum*; and newly created insects play a part in the delusions (Macalpine and Hunter, 1955, p. 2). And above (page 293) I mentioned Niederland's discovery that the names of Paul Schreber's grandmother appear in the *Memoirs* in masculine form (Niederland, 1963, p. 204). It is relatively easy to add to this brief list links with aspects of Paul Schreber's life that stand apart from Moritz Schreber—for example, there are the war experiences in Alsace (see page 141), or there is the god Ariman, who mutters about "David and Solomon" (D. P. Schreber, 1903, p. 181 = 1955, p. 151), names which also occur in the Schreber family tree.

As I said: many of these links had already been established. Schatzman did not mention them, nor did he mention the fact that he did not mention them. If Schatzman thinks that this lends force to his argument, he is of course mistaken: A hypothesis can prove its strength precisely through a confrontation with the evidence which appears to be least in accordance with it.

The general question accompanying Schatzman's parallels is

whether the traces of Paul Schreber's upbringing in his psychosis also
mean that that upbringing had a part in causing the psychosis. If
Schatzman is right, i.e., if the fact that we can recognize real events
in the delusions means that those events helped to make Paul Schreber
go mad, then the parallels that are unconnected with Moritz Schreber
imply that it was not *only* Paul Schreber's upbringing that was to
blame. This reservation in respect of Schatzman does not of course
detract from the fact that the parallels between upbringing and madness
are much more numerous than all the other parallels so far found.

Anyone who wonders whether the traces of an early reality in the
delusions also mean that precisely that reality was a contributing factor
in the origination of the mental illness cannot escape general theoretical
thinking about schizophrenia—the comprehensive term which would
nowadays be applied to Paul Schreber's psychosis. However, theoretical thinking on schizophrenia is a subject that goes far beyond the
pretensions of this book. I want to look only at one aspect of the
subject, i.e., research into the genetics of schizophrenia. My impression is that this is the only branch of research into schizophrenia that
has produced "hard" results: results that are indisputable irrespective
of the school of psychiatry to which one belongs. I also mention this
sort of research here because there is no doubt that the Schreber literature has failed to do it justice. The psychoanalysts simply never
mention it,[2] and Schatzman merely made the occasional disparaging
remark on it.[3] Such reactions betray a fear of the results of research
into heredity that is quite unfounded. For genetic research has shown
that in over half of all cases, schizophrenia cannot be accounted for
by genetic factors. Of course, it does not necessarily follow from this
that social factors play a part: There may be other biological influences
at work. Incidentally, even if a tendency to schizophrenia were totally
determined by genetic factors, it would still be possible to carry out
research like Niederland's or Schatzman's: Even then there would have
to be traces of the patient's ordinary life in his illness, for what other
material does the patient have from which to construct his delusions?
At the same time this thought makes it clear that identifying traces of
a patient's former life in his psychosis is not necessarily an argument
against a biological explanation for schizophrenia. Neither is the dominant influence of Moritz Schreber in his son's psychosis surprising:
In the scarcely shocking sort of life that Paul Schreber led before his
illness, his father's was certainly the most powerful impression, and

nothing in his "normal" life is so precisely documented as the manner in which he was brought up.

Having gone over these doubts which the parallels between up-bringing and psychosis arouse in me, I shall now turn to my next argument against Schatzman. For even if one accepts his interpretation of the parallels, one question still remains to be answered, viz.: Why could Paul Schreber not simply remember his dreadful upbringing; why did he transform his hate for his father into religious mania, into madness?

The transformation from hate to religious mania

The answer Schatzman offers appears throughout his book. I have already mentioned one remark (page 231): According to Schatzman, Paul Schreber's contemporaries more or less deified his father, and that helped make possible the transformation from father to deity. A reader attaching much importance to this theory might thus imagine that Paul Schreber's mental illness began when he was living in Leipzig, since it was only there that his father's name had any particular popular associations at that time. But Paul Schreber's illness began first when he was living in Chemnitz, and subsequently during his two periods of living in Dresden.

However, this deification is not Schatzman's main argument. Instead, he looked for the cause of Paul Schreber's transformation of his father into a God in the father's methods of childrearing, which, Schatzman believed, included a curious sort of brain-washing. Not only did Moritz Schreber have a precise notion of the model to which he wished to shape a child: In addition, part of the model was that the child, once trained, should not be aware that it had been trained. In other words, the intention was that the in-depth programming by the educator had to be forgotten, so that the child would perceive "good" behavior as its own preferred, free choice. Having been brought up in this way, Paul Schreber would then have been unable to see the true figure underlying the forces inside his head, so that he ended up constructing all sorts of gods.

Schatzman believed that he could demonstrate this policy in Moritz Schreber's educational methods by an analysis of the manner in which such terms as "true freedom" or "noble independence" are employed in them. To this end he chose a passage in which Moritz

Schreber argued that as a child gets older it must learn to obey of its own free will.

> The child must gradually learn to recognize more and more that he has the physical possibility of wishing and acting otherwise, but that he elevates himself through his own independence to the moral impossibility of wishing or acting otherwise. This is achieved . . . by illustrative references to the freedom of will present in the child: "You could act differently, but a good child does not *want* to act differently" [D. G. M. Schreber, 1858a, p. 135; also quoted in Schatzman, 1973a, p. 29].

Schatzman then set out what these thoughts of Moritz Schreber's actually mean.

> The child, "physically" free now, unlike before, to wish to disobey and to disobey parents, must learn the "moral impossibility" of either; he becomes free in potential, not in practice. The child must think he "elevates himself through his own independence" to reach this state, while in fact the parent brings him to it. The parent's statement in this passage can be decomposed into its secret, elementary premises: "You could act differently, but I tell you who you are, and I say you are a child who (a) wishes to be good, (b) agrees with my definition of good, (c) does not see my definition to be mine only, and (d) suspects no secret premises in what I say." The aim is for the child to do what his *parent* wants, while thinking he does what *he* wants. Freedom is free not to be free and to see its unfreedom as freedom; that is all [Schatzman, 1973a, p. 20].

Schatzman observed this kind of "misleading" use of words in Moritz Schreber in such terms as "independence" or "self-control," and then turned to the consequences of it: Paul Schreber, he said,

> never connects the coercion [while in the psychiatric clinics] with his father. He cannot, possibly because his father masked (probably unawares) the source of control by defining the state of being controlled by parents as *self*control [*ibid.*, p. 22].

Schatzman offered this criticism of Moritz Schreber from the point of view of an ideal which is in fact only to be found in his book in a negative sense: Schatzman "projects through the negative of the Schreber family that other possibility of communal life within the family, in which there is no fear of fathers and no oppression by fathers,'' according to the dustjacket text of the German translation of *Soul Murder* in 1974 (1974a). Schatzman himself wrote:

Self-determination means that self, not someone else, determines who self is. Dr Scheber means by it (and by ''selfreliance'' and ''free will'') that state in which one no longer needs parents to determine oneself, since they already have done so [1973a, p. 18].

Moritz Schreber started from the old-fashioned idea that there are such things as objective values, rooted in nature and religion. Schatzman, by contrast, used a modern ideal of freedom, believing that every individual should be able to determine the course of his own life, and from this angle he exposed Moritz Schreber's attitude as subtle coercion, manipulation: Moritz Schreber, in other words, forced his own values onto others so thoroughly that those others perceived them as part of their own personality. It is in this falsification of personality that Schatzman sought the answer to the question of why Paul Schreber arrived at the construction of his own peculiar theology, and why he was unable to see that it was his father who lay behind his problems.

That is Schatzman's view. My view, by contrast, is that Schatzman's perception of ''free'' upbringing is even wider of the mark, even more confusing, than Moritz Schreber's. There is no need for me to set out the details of why Moritz Schreber's belief in objective values is misguided: The ''invention of nihilism''[4] has long since become public property. However, the discovery that objective values do not exist has led to the illogical conclusion that therefore every individual, in the fearful realization of the total absence of anything solid for support, must choose the direction of his own life himself, and that the man who says his choice is based on anything else is mistaken or lying. This is a false conclusion because nihilism commits one to nothing, not even to a rational attitude toward one's own values. (On the contrary, nihilism is rather a product of that rationalism.)

Neither is there any reason whatsoever to assume that one's own ideas about good and evil, ideas which are perceived as belonging to the most essential part of one's own personality, are not themselves conditioned. The construction of a ''self'' which ''chooses'' these ideas merely shifts the problem: Is this ''self'' then not determined like all other things?

It is difficult to refute the argument of the man who says that an individual must be free to choose his own values. But I do want to point to an inconsistency in Schatzman: the problem that a choice for the free individual does not necessarily mean a painless farewell to the outdated idea of objective values. Schatzman opined that Paul Schreber's mental illness has never been accounted for by his father's ideas of child-rearing, since such ideas were widespread at the time and were therefore not seen as inhuman:

> Many of the persons who treated or wrote about Schreber, the son, later on, without linking his "nervous illness" to his father's activities, failed to assert a higher or wider rationality against which to measure certain elements in the prevailing one [1973a, p. 147].

But when Schatzman referred to a "higher or wider rationality," all he means is the *later* "rationality," the more modern, "freer" ideas of child-rearing. Why should they be "higher"? I can make my critique of the idea of freely chosen values only more concrete by saying something about the question of how values do come into being, how people do arrive at their choice of life-path, and which laws morality does adhere to.

At the cradle of morality stands men's coercion of men. In order not to go under in a given form of society, certain behavior is undesirable, and certain behavior desirable. To put this another way: morality has its origins in the chances of power within a given figuration. Let me take a well-worn but none the less illuminating example—well-worn because it is the chief theme of a book which some readers may have guessed is the background to these thoughts: *The Civilizing Process* by N. Elias. The example is the change in the circumstances of the French nobility from the Middle Ages until the absolutism of Louis XIV. From a figuration of "free" knights in permanent conflict with one another there eventually evolved a centralistic kingdom under an absolute ruler, in which the nobles could do little else but hope for favors at court. This change in the nobles' chances of power led to a change in their code of conduct: The expression of aggression became increasingly pointless and hence came to be regarded increasingly as uncivilized; the court society stimulated quite different means toward power: Intriguing for the favor of the sovereign demands psychological insight more than anything else. Thus a different personality structure was stimulated. I shall confine myself here to only one facet of this: the increase in the number and severity of prohibitions on expressions of aggression. This is a readily appreciable aspect, and it will do for what I have to say. At the same time I would mention a change in the nature of the coercion behind this shaping of behavior. Behavior that was to a high degree determined by the direct threat of violence evolved into a pattern of behavior in which those concerned anticipated the consequences of their behavior; true, this meant that behavior was determined just as much with an eye to the available opportunities for power as it had been previously, but with the increased internalization of the demands of others this modelling of behavior also came increasingly to be perceived as one of the constituents of the individual's own personality. To denote this shift, Elias used the expressions "constraint through others" and "self-constraint"—in which constraint through others is internalized, becoming increasingly automatic and unconscious. This entire development—the decline in expression of aggression, and the shift from constraint through others to self-constraint—is not, incidentally, confined to the French nobility between Middle Ages and absolutism, but is more generally true of the whole of Western culture, where the increase in bonds between individuals makes the attuning of behavior to others increasingly necessary.

To return to the question of where ideas about life-paths and behavioral codes come from: such ideas are not eternal, objective, or natural, as Moritz Schreber thought, nor are they the product of individual free choice, as Schatzman would have it; they depend on the chances of power existing in the society in question. It is in these terms, and not in terms of "free" choices, that the high degree of consensus in the field of morality is to be explained, and the rate at which such ideas change, i.e., the rate of change of the structure of society; which is quite different from (usually much slower than) the rate of individual development. The attitude toward Moritz Schreber's educational ideas is an example of this: no one chooses his attitude to these ideas "freely" or "of himself," but the ideas concerning authority and similar concepts that are contained within Schreber's ideas show a development over longer periods of time: the modern aversion to authority is no more a "free" choice than was the general acceptance of such ideas a century ago.

The attitude of psychoanalysts toward Moritz Schreber may teach us something about the "power" of such developments in morality. In the last chapter we saw how strong was the loyalty of the psychoanalysts toward Freud: It proved often to be stronger than reason. But the urge of loyalty to Freud cannot hope to compete with the changes that have taken place since Freud's time in attitudes toward education, upbringing, authority, and the like: There is now not one psychoanalyst who shares Freud's favorable opinion of Moritz Schreber.

I believe that in the foregoing I have succeeded in answering Schatzman, from whose "freedom" perspective the approach of Moritz Schreber is "confusing"; I believe also that in looking at it my way I shall be able to some extent to explain the change in ideas on education and upbringing, and hence Schatzman's indignation toward Moritz Schreber. Before I do this, however, I shall first have to make a general observation about the place occupied by upbringing in the development of a society.

Elias's vision of developments in society spanning many generations, and of concomitant changes in the personality structure of the members of those societies, implies that each new generation of adults takes over the thread of development from the previous generation. Each new generation, therefore, must be educated to the then prevailing personality structure, and this education or training, this "socialization" of children, is termed "upbringing." This idea implies that every child in developing toward adulthood passes through something of the development spanning many generations in the history of mankind.

This idea—that in a certain sense "psychogenesis" repeats "sociogenesis"—may be illustrated by reference to Moritz Schreber's educational thinking, where it is not difficult to show that self-constraint is the product of constraint through others, and that—literally in this case—constraint stands at the cradle of morality.

Moritz Schreber's advice to parents of an infant was: "Suppress every trace of false qualities which you may discover in the child; that is, all bad behavior" (D. G. M. Schreber, 1861a, p. 19). Equally clearly, Moritz Schreber realized that this coercion will eventually have to be internalized by the child:

> In the first years of your child's life *you* guided and governed its will. But in a sensible education this is regarded merely as the transition to the actual, higher objective: from year to year the child must want to learn Good, Right and Truth more and more *of its own accord* [*ibid.*, p. 60].

Schreber believed that it is possible to start this process as early as infancy.

You must never fulfil a child's wish, not even one that is in itself permissible, while it is crying or behaving badly, but wait until the child is in a calm and good temper. Otherwise the idea will fix itself in the child that it can force you to give it something by crying and behaving badly, so that the child's respect is destroyed for a long time, and the child rules you, not you the child [*ibid.*, p. 19].

The child, then, is already learning to adjust its behavior itself, first of all to the behavior to be expected from its parents.

There is a nice example of the transition to self-constraint in the "register of sins" which Moritz Schreber advised for children between seven and fifteen.

Hang a slate in your children's day-room, with the name of each child inscribed on it. Under each name note every fault that occurs, with a simple stroke for mere carelessnesses, forgetfulness or other oversights, and in the case of more serious misdemeanours, particularly faults of character, with a stroke with 1, 2 or more crossbars, or whatever, according to the degree of guilt, or perhaps by a note written alongside. At the end of the month, you take the table down for ten minutes or a quarter of an hour and go through the register of sins in everyone's presence. According to circumstances you express reproof or appreciation, and draw particular attention, with real emphasis, to the bad habits which may characterize one or other child [*ibid.*, p. 59].

In this way the ideals of upbringing are already beginning to separate from the parents and assume a somewhat objective form. If the reader should feel inclined here to interpose that the development toward self-constraint is one toward a more *subjective*, not a more *objective* form of constraint, I would remind him that it is precisely in the case of the most subjective of all forms of constraint, constraint by one's own conscience, that the standards applied are often perceived to be the most objective, as, for example, in the view that conscience is the voice of God.

Moritz Schreber used the term "sense of honor" to mean that the child feels superior on account of its good behavior. Here, then, the child is already beginning to identify itself with the life of its parents.

Once the sense of honor is cultivated, it will save the stick and the rod. You can rule the child with a word.

So at first *take care* of the sense of honor. . . . Do not blunt the sense of honor, certainly not by unconsidered terms of abuse. Even when names like "lazybones, coward, lout" etc. may be deserved, they must not in every case, but only after repeated instances, be used as intensification, like heavy artillery. The expression "you should be ashamed of yourself" should already be considered a severe punishment [*ibid.*, p. 58].

"You should be ashamed of yourself" is indeed a much better way of sparing the sense of honor. It reaffirms the educating authority in the child itself; it expresses the fact that there are two different things to be considered: both reprehensible childish behavior and a child that is ashamed of it. This duality in the child is absent in such terms of abuse as "lout."

At the same time it should be borne in mind that in cases where punishment becomes necessary, corporal punishment, which in the early years may be hard to avoid entirely, in the more advanced years of childhood (towards the age of 10-12), should be abstained from completely, if at all possible, because the already more *refined sense of honour* may all too easily be more or less blunted by it [*ibid.*, p. 255].

To Schatzman this internalization of parental constraint in Moritz Schreber's educational thinking must be more grist to his mill. Doubtless he would consider that here is yet more proof of the degree to which Moritz Schreber's pretension—a system of upbringing to independence—is a farce, yet more evidence of how much the parental authority, now become internal in the individual, underlies this apparent independence. Schatzman is not the only person to whom the directness with which Moritz Schreber assumes that good behavior by children is a product of constraint appears almost embarrassing—any modern reader will feel the same way. In this respect ideas about upbringing have changed drastically since Moritz Schreber's day. Nowadays we no longer join in his lamentation that during the first few years upbringing simply is not possible without corporal punishment. This change of mentality points to quite a different way in which upbringing also constitutes part of the general development of society: Parents are less and less able, in their attitudes toward children, to return effortlessly to all the stages in the development of mankind, for example, to a degree of cruelty such as was usual during the Middle Ages. As a result the child in its upbringing will likewise no longer pass through all the historical stages of the development of mankind. Today the notion of constraint in upbringing has been suppressed to such an extent that it is possible for Schatzman to conceive an ideal of education as a process without constraint. It is of course understandable that Schatzman, as the latest link in the chain of this evolution, should see an earlier stage as a morally lower stage. Yet all that has happened here is that a historical development has become the basis for a system of morality. Schatzman's inability to see his own position in historical perspective, his incapacity to distance himself from his own morality, means also that he makes Moritz Schreber exemplify the opposite of his own concept of freedom. That, of course, is wrong: In Moritz Schreber constraint in upbringing is much more obvious than today, but even he does not stand at the beginning of this development; in his case beating children has already been relegated to the first stage in a child's upbringing. This same development is the origin of the most striking feature of modern child-rearing, namely, the declining difference in the relationships of power between parents and children. To take the same example again: If adults start prohibiting themselves from beating children, they deny themselves a means of exercising power over their children. This reduction in power ratios works in favor not only of children, but also of all sorts of other "underprivileged" sections of the community—to use a term which itself is a part of this development.[5] Schatzman, with his implicit sympathy for the child and the mad Paul Schreber, is an extreme example of this development.

As I have said: Schatzman does not see himself as part of such developments. Against an upbringing with constraint he places his ideal of freedom, which I claim cannot exist in the real world. It does not surprise me, therefore, that Schatzman finds the essence of unfreedom which he has discerned in Moritz Schreber wherever he looks at other systems of upbringing: in Luther, Fichte, Skinner, and in the Soviet Union (1973a, pp. 144-147, 155 157). What *does* surprise is that he believes he has found support in one educator, namely Friedrich Fröbel. Is Fröbel the opposite of Moritz Schreber, and does he refute my model of the development of upbringing?

It is curious that the antithesis between the good Fröbel and the evil Moritz Schreber escaped everyone at the time. I have already quoted the subtitle of the magazine *Der Schrebergärtner*, "A weekly magazine for the enlightenment of the people and the education of children according to the ideas of Fröbel, Schreber and Hauschild."

And Moritz Schreber (1861d) also published an article in *Die Erziehung der Gegenwart*, a magazine whose subtitle was "Contributions to the solution of its task [i.e., of "Modern Education"] taking into account the principles of Friedrich Fröbel." The motto "Come, let our children live" on the Schreber-Hauschild processional float (see Fig. 55) is taken from Fröbel. I could continue with such examples.

Schatzman was right when he said that Fröbel put heavy emphasis on leaving the child to its own devices. And Moritz Schreber had another hobby-horse, namely the child's physical development, which must not be forgotten any more than its mental development. But I do not know whether there is really so much difference between the two educators when it comes to constraint and leaving children to their own devices. Fröbel's emphasis on allowing the child to develop freely and the favorable reception of his ideas show that in those days the balance of power already was shifting in the children's favor. And it is not too difficult to show that Moritz Schreber was also part of the same development. Let me return, for the last time, to Schatzman's question, with which this subsection began: Why did Paul Schreber disguise his hatred of his father as persecution mania, and why did he transform his memories into "divine miracles"?

> Why did [Paul] Schreber turn memories into "miracles"? My hypothesis is that he did because his father had forbidden him to see the truth about his past. His father had demanded that children love, honour, and obey their parents. As I illustrate later, he taught parents a method explicitly designed to force children not to feel bitterness or anger towards their parents, even when the feelings might be justified [Schatzman, 1973a, p. 47].

Schatzman illustrated this with a text from Moritz Schreber:

> It is generally healthy for the sentiments if the child after each punishment, after he has recovered, is gently prodded (preferably by a third person) to offer to shake the hand of the punisher as a sign of a plea for forgiveness . . . From then on everything should be forgotten [*ibid.*, p. 120].

Can such a procedure, which to modern eyes must surely seem extremely humiliating for a child, be held largely responsible for causing Paul Schreber's mental illness? It is interesting to see what Schatzman has left out with his three dots: According to Schreber it is healthy for the child "to offer to shake the hand of the punisher as a sign of a plea for forgiveness (and not, as used to be required, to thank him). From then on everything should be forgotten" (D. G. M. Schreber, 1858a, p. 142). It may be unpleasant for the child to have to ask its punisher for forgiveness, but at least it is less unpleasant than thanking him for the punishment.[6] This quotation demonstrates that Moritz Schreber did not represent the most extreme form of authoritarian upbringing. If Moritz Schreber's day was preceded by a time of educational practices even more confusing to modern eyes, then surely it really is unlikely that his practices, already milder than their predecessors, should have caused his son's illness. What sort of mental deformities would not the earlier, even more "confusing" method of upbringing have caused?

With the foregoing I have ventured as a layman into the field of psychiatry and hope that I have shown how weak this psychiatric theory is. However, I do not have an alternative to offer. I have tried to place the relationship of Schatzman to Moritz Schreber in the context of the history of education. In so doing, I have ventured—again as a layman—into the field of the history of education. All this ties up neatly with the general response which Schatzman's book has elicited. It has not called forth anything in the way of new psychiatric theories, but at least Schatzman's book has retrieved the educator Moritz Schreber from extrapsychiatric oblivion. My final section is devoted to this reception of Schatzman's work. There I also criticize the scientific specialty called "history of education," which is also currently taking an interest in Moritz Schreber.

2. THE RESPONSE TO SCHATZMAN'S WORK

This section is concerned with the fame which Moritz Schreber has acquired through the work of Morton Schatzman. The comparatively great influence of Schatzman's book *Soul Murder* is not immediately apparent from the sales figures. The total press run as a Pelican paperback was no more than seven thousand. However, the book has been repeatedly translated, even into Japanese. The Dutch translation has been remaindered, but in Italy the book spent some considerable time on the list of the top ten sellers, while the German translation had a print run several times the size of the original British edition. The article on father and son Schreber that Schatzman first published two years before *Soul Murder* has also appeared in many periodicals and been translated into several languages. Moreover, *Soul Murder* received many reviews, including long ones in such prominent publications as the *Times Literary Supplement*, the *New York Review of Books*, and *Der Spiegel*.[7]

I have already dealt with the psychoanalysts' reactions to Schatzman's work in Chapter 23: All they taught us was something about the sectarianism of psychoanalysis; they had nothing to do with serious psychiatric discussion. In the other reactions to Schatzman, too, no new psychiatric insights have emerged. The chief consequence of his work has been that Moritz Schreber the educator (as opposed to Moritz Schreber the "founder" of the German allotment gardening movement) has at last, more than a century after his death, become to some extent well-known—or rather: notorious. Here are two examples, chosen at random. Moritz Schreber had

> devised a scale of punishments, exercises and weird contraptions which would not be out of place in a torture chamber [Slikker and Meijer, 1975, p. 16].

> In the elder Schreber's widely-read books are found rigid schedules of exercise, forced winter swimming, arbitrary parental authority, and many aspects of fascist life which were then generally accepted [Brown, 1973, p. 19].

Not only does the awfulness attributed to Moritz Schreber reach its zenith in the response to Schatzman: His fame as an educator also gets blown up out of all proportion. In previous chapters I have shown how Moritz Schreber's real influence as an educator was already being wildly exaggerated in the allotment literature, and how in the psychoanalytic literature we begin to find him described even as "the leading expert in all Germany on childrearing." But Schatzman's book took these developments to even greater heights: To judge by *Soul Murder*, one would think that Moritz Schreber was really a famous educator. As a result, the reactions to Schatzman's work refer *en masse* about Moritz Schreber's great influence. Indeed, this misconception is now so widespread, thanks to Schatzman, that I can easily compile a list of examples even if I impose three restrictions on my selection by choosing only reviews of *Soul Murder*, and of those taking only the ones which give Schreber's name wrongly, and of *those* taking only the ones that compare him with Dr. Spock:

Daniel Schreber was the Dr. Spock of the 1840s in Germany [Cohen, 1973].

Dr. Daniel Gottlieb Schreber was the Dr. Spock of his times [*Periscoop* 1975 = *Trouw* 1975].

Schreber's father—Dr Daniel Gottlieb Schreber—was in terms of influence the Dr Spock of mid-nineteenth-century Germany [Gillie, 1973].

His father, Daniel Gottlieb Moritz Schreber, wrote books on child-rearing that were as popular in the mid-19th-century as Dr. Spock's were here a few years ago [*Morning News*, 1973].

Comparisons of this kind are mere curiosities, having very little to do with reality. But before I move from the reviews to a less transient field in which Schatzman's work has been influential, the history of education, I want, purely for the sake of curiosity, to look briefly at one or two other consequences of Schatzman's work.

Anyone who has read *Soul Murder* will not easily forget the child-rearing devices illustrated in it. This strongly visual aspect of the drama between father and son Schreber makes Schatzman's book an attractive proposition for adaptation to the stage. The first play about the Schrebers appeared in Italy. This was followed by a work by the Dutch writers Meijer and Rijnders, in which we are shown how father Schreber tormented his son with all sorts of contrivances. The play was performed in Holland in 1977 and was awarded a dramatic prize. In 1980 it was performed in Belgium. In 1978, meanwhile, television viewers were treated to a play on "the Schreber case," in which, among other things, there was a scene of the Schreber family at table. The children were held tight to their chairs by cruel-looking iron harnesses—harnesses totally divorced from the real Moritz Schreber and evidently the product of the sadistic imagination of the author, G. Eigler. So here we see the Schreber devices gradually taking on a separate identity of their own. Just as the Schreber gardens have become part of the everyday life of Germany without the word *Schrebergarten* immediately calling to mind a famous man, so too, perhaps, do his devices have a shining future ahead of them as symbols of everything that is bad.

For the remainder of this section I shall confine myself to Moritz Schreber's fame as an educator, as acquired through Schatzman's work in the field in which one might expect the greatest degree of competence, i.e., the history of education. I wrote above (page 243) that Moritz Schreber's name does not appear in the kind of literature which was prevalent in the history of education still some ten or twenty years ago; he never became one of the really famous educators like Fröbel or Rousseau, for example. I also tried to explain this fact, by looking at, among other things, the principles underlying this sort of historical writing: from the more or less unbroken line of development which may be discerned in the history of educational thinking, the historians of education have always tended to assume that their own ideas on education are "scientifically" the most correct. They have thus morally raised, but at the same time scientifically degraded, it to a teleology, a process of giving birth to the ideas of today, in which the only interesting educators are those who anticipated the ideas of the period being studied. And Moritz Schreber was not ahead of his times.

Moritz Schreber is now beginning to attract some attention in the history of education. The fact that this is possible is due to a radical change which that branch of scholarship has undergone. It is a change that is part of the process of emancipation to which I referred in the previous section: the growing power of children with regard to their educators, or of "ordinary" people as compared with the elite. Coupled with this there is increasing attention to, and admiration of, those sections of society. Because of this development, with its catalyst, the student movement, which itself is part of it, a title like "Great Educators" now appears hopelessly outmoded. Literature about educators has been superseded by literature about children—preferably children of "ordinary folk," i.e., from proletarian backgrounds, and so on. The study of the history of education has also seen another radical change which, however, I cannot account for so easily: Whereas in the past educational historians always looked for signs of progress, for the points of light in the darkness of history, modern authors are by preference "critical," laying every emphasis on the blackest episodes in that same history. To take an example more or less at random, look at Shorter's book, currently enjoying enormous popularity, *The Making of the Modern Family*. Shorter wrote, not about the elite but about "the classes in which we are interested, the other 95% of the population" (1977, p. 19), and he is fond of using the term "the Bad Old Days."

On all counts, modern studies of the history of education appear to be quite the opposite of the old genre: They do not construct but demolish; they do not try to understand the educators but take the side of the children; they concentrate not on slightly esoteric theoretical systems or principles but on the people, the proletariat, the fringe groups. Yet the basic structure, the fundamental error, has remained precisely the same. The unstated premise is still that the author's own ideas of education must be the right ones: And whether one then, as in the past, hands out pats on the back to predecessors who had vaguely similar ideas, or, as now, curses history because it deviates from one's own ideals—in either case it is the most recent point in any development that is taken to be the fulcrum. A sentence from DeMause exemplifies the modern view: "The history of childhood is a nightmare from which we have only recently begun to awaken" (1975, p. 1). This whole change in the history of education has made the climate extremely unfavorable for educators from the past. And if they are to be allowed to make an appearance at all, then it must be as a salutary warning: a description which precisely fits Moritz Schreber as he is presented by Schatzman.

Thanks again to Schatzman, Moritz Schreber is also beginning to attract attention from writers on the history of education who are also interested in psychiatry. In this genre of literature, incidentally, not even the slightest attempt is made to shade the total blackness with which he is depicted by Schatzman. For example, he figured repeatedly in the chamber of horrors presented by Rutschky in her book significantly entitled *Schwarze Pädagogik* (Black Pedagogics) (1977). And in Ottmüller's eyes he served as "a promiment example" of the type of educator who sees the child as "the potential domestic tyrant filled with evil and asocial desires, whose will must be broken at all costs" (1979, p. 13). "The ineffable Dr. Schreber never mentioned masturbation in his exposition of total control over the child," according to Robertson (1975, p. 420) in her survey of education and upbringing in nineteenth-century Europe. This is not true (see, e.g., D. G. M. Schreber [1839, p. 243]); moreover, it is not a particularly good idea to take Schatzman's article on the Schreber case as one of the most important sources for education and upbringing in nineteenth-century Germany, as Robertson does. In Kern, Schatzman's argument has become more or less archetypal for an entire period (1975, pp. 117-119): according to him, father and son Schreber reveal something about "the most intense family psychodynamics of the Victorian period" (*ibid.*, p. 117). Furthermore, Kern went on, Moritz Schreber, "a sadistic father," was of the opinion that "corporal punishment should be freely employed.'' This no longer has anything to do with Moritz Schreber: It is merely the product of Kern's own moral indignation.[8]

Again, this total blackening of Moritz Schreber suits the structure of the modern study of the history of education. It is the primarily moral preoccupation that appears to increase the "relevance" of one's own work by placing all the emphasis on the "bad" things in history, i.e., everything that deviates from the present norm. If one were to examine the history of education over a longer period, one would unquestionably find that it is a process of evolution in which Moritz Schreber in modern eyes is very definitely to be preferred, in many ways, to still earlier educators.

But even though that kind of approach would be an improvement, it is still far from what I should like to see. It must be remembered that the idea of progress in education can be no more than an object of academic study: it presupposes criteria against which progress may be measured; it is one of the tasks of the history of education to show why it is that in general the history of education is seen as a process of progress. In order to do this, it must study two things: on the one hand the factual history of education itself, and on the other hand the criteria by which judgments are made, i.e., the modern ideals of education and upbringing as those ideals have become as a product of that history. One of the most important routes by which we may approach the factual history of education, it seems to me, is the study of those educators whose writings were not at the time revolutionary in their theories but who wrote more for direct application in the home. Moritz Schreber is an example of such a writer. A history of education on these lines would also have to take account of the simple thought that changing habits and customs in education and upbringing must also be explained in terms of the way in which the adults concerned have themselves changed. In short: Educational history ought to be part of a historically oriented sociology.

This sociological imperialism almost certainly renders my remarks quite indigestible to every right-minded educator. As an academic discipline education is older and more established than sociology. This is tied up with the practical and moral functions which education has always had, and still has, and it is precisely this moral function which, in my view, education should relinquish first. However, letting go of this moralizing function would also mean, precisely because of the absence of any scientific theoretical foundation, that there would be no basis left for all the activities of educators and students of education hitherto.

In short, I think it is safe to regard the chances of my remarks concerning the history of education ever having any influence as negligible. In the other field of science into which I have ventured, psychiatry, my chances must be if anything still worse, since there I have not been able to suggest even one alternative: All I ask for there is greater modesty. I do not see why psychiatrists should accept such an attack on their sense of dignity and on their bank accounts. Thus everything in this book that goes beyond the facts is written not in the hope of being a lesson to others, but solely as a test of proficiency.

NOTES TO CHAPTER 24

[1]Sometimes Schatzman was perhaps a little *too* quick to find parallels between the "divine miracles" and Paul Schreber's upbringing. Just as he linked the "cold miracles" with the cold baths that Paul Schreber had to take in his youth, so too he linked the "heat miracles" with the hot baths that Moritz Schreber (1852c, p. 40) recommended for babies up to the age of six months. However, even at their hottest these baths were no more than 35° C. Is it really plausible that this kind of "heat" could have such a traumatic effect?

[2]The only exception is Baumeyer (1956, p. 74). But then, he is not an orthodox psychoanalyst: The school to which he belongs—the circle around Schultz-Hencke—has been expelled by the official psychoanalytic association.

Incidentally, Baumeyer referred to a pre-war author and a heredity percentage for schizophrenia of 70 per cent which is also very outdated.

[3]Genetic research into schizophrenia eliminates nongenetic factors by looking at the differences between monozygotic and dizygotic twins with regard to the frequency of schizophrenia in one member of the pair when the other member is schizophrenic. Schatzman (1973a, p. 138) wrote:

> Martti Siirala, a Finnish psychiatrist, maintains many so-called symptoms of schizophrenia might be occasioned by an inherited predisposition, not of the patient, but of people around him, to combat unusual tendencies in him that disturb their view of reality (1961, p. 73). If Siirala were right, geneticists would need to revise their premises about what it is that runs in families of schizophrenics. Siirala's views are highly speculative and would be hard to test. I mention them to jog loose any too-fixed, too-pat assumptions you may have.

But Siirala's views are in fact very easily tested: They are refuted by the great differences between monozygotic and dizygotic twins.

[4]The term comes from Goudsblom (1980).

[5]My thesis is aimed at the community of Schreber experts, i.e., a few psychiatrists scattered over Europe and North America. Now that I am discussing such subjects as freedom, morality, and power, I have suddenly arrived in quite a different forum of discussion, namely, the still relatively small circle of sociologists centred round Professor J. Goudsblom in Amsterdam, where the work of Norbert Elias is the main source of inspiration. Further elaboration of my remarks means that I am addressing myself to this quite different readership: which is a good enough reason for keeping

it short. In *The Civilizing Process* Elias provided another explanation of the reduction in differences of power, namely, the increased degree to which the elite are dependent on the human apparatus needed to do the work. However, this does not immediately explain the increase in the power of groups outside the work process.

⁶Despite his severely moralistic view, Schatzman did not allow himself to be beguiled into making many factual errors. Here, for example, he correctly inserted ellipses where he has omitted something in a quotation from Moritz Schreber. In this he distinguished himself favorably from most authors on Moritz Schreber. An example is Schatzman's own German translator, who left these points out (Schatzman, 1978, p. 115). This is worse than careless, for the translator had taken the effort to reproduce the passages concerned straight from the work of Moritz Schreber.

⁷I owe my figures for *Soul Murder* to Schatzman's British literary agents, Deborah Rogers Ltd. Schatzman appears in the top ten books in Italy in *Panorama* for 21 March 1974, 11 April 1974, and 25 April 1974, and in *Il Milanese* for the first week in February 1974 (p. 73).

⁸Kern's text is also remarkable for another reason. I have presented it as a consequence of Schatzman's work. He also gives a Schatzmanian interpretation. But in his pages about father and son Schreber the name Schatzman is nowhere to be seen. Instead, there are favorable references to Niederland and Freud. For example, Kern wrote:

> The Schreber case has historical significance beyond an account of the individual problems of a man subjected to experimentation by a sadistic father. Schreber's body acted as a spokesman for his age and revealed many of the pressures that severely inhibited the free development and enjoyment of the human body [1975, p. 119].

And then Kern went on to say that this insight comes from Freud! But Freud saw things in quite a different light: He did not see Moritz Schreber as a malefactor at all. Is this an isolated mistake by the psychoanalytically oriented Kern? No: In Chapter 23 we saw that this is general psychoanalytic policy with regard to Freud and Schatzman. (I cannot *prove* that Kern learned of the Schreber case through Schatzman's work. But I can produce very plausible evidence for it: Where Kern quoted a passage from Moritz Schreber, it emerges from his note [1975, p. 277] that he borrowed it from Schatzman. And Schatzman's article about father and son Schreber appeared in *The History of Childhood Quarterly*; in the same year the journal also carried an article by Kern.)

BIBLIOGRAPHY

Some of the texts cited are difficult to find. For information ask the author: Han Israëls, Post box 15185, Amsterdam. The brackets indicate interpolation of the names by the author.

A[ckermann, W.] (1943), Volksbelehrung als Grundlage der Volksgesundheit: Zum Gedächtniss von Daniel Gottlieb Moritz Schreber. *Die Gesundheits-Führung, Ziel und Weg: Monatsschrift des Hauptamtes für Volksgesundheit der NDSAP*, 218-219.

Ackermann, W. (1943), Daniel Gottlieb Moritz Schreber. *Der Landarzt* 24:287-289.

"Acta der Frau Louise Henriette Pauline verw. Dr. Schreber geb. Haase: Heimathschein für's Ausland betr." (1863), Manuscript. Municipal Archives, Leipzig.

Adelmann, Georg (1854), *Ernst August Carus: Eine biographische Skizze*. Dorpat.

Allgemeine deutsche Biographie (1891), vol. 32. Leipzig: Duncker & Humblot.

"Allgemeiner Verband der Schrebervereine Leipzig: Photo's, Postkarten, Zeitungsausschnitte u.ä. um 1900." Library of the Museum der Geschichte der Stadt Leipzig.

Allgemeines Lexikon der bildenden Künstler von der Antike bis zum Gegenwart (1934), Begründet von Ulrich Thieme und Felix Becker, herausgegeben von Hans Vollmer, vol. 28. Leipzig: E. A. Seemann.

Arnemann-Großschweidnitz (1903), Review of *Denkwürdigkeiten eines Nervenkranken* by Daniel Paul Schreber. *Psychiatrisch-neurologische Wochenschrift*, 5:422-423.

Aschaffenburg (1903), Review of *Denkwürdigkeiten eines Nervenkranken* by Daniel Paul Schreber. *Centralblatt für Nervenheilkunde und Psychiatrie*, 14 = 26:500.

B., H. (1940), Schrebers Tochter wird hundert Jahre alt: Frau Anna Jung erlebte das Jahr 1848 als achtjähriges Mädchen. *Neue Leipziger Zeitung*, 30/12/1940.

B., K. See Bornstein, Karl.

Baginsky, Adolf (1883), *Handbuch der Schul-Hygiene*, 2d ed. Stuttgart: Enke.

Bakx, Hans (1977), Schreber, een klassiek psychiatrisch ziektegeval. *NRC-Handelsblad* (Holland), 12/3/1977, p. 12.

Bankhofer, Hademar (1977), Gepachtete Natur—wieder sehr gefragt. *Wochenschau* (Austria), 27/3/1977, p. 15.

Bauer, Wilhelm (1937), *Deutsche Kultur von 1830 bis 1870*. Handbuch der Kultur-

341

geschichte, erste Abteilung, vol. 8. Potsdam: Akademische Verlagsgesellschaft Athenaion.

Baumeyer, Franz (1952), New Insights into the Life and Psychosis of Schreber. *International Journal of Psycho-Analysis*, 33:262.

—— (1955), Der Fall Schreber. *Psyche*, 9:513-536.

—— (1956), The Schreber case. *International Journal of Psycho-Analysis*, 37:61-74.

—— (1970), Noch ein Nachtrag zu Freuds Arbeit über Schreber. *Zeitschrift für psychosomatische Medizin und Psychoanalyse*, 16:243-245.

—— (1973), Nachträge zum "Fall Schreber." In *Bürgerliche Wahnwelt um Neunzehnhundert*, herausgegeben von Peter Heiligenthal und Reinhard Volk. Wiesbaden: Focus-Verlag.

—— (1979), "Le cas Schreber." In *Le cas Schreber*, edited by Eduardo Prado de Oliveira. Paris: Presses universitaires de France.

Bayerisches Ärzteblatt (1961), Der Arzt der Kleingärten: Zu Dr. Schrebers 100. Todestag. 16:394-395.

Bdt., E. (1859), "Zur Geschichte des Turnwesens in Leipzig." *Deutsche Turn-Zeitung*, 4:70-71.

[Beneke, F.] (1912), *Geschichte des Corps Saxonia zu Leipzig 1812 bis 1912*. Herausgegeben von der Genossenschaft "Corps Saxonia." Leipzig.

Benjamin, Walter (1972), *Gesammelte Schriften*, vol. 4. Frankfurt am Main: Suhrkamp.

Berliner Lehrerzeitung: Organ des Berliner Verbands der Lehrer und Erzieher in der Gewerkschaft Erziehung und Wissenschaft (1954), Dr. med. D. G. H. Schreber (1808-1861): Ein Pionier für naturgebundene Erziehung. Vol. 8, p. 502.

Bernhardt, Walter (1929), G. M. Schreber und seine Bedeutung für die Entwicklung der Idee der Leibesübungen im 19. Jahrhundert. Staatsexamensarbeit, Institut für Leibesübungen, Leipzig.

Biedermann, Karl (1845) Allgemeines Turnen. *Leipziger Tageblatt*, 7/12/1845, p. 3541-3542.

—— (1886), *Mein Leben und ein Stück Zeitgeschichte*, vol. 1, 1812-1849. Breslau: G. Schottländer.

[Biedermann, Karl] (1896), Karl Biedermann, von ihm selbst. In *Nachrichten aus dem Allgemeinen Turnverein zu Leipzig für das Jubeljahr 1895*. Leipzig: Allgemeine Turnverein.

Bilz, Friedrich Eduard (1895), *Lehr- und Nachschlagebuch der naturgemässen Heilweise und Gesundheitspflege: Das neue Naturheilverfahren*, 9th ed. Leipzig: F. E. Bilz (1895).

—— (1927/28), *Das neue Naturheilverfahren: Lehr- und Nachschlagebuch der naturgemässen Heilweise und Gesundheitspflege sowie aller verwandten Reformheilmethoden*. Neubearbeitung. Dresden-Radebeul and Leipzig: F. E. Bilz.

Biographisches Lexikon der hervorragenden Ärzte aller Zeiten und Völker. See Hirsch, August.

Blum, Hans (1907), *Lebenserinnerungen*, vol. 1, 1841-1870. Berlin: Vossische Buchhandlung.

Böhmert, Wilhelm (1898), *Die Verteilung des Einkommens in Preussen und Sachsen, mit besonderer Berücksichtigung der Großstädte und des Landes*. Dresden: O. V. Böhmert.

Bormann, Friedrich Adolph (1859), *Besprechung der Dr. Schreberschen Schrift: "Ein ärztlicher Blick in das Schulwesen" mit besonderer Berücksichtigung des Turnens in der Volksschule*. Döbeln.

B[ornstein], K[arl] (1931), Dr. Daniel Gottlieb Moritz Schreber, Leipzig. *Blätter für Volksgesundheitspflege*, 31:161-162.

Bornstein, Karl (1931), Dr. Daniel Gottlieb Moritz Schreber, ein Kämpfer für Volkserziehung. *Zeitschrift für ärztliche Fortbildung*, 28:798.

Brauchle, Alfred (1937), *Naturheilkunde in Lebensbildern*. Leipzig: Philipp Reclam Jun.

—— (1944), *Grosse Naturärzte*, 2d rev. ed. of *Naturheilkunde in Lebensbildern*. Leipzig: Philipp Reclam Jun.

—— (1951), *Die Geschichte der Naturheilkunde in Lebensbildern*, 3rd rev. ed. of *Naturheilkunde in Lebensbildern*. Stuttgart: Reclam.

—— (1971), *Zur Geschichte der Physiotherapie: Naturheilkunde in ärztlichen Lebensbildern*. 4th ed. of *Naturheilkunde in Lebensbildern*, revised by Walter Groh. Heidelberg: Karl F. Haug.

Bregman, Lucy (1977), Religion and madness: Schreber's Memoirs as personal myth. *Journal of Religion and Health*, 16:119-135.

Brehme, Louis (1889), Dr. med. Carl Hermann Schildbach†. *Jahrbücher der deutschen Turnkunst* 35:8-13.

Brocke, Hiltrud (1977), *Jugend- und Kindergruppenarbeit: Anregungen und Beispiele für unsere Gruppenleiter und -helfer*. Herausgegeben von der Deutschen Schreberjugend, Bundesverband. Krefeld.

Brown, Phil (1973), Review: Recent Anti-Psychiatry Books. *Rough Times*, April-May, p. 19.

Buchheim, Karl (1966), *Deutsche Kultur zwischen 1830 und 1870*. Handbuch der Kulturgeschichte, Abteilung 1 (vol. 9). Frankfurt am Main: Akademische Verlagsgesellschaft Athenaion.

Buchner, W. (1869), *Zur Schulbankfrage*. Berlin: Guttentag.

Calasso, Roberto (1974a), "Nota sui lettori di Schreber." In *Memorie di un malato di nervi* by Daniel Paul Schreber. Milano: Adelphi.

—— (1974b), *L'impuro folle*. Milano: Adelphi.

Canetti, Elias (1972) *Macht und Überleben: Drei Essays*. Berlin: Literarisches Colloquium.

—— (1976a), *Die Provinz des Menschen: Aufzeichnungen 1942-1972*. Frankfurt am Main: Fischer Taschenbuch.

—— (1976b), *Wat de mens betreft: Aantekeningen, 1942-1972*. Amsterdam: De Arbeiderspers.

Carr, Arthur C. (1974), Observations on Paranoia and their Relationship to the Schreber Case. In *The Schreber Case* by William G. Niederland. New York: Quadrangle/The New York Times Book Co.

Catalogus van de paedagogische bibliotheek van het Nederlandsch Onderwijzers-Genootschap. Amsterdam: 1891.

Chasseguet-Smirgel, Janine (1975), A propos du délire transsexuel du président Schreber. *Revue française de psychanalyse*, 39:1013-1025.

Chazaud, J. (1966), Contribution à la théorie psychanalytique de la paranoïa. *Revue française de psychanalyse*, 30:93-120.

Clare, Anthony (1974), Love or Hatred. *New Society*, 27:270-271.

Cohen, David (1973), The Dr Spock of the 1840s. *Times Educational Supplement*, 4/5/1973. (Source: M. Schatzman.)

Colas, Dominique (1975), Le despotisme pédagogique du docteur Schreber. *Critique: Revue générale des publications françaises et étrangères*, 31:78-91.

Croufer, Francis (1970), La vie du Président Schreber, une ordalie relative à la paternité? *Les feuillets psychiatriques de Liège*, 3:214-251.

Daniels, George Eaton (1975), Review of *The Schreber Case* by William G. Niederland. *Bulletin of the New York Academy of Medicine*, 51:1331-1343.

Deleuze, Gilles, and Guattari, Félix (1972), *L'anti-Oedipe*, vol. 1 of *Capitalisme et schizophrénie* by Gilles Deleuze and Félix Guattari. Paris: Les éditions de minuit.

deMause, Lloyd (1975), The Evolution of Childhood. In *The History of Childhood*, edited by Lloyd deMause. Reprint. New York, Hagerstown, San Francisco, London: Harper & Row.

Deutsche Schreberjugend, Herausgeber (c. 1958), Arbeitshilfen für den Gruppenleiter. Mimeographed. n.p., n.d.

―――― (1979), Over 100 Years of the German Schreberyouth Organization. Mimeographed n.p., n.d. (1979 or a little earlier).

―――― Landesgruppe Berlin, Herausgeber (n.d.), Selbstdarstellung der Deutschen Schreberjugend. Mimeographed. Berlin.

Devreese, Daniel (1981), De "Personalakte" van Daniel Paul Schreber bij het "Königliche Justizministerium" te Dresden. *Psychoanalytische Perspektieven* (Ghent), Nr. 1:17-97.

Diem, Liselott (1958), Aus Schrebers Kallipädie 1858: Das Kind in seinen Spielen. *Die Leibeserziehung*, 7:390-393.

Donadeo, John (1960), Report of the talk on 29/9/1959 by William G. Niederland, "The 'Miracled-Up' World of Schreber's Childhood" and of the subsequent discussion. *Psychoanalytic Quarterly*. 29:301-304.

Dresdner Zeitung (1944), Die älteste Leipzigerin gestorben. No. 277 p. 3. (Source: Sächsische Landesbibliothek, Dresden.)

Ehrenwald, Jan (1960), The Symbiotic Matrix of Paranoid Delusions and the Homosexual Alternative. *The American Journal of Psycho-Analysis*, 20:49-59.

―――― (1963), *Neurosis in the Family and Patterns of Psychosocial Defense: A Study of Psychiatric Epidemiology*. New York: Hoeber.

Eickhoff, F.-W. (1979), Review of *Der Fall Schreber* by William G. Niederland. *Psyche*, 33:1058-1062.

Eigler, Gernot (1978), Die Wunder der Erziehung. Television play ZDF West Germany 21/9/1978, 22.05-23.15.

Elias, Norbert (1978), *The Civilizing Process: The History of Manners*. Oxford: Blackwell.

Elliott-Smith, Monique (1973), La pédagogie Schreberienne. *Le coq-heron*, no. 37-38, June-July, pp. 4-8.

Engelsing, Rolf (1973), *Analphabetentum und Lektüre: Zur Sozialgeschichte des Lesens in Deutschland zwischen feudaler und industrieller Gesellschaft*. Stuttgart: Metzler.

―――― (1978), *Zur Sozialgeschichte deutscher Mittel- und Unterschichten*. Kritische Studien zur Geschichtswissenschaft, vol. 4, 2d rev. ed. Göttingen: Vandenhoeck & Ruprecht.

Eschner, Max, Herausgeber (1910), *Leipzigs Denkmäler: Denksteine und Gedenktafeln*. Leipzig: Otto Wigand.

Eulenberg, Hermann, and Bach, Theodor (1891), *Schulgesundheitslehre: Das Schulhaus und das Unterrichtswesen, vom hygienischen Standpunkte für Ärzte, Lehrer, Verwaltungsbeamte und Architekten*. Berlin: J. J. Heines Verlag.

Euler, Carl, Herausgeber (1895), *Encyklopädisches Handbuch des gesamten Turnwesens und der verwandten Gebiete*, vol. 2. Wien, Leipzig: A. Pichler's Witwe & Sohn.

F., C. (1908), Ein Vorkämpfer für das Jugendspiel: Zur Erinnerung an Dr. Daniel Gottlieb Moritz Schreber. *Gartenlaube*, pp. 891-892.

Fahrner (1865), *Das Kind und der Schultisch: Die schlechte Haltung der Kinder beim*

Schreiben und ihre Folgen, sowie die Mittel, derselben in Schule und Haus abzuhelfen, 2d ed. Zürich: Schulthess.

Festschrift für Paul Flechsig: Zur Feier seines 25 jährigen Jubiläums als ordentlicher Professor an der Universität Leipzig (1909), *Monatsschrift für Psychiatrie und Neurologie* 26, Ergänzungsheft. Berlin: S. Karger.

Festschrift zur fünfzigjährigen Jubelfeier des allgemeinen Turnvereins zu Leipzig 1845-1895 (1895), Leipzig: Allgemeine Turnverein.

Finke, Wilko (1975), Leben und Wirken Dr. Daniel Gottlob Moritz Schrebers. Diplomarbeit, Deutsche Hochschule für Körperkultur, Leipzig.

Flechsig, Paul (Emil) (1927), *Meine myelogenetische Hirnlehre: Mit biographischer Einleitung*. Berlin: Julius Springer.

Foerster, O. G. (1933), Moritz Schreber: Zur 125. Wiederkehr seines Geburtstages am 15. Oktober. *Allgemeine deutsche Lehrerzeitung*, 62:680-681.

Fortuin, Johanna (1976), Review of *De ondergang van Daniel Paul Schreber* by Morton Schatzman and Sigmund Freud. *Jeugd en samenleving*, 6/2/1976, pp. 143-144.

Freiheitskampf, Der (1944), Die älteste Leipzigerin gestorben. No. 311, p. 3. (Source: Sächsische Landesbibliothek Dresden.)

Freud, Sigmund (1911a), Psychoanalytische Bemerkungen über einen autobiographisch beschriebenen Fall von Paranoia (Dementia paranoides). *Jahrbuch für psychoanalytische und psychopathologische Forschungen*, 3 (1st half): 9-68.

——— (1911b), Psycho-analytic notes on an autobiographical account of a case of paranoia (dementia paranoides). *Standard Edition*, 12:1-82. London: Hogarth Press, 1958.

——— (1964), *Werke aus den Jahren 1909-1913*. Gesammelte Werke, vol. 8, 4th ed. Frankfurt am Main: S. Fischer Verlag.

——— (1973), *Zwang, Paranoia und Perversion*. Studienausgabe, vol. 7. Frankfurt am Main: S. Fischer Verlag.

——— and Jung, Carl Gustav (1974), *Briefwechsel*. Frankfurt am Main: S. Fischer Verlag.

Freund der Schreber-Vereine 4, Der (1908), Dr. Daniel Gottlieb Moritz Schreber. pp. 210-212.

Friedreich's Blätter für gerichtliche Medicin und Sanitätspolizei (1904), 55:239 and 392. Reviews of *Denkwürdigkeiten eines Nervenkranken* by Daniel Paul Schreber.

Friedrich, Edm. (1861), Dr. Moritz Schreber †. *Neue Jahrbücher für die Turnkunst*, 7:321-322.

Friedrich, Günther (1932), Stammbaum der Familie Schreber. Manuscript. n.p.

——— (1932/33), Ahnentafel der Familien Wenck und Haase. Manuscript. n.p.

——— (1933), "Stammtafel der Familie Jung." Manuscript. n.p.

——— (1956), Über den Ursprung der "Schrebergärten." *Schleswiger Nachrichten*, 25/4/1956. (Source: G. Friedrich.)

[Fritzsche, Hugo] (1903), *Dr. med. Schreber und die Leipziger Schreber-Vereine mit besonderer Berücksichtigung des Schreber-Vereins der Nordvorstadt: Denkschrift zur Deutschen Städteausstellung zu Dresden*. Herausgegeben vom Schreber-Verein der Nordvorstadt. Leipzig.

Fritzsche, Hugo (1907), Schreberverein oder Gartenverein? *Der Freund der Schreber-Vereine*, 3:279-282.

——— (1911), Dr. Daniel Gottlieb Moritz Schreber, ein Kämpfer für Volkserziehung: Zur 50. Wiederkehr seines Todestages († 11.Nov. 1861). *Der Freund der Schrebervereine*, 7:179-181 and 195-198.

——— (1926), Aus Dr. Moritz Schrebers Leben. *Garten und Kind: Zeitschrift der mitteldeutschen Schrebergärtner* 6:12-14.

———— and Brückner, G. A. (1903), *Dr. med. Schreber und die Leipziger Schreber-Vereine mit besonderer Berücksichtigung des Schrebervereins der Nordvorstadt: Denkschrift zur Deutschen Städteausstellung zu Dresden.* Herausgegeben vom Schreber-Verein der Nordvorstadt. Leipzig.

G., W. Griff in die Geschichte. *Die geistige Welt*, 11/10/1958. (Source: G. Friedrich.)

Gasch, F. Rudolf (1896), Moritz Schreber. In *Nachrichten aus dem allgemeinen Turnverein zu Leipzig für das Jubeljahr 1895.* Leipzig: Allgemeiner Turnverein.

Gasch, (F.) Rudolf, Herausgeber (1920), *Handbuch des gesamten Turnwesens und der verwandten Leibesübungen.* Wien, Leipzig: A. Pichlers Witwe & Sohn.

———— Herausgeber (1928), *Handbuch des gesamten Turnwesens und der verwandten Leibesübungen*, vol. 2, 2nd ed. Wien, Leipzig: A. Pichlers Witwe & Sohn.

Gesundheitswesen und Desinfektion (1972), In Memoriam Dr. Schreber. 64:160-161.

Gillie, Oliver (1973), Freud's Missing Link. *The Sunday Times*, 25/3/1973, p. 27.

Gmelin, W. (1961), Moritz Schreber zum Gedenken. *Der Naturarzt: Zeitschrift für naturgemässe Lebens- und Heilweise*, 83:341.

Goudsblom, Johan (1977), *Sociology in the Balance: A Critical Essay.* New York: Columbia University Press.

———— (1980), *Nihilism and Culture.* Oxford: Blackwell.

Gr., A. (1958), Die Menschennatur als Ganzes auffassen: Moritz Schreber forderte die Einheit von verstandesgemässer Erziehung und praktischer Lebensertüchtigung. *Thüringische Landeszeitung*, 25/10/1958, n.p.

Graefe, Rudolf (1902), Vorwort zur sechsundzwanzigsten Auflage. In *Ärztliche Zimmergymnastik* by Daniel Gottlob Moritz Schreber. 28th ed. Leipzig: Friedrich Fleischer.

Green, André (1977), Transcription d'origine inconnue. *Nouvelle Revue de Psychanalyse*, no. 16:27-63.

Groh, Walter (1960), *Priessnitz, Grundlagen des klassischen Naturheilverfahrens.* Herausgegeben von Hans Haferkamp. Schriftenreihe des Zentralverbandes der Ärzte für Naturheilverfahren, vol. 3. Hamburg: Medizinisch-literarischer Verlag Dr. Blume & Co.

Grosse, Karl (1897), *Geschichte der Stadt Leipzig von der ältesten bis auf die neueste Zeit.* Rev. ed., vol. 1. Leipzig: Alwin Schmidt's Verlag.

———— (1898), *Geschichte der Stadt Leipzig von der ältesten bis auf die neueste Zeit.* Rev. ed., vol. 2. Leipzig: Alwin Schmidt's Verlag.

H., K. F. (1959), Bock und Schreber—Gesundheitserzieher vor hundert Jahren. *Ärztliche Praxis: Die Wochenzeitschrift des praktischen Arztes*, 11:1078.

Haeckel, Ernst (1868), *Natürliche Schöpfungsgeschichte: Gemeinverständliche wissenschaftliche Vorträge über die Entwickelungslehre im Allgemeinen und diejenige von Darwin, Goethe und Lamarck im Besonderen, über die Anwendung derselben auf den Ursprung des Menschen und andere damit zusammenhängende Grundfragen der Naturwissenschaft.* Berlin: Reimer.

Hagen, Reinhard von dem (1929a), Dr. Schreber und sein Werk: Zum allgemeinen sächsischen Schrebertag am 25. August. *Dresdner Anzeiger*, 23/8/1929a, p. 6.

———— (1929b), Dr. Schreber und sein Werk. *Dresdner Nachrichten*, 23/8/1929b, p. 6.

Hänsch, Rudolf (1925), Moritz Schreber, Ernst Innocenz Hauschild und die Entstehung der Schrebervereine." *Leipzig*, 2:288-291.

Harding, D. W. "Crazy Mixed-Up Kids." *New York Review of Books*, 14/6/1973, pp. 24-27.

Hartmann, Ph. Karl (1861), *Glückseligkeitslehre für das physische Leben des Menschen: Ein diätetischer Führer durch das Leben.* Revised by (Daniel Gottlob) Moritz Schreber. 4th ed. Leipzig: Carl Geibel.

Hartung, D. (1907), Trauerrede beim Begräbnis der Frau verw. Dr. Schreber. Mimeographed. Leipzig, 17/5/1907.

Hauschild, Ernst Innocenz (1862), *Vierzig pädagogische Briefe aus der Schule an das Elternhaus*. Leipzig: Gustav Grädner.

—— (1865), *Dreissig Pädagogische Briefe aus der Schule an das Elternhaus*. Leipzig: M. G. Priber.

Heijer, Jac (1976), Paul Gallis: Het decor is meer dan een plaatje. *NRC-Handelsblad* (Holland), 27/8/1976, p. CS3.

Heilbrunn, Kurt (1922), Die Entwicklung der Kleingartenbewegung bis zum Jahre 1921 und ihr Einfluss auf die Volksernährung. Dissertation, Rostock.

Heiligenthal, Peter, and Volk, Reinhard, Herausgeber (1973), *Bürgerliche Wahnwelt um Neunzehnhundert: "Denkwürdigkeiten eines Nervenkranken"* von Daniel Paul Schreber, mit Aufsätzen von Franz Baumeyer, einem Vorwort, einem Materialanhang und sechs Abbildungen. Der Fall Schreber, vol. 1. Wiesbaden: Focus-Verlag.

Heilmann, Ernst (1911), *Geschichte der Arbeiterbewegung in Chemnitz und dem Erzgebirge*. Chemnitz: Sozialdemokratischer Verein für den 16. sächsischen Reichstagswahlkreis Max Müller.

Heindl, Joh. Bapt., Herausgeber (1859), *Galerie berühmter Pädagogen, verdienter Schulmänner, Jugend- und Volksschriftsteller und Componisten aus der Gegenwart in Biographien und biographischen Skizzen*, Vol. 2. München: Joseph Anton Finsterlin.

Hemelrijk, Jan (1965), *Er is een weg naar de vrijheid: Zeven maanden concentratiekamp*. Hilversum, Antwerpen: W. de Haan and Standaard-Boekhandel.

Hennig, Carl (1882), Vorwort zur zweiten Auflage. In *Das Buch der Erziehung an Leib und Seele* by Daniel Gottlob Moritz Schreber, 2d rev. ed. of *Kallipädie*. Leipzig: Friedrich Fleischer. (1882).

Hirsch, August, Herausgeber (1887), *Biographisches Lexikon der hervorragenden Ärzte aller Zeiten und Völker*, vol. 5. Wien, Leipzig: Urban & Schwarzenberg.

[Hirschfeld, Adolf, and Franke, August] (1879), *Geschichte der Leipziger Burschenschaft Germania 1859-1879: Festgabe zum zwanzigsten Stiftungsfeste am 25., 26., 27. und 28. Juli 1879*. (Leipzig: G. G. Naumann.)

Hirth, Georg, Herausgeber (1865), *Das gesammte Turnwesen: Ein Lesebuch für deutsche Turner, enthaltend gegen 100 abgeschlossene Muster-Darstellungen von den vorzüglichsten älteren und neueren Turnschriftstellern*. Leipzig: Ernst Keil.

Hoffmann (1940), Aus der Geschichte der Medizin: Daniel Gottlob Moritz Schreber, ein Gesundheitserzieher des deutschen Volkes im 19. Jahrhundert. *Der Landarzt*, 21:5-8.

Hoffman, Carl Sam. (1815), *Historische Beschreibung der Stadt, des Amtes und der Dioces Oschatz in ältern und neuern Zeiten*, vol. 1. Oschatz.

Hoffman, Walther Gustav (1965), *Das Wachstum der deutschen Wirtschaft seit der Mitte des 19. Jahrhunderts*. Enzyklopädie der Rechts- und Staatswissenschaft, Abteilung Staatswissenschaft. Berlin, Heidelberg, New York: Springer-Verlag.

Illustrierte Zeitung (1862), Daniel Gottlob Moritz Schreber. 1/2/1862, pp. 80-82.

Infeld (1905), Review of *Denkwürdigkeiten eines Nervenkranken* by Daniel Paul Schreber. *Wiener Medizinische Presse*, 46:1660.

Israëls, Han (1980), *Schreber, vader en zoon*. Thesis, University of Amsterdam.

—— (1984), Il padre di Schreber secondo Freud, evvero: c'è da fidarsi degli psicanalisti? In: *Freud: Gerusalemme nella psicanalisi*. Milan: Spirali/Vel Edizioni.

J. (1861), Nekrolog: Dr. med. Daniel Gottlob Moritz Schreber. *Leipziger Tageblatt*, 15/11/1861, pp. 5813, 5814.

Jaccard, Roland (1979), Sciences humaines: Schreber père et fils. *Le Monde*, 6/4/1979, p. 23.

Jahn, Walter (1936), Vater der Laubenkolonie: Zum heutigen 75. Todestage des Arztes Schreber. *Berliner Lokal-Anzeiger*, 10/11/1936, 4. Beiblatt, p. 1.

Janssen, J. J. (1973), Garden Club. *Sunday Times*, 1/4/1973, p. 13.

Juhnke, Klaus (1975), Darstellung und Einschätzung Dr. Daniel Gottlob Moritz Schrebers in der deutschsprachigen sporthistorischen Literatur. Diplomarbeit, Deutsche Hochschule für Körperkultur, Leipzig.

Jung, Anna, geb. Schreber; Jung, Carl; Schreber, (Daniel) Paul; Schreber, Sidonie; and Krause, Klara, geb. Schreber. Letter "an das Polizeiamt zu Leipzig." Typescript. Leipzig und Dresden, Juni 1907. Municipal Archives Leipzig.

Jung, Carl (1901), Letter beginning "Sehr geehrter Herr!" Leipzig, 26/3/1901. Manuscript collection, Staatsbibliothek Preussischer Kulturbesitz.

Jung, Käte, geb. Metsch (1907), Erinnerungen an alt Leipzig und die Grossmama (Pauline) Schreber (geb. Haase). Transcript. n.p. n.d.

Katan, Maurits (1959), Schreber's Hereafter: Its Building-Up (Aufbau) and Its Downfall. *The Psychoanalytic Study of the Child*, 14:314-382. New York: International Universities Press.

———— (1974), Schreber's Hereafter: Its Building-Up (Aufbau) and Its Downfall. In *The Schreber Case* by William G. Niederland. New York: Quadrangle/The New York Times Book Co.

———— (1975), Childhood Memories as Contents of Schizophrenic Hallucinations and Delusions. *The Psychoanalytic Study of the Child*, 30:357-374. New Haven: Yale University Press.

———— (1978), Schrebers Jenseits: Sein Aufbau und Untergang. In *Der Fall Schreber* by William G. Niederland. Frankfurt am Main: Suhrkamp Verlag.

———— (1979), Schreber: l'au delà, sa construction (Aufbau) et sa chute. In *Le Cas Schreber*, edited by Eduardo Prado de Oliveira. Paris: Presses universitaires de France.

K-d, E. M. (1936), Der Arzt der Kleingärten: Zu Dr. Schrebers 76. Todestag am 10. November. *Wiener Medizinische Wochenschrift*, 86:1262-1263.

Keilman (Bernd Carson) (1973), Die Idee des Dr. Schreber. Kleingärtner und Oho, instalment 6. *Die Leipziger Abendzeitung*, 24/12/1973, p. 4.

Kern, Stephen (1975), *Anatomy and Destiny: A Cultural History of the Human Body*. Indianapolis, New York: The Bobbs-Merril Company.

Kilian, G. Werner, (gwk) (1958a), Zum 150. Geburtstag von Moritz Schreber: Ein Leben "dem Heile künftiger Geschlechter." *Union* (Leipzig), 15/10/1958, n.p.

———— (1958b), Vorkämpfer des Gesundseins: Vor 150 Jahren am 15. Oktober wurde Dr. Moritz Schreber geboren. *Neue Zeit* (Deutschland-Ausgabe), 15/10/1958, p. 8.

———— (1960), Ist Moritz Schreber noch gegenwartsnah? *Beiträge zur Orthopädie und Traumatologie*, 7:416-421.

Kilian, [G.] Werner (1977), 1. Die Anfänge der Orthopädie in Leipzig bis zur Gründung des Universitätsinstitutes. Typescript. (Leipzig.)

Kilian, G. Werner and Uibe, Peter (1958), Daniel Gottlob Moritz Schreber. *Forschungen und Fortschritte*, 32:335-340.

Kitay, Philip M. (1963), Introduction to Symposium on "Reinterpretations of the Schreber Case: Freud's Theory of Paranoia." *International Journal of Psycho-Analysis*, 44:191-194.

Kleine, Hugo Otto (1942), *Ärzte kämpfen für Deutschland: Historische Bilder aus fünf Jahrhunderten deutschen Arztwirkens*. Stuttgart: Hippokrates-Verlag.

——— (1958), *Ärzte in den Sturmen der Zeit: Medizin-historische Miniaturen aus 5 Jahrhunderten*. Ulm/Donau: Haug.

Kliem, Manfred (1977), *Friedrich Engels: Dokumente seines Lebens, 1820-1895*. Leipzig: Philipp Reclam Jun.

Kloss, M. (1862), Dr. med. D. G. M. Schreber, geb. den 15. October 1808, † den 10. November 1861. *Neue Jahrbücher für die Turnkunst*, 8:10-16.

Knight, Robert P. (1940), The Relationship of Latent Homosexuality to the Mechanism of Paranoid Delusions. *Bulletin of the Menninger Clinic*, 4:149-159.

Knorr. (1858), "Reisebericht über den Besuch gymnastischer Anstalten Nord- und Süddeutschlands." *Neue Jahrbücher für die Turnkunst*, 4:18-28.

Kochendorf, Richard (1907a), *Heilgymnastik gegen Nervosität nach dem von Daniel Gottlob Moritz Schreber entworfenen System*. Leipzig: Siegbert Schnurpfeil.

——— (1907b), *Lungen-Gymnastik ohne Geräte: Nach dem System von Dr. med. Daniel Gottlob Mortiz Schreber*. Leipzig: Siegbert Schnurpfeil.

Koetschau, K. (1924), August Richter. *Wallraf-Richartz-Jahrbuch*, 1:151-157.

Kohut, Heinz (1971), *The Analysis of the Self: A Systematic Approach to the Psychoanalytic Treatment of Narcissistic Personality Disorders*. The Psychoanalytic Study of the Child, Monograph 4. New York: International Universities Press.

——— (1978), *The Search for the Self: Selected Writings, 1950–1978*. Edited by Paul H. Ornstein, 2 vols. New York: International Universities Press.

Kötzschke, Rudolf, and Kretzschmar. Hellmut (1965), *Sächsische Geschichte: Werden und Wandlungen eines deutschen Stammes und seiner Heimat im Rahmen der deutschen Geschichte*. 1935. Reprint. Frankfurt am Main: Weidlich.

Krause, Klara, geb. Schreber (1909), Passage from a letter to G. Richard Siegel. *Der Freund der Schreber-Vereine*, 5:75.

Krey, Bernh. (1913), Schrebers Traum: Ein szenischer Prolog mit Spiel und Reigen. *Der Freund der Schreber-Vereine*, 9:4-7.

Kron, H. (1903), Review of *Denkwürdigkeiten eines Nervenkranken* by Daniel Paul Schreber. *Deutsche Medizinal-Zeitung*, 24:918.

Kuppe, K. O. (1976), Dr. med. Daniel Gottlieb Moritz Schreber. *Kneipp-Blätter*, 85:88-90.

L., A. (1938), "Alt zu werden kann schön sein!" Letzte Tochter Dr. Schrebers wird 98 Jahre alt. *Leipziger Neueste Nachrichten*, 30/12/1938. (Source: G. Friedrich.)

——— (1940), Eine hundertjährige Leipzigerin. *Leipziger Neueste Nachrichten*, 30/12/1940. (Source: descendants of Moritz Schreber.)

L., H. (1845), Leipziger Stadttheater: "Der ewige Jude." *Leipziger Tageblatt*, 28/12/1845, pp. 3806, 3807.

Lacan, Jacques (1971), *Écrits 2*. Paris: Éditions du Seuil.

Lange, P. (1968), Die Kleingärtnerbewegung lebt heute noch: Dr. Schreber zum Gedächtnis. *Leipziger Neueste Nachrichten: Mitteldeutsche Rundschau, unabhängige Heimatzeitung für Sachsen, Thüringen, Provinz Sachsen und Anhalt*, May 1968, no. 9, p. 3.

Lange, Walter (1927), Durch Befreiung und Einigung zur modernen Großstadt. In *Heimatgeschichte für Leipzig und den Leipziger Kreis*, herausgegeben von Karl Reumuth. Leipzig: Dürr'sche Buchhandlung.

Lehmann (1910), Sachsen: Städtische Anstalt Dösen. In *Deutsche Heil- und Pflegeanstalten für Psychischkranke*, herausgegeben von J. Bresler, vol. 1. Halle: Carl Marhold Verlagsbuchhandlung.

Lehmann, Friedrich (1910), Lindenhof: Privatanstalt in Coswig bei Dresden. In

Deutsche Heil- und Pflegeanstalten für Psychischkranke, herausgegeben von J. Bresler, vol. 1. Halle: Carl Marhold Verlagsbuchhandlung.

Lehmann, O. (1914), Ein halbes Jahrhundert echter Schrebervereinsarbeit. *Der Freund der Schreber-Vereine*, 10:158-165.

Leipzig: Ein Blick in das Wesen und Werden einer deutschen Stadt.(Leipzig: Poeschel & Trepte) 1914.

Leipzig im Jahre 1904 (1904). Leipzig: J. J. Weber.

Leipziger Neueste Nachrichten (1931), Dr. Moritz Schrebers 70. Todestag. 10/11/1931, p. 9.

Leipziger Tageblatt (1845), Die Eröffnung des Turnplatzes zu Leipzig. 26/8/1845, p. 2273.

Leipziger Tageblatt (1907a), erste Beilage, n.p. "Frau Dr. Pauline Schreber †." 17/5/1907.

Leipziger, Tageblatt (1907b), erste Beilage, n.p. Two mourning advertisements from Schreber Associations regarding Pauline Schreber. 17/5/1907.

Leipziger Tageblatt (1907c), erste Beilage, n.p. Two mourning advertisements from Schreber Associations regarding Pauline Schreber. 18/5/1907.

Leonhardt, Hans, Zusammensteller (1928), *Geschichte der Leipziger Burschenschaft Germania*. Leipzig: Selbstverlag der Burschenschaft.

Leucker, Peter (1979), "Herzlichen Glückwunsch." *Wir: Informationen der Deutschen Schreberjugend aus Bund und Ländern*, March, n.p.

Lewis, Dio (1862), *The New Gymnastics for Men, Women, and Children: With a Translation of Prof. Kloss's Dumb-bell Instructor and Prof. Schreber's Pangymnastikon*. Boston: Ticknor and Fields.

Lidz, Theodore (1975), Review of *The Schreber Case* by William G. Niederland. *Psychoanalytic Quarterly*, 44:653-656.

Liebling, Friedrich (1956), Zum Geleit. In *Grosse Pädagogen* by Josef Rattner. München, Basel: E. Reinhardt.

Lion, J. C. (1857), Review of *Kallipädie* by Daniel Gottlob Moritz Schreber. *Deutsche Turnzeitung*, 2:111-112.

Lipsius (1908a), Dr. Moritz Schreber: Zum hundertjährigen Geburtstage (15. Oktober 1808). *Dresdener Anzeiger*, no. 286, p. 5.

—————— (1908b), Dr. Moritz Schreber: Zum hundertjährigen Geburtstage (15. Oktober 1808). *Sächsische Dorfzeitung und Elbgaupresse*, no. 241, pp. 1-2.

Listener (1973), Out of the Air: Pollutions. 17/5/1973, p. 652.

Loeffler, Friedrich, Herausgeber (1955), *Festschrift zum 25-Jahr-Feier der orthopädischen Klinik der Karl-Marx-Universität Leipzig*. Berlin, VEB Verlag Volk und Gesundheit.

London, N.Y. (1976), Review of *The Schreber Case* by W. G. Niederland. *J. Amer. Psychoanal. Assn.*, 24:697-706.

Lubach, D., and Coronel, S. Sr. (1870), *De opvoeding van den mensch van zijne kindsheid tot den volwassen leeftijd: Eene handleiding voor ouders en onderwijzers*. Haarlem: De Erven F. Bohn.

Lübbing, Hermann (1952) Die Familie Schreber-von Schreeb in Oldenburg und Hatten (1667-1845). *Oldenburger Balkenschild*, no. 3-4, pp. 15-22.

Macalpine, Ida, and Hunter, Richard A. (1955) Introduction. In *Memoirs of my Nervous Illness* by Daniel Paul Schreber. London: Wm. Dawson & Sons.

Mangner, (K.F.) Eduard (1876), Dr. D. G. M. Schreber, ein Kämpfer für Volkserziehung. *Cornelia: Zeitschrift für häusliche Erziehung*, 26:129-141.

—————— (1877), *Dr. D. G. M. Schreber, ein Kämpfer für Volkserziehung*. Leipzig: C. F. Winter'sche Verlagshandlung.

—————— (1884), *Spielplätze und Erziehungsvereine: Praktische Winke zur Förderung harmonischer Jugenderziehung nach dem Vorbilde der Leipziger Schreberver- eine.* Leipzig: Friedrich Fleischer.

Mannoni, Maud (1973), *Education impossible.* Paris: Éditions du Seuil.

Mannoni, Octave (1974), Président Schreber, Professeur Flechsig. *Temps modernes*, 30:624-641.

———— (1978), *Fictions freudiennes.* Paris: Éditions du Seuil.

———— (1979), Le Cas Freud. *Le quinzaine litteraire*, 15/5/1979, pp. 21-22.

Masson, J. L. (1973), Schreber and Freud: A review of *Soul Murder.* Mimeographed. University of Toronto.

Masson, J. M. (1982), Schreber and Freud. Unpublished manuscript.

Mayrhofer, B. (1937), *Kurzes Wörterbuch zur Geschichte der Medizin.* Jena: Gustav Fischer.

McCawley, Austin (1971), Paranoia and Homosexuality: Schreber Reconsidered. *New York State Journal of Medicine*, 71 = 12:1506-1513.

Medical History (1974), Review of *Soul Murder* by Morton Schatzman. October 1974, p. 381.

Meijer, Mia and Rijnders, Gerardjan (1976), Schreber: een stuk over de waanwereld van een 19e eeuwse rechter. Typescript. (Amsterdam)

———— ———— (1977), President Schreber: gek, kunstobject, fascist. *Hollands Diep*, 12/3/1977, p. 22-25.

Melman, Charles (1980), "De l'aventure paranoiaque." *Analytica: Cahiers de re- cherche du champ freudien*, 18:3-32.

Mencken, Franz Erich, Herausgeber (1965), *Dein dich zärtlich liebender Sohn: Kin- derbriefe aus 6 Jahrhunderten.* München: Heimeran.

Menninger, Karl Augustus and Menninger, J. L. (1942), *Love Against Hate.* New York: Harcourt.

Mette, Julius (1955), Daniel Gottlieb Moritz Schreber. *Der Naturarzt: Zeitschrift für naturgemässe Lebens- und Heilweise*, 77:135-136.

Milczewsky, Renate. Text for a radio programme on Litfass and Schreber. Type- script. Sender Freies Berlin, Nr. T-227 475. (Broadcast some time between 1960 and 1970.)

Mittenzwey, L. (1896), *Die Pflege des Bewegungsspieles insbesondere durch die Schrebervereine: Zugleich eine Darstellung der Entwickelung und Einrichtung, sowie der Ziele und Aufgaben dieser Vereine.* Leipzig: Eduard Strauch.

Möbius (1903), Review of *Denkwürdigkeiten eines Nervenkranken* by Daniel Paul Schreber. *Schmidt's Jahrbücher der in- und ausländischen gesammten Medicin*, 279:105.

Moreau, Pierre F. (1974), Une bonne éducation au XIXe siècle: Des principes et des méthodes à rendre fou. *Psychologie*, June, pp. 43-48.

Morning News (1973), Unpeeling the Masks of Madness. 29/3/1973, p. 18.

Müller, J. P. (1906), *Mein System· 15 Minuten tägliche Arbeit für die Gesundheit*, 5th ed. Leipzig: Tillge.

Nagler, Georg Kaspar (1924), *Neues allgemeines Künstler-Lexikon oder Nachrichten von dem Leben und den Werken der Maler, Bildhauer, Baumeister, Kupfer- stecher, Lithographen, Formschneider, Zeichner, Medailleure, Elfenbeinarbeiter etc.* Vol. 14. Orig. pub. between 1841 and 1846. 3d ed. Leipzig: Schwarzenberg & Schumann.

Neue Gartenlaube, Die (1942), "Wer war Herr Schreber?" p. 505.

Neue Leipziger Tageszeitung (1944), Die älteste Leipzigerin gestorben. 21/11/1944, p. 3.

Neue Leipziger Zeitung (1938), Wie die Schrebergärten zu ihren Namen kamen. 13/3/1938, p. 26.

——— (1939), Stadtanzeiger: Besuch bei einer Neunundneunzigjährigen. 30/12/1939, p. 3.

Neues Wiener Tagblatt (1944), Wer war Dr. Schreber? 23/11/1944, p. 3.

Niederland, William G. (1951), Three Notes on the Schreber Case. *Psychoanalytic Quarterly*, 20:579-591.

——— (1959a), Schreber: Father and Son. *Psychoanalytic Quarterly*, 28:151-169.

——— (1959b), The 'miracled-up' world of Schreber's childhood. *The Psychoanalytic Study of the Child*, 14:383-413. New York: International Universities Press.

——— (1960), Schreber's father. *Journal of the American Psychoanalytic Association*, 8:492-499.

——— (1963), Further Data and Memorabilia Pertaining to the Schreber Case. *International Journal of Psycho-Analysis*, 44:201-207.

——— (1968), Schreber and Flechsig: A Further Contribution to the 'Kernel of Truth' in Schreber's Delusional System. *Journal of the American Psychoanalytic Association*, 16:740-748.

——— (1972), The Schreber case: Sixty years later. *International Journal of Psychiatry*, 10:79-84.

——— (1974), *The Schreber Case: Psychoanalytic Profile of a Paranoid Personality*. New York: Quadrangle/The New York Times Book Co.

——— (1978), *Der Fall Schreber: Das Psychoanalytische Profil einer paranoiden Persönlichkeit*. Frankfurt am Main: Suhrkamp Verlag.

Niemann, Edgar H. (1961), Förderer der Jugenderziehung und des Volkssports: Zum 100. Todestag des hervorragenden Arztpädagoge und Orthopäde Dr. Schreber. *Sächsisches Tageblatt* (Leipzig), 9/11/1961, n.p.

Noordam, N. F. (1968), *Inleiding in de historische pedagogiek*. Groningen: Wolters-Noordhoff.

Ottmüller, Uta (1979), 'Mutterpflichten'—Die Wandlungen ihrer inhaltlichen Ausformung durch die akademische Medizin. Mimeographed. Berlin: Max-Planck-Institut für Bildungsforschung. *Gesellschaft: Beiträge zur Marx'schen Theorie*, in press.

P., E. (1867), Ein Atelier im Irrenhaus. *Gartenlaube*, pp. 14-16.

Pelman (1903), Review of *Denkwürdigkeiten eines Nervenkranken* by Daniel Paul Schreber. *Allgemeine Zeitschrift für Psychiatrie*, 60:657-659.

——— (1904), Review of *Denkwürdigkeiten eines Nervenkranken* by Daniel Paul Schreber. *Deutsche medizinische Wochenschrift*, 30:563.

Periscoop (1975), Review of *De ondergang van Daniel Paul Schreber* by Morton Schatzman and Sigmund Freud. May, p. 12.

"Personalakte" about Daniel Paul Schreber of the Saxony "Justiz-Ministerium" 1864-1911. State Archives, Dresden.

Pfeiffer, Kurt (1937), *Daniel Gottlob Moritz Schreber und sein Wirken für die Volksgesundheit*. Dissertation, Medizinische Akademia Düsseldorf. Düsseldorf: Dissertations-Verlag G. H. Nolte.

Pfeiffer, R. (1904), Review of *Denkwürdigkeiten eines Nervenkranken* by Daniel Paul Schreber. *Deutsche Zeitschrift für Nervenheilkunde*, 27:352-353.

Pierer's Jahrbücher der Wissenschaften, Künste und Gewerbe: Ergänzungswerk zu sämmtlichen Auflagen des Universal-Lexikons (1873), vol. 3. Oberhausen: Spaarmann.

Politzer, L. M. (1862), Nekrolog. *Jahrbuch für Kinderheilkunde und physische Erziehung* 5:Nekrologe 1-7.

"Polizeiamt der Stadt Leipzig 11." Municipal Archives, Leipzig.

"Polizeiamt der Stadt Leipzig 105." Fo. 119. Municipal Archives, Leipzig.

"Polizeimeldebuch Chemnitz." Municipal Archives, Karl-Marx-Stadt.

Prado de Oliveira, Eduardo (1979a), Présentation. In *Le Cas Schreber*, edited by Eduardo Prado de Oliveira. Paris: Presses universitaires de France.

——, ed. (1979a), *Le cas Schreber: Contributions psychanalytiques de M. Katan, W. G. Niederland, H. Nunberg, I. Macalpine, R. A. Hunter, F. Baumeyer, W. R. D. Fairbairn, R. B. White, Ph. M. Kitay, A. C. Carr, J. Nydes*. Sous l'orientation de Jean Laplanche. Paris: Presses universitaires de France.

—— (1979b), Trois études sur Schreber et la citation. *Psychanalyse à l'université*, 4:245-282.

Psychotherapy Review (Spring 1974), Review of *Soul Murder* by Morton Schatzman. (Source: M. Schatzman.)

R. (1905), Review of *Denkwürdigkeiten eines Nervenkranken* by Daniel Paul Schreber. *Wiener medizinische Wochenschrift*, 55:105.

Rabant, Claude (1978), *Délire et théorie*. Paris: Aubier-Montaigne.

Racamier, P. C., and Chasseguet-Smirgel, Janine (1966), La révision du cas Schreber: revue. *Revue française de psychanalyse*, 30:3-26.

Randschau, Ilse (1974), Verrückt durch väterliche Zucht. *Stern*, 18/4/1974, pp. 198, 199.

Rattner, Josef (1956), *Grosse Pädagogen: Erasmus, Vives, Montaigne, Comenius, Locke, Rousseau, Kant, Salzmann, Pestalozzi, Jean Paul, Goethe, Herbart, Fröbel. Kerschensteiner, Aichhorn*. München, Basel: E. Reinhardt.

Reumuth, Karl (1926), Wesen und Aufgaben der Schreberjugendbewegung. *Schriften des Landesverbandes Sachsen der Schreber- und Gartenvereine*, no. 3. Leipzig: Landesverband Sachsen der Schreber- und Gartenvereine.

——, Herausgeber (1927), *Heimatgeschichte für Leipzig und den Leipziger Kreis*. Leipzig: Dürr'sche Buchhandlung.

Richter, Gerhard (1913), Ein erfüllter Traum. *Der Freund der Schreber-Vereine*, 9:39-41.

—— (1914a), *Geschichte des Schrebervereins der Westvorstadt zu Leipzig: Festschrift zur Feier des 50-jährigen Stiftungsfestes am 13. und 14. Juni 1914*. Leipzig.

—— (1914b), Aus Vergangenheit und Gegenwart des ersten Schrebervereins. *Der Freund der Schreber-Vereine*, 10:106-113.

—— (1925), *Das Buch der Schreber-Jugendpflege*. Leipzig: Verlag des Kreisverbandes der Schreber- und Gartenvereine.

—— (1930), *Deutsche Schreberjugendpflege*. Schriften des Reichsverbands der Kleingartenvereine Deutschlands, vol. 19. Frankfurt am Main: Reichsverband der Kleingartenvereine Deutschlands.

—— (1935), Report of a visit to Anna Jung at 14/3/1935. Typescript. (Leipzig).

—— (1936a), ''Wie die erste Schreberanlage der Welt entstand.'' *Der Kleingärtner und Kleinsiedler*, 1:5-7.

—— (1936b), Report of a visit to Anna Jung at 15/10/1936. Typescript. (Leipzig.)

—— (1939a), Report of a visit to Anna Jung at 9/5/1939. Typescript. Leipzig.

—— (1939b), *Geschichte des ältesten Schrebervereins, 1864-1939: Festschrift zum 75jährigen Bestehen des Kleingärtnervereins Dr. Schreber*. Leipzig.

—— (1940), Leipzig, die Urzelle des Schrebergartenwesens: Ein Gedächtnissblatt für Dr. Schreber und Dr. Hauschild. *Leipziger Jahrbuch*, 1:48-51.

—— and Dietze (1928), Denkschrift über die Schreberjugendpflege im Freistaat Sachsen zwecks Erlangung von Staatsmitteln. *Schriften des Landesverbandes Sachsen der Schreber- und Gartenvereine*, no. 7. Leipzig: Landesverband Sachsen der Schreber- und Gartenvereine.

—— and Wahl, Günter (1973), Dr. med. Daniel Gottlieb Moritz Schreber, der Kämpfer für wahre Volkserziehung, der Pionier der Jugendpflege. *Wir: Infor-*

mationen der Deutschen Schreberjugend aus Bund und Ländern. April 1973, n.p.

Richter, H. E. (1858), Vom Gränzgebiet der erzieherischen und Heilgymnastik. *Neue Jahrbücher für die Turnkunst,* 4:1-6.

―――― (1863), Der Vater des Leipziger Turnwesens. *Gartenlaube,* 11:484-489.

Ringpfeil, K. (1927), Was bieten wir unseren Schreberkindern an Leib und Seele? *Schriften des Landesverbandes Sachsen der Schreber- und Gartenvereine,* no. 5. Leipzig: Landesverband Sachsen der Schreber- und Gartenvereine.

Ritter, Alfons (1936a), *Schreber: Das Bildungssystem eines Arztes.* Dissertation, Erlangen, 1935. Erfurt: Verlag Ohlenroth.

―――― (1936b), *Schreber: Künder und Streiter für wahre Volkserziehung.* Erfurt: Verlag Ohlenroth.

Robertson, Priscilla (1975), Home As a Nest: Middle Class Childhood in Nineteenth-Century Europe. In *The History of Childhood,* edited by Lloyd deMause. Reprint. New York, Hagerstown, San Francisco, London: Harper & Row.

Romein, Jan (1946), *De biografie: Een inleiding.* Daad en droom, een reeks biografieën onder redactie van Annie Romein-Verschoor, vol. 1. Amsterdam, Uitgeverij Ploegsma.

Rondagh, Ferd. (1975), Psychiater beschrijft hoe een strenge vader zijn zoon gek maakte. *Volkskrant,* 1/2/1975, p. 31.

Rosenkötter, Lutz (1975), Review of *The Schreber Case* by William G. Niederland, *Die Angst vor dem Vater* by Morton Schatzman, and *Bürgerliche Wahnwelt um Neunzehnhundert,* herausgegeben von Peter Heiligenthal und Reinhard Volk. *Psyche,* 29:184-186.

Rösler (1911), Letter beginning "Sehr geehrter Herr College!" Leipzig, 13/4/1911. In "Krankengeschichte" on Daniel Paul Schreber. Archives Bezirkskrankenhaus für Psychiatrie Leipzig-Dösen.

Rühl, Hugo (1901), *Deutsche Turner in Wort und Bild.* Leipzig, Wien: A. Pichlers Witwe & Sohn.

Rutschky, Katharina, Herausgeberin (1977), *Schwarze Pädagogik: Quellen zur Naturgeschichte der bürgerlichen Erziehung.* Frankfurt am Main, Berlin, Wien: Ullstein.

Saalfeld, Diedrich (1974), Einkommensverhältnisse und Lebenshaltungskosten städtischer Populationen in Deutschland in der Übergangsperiode zum Industriealter. In *Wirtschaftliche und soziale Strukturen in saekularen Wandel.* Vol. 2, *Die vorindustrielle Zeit: Ausseragrarische Probleme.* Hannover: M. & H. Schaper.

Sächsische Kurier (1933), Gedenkblatt für Dr. Schreber: Zum 125. Geburtstage am 15. Oktober. No. 241.

Sächsische Ordenskanzlei 61. State Archives, Dresden.

Sächsische Vaterlandsblätter 3 (1843), Leipzig: Universität-Turnerei. p. 559.

―――― 5 (1845), Leipzig: Die Wahlmänner der Stadtverordneten. p. 833.

Schalmey, Peter (1977), *Die Bewährung psychoanalytischer Hypothesen.* Wissenschaftstheorie und Grundlagenforschung, no. 7. Kronberg/Ts.: Scriptor Verlag.

Schatzman, Morton (1971), Paranoia or Persecution: The Case of Schreber. *Family Process,* 10:177-207.

―――― (1973a), *Soul Murder: Persecution in the Family.* London: Allen Lane.

―――― (1973b), Author's Reply to 'The Schreber Case, Sixty Years Later'. *International Journal of Psychiatry,* 11:126-128.

―――― (1974a), *Die Angst vor dem Vater: Langzeitwirkungen einer Erziehungsmethode, eine Analyse am Fall Schreber.* Reinbek: Rowohlt Verlag.

―――― (1974b), Review of *The Schreber Case* by William G. Niederland. *The History of Childhood Quarterly,* 2:453-457.

―――― (1974c), *L'esprit assassiné*. Paris: Éditions Stock.

―――― (1976), *Soul Murder: Persecution in the Family*. Middlesex, Penguin Books.

―――― (1977), *El asesinato del alma: la persecucion del nino en la familia autoritaria*. Madrid: Siglo Veintiuno de Espana Editores.

―――― (1978) *Die Angst vor dem Vater: Langzeitwirkungen einer Erziehungsmethode, eine Analyse am Fall Schreber*. Reinbek: Rowohlt Taschenbuch.

―――― and Freud, Sigmund (1974), *De ondergang van Daniel Paul Schreber: Een klassiek geval van paranoia en schizofrenie; and Psychoanalytische aantekeningen over een autobiografisch beschreven geval van paranoia (dementia paranoides)*. Amsterdam: Van Gennep.

Scheff, Thomas J., ed. (1975), *Labelling Madness*. Engelwood Cliffs, N. J.: Prentice-Hall.

Schildbach, Carl Hermann (1861), *Bericht über die gymnastisch-orthopädische Heilanstalt der DD. Schreber und Schildbach zu Leipzig, Zeitzer Strasse 43*. Leipzig: J. C. Hinrichs'sche Buchhandlung.

Schildbach, (Carl Hermann) (1862a), "Schreber." *Deutsche Turn-Zeitung*, 7:4-6.

―――― (1862b) Nachtrag zu Schrebers Nekrolog. *Neue Jahrbücher für die Turnkunst*, 8:16-18.

Schildbach, Carl Hermann (1864), *Zweiter Bericht über die gymnastisch-orthopädische Heilanstalt zu Leipzig, nebst Mittheilungen über die Grundsätze und Erfolge bei der Behandlung der Rückgratsverkrümmungen*. Leipzig: J. C. Hinrichs'sche Buchhandlung.

―――― (1867), Eine orthopädische Heilanstalt. *Cornelia*, 7:95-102.

―――― (1872), *Die Skoliose: Anleitung zur Beurtheilung und Behandlung der Rückgratsverkrümmungen für praktische Ärzte*. Leipzig: Veit & Co.

―――― (1877), *Orthopädische Klinik: Mittheilungen aus der Praxis der gymnatish-orthopädischen Heilanstalt zu Leipzig*. Leipzig: Veit & Co.

Schilling, Kurt (1924), *Das Kleingartenwesen in Sachsen*. Dresden: Eigenverlag des Verfassers.

―――― (1950), Dr. Schreber und der Schrebergarten. *Kleingärtner-Jahrbuch*, pp. 33-39.

―――― (1961), Dr. Schreber. *Deutscher Kleingärtner*, 218.

―――― (1964), Dr. D. G. M. Schreber und wir: Ein Leben für die Jugend und ein offenes Wort an alle. *Der Fachberater für das deutsche Kleingartenwesen*, June, pp. 1-23.

Schmidt, Karl (1867), *Die Geschichte der Pädagogik von Pestalozzi bis zur Gegenwart*. Geschichte der Pädagogik, vol. 4, 2nd ed. Göthen: Schettler.

Schreber, Daniel Gottlieb Moritz* (1852a), *Kinesiatrik oder die gymnastische Heilmethode: Für Ärzte und gebildete Nichtärzte nach eigenen Erfahrungen dargestellt*. Leipzig: Friedrich Fleischer.

Schreber, Daniel Gottlob Moritz, 1826, 1833a, and 1833b. See: Schreber, Danielis Gottlobus Mauritius.

Schreber, [Daniel Gottlob Moritz] (1835a), Letter to his parents. Dresden, 25/9/1835. Archives Kleingartensparte "Dr. Schreber" Leipzig.

[Schreber, Daniel Gottlob] Moritz (1835b), Letter to his parents. Dresden, 30/9/1835. Archives Kleingartensparte "Dr. Schreber" Leipzig.

Schreber, [Daniel Gottlob] Moritz (1839), *Das Buch der Gesundheit: Eine Orthobiotik*

*D.G.M. Schreber's publications are listed alphabetically, and thus the erroneous German listing. ["Gottlieb"] precedes correct ones ["Gottlob"], which in turn precede Latin renderings.

nach den Gesetzen der Natur und dem Baue des menschlichen Organismus.
Leipzig: Friedrich Volckmar.

Schreber, Daniel Gottlob Moritz (1840), *Die Normalgaben der Arztneimittel: Zum Gebrauche für praktische Ärzte und Kliniker übersichtlich dargestellt.* Leipzig: Friedrich Volckmar.

——— (1842), *Die Kaltwasser-Heilmethode in ihren Grenzen und ihrem wahren Werthe.* Leipzig: Bernh. Hermann.

——— (1843), *Das Turnen vom ärztlichen Standpunkte aus, zugleich als eine Staatsangelegenheit dargestellt.* Leipzig: Mayer und Wigand.

Schreber, [Daniel Gottlob] Moritz (1845a), *Fyra gyllene reglor för barna-uppfostran.* Upsala: Torssell.

Schreber, [Daniel Gottlob Moritz] (1845b), Das Turnen. *Leipziger Tageblatt,* 20/8/1845, pp. 2225, 2226.

Schreber, [Daniel Gottlob Moritz] (1848). Review of *Beiträge zur Heilgymnastik* by A. O. Neumann. *Schmidt's Jahrbüch der in- und ausländischen gesammten Medicin,* 59:207-211.

[Schreber, Daniel Gottlob Moritz] (1849), Manuscript of a speech for the Leipziger Allgemeiner Turnverein. (Leipzig.) Archives Kleingartensparte "Dr. Schreber" Leipzig.

Schreber, Daniel Gottlob Moritz (1852a), See: Schreber, Daniel Gottlieb Moritz.

Schreber, [Daniel Gottlob] Moritz (1852b), Letter to the police of Leipzig. Leipzig, 30/3/1852. In "Polizeiamt der Stadt Leipzig 11." Municipal Archives Leipzig.

Schreber, Daniel Gottlob Moritz (1852c), *Die Eigenthümlichkeiten des kindlichen Organismus im gesunden und kranken Zustande: Eine Propädeutik der speciellen Kinderheilkunde.* Leipzig: Friedrich Fleischer.

——— (1853a), *Die schädlichen Körperhaltungen und Gewohnheiten der Kinder nebst Angabe der Mittel dagegen: Für Ältern und Erzieher.* Leipzig: Friedrich Fleischer.

——— (1853b), *Nadeelige ligchaamshoudingen en kwade gewoonten der kinderen, benevens opgave der middelen daartegen, ten dienste van ouders en opvoeders.* Utrecht: W. F. Dannenfelser.

——— (1855a), *Ärztliche Zimmergymnastik oder Darstellung und Anwendung der unmittelbaren—d.h. ohne Geräth und Beistand, mithin stets und überall ausführbaren—heilgymnastischen Bewegungen für jedes Alter und Geschlecht und für die verschiedenen speciellen Gebrauchszwecke als ein einfach natürliches System entworfen.* Leipzig: Friedrich Fleischer.

Schreber, [Daniel Gottlob] Moritz (1855b), Letter beginning "An den Stadtrath zu Oschatz." Leipzig, 25/8/1855.

Schreber, [Daniel Gottlob Moritz] (1857a), "Macht nicht das Turnen grosse Hände?" *Neue Jahrbücher für die Turnkunst,* 3:210-212.

Schreber, Daniel Gottlob Moritz (1857b), *Onze kinderen: Hunne kwade gewoonten en nadeelige ligchaamshoudingen, benevens opgave der middelen daartegen.* Utrecht: W. F. Dannenfelser.

——— (1857c), *Aerztliche Zimmer-Gymnastik oder Darstellung und Anwendung der unmittelbaren heilgymnastischen Bewegungen für jedes Alter und Geschlecht,* 3rd rev. ed. Leipzig: Friedrich Fleischer.

——— (1858a), *Kallipädie oder Erziehung zur Schönheit durch naturgetreue und gleichmässige Förderung normaler Körperbildung, lebenstüchtiger Gesundheit und geistiger Veredelung und insbesondere durch möglichste Benutzung specieller Erziehungsmittel: Für Ältern, Erzieher und Lehrer.* Leipzig: Friedrich Fleischer.

Schreber, [Daniel Gottlob] Moritz (1858b), Über Anwendung der Sonnenbäder zu Heilzwecken, insbesondere gegen gewisse chronische Krankheiten des kindlichen

Alters. *Jahrbuch für Kinderheilkunde und physische Erziehung* 1:Original-Aufsätze, 169-171.

Schreber, [Daniel Gottlob Moritz] (1858c), Letter to Joh. Bapt. Heindl. Leipzig, 27/5/1858. Manuscript. Bayerische Staatsbibliothek.

——— (1858d), Die Turnanstalt als Schule der Männlichkeit. *Neue Jahrbücher für die Turnkunst*, 4:169-170.

Schreber, Daniel Gottlob Moritz (1858e), *Ein ärztlicher Blick in das Schulwesen in der Absicht: zu heilen, und nicht: zu verletzen.* Leipzig: Friedrich Fleischer.

——— (1859a), *Anthropos: Der Wunderbau des menschlichen Organismus, sein Leben und seine Gesundheitsgesetze; ein allgemein fassliches Gesammtbild der menschlichen Natur für Lehrer, Schüler, sowie für Jedermann, der nach gründlicher Bildung und körperlich geistiger Gesundheit strebt.* Leipzig: Friedrich Fleischer.

——— (1859b), *Die plannmässige Schärfung der Sinnesorgane als eine Grundlage und leicht zu erfüllende Aufgabe der Erziehung, besonders der Schulbildung.* Leipzig: Friedrich Fleischer.

Schreber, [Daniel Gottlob Moritz] (1860a), Die Jugendspiele in ihrer gesundheitlichen und pädagogischen Bedeutung. *Gartenlaube*, 8:414-416.

——— (1860b), Die Jugendspiele in ihrer gesundheitlichen und pädagogischen Bedeutung und die Nothwendigkeit ihrer Beachtung von Seite der Schulerziehung. *Jahrbuch für Kinderheilkunde und physische Erziehung*, 3:Original-Aufsätze 247:254.

——— (1860c), *Die deutsche Turnkunst in der Gegenwart und Zukunft: Wesen, Bedeutung und Grundregeln bei Ausübung derselben.* Leipzig: Hermann Fries.

Schreber, [Daniel Gottlob] Moritz (1861a), *Der Hausfreund als Erzieher und Führer zu Familienglück, Volksgesundheit und Menschenveredelung für Väter und Mütter des deutschen Volkes.* Leipzig: Friedrich Fleischer.

——— (1861b), An ein hohes Staatsministerium des Cultus und Erziehungswesens. Leipzig.

——— (1861c), Letter to the king of Prussia. Leipzig, January 1861. Manuscript. Staatsbibliothek Preussischer Kulturbesitz.

Schreber, [Daniel Gottlob Moritz] (1861d), Die Jugendspiele in ihrer gesundheitlichen und pädagogischen Bedeutung und die Nothwendigkeit ihrer Beachtung von Seiten der Schulerziehung. *Die Erziehung der Gegenwart: Beiträge zur Lösung ihrer Aufgabe mit Berücksichtigung von Friedrich Fröbels Grundsätzen* 1:137-140.

Schreber, Daniel Gottlob Moritz (1861e), *Das Buch der Gesundheit oder die Lebenskunst nach der Einrichtung und den Gesetzen der menschlichen Natur*, 2d rev. ed. Leipzig: Hermann Fries.

——— (1862a), *Das Pangymnastikon oder das ganze Turnsystem an einem einzigen Geräthe ohne Raumerforderniss als einfachstes Mittel zur Entwickelung höchster und allseitiger Muskelkraft, Körperdurchbildung und Lebenstüchtigkeit: Für Schulanstalten, Haus-Turner und Turnvereine.* Leipzig: Friedrich Fleischer.

Schreber, [Daniel Gottlob] Moritz (1862b), *Beknopte opvoedingsleer: Een boek voor vaders en moeders.* Vrij naar het hoogduitsch door Frans de Cort. Brussel, Zutphen: Ferdinand Claassen, P. B. Plantenga.

Schreber, Daniel Gottlob Moritz (1864), *Leerwijze om de ligchaamsbouw van kinderen te regelen, en hunne gezondheid te bevorderen.* Amsterdam: G. D. Funke.

——— (1882), *Das Buch der Erziehung an Leib und Seele: Für Ältern, Erzieher und Lehrer*, 2d ed. Erweitert von Carl Hennig. Leipzig: Friedrich Fleischer, (1882).

——— (1891), *Das Buch der Erziehung an Leib und Seele: Für Eltern, Erzieher und Lehrer*, 3d ed. Erweitert von Carl Hennig. Leipzig: R. Voigtländer.

Schreber, [Daniel Gottlob Moritz] (1909), ''Vaterworte an meine liebe Anna bei ihrem

358 HAN ISRAELS

Übergange aus den Kinderjahren in das Jungfrauenalter.'' Leipzig, Eastern 1856. *Der Freund der Schreber-Vereine*, 5:73-75.

Schreber, [Daniel Gottlob Moritz] (n.d.), Letter beginning "Lieber Freund!'' n.p., n.d. University Library, Leipzig.

Schreber, Daniel Gottlob Moritz, and Neumann, A. C. (1858), *Streitfragen der deutschen und schwedischen Heilgymnastik: Erörtert in Form myologischer Briefe*. Leipzig: A. Förstner'sche Buchhandlung (Arthur Felix), 1858.

Schreber, Danielis Gottlobus Mauritius (1826), Letter beginning "Rector Academiae Magnifice, Viri Summe Reverendi, Illustrissimi, Doctissimi, Honeratissimi.'' Manuscript. Lipsiae, 3/11/1826.

———— (1833a), *De tartari stibiati in inflammationibus organorum respirationis effectu atque usu*. Dissertatio inauguralis medica. Lipsiae.

———— (1833b), Curriculum vitae. In *Annotationes anatomicae et physiologicae*, Prol. XX by Ernestus Henricus Weber. Leipzig.

Schreber, (Daniel) Paul (1865), Letter to the Saxony ministry of justice. Leipzig, 22/3/1865. In "Personalakte" about Daniel Paul Schreber of the Saxony "Justiz-Ministerium.'' State Archives, Dresden.

———— Den 26. Juli 1889. Poem for the silver wedding of Anna and Carl Jung. Written down by a brother or sister of Paula Jung.

Schreber, Daniel Paul (1892), Letter to the Saxony ministry of justice. Freiberg, 12/11/1892. In "Personalakte" about Daniel Paul Schreber of the Saxony "Justiz-Ministerium.'' State Archives, Dresden.

———— (1903), *Denkwürdigkeiten eines Nervenkranken nebst Nachträgen und einem Anhang über die Frage: "Unter welchen Voraussetzungen darf eine für geisteskrank erachtete Person gegen ihren erklärten Willen in einer Heilanstalt festgehalten werden?''* Leipzig: Oswald Mutze.

[Schreber, Daniel Paul] (1904), Speech. Manuscript. n.p. 26/12/1904.

———— (1905), Zum 29. Juni 1905. Poem for his mother's ninetieth birthday. Mimeographed. n.p.

[Schreber, Daniel] Paul (1907a), Seinen lieben Sabchen zum neunzehnten Juni 1907 gewidmet. Poem for his wife's fiftieth birthday. Manuscript. (Dresden).

Schreber, [Daniel] Paul (1907b), "Erklärung.'' *Der Freund der Schreber-Vereine*, 3:292-293.

Schreber, Daniel Paul (1955), *Memoirs of my Nervous Illness*. Edited by Ida Macalpine and Richard A. Hunter. London: W. Dawson & Sons.

———— (1973a), Denkwürdigkeiten eines Nervenkranken nebst Nachträgen. In *Bürgerliche Wahnwelt um Neunzehnhundert*, herausgegeben von Peter Heiligenthal und Reinhard Volk. Wiesbaden: Focus-Verlag.

———— (1973b), *Denkwürdigkeiten eines Nervenkranken*. Herausgegeben von Samuel M. Weber. Frankfurt am Main, Berlin, Wien: Ullstein.

———— (1974), *Memorie di un malato di nervi*. A cura di Roberto Calasso. Milano: Adelphi edizioni.

———— (1975), *Mémoires d'un névropathe avec des compléments et un appendice sur la question "A quelles conditions une personne jugée aliénée peut-elle être maintenue dans un établissement hospitalier contre sa volonté évidente?''* Le champ freudien. Paris: Éditions du Seuil.

[Schreber, Daniel Paul] (n.d.), Poem, with explanatory note dating from 1937: Vorstehende Zeilen schrieb mein Onkel Paul Schreber († 1911) als Grossmutter Schreber uns zwei Schwäne schenkte. Manuscript. n.p., n.d.

Schreber, Johann Christian Daniel (1760), *Novae species insectorum*. Lipsiae: Fritsch.

[Schreber, Johann Gotthilf Daniel] (1812), Stammbaum. Manuscript. Leipzig.

———— (1829), Letter "an den Rathskämmerer Herrn Georg Friedrich Valz zu Os-
chatz." Transcript. Leipzig, 12/5/1829.
Schreber, Johann Gotthilf Daniel (1830), Kurze Geschichte meines Lebens. Manu-
script. Leipzig.
[Schreber, Louise Henriette Pauline, geb. Haase] (1899), Letter beginning "Liebe
Käte!" n.p., 7/8/1899.
———— (1904), Poem for the christening of a grand-granddaughter at 26/12/1904. n.p.
Schreber, Moritz. See: Schreber, Daniel Gottlob Moritz.
Schreber, Ottilie Sabine, geb. Behr. Letter to the Saxony "Justiz-Ministerium".
Dresden, 10/5/1911. In "Personalakte" about Daniel Paul Schreber of the Saxony
"Justiz-Ministerium." State Archives, Dresden.
Schreber, Paul. See: Schreber, Daniel Paul.
Schrebergärtner, Der (1924), Mitteilungsblatt des Schrebergarten-Vereins zu Stral-
sund, 16/6/1924, p. 33. "Sechzig Jahre Schrebertum."
Schreiber, Emil O. (1894), Geschichte des Schrebervereins der Westvorstadt zu Leip-
zig: Festschrift zur Feier des 30-jährigen Stiftungsfestes. Leipzig.
Schreiber, Emil O. (1895), 3. Die Schrebervereine zu Leipzig. Jahrbuch für deutsche
Jugend- und Volksspiele, 4:122-128.
Schultze, [Ernst] (1904), Review of Denkwürdigkeiten eines Nervenkranken by Daniel
Paul Schreber. Ärztliche Sachverständigen-Zeitung, 10:298.
Schultze, Ernst (1905), Review of Denkwürdigkeiten eines Nervenkranken by Daniel
Paul Schreber. Zeitschrift für Psychologie und Physiologie der Sinnesorgane,
37:469.
Schultz-Hencke, Harald (1952), Das Problem der Schizophrenie: Analytische Psy-
chotherapie und Psychose. Stutgart: G. Thieme.
Schütze, Rudolf (1936a), Moritz Schreber—der Leipziger Arzt und Pädagoge.
Deutsches Ärzteblatt, 36:1167.
———— (1936b), Moritz Schreber und sein Werk: Aus Anlass der 75. Wiederkehr
seines Todestages am 10. November. Münchener medizinische Wochenschrift,
83:1888-1890.
———— (1936c), Moritz Schreber—der geistige Vater der Schrebervereine: Zur 75.
Wiederkehr seines Todestages am 10. November. Politische Erziehung: Mitteilungsblatt des nationalsozialistischen Lehrerbundes Gauverband Sachsen, pp.
527-528.
Schwägrichen, (Christian) Frid(rich S.). (1828), Letter. Manuscript. Lipsiae, 14/2/1828.
Schwatlo, Hellmut (1938), Nie sah Herr Schreber Schrebergärten. Neue Leipziger
Zeitung.
Schweighofer, Fritz (1976), Psychoanalyse und Graphologie, dargestellt an den Hand-
schriften Sigmund Freuds und seiner Schüler. Stuttgart: Hippokrates Verlag.
Searles, Harold F. (1965), Collected Papers on Schizophrenia and Related Subjects.
The International Psycho-analytical Library, edited by John D. Sutherland, no.
63. London: Hogarth Press.
Ségur, Sophie de (1866), Comédies et proverbes, 2d ed. Paris: Librairie de L. Hachette
et Co.
Seidel, Peter (1974a), Die Idee mit dem Spielplatz. Kinderfreude in kleinen Gärten,
instalment 1, eine MNN-Serie über Dr. Schreber. Mitteldeutsche Neueste Nachrichten: Bezirkszeitung der National-Demokratischen Partei Deutschlands,
24/10/1974a, n.p.
———— (1974b), Berühmt auch als Begründer der helfenden Heilgymnastik. Kinderfreude in kleinen Gärten, instalment 2, eine MNN-Serie über Dr. Schreber.
Mitteldeutsche Neueste Nachrichten: Bezirkszeitung der National-Demokratischen Partei Deutschlands, 30/10/1974, n.p.

——— (1977), Nach der MNN-Serie über Dr. Schreber: Ein unerwarteter Fund. *Mitteldeutsche Neueste Nachrichten: Bezirkszeitung der National-Demokratischen Partei Deutschlands*, 15-16/10/1977, n.p.

Shengold, Leonard (1961), Chekhov and Schreber. *International Journal of Psycho-Analysis*, 42:431-438.

——— (1974), Soul Murder: A Review. *International Journal of Psychoanalytic Psychotherapy*, 3:366-373.

——— (1975), An Attempt at Soul Murder: Rudyard Kipling's Early Life and Work. *The Psychoanalytic Study of the Child*, 30:683-724. New Haven: Yale University Press.

Shorter, Edward (1977), *The Making of the Modern Family*. Glasgow: Fontana/Collins.

Shraberg, David (1975), Review of *The Schreber Case* by William G. Niederland. *The Journal of the American Academy of Psychoanalysis*, 3:343-346.

Shulman, Bernard H. (1959), An Adlerian view of the Schreber case. *Journal of Individual Psychology*, 15:180-192.

Siegel, [G.] Richard (1907a), Die Leipziger Schrebervereine, ihre Entstehung, ihr Wesen und Wirken. *Der Freund der Schreber-Vereine*, 3:2-10.

——— (1907b), Speech. In "Trauerrede beim Begräbnis der Frau verw. Dr. Schreber" by D. Hartung. Leipzig.

Siegel, G. Richard (1907c), Frau Pauline verw. Dr. Schreber †. *Der Freund der Schreber-Vereine*, 3:126-128.

——— (1907d), Zur Abwehr. *Der Freund der Schreber-Vereine*, 3:218.

Siegel, [G.] Richard (1907e), Dr. Schreber und die Schrebervereine. *Der Freund der Schreber-Vereine*, 3:251-255.

Siegel, G. Richard (1907f), Die Wochenschrift 'Der Schrebergärtner' und die Leipziger Schrebervereine. *Der Freund der Schreber-Vereine*, 3:289-292.

Siegel, [G.] Richard (1908a), Zur Geschichte des "Verbandes Leipziger Schrebervereine" und des "Allgemeinen Verbandes der Schrebervereinen." *Der Freund der Schreber-Vereine*, 4:3-6.

S[iegel, G. Richard] (1908b), Direktor Dr. Karl Vogel über Dr. Schreber. *Der Freund der Schreber-Vereine*, 4:25-26.

——— (1908c), Zur einhundertjährigen Wiederkehr des Geburtstages Dr. Schrebers und Dr. Hauschilds. *Der Freund der Schreber-Vereine*, 4:205-210.

Siegel, G. Richard (1908d), Gedenkfeier zur einhundertjährigen Wiederkehr des Geburtstages Dr. Schrebers und Dr. Hauschilds. *Der Freund der Schreber-Vereine*, 4:220.

Siegel, [G.] Richard (1909a), Comments on Daniel Gottlob Moritz Schreber 1909. *Der Freund der Schreber-Vereine*, 5:75.

——— (1909b), Erinnerungen an Dr. Moritz Schreber: Nach Berichten von seinen Töchtern. *Der Freund der Schreber-Vereine*, 5:205-209.

Siegel, G. Richard (1914), Schreber-Worte. *Der Freund der Schreber-Vereine*, 10:17-19.

Siemens, Hermann Werner (1966), Über unbekannte Ahnen von Werner Siemens. *Mitteilungen der Arbeitsgemeinschaft für Familiengeschichte im Kulturkreis Siemens E.V*, no. 46, pp. 73ff.

Slikker, Mia, and Meijer, Quint (1975), Review of *De ondergang van Daniel Paul Schreber* by Morton Schatzman and Sigmund Freud. *Pharetra*, 17/11/1975, p. 16.

S-r (1863), Über das Abhärten der Kinder, und dessen methodische Durchführung. *Jahrbuch für Kinderheilkunde und physische Erziehung*, 6:Original-Aufsätze 247-256.

Starke, Werner (1976), Väter der Schrebergärten. In a Leipzig newspaper, 3-4/7/1976.

Stephani, Eberhard (1980), Die Laubenpieper. *Stern*, 8/5/1980, pp. 40-58.

Stone, Irving (1972), *The Passions of the Mind: A Biographical Novel of Sigmund Freud*. New York: Signet/The New American Library.

Storr, Anthony (1973), All in the Family. *Book World*, 4/2/1973, pp. 4 and 10.

Stötzner, E. (1883), Auf Leipzigs Schreberplätzen. *Gartenlaube*, 31:368-373.

Striegler, B. (1904), Leipzig als Turnerstadt. *Leipziger Kalender*, 91-97.

[Tabouret-Keller, Andrée] (1973), Une étude: La remarquable famille Schreber. *Scilicet*, no. 4, pp. 287-321.

This, Bernard. La race Schreberienne. *Le coq-heron*, no. 37/38, June/July, pp. 2-3, 1973a; no. 40, November, pp. 2-12, 1973b; no. 41/42, December 1973/January 1974, pp. 9-17.

Times Literary Supplement (1973), The over-Spartan Schrebers. 13/7/1973, p. 803.

Troitzsch, Rudolf (1963-68), Erinnerungen. Typescript. n.p. (written between 1963 and 1968).

——— (1974), Letter to Peter Heiligenthal and Reinhard Volk. Typescript. Hoxhohl, 14/1/1974.

Trouw (1975), stadseditie, 6/3/1975, p. 12. Review of *De ondergang van Daniel Paul Schreber* by Morton Schatzman and Sigmund Freud.

Uibe, Peter (1959), Schreber als Orthopäde. *Hippokrates*, 30:216-218.

Union, Die (1964), Entdecker der grossen Liebe zum kleinen Garten: Vor nunmehr 100 Jahren wurde in Leipzig der erste Schreber-Verein gegründet. Vol. 19, No. 135 (Leipzig).

Ussel, Jozef Maria Willem van (1968), *Geschiedenis van het seksuele probleem*. Meppel: J. A. Boom en Zoon.

Valentin, Bruno (1961), *Geschichte der Orthopädie*. Stuttgart: Georg Thieme Verlag.

Vogel, (Karl) (1861), Dr. D. G. M. Schreber, geb. 1808 † 1861: Eines bewährten Kinderfreundes letzter Rath und Wunsch. *Mittheilungen der allgemeinen Bürgerschule zu Leipzig an das Elternhaus ihrer Zöglinge*, 16/12/1861, p. 37-44.

Volhard, (J.) (1912), Allgemeiner Familienabend im "Sanssouci": Dienstag, den 22. Oktober 1912. *Der Freund der Schreber-Vereine*, 8:169-171.

Volhard, J. (1914), 50jährige Jubelfeier im Schreberverein der Westvorstadt. *Der Freund der Schreber-Vereine*, 10:115-118.

Vries, Leonard de (1976), *Ha dokter Ho dokter: Knotsgekke geneeskunde uit grootvaders tijd*, 2d ed. Haarlem: De Haan.

W., G. (1908), Zum hundertsten Geburtstag Dr. Moritz Schreber. *Leipziger Tageblatt*, 13/10/1908, p. 3.

Wahrig, Gerhard (1973), *Deutsches Wörterbuch*. Gütersloh, Berlin, München, Wien: Bertelsmann Lexikon-Verlag.

Weber (1894), Medical report for the "Oberlandesgericht" Dresden on Daniel Paul Schreber. (Pirna,) 21/11/1894. Transcript in "Personalakte" on Daniel Paul Schreber of the Saxony "Justiz-ministerium." State Archives, Dresden.

Weber (1895), "Ärztliches Gutachten" on Daniel Paul Schreber. (Pirna,) 7/11/1895. In "Personalakte" on Daniel Paul Schreber of the Saxony "Justiz-Ministerium." State Archives, Dresden.

Weber (1899), "Gerichtsärztliches Gutachten" on Daniel Paul Schreber. (Pirna) 9/12/1899. In *Denkwürdigkeiten eines Nervenkranken* by Daniel Paul Schreber. Leipzig: Oswald Mutze, 1903.

Weber (1900), Anstaltsbezirkärztliches Gutachten. (Pirna) 28/11/1900. In *Denkwürdigkeiten eines Nervenkranken* by Daniel Paul Schreber. Leipzig: Oswald Mutze.

Weber (1902), "Gutachten" on Daniel Paul Schreber. (Pirna) 5/4/1902. In

362 HAN ISRAELS

Denkwürdigkeiten eines Nervenkranken by Daniel Paul Schreber. Leipzig: Oswald Mutze.

Weber (1910), "Die Heil- und Pflegeanstalt Sonnenstein bei Pirna." In *Deutsche Heil- und Pflegeanstalten für Psychischkranke*, herausgegeben von J. Bresler, vol. 1. Halle: Carl Marhold Verlagsbuchhandlung.

Weber, Ernestus Henricus (1833), *Annotationes anatomicae et physiologicae*. Prol. XX. Lipsiae.

Weber, Samuel M. (1973), Die Parabel. In *Denkwürdigkeiten eines Nervenkranken* by Daniel Paul Schreber. Frankfurt am Main, Berlin, Wien: Ullstein.

Wehlitz, H. (1927), Schreber über körperliche Erziehung: Ein Auszug. *Deutsche Turn-Zeitung*, 812.

Weinmeister, R. (1939), Schreber, Hauschild und die Schrebervereins-Bewegung: Zum 75-jährigen Bestehen des Kleingärtnervereins Dr. Schreber in Leipzig. *Leipziger Beobachter*, 20/5/1939, pp. 93-95.

Werner, Carl Edmund (1894), Letter to the Saxony ministry of justice. Dresden, 26/11/1894. In "Personalakte" on Daniel Paul Schreber of the Saxony "Justiz-Ministerium." State Archives, Dresden.

White, Robert B. (1961), The Mother-Conflict in Schreber's Psychosis. *International Journal of Psycho-Analysis*, 42:55-73.

———— (1963), The Schreber Case Reconsidered in the Light of Psychosocial Concepts. *International Journal of Psycho-Analysis*, 44:213-221.

Wiener Neueste Nachrichten (1943), Vom Schrebern zum Schrebergarten. 12/7/1943, p. 3.

Wilden, Anthony (1972), *System and Structure: Essays in Communication and Exchange*. London: Tavistock Publications.

Windscheid (1904), Review of *Denkwürdigkeiten eines Nervenkranken* by Daniel Paul Schreber. *Monatsschrift für Psychiatrie und Neurologie*, 15:399.

Wulff, L. (1929), *Was können Schreber's Zimmergymnastik-Übungen, auch teils abgeändert, für Alte, Schwache und Kranke leisten?* Parchim: Kommissionsverlag H. Wehdemann's Buchhandlung.

Zitz-Halein, Kathinka (1841), *Dictionnaire des gallicismes oder Taschenwörterbuch aller Ausdrücke der französischen Sprache, welche sich nicht wörtlich übersetzen lassen*. Revised by Christian Ferdinand Fliessbach. Leipzig: Ch. E. Kollmann.

INDEX